The Province of Sharīʿah Determined

The Province of Sharīʿah Determined

Fundamental Rethink of the Sharīʿah

Mohd Faiz Abdullah

TOP
The Other Press
Kuala Lumpur

Published by
The Other Press Sdn. Bhd.
607 Mutiara Majestic
Jalan Othman
46000 Petaling Jaya
Selangor, Malaysia
www.ibtbooks.com

The Other Press is affiliated with Islamic Book Trust.

Perpustakaan Negara Malaysia   Cataloguing-in-Publication Data

Mohd. Faiz Abdullah
The Province of Shariʿah Determined : Fundamental Rethink of the Shariʿah / Mohd Faiz Abdullah.
Includes index
Bibliography: p. 369
ISBN 978-967-0957-09-8 (paperback)
ISBN 978-967-0957-10-4 (hardback)
1. Islamic law. I. Title.
340.59

Printed by
SS Graphic Printers (M) Sdn Bhd
Lot 7 & 8, Jalan TIB 3, Taman Industri Bolton,
68100 Batu Caves, Selangor Darul Ehsan.

Contents

Preface

This monograph is not a study calling for the reformation of Islam. That would be audacity of the highest order. The reformation of any religion advocated by ordinary mortals who may have the gift of demagoguery spells doom, bringing forth the voices of wreck and ruin and tearing communities apart. The reformation of a religion must be left to the prophets. It is about authority and legitimacy from on high—for a revealed religion can only be "reformed" by another even greater. The religion of Islam brought by Prophet Muḥammad (ṣ) as a blessing, a mercy and a guide for mankind is in no need of reform. However, the Muslim world and its *ummah*, that is, the myriad Muslim communities and nations throughout the world where Muslims comprise the majority are in dire need of reform and renewal. This will have to be multi-dimensional. Apart from the political, social and economic spheres that must be examined with a view for reform and renewal, there is a pressing need for an ideational paradigm change. And within this matrix, the conception of the *Sharīʿah* as being doctrinaire, legalistic and one-dimensional needs to be deconstructed, hence *A Fundamental Rethink of the Sharīʿah.*

The main title, *The Province of Sharīʿah Determined*, was inspired by John Austin's famous tome on jurisprudence, published in 1832, in which he expounded the command theory of law. My position, as will be made clear from Chapter 1 onwards, is that while indeed God's law, particularly as gleaned from the Qur'ān, does seem to be couched in the language of commands and prohibitions, an Austinian command theory nevertheless is neither adequate nor capable of encapsulating the multidimensionality of the *Sharīʿah*.

The word "*Sharīʿah*" has long been used in ways which betray certain underlying preconceptions as well as misconceptions regarding its purport, scope and real meaning. Arising from this anomalous usage and insufficient clarity, much debate and rancorous polemics have been generated by scholars and laypeople alike leading to finger-pointing, mudslinging, charges of heresy or even outright apostasy. This study examines the etymology, concept and scope of *Sharīʿah* in both its historical and contemporary contexts with a view to bringing some clarity to the subject and determining its province. The epistemology of the doctrine of the *madhhab* (school of jurisprudence) with the cognates of *ijtihād, taqlīd* and *ikhtilāf* is examined to shed greater light on the *Sharīʿah* as divine guidance to the *ummah* as well as canonical law. This invariably warrants a study of the concepts of *fiqh, ʿilm al-fiqh* and *uṣūl al-fiqh*, which tend to be erroneously interchanged with *Sharīʿah,* which in turn blurs the distinction between divine law and juristic law. This study takes the position that the canonical law that results from the exercise of *ʿaql* (reason/intellect) through the mechanism and processes of *ijtihād, taqlīd* and *ikhtilāf* provides substantive ground for departing from the general understanding of the *Sharīʿah* as immutable. Following this discussion, I have incorporated a chapter on theology and philosophy—*kalām* and *falsafah*—which are often excluded from the conventional discourse on the *Sharīʿah*. Indeed, there is no need to reinvent the wheel of harmonizing religion with philosophy. This was accomplished more than 1,000 years ago by the *falāsifah*, from al-Fārābī onwards and finally synthesized by Ibn Rushd. My sole purpose in including the two subjects, *kalām* and *falsafah*, is to provide a contextual paradigm for a more meaningful and inclusive *Sharīʿah* discourse, moving it away from an overly *fiqh*-centric (legalistic/juristic) polemic. I have also devoted some space for a discussion on the bifurcation between church and state, which I believe is partly contributing to the general misunderstanding about

Islam and the concept of the Islamic state, though I have made it clear that such a subject (on the Islamic state and political Islam) would necessitate another serious study on its own in order to do justice to its doctrinal significance as well as practical implications. Furthermore, contrary to the conventional approach, the phenomenon of *siyāsah al-shar'iyyah* is postulated as "*Sharī'ah* in action" and discoursed as an umbrella doctrine incorporating, and not circumscribed by, the doctrine of the *maqāṣid al-Sharī'ah*. In revisiting the *Sharī'ah* sources, I have attempted to provide a fresh perspective on the classical fonts of *Sharī'ah* law, and this is followed immediately by an essay on the processes of the evolution of the law, with the stress on the inherent dynamism of *Sharī'ah* law as opposed to the myth of its passivity and ossification. Finally, a case is made for a fundamental rethinking of the *Sharī'ah* and how it should be adopted in the contemporary world.

In this study, reference to the word "*Sunnah*" without more means the *Sunnah* of the Prophet. And reference to the word "Prophet" without more means Muḥammad, the Messenger of Allah (ṣ). Readers will find in almost every page Arabic terms and phrases transliterated with their translations in parentheses or vice versa, while the citation of Qur'ānic verses is generally taken from *The Message of the Qur'ān* by Muhammad Asad, together with the annotations whenever appropriate. I have also occasionally used Muhammad Marmaduke Pickthall's *The Meaning of the Glorious Koran: An Explanatory Translation* and Abdullah Yusuf Ali's *The Meaning of the Holy Qur'ān* when the situation warranted it. Chapter and verse references are generally cited in the endnotes of each chapter. With the recent publication of *The Study Quran* by a team led by the world-renowned Muslim scholar Seyyed Hossein Nasr, I have benefited tremendously from its encyclopedic commentaries and have on various occasions used them particularly in situations which require variant expositions arising from differences of opinions.

When I began this project, I had set out to write about the *Sharī'ah* with a view to elucidating what it is or what it ought to be from a scholarly point of view. With that in mind, I had attempted to maintain as much academic detachment as I possibly could, making every effort to stay out of religious polemics. Now, having read through the draft, I realize that there were occasions where some degree of subjectivity had crept in which would be indicative of my personal perceptions of what I believe the *Sharīʻah* ought to be. On further reflection, I have decided that there is no necessity to review those parts or to decouple them from the otherwise generally non-polemical and impartial viewpoints. After all, the *Sharīʻah* inspires, and while sobriety of thinking must be the order of the day if one is to be taken seriously, some sparks must fly when the hammer hits the anvil—provided, as Hamlet reminds us, that in the very torrent of our passion, we are able to "acquire and beget a temperance that may give it smoothness."

Mohd Faiz bin Abdullah, PhD.
2 Ramaḍān, 1437 / June 7, 2016
Shah Alam, Selangor, Malaysia

Chapter 1

The Sharīʻah[1]

Etymology of Sharīʻah

There are a few ways of defining the word "*Sharīʻah,*" but this is easier said than done as will be apparent as we embark on this journey. The title of this monograph notwithstanding, it must be stressed from the start that the purpose of attempting a definition of the *Sharīʻah* is not to put limits to its meaning but, on the contrary, to test how far its province may be extended. The "few ways" to be used are not cut and dry and it is not merely a question of personal choice which one way represents the best definition. If defining *Sharīʻah* is just about arranging in order of preference and importance the "constituents" of the *Sharīʻah* as if they are already spelt out clearly, then all that has to be done is to enumerate them. However, finding out the constituents of the *Sharīʻah* is the very function of attempting to define it.

As a starting point, the etymology of the word may be traced to "*shirʻah*" as it occurs in the Qur'ān:

> "Unto each community we have given a divine law and a traced-out way" (*Li kullin jaʻalnā minkum shirʻatan wa minhājā*).[2]

Shirʻah is often referred to in its literal usage as "a road to the watering place," or in the context of *tashrīʻ*, to signify "bringing camels to the watering place to drink without requiring to draw with the pulley and its appurtenances, nor to give them to drink in a watering trough or tank." Metaphorically, it applies to "him who takes an easy way to perform an affair and does not exert himself therein." It could also mean "to make manifest," as in *Shara'a Allāhu lanā kadhā* (God made apparent to us such a thing), hence the Qur'ānic reference to fish appearing on the surface of the water as "*Idh ta'tīhim ḥītānuhum yawma sabtihim shurra'ā*" (When their fish came to them on their Sabbath openly), *shurra'ā* in this case signifying "openly," "manifestly."[3]

In the full context of the verse in Sūrah al-Mā'idah, bearing in mind the deserts of Arabia, the meaning is much more profound even in its literal sense: a path to salvation from death. Metaphorically, it therefore means a straight path by which God leads people to the truth.[4] Translators and commentators generally translate *shir'ah* here as "divine law" or "Law" with a capital "L" or just "law."[5] It matters not that the Arabic script does not have lower or upper case because the upper case here employed by the translators is to signify Divine law, not law in the ordinary sense. It could be argued at the same time that adding "divine" to the word "law" is superfluous, considering the context of the assertion: coming from God, it cannot be anything else but divine. But that is nitpicking. What is more important is that the debate begins from the word "go," for there are diverse interpretations as to what exactly this divine law is. It centres not just on the scope and purport of "divine law" but also on the contextual reference to mankind, that is, to whom this law is applicable. From the expression *li kullin* (every one of you), it would not be a stretch to infer that this *āyah* is addressed not to just one community but to "each and every" community, dispelling the notion that *shir'ah* here refers only to the *Sharī'ah* of the *ummah* (Muslim community). This is indicative of God having ordained different ritual and legal formulations for the different religious communities, and "each religious community is independent of the laws of other such communities, even if the essential truths and principles are the same."[6] In this regard, the rendering of the word *Sharī'ah* such as that given by Ibn Kathīr to refer it exclusively to the Qur'ān is therefore inconsistent with the plain meaning of the text.[7]

In any event, the rest of the *āyah* shows that God has revealed not just one "Law" but various divine laws to the multifarious communities of mankind, for "had Allah willed, He would have made you one nation (united in religion) …"[8] Nasr suggests that this is a "counterfactual conditional statement showing that human beings do not exist as one community because God has not willed it as such."[9] That means that *shirʿah* as divine law had been in usage with reference to other communities such as the Jews and the Christians before the establishment of the community of Muslims, that is, before the advent of Islam as a system of beliefs and rituals based on the Qur'ān and the Sunnah. In other words, in terms of the *shirʿah*, Islam is preceded by Christianity and Judaism, as the following *āyah*[10] makes clear:

> "He hath ordained for you that religion which He commended unto Noah, and that which We inspire in thee (Muhammad), and that which We commended unto Abraham and Moses and Jesus, saying: Establish the religion, and be not divided therein …"[11]

By inductive reasoning, this term could be extended to include the Zoroastrians, Hindus, Jains, Buddhists, Taoists and so on, though the Literalists would consider such an opinion to be purely speculative. Indeed, this is a *ra'y*, but it is opinion based on related evidence. The Qur'ān has made it clear that God has not only appointed a divine law but also a "*minhāj*," that is, "an open road," in the sense of "a way of life." However, this is not to suggest that all religions are the same but that the Almighty in His infinite wisdom, as declared in the Qur'an, has dispatched to the diverse communities of mankind their prophets to teach and guide them, for "there is not a nation but a warner hath passed among them."[12] Furthermore, Allah has "never sent a messenger save with the language of his folk, that he might make (the message) clear for them …"[13] According to Asad, because every divine writ was meant to be understood by man, each had to be formulated in the language of the people whom the particular prophet was addressing in the first instance, and the Qur'an being revealed in the Arabic language is no exception in this respect, notwithstanding its universal import. It is universal in a geographical sense as well, for within every community, God has "raised up an apostle." *Ummah,* as used here, may be taken to denote "civilization."[14]

Hallaq renders "*minhāj*" as the "normative way," drawing attention to the Hebraic cognate "*minhag*," meaning "the Law," and concludes that "the creation of an Islamic legal parallel here speaks for itself."[15] I beg to differ. To my mind, that appears to be a premature conclusion in as far as it purports to set "*minhāj*" within the province of law only. There is already the reference to "*shir'ah*" as divine law, which by definition is normative. Hence, to add "normative way" within the same conjunction is, linguistically speaking, tautologous. It may be understandable, even spot-on, as it were, to talk of "*minhag*" as enjoining the establishment of a Judaic legal paradigm on account of the Torah itself being commonly referred to as "the Jewish written law," but nowhere would one find in the established commentaries any reference of the Qur'ān being referred to as "the Islamic written law." Also known as the Pentateuch (the five vessels), as it comprises the five books of the Hebrew Bible, the Torah was given to Moses on Mount Sinai, ordaining all the biblical laws of Judaism. Indeed, a plurality of meanings is associated with the Torah, but all find a semantic nexus in the Judaic legal corpus, which may also include the Oral Law. The preeminent medieval Sephardic Jewish polymath Mūsā ibn Maymūn (d. 1204), known in the Latin West as Maimonides, went further and postulated that the ultimate purpose of the Torah is political, being crucial in the administration of a Jewish state. His magnum opus, the voluminous *Mishneh Torah*, remains the canon for Talmudic law, and his postulation on the Torah as a rationalizing force resonated with the more spiritually inclined philosophers of seventeenth-century Europe, in particular another Sephardic Jew, Baruch Spinoza (Portuguese: Benedict de Spinoza), who had challenged Cartesian dualism. But that is getting ahead of the game, for we shall have more of that in Chapter 3. Coming back to the question of "*minhāj*" as law, there is the view that in the classical formulations, there appears to be mutuality between Islam and Judaism on the religious regulation of everyday life in order to establish a God-fearing society modelled on the basis of bowing to the will of God.[16] But that is a subjective assessment which, taken to its logical conclusion, goes beyond merely rules and regulations to a paradigm of a State governed by God's law. That line of argument will draw us inevitably to the fundamental polemics of the *Sharī'ah* being the be-all and end-all of Islam, which we shall deal with later. For now, we will give it a far wider semantic berth, treating it as referring to the body of laws promulgated and "the way of life recommended" to a particular religion which naturally "varied in accordance with the exigencies of the time and of each community's cultural development," and these two terms should not be confused with the term "*dīn*," which relates to "the unchanging spiritual truths … preached by every one of God's apostles."[17]

Finally, from the perspective of the Shaykh al-Akbar Muḥyī al-Dīn Ibn al-'Arabī (d. 638/1240), the term *shar'* does not necessarily denote the revealed law of Islam, since every religion sent by God is a *shar'*, and religion in general may also be called *shar'*, especially when it is being contrasted with the path of reason. The term *Sharī'ah* may be used in the same way, though mainly in the plural *sharā'i'*, when it can best be translated as "revealed religions."[18] Ibn al-'Arabī asserts that the validity of other religions other than Islam is found in the Qur'ān itself:

> "And We sent no messenger before thee but We inspired him, (saying): There is no God save Me (Allah), so worship Me."[19]

Sharī'ah as Dīn

Asad's explanation needs further analysis for it appears to create more confusion than clarity because if one is not to equate "*dīn*" with "*shirʿah* as divine law," then the question is: at which point does the meaning of one depart from the other because both are divine? How could "the unchanging spiritual truths" differ from the "laws promulgated and the way of life recommended," for the latter must also be founded on the same unchanging truths? The answer lies in accepting the bifurcation of "*dīn*" as "religion per se" on the one hand and "*shirʿah*" and "*minhāj*" on the other as an aggregation of "law, culture, economy and political system."

God commands the Prophet to follow the *Sharīʿah*:

> "And now have We set thee (O Muhammad) on a clear road of commandment; so follow it and follow not the whims of those who know not."[20]

The key issue here is the interpretation to be given to the word as it occurs in the phrase *ʿalā sharīʿatin min al-amr*. It is noteworthy that this is the only time that *sharīʿah* is used in the Qurʾān, and as noted earlier, it is generally seen as "clear road," incorporating the meaning of "*minhāj*." Read in light of the earlier meaning of road in a metaphorical sense as well as juxtaposed with the *āyah* concerning "*ahwāʾ*" (caprice), a fuller meaning of *Sharīʿah*, therefore, would include the moral and spiritual implications associated with the path ordained by God, going beyond the legalistic definition.[21] To be precise, there should in fact be no legal connotation to the word as yet because, as some exegetes point out, the *āyah* is part of a middle-period Meccan *sūrah*. The word here means "the way of religion," that is, "*dīn*," wider than the mere formal rites and legal provisions, which mostly came in the Medinan period, long after this Meccan *āyah* had been revealed.[22] This is also clear in Asad's rendering.[23]

The concept of *dīn* itself has been subject to various expositions. There are generally two polarities here: the narrow view which looks at *dīn* from the prism of the religion of Islam as the only true religion and other religions as having "gone astray," and there is also the broad view which does not denigrate other religions and in particular considers the Abrahamic faiths, such as Christianity and Judaism, as being part of the same monotheistic tradition as that inherited by Islam. Naquib al-Attas, for instance, begins the exposition by resorting to stamping *dīn* with the halo of exclusivity by asserting that *dīn* in the Islamic religion "is not the same as the concept *religion* as interpreted and understood throughout Western religious history." *Dīn* in Islam has "all the basic connotations … conceived as gathered into a single unity of coherent meaning as reflected in the Holy Qur'ān and in the Arabic language to which it belongs." Al-Attas then proceeds to give it an extensive semantic treatment, positing that its primary significations may be reduced to four: indebtedness, submissiveness, judicious power and natural inclination,[24] and the rest of the chapter is devoted to their exposition, including a brief discourse on knowledge. Quoting from the Qur'ānic passages where *dīn* and Islam are referred to, al-Attas makes the proposition that "the *dīn* referred to is none other than Islam." While conceding that there are "other *forms* of *dīn*," al-Attas maintains that "the one in which is enacted total submission (*istislām*) to God alone is the best, and this one is the only *dīn* acceptable to God…."[25] Inter alia, the oft-quoted line from Sūrah Āl ʻImrān, *āyah* 19, is given as follows:

> "Verily the Religion (*al-dīn*) in the sight of God is Islam (*al-Islām*)."[26]

Al-Attas says that "the term *dīn* is also used, albeit metaphorically, to denote religions other than Islam," but adds the rider that "what makes Islam different from the other religions, is that the submission according to Islam is sincere and total submission to God's will, and this is enacted willingly as absolute obedience to the law revealed by Him." He says this view is "implicitly supported" by the *āyah* "Do they seek for other than the religion (*dīn*) of God? While all creatures in the heavens and on earth have, willing or unwilling, submitted (*aslam*) to His Will, and to Him shall they all be returned."[27] As for the broad view concerning *dīn*, Sūrah al-Mā'idah, *āyah* 48, as has been cited from the outset, remains pivotal. Just to reiterate, it is clear that from the Qur'ānic viewpoint, there is certainly more than one way of revering and worshiping God on account of the myriad human communities that God has created. Thus, it is not one law, but many laws, and to each law a particular path takes shape as reflected in the performance of rites, particular to that form of worship.[28] Thus,

> "Unto every community have We appointed [different] ways of worship, which they ought to observe. Hence, [O believer,] do not let those [who follow ways other than mine] draw thee into disputes on this score, but summon [them all] unto thy Sustainer: for, behold, thou art indeed on the right way. And if they [try to] argue with thee, say [only]: 'God knows best what you are doing.' [For, indeed,] God will judge between you [all] on Resurrection Day with regard to all on which you were wont to differ."[29]

Does this view imply a liberal agenda where revealed religion is secondary to personal opinion and individuals must be given the freedom of interpretation of the scriptures? The answer is firmly in the negative. This approach is not carte blanche for freedom "to invent new creeds, laws, and ways" but rather that it is indicative that "God has revealed many ways and many religions for humanity." Rather than donning the cloak of exclusivity in religion before God, one can and should look beyond outward differences and value people for the degree of their reverence and piety towards God. The Qur'ān commends those who continue to submit to the way ordained by former prophets:

> "Truly those who believe and those who are Jews, and the Christians, and the Sabeans[30]—whosoever believes in God and the Last Day and works righteousness shall have their reward with their Lord. No fear shall come upon them, nor shall they grieve."[31]

This position recurs in the Qur'ān several times and, according to Asad, lays down a fundamental doctrine of Islam that the idea of "salvation" is conditional upon three elements only: belief in God, belief in the Day of Judgment, and righteous actions in life. While contextually this passage is an admonishment against the *banū Isrā'īl* (children of Israel) and the false Jewish belief that their descent from Abraham entitles them to be regarded as "God's chosen people," the same warning may be directed against Muslims who consider themselves the only *ummah* (among the many communities created by Allah) following "the true religion."

This broad view concerning *dīn* is supported by none other than the prominent and influential Persian polymath al-Ṭabarī[32] (d. 310/923), who, citing the above *āyah*, says that "God has not singled out some of His creatures as opposed to others concerning the bestowal of rewards for virtuous actions with faith." The broad view posits that submission (*islām*) cannot be confined to any single form, that observing God's covenant was a fundamental reality that predates the religion that formally takes the name of Islam. Indeed, the contrarian argument posits that there are verses, such as *āyah*s 65-67 of Sūrah Āl ʿImrān, that manifest a rejection of Judaism and Christianity in favour of Islam, but these and many similar verses can also be read as an affirmation of all forms of submission, which has been ordained as part of God's covenant with the different communities established from all revealed religions. The contention that, with the Qur'ān, the covenant attached to the other revealed religions before Islam has been abrogated or rendered obsolete is not supported by textual evidence. On the contrary, the Qur'ānic verses positively point to a reaffirmation of the covenant of those who came before Islam, enjoining all people to follow the way that precedes sectarian associations,[33] that is, the way of Prophet Ibrāhīm:

> "Say, God has spoken true. So follow the creed of Abraham, a *ḥanīf*, and he was not of the idolaters."[34]

Ḥanīf has been variously translated as "the upright," "who turned away from all that is false," "the sane in faith" and "sincere" in faith in submission to God. Prophet Ibrāhīm was chosen not because he followed a particular creed but because he submitted himself entirely to God.[35] The ultimate goal of religious practice is not blind adherence to a particular religious form but to be constantly God-fearing or God-conscious, for

> "verily, the noblest of you in the sight of God is the one who is most deeply conscious of Him. Behold, God is all-knowing, all-aware."[36]

There is, therefore, a strong foundation for the view that Sharī'ah is used in the Qur'ān in a general sense, neither technical nor restrictive, and carries a wider purport than its association, later, with formal rites and legal provisions.[37] According to this generic approach, Sūrah al-Mā'idah, *āyah* 48, taken contextually, enjoins Muslims to follow the right way of religion—and not the wrong way—and is therefore no authority for the proposition that "*sharī'ah*" refers to *sharī'ah* as law and that the legal systems of Muslim societies must be based on the *Sharī'ah*, organized according to the pattern of a *Sharī'ah* or Islamic state. The "*Sharī'ah*" as stated in this oft-quoted *āyah* therefore precedes the *Sharī'ah* law as is generally understood by the *'ulamā'*.

Sharī'ah as "Categorizations of Human Acts"

In the context of the Sharī'ah as law in a technical sense, al-Ṭabarī offers a "practical" definition by enumerating its constituents, as in his *al-Musammā Jāmi' al-Bayān fī Ta'wīl al-Qur'ān*, where he deals with the reference to *Sharī'ah* in Sūrah al-Jāthiyah, *āyah* 18, as follows:

> "The *Sharī'ah* comprises the law of inheritance (*farā'id*), the *ḥadd* punishments (*ḥudūd*), the commandments and prohibitions."[38]

Unlike *dīn*, where he takes the broad view, al-Ṭabarī equates *Sharī'ah* with the law, and in this regard, it typifies the conservative, restrictive view of the term and is often cited by other traditional *'ulamā'* as the authority for the classic definition of *Sharī'ah*, which, as suggested at the outset, views it as "law," implying that defining the *Sharī'ah* is a matter of identifying its legal components.

It is contended that even within the matrix of a legalistic doctrine, referring to the *Sharīʿah* as God's commandments and prohibitions is correct but not completely explicative of the concept. This is because the *Sharīʿah* is the sum total of God's "categorizations of human acts" (*al-aḥkām fī al-afʿāl* or *al-aḥkām al-ʿamaliyyah*), and in these are commandments and prohibitions as well as other divisions, according to the classic definition by the great thirteenth-century *faqīh* and *mutakallim* Sayf al-Dīn al-Āmidī (d. 631/1233).[39] These categorizations are constituted into two sets: normative (*taklīfī*) categories and non-normative (*waḍʿī*) categories. It should be noted that rather than speaking simply of the *Sharīʿah*, the *fuqahā'* (jurists) would frequently speak of *Sharīʿah* categorizations (*al-aḥkām al-sharʿiyyah*).[40] Of the normative, there are five *Sharīʿah* categories: mandatory (*wājib*), recommended (*mandūb*), permissible (*mubāḥ*), discouraged (*makrūh*) and forbidden (*ḥarām*). So there are three shades of human acts which are neither mandatory (commanded) nor forbidden (prohibited). As for the latter two, they may be rightly termed rules of law in conformity with a command theory of law: commands and prohibitions are prescriptions that leave individuals with no choice but to comply. For the other three, they are unique and do not fit under the "rules of law" rubric in that they do not order behaviour but only seek to influence it while offering the choice of non-compliance.[41] It is here that *Sharīʿah* as *fiqh* parts company with *kalām* with regard to the categorizations of human acts. As the subject of *kalām* will be dealt with in Chapter 3, it is premature to go deeper into this except to state that the *kalām* approach differs from *fiqh* in its epistemological treatment of the categorizations as well as in the conceptualization of knowledge.

For the non-normative categories, there are two main subsets: valid/invalid (*ṣaḥīḥ/bāṭil*), unaffected by extenuating circumstances (*ʿazīmah*) and affected by extenuating circumstances (*rukhsah*). While the first subset is self-evident (*e.g.* valid or invalid transaction, act of worship), the second is slightly more complicated. The second subset applies generally to an obligatory act, the question being whether it is affected by extenuating circumstances, which may then remove the obligation or attenuate it in some way. A basic example is the relief from the obligation of observing the Ramaḍān fast and a reduction in the number of *rak'ah*s (bowing-prostration sequences) in the *ṣalāh* (ritual prayer) while on a journey beyond a prescribed distance.[42]

In terms of a command theory of law, this definition of *Sharī'ah*, at least in part, may be said to foreshadow the Austinian definition of law in English jurisprudence.[43] Indeed, this is an oversimplification. The Austinian command theory posits laws as commands of a sovereign backed by sanctions if not complied with. Positive law consists of those commands laid down by a sovereign, to be contrasted to other lawgivers, like God's general commands.[44] Indeed, there is greater merit in the Austinian linkage with the Torah, but not the Qur'ān *per se*, as a law of commands and prohibitions. Within "the province of jurisprudence," Austin placed certain "exceptions," which are items prescribing action but do not carry the force of sanctions. He also excluded from the province of law religion, morality, convention and custom. A common misconception is that Austin advocates the separation of law and morality, whereas he is merely stating that there is a substantive body of law that is not moral.[45] As for such a separation in the *Sharī'ah* as advocated by certain quarters, it would be a contradiction in terms in view of the definition of the *Sharī'ah* itself. This issue is taken up more substantively in Chapter 4.

Austin's analytical jurisprudence entailed common-law reasoning by way of expounding the *ratio decidendi* of a case, which eventually not only became the foundation for setting precedents but also provided the basis for producing judge-made law. More significantly, in the context of the *Sharī'ah* as defined by al-Ṭabarī, Austin's legal theory is among the first in modern Western jurisprudence that is "imperium oriented"—law imposed from on high—and significant, bearing in mind that the command theory was quite influential in the latter part of the twentieth century. All things considered, however, the Austinian command theory is fundamentally inadequate to support the definition of *Sharīʻah*. In any event, al-Ṭabarī's characterization of the *Sharīʻah* as "commands and prohibitions"—pertaining predominantly to matters of religious observances—plus issues on inheritance and the fixed punishments for crimes do not go far enough to provide for a legal system that would be required for the administration of the vast Muslim empire that was to grow from the modest beginnings of Medina, regardless that it was no doubt the first city-state founded on the Qur'ān under the direct "government" of the Prophet. Whether or not this would be considered a "theocracy" and thus set the model for an "Islamic state" is a subject worth pursuing, perhaps in another enterprise, in order to do justice to its importance. Nevertheless, al-Ṭabarī's approach provides a good starting point.

Along these lines, Joseph Schact has defined the *Sharīʻah* as "an all-embracing body of religious duties, the totality of Allah's commands that regulate the life of every Muslim in all its aspects."[46] Traditional Muslim scholars, legalistic-minded *'ulamā'* and generally the conservative side of the *ummah* would have no serious issue with such a definition, what more with sound bites like "all-embracing" and "totality of Allah's commands." I have some issues. The emphasis in this definition is on rules and regulations, that is, law as encapsulated in Schacht's assertion that "Islamic law is the epitome of Islamic thought, the most typical manifestation of the Islamic way of life, the core and kernel of Islam itself."[47] Schacht contends that the "very term *fiqh* for knowledge shows that early Islam regarded knowledge of the sacred Law as the knowledge par excellence" and that theology (that is, *uṣūl al-dīn* or *uṣūl al-kalām* as used interchangeably[48]) has never been able to achieve comparable importance in Islam and it is impossible to understand Islam without understanding Islamic law. The claim by Schacht that "early Islam" placed "*fiqh*" (as knowledge of the Divine Law) as the knowledge par excellence is incorrect as will be made clearer in due course. Suffice at this juncture to say that *fiqh* as a study of the *Sharīʻah* as law exemplified by the use of *qiyās* (initially employed by Imām Abū

Ḥanīfah (d. 150/767) and later fine-tuned to a precise methodology under Imām al-Shāfiʿī (d. 204/820) came later in Islamic history. Even then, as would be made clear from the initial work of Abū Ḥanīfah, there is nothing to support the assertion that he regarded "knowledge of the Divine Law" as "knowledge par excellence." On the contrary, as will be established in Chapter 2, he regarded *fiqh* as *kalām*, albeit a proto version. Nevertheless, I am not suggesting that law in Islam is not important, but the point must be made that *Sharīʿah* and *fiqh*, used interchangeably, included ethics, morality, society and law, and in early Islam there is evidence to point to the fact that knowledge of law was not of the highest importance. According to Ibn Khaldūn, (d. 808/1406) the early Muslims never had the need to resort to legal reasoning or to derive rules from complicated juristic processes. To them, nothing more than linguistic habit was needed for deriving ideas from words. They had no need to study the chains of transmitters, for they themselves were the source for most of the norms needed in cases where the need arose for *ijtihād* to derive laws.[49] And even as *fiqh* started to become a subject of study, it was not always seen in the matrix of the *Sharīʿah* as "law," as in rules and ordinances of God. Schact's predilection in this reflects the predominance of the position given to the *fuqahā'* over the *mutakallimūn* (scholastic/dialectic theologians), particularly the importance of al-Shāfiʿī over that of Abū Ḥanīfah. There should not be any issue as to who is greater than the other for both were undoubtedly unsurpassed in their positions as the leading *mujtahid*s of their time. While both were canonized as founders of two of the four major Sunni schools of jurisprudence, they were distinguished by different approaches. The distinction goes back to Ibn Khaldūn, who said that the treatment by the *fuqahā'* "is more germane to jurisprudence and more suited for special cases" than the treatment by the *mutakallimūn*, because while the *fuqahā'* based their analysis on legal points, the *mutakallimūn* "present them in their bare outlines without reference to *fiqh*." They were also inclined to use logical deduction.[50]

The earlier reference to al-Āmidī's definition of the *Sharīʿah* in terms of the categorizations does not, however, place al-Āmidī necessarily into the category of *fuqahā'* who were opposed to the *mutakallimūn* in as much as it is erroneous to see them as representing mutually exclusive groups. In medieval Islam, many *ʿulamā'* wore both hats, as it were, and the question was one of emphasis or orientation. As for orientation, there is also the question of the ascent of a group in early Islam who were the practitioners of *taṣawwuf*, and over the ages the term Sufi became associated with them alongside the term Sufism. That indeed is a specialized subject not advisable to be commented upon by those who are not themselves steeped in the tradition and armchair commentators like the author do not fit the description of adepts in the field. Suffice it to say that this monograph will have occasion to include incidental commentaries pertaining to it, whenever relevant, but done purely as detached transmission. Be that as it may, the *ʿulamā'* and the adepts from all three groups regard the *Sharīʿah* as the *sine qua non* to the establishment of Islamic civilization. The difference indeed is one of degree of preponderance towards viewing the *Sharīʿah* as law.

All-Encompassing Law

Classical Muslim jurisprudence treats law as the revealed will of God, and because direct access to revelation had ceased with the passing of the Prophet of Islam, "the *Sharīʿah*, having once achieved perfection of expression, was in principle static and immutable."[51] According to this approach, *Sharīʿah* law, being the embodiment of God's will, is therefore cast in stone and the pivotal role of the jurist is not of expounder but discoverer "of the divine command."[52] Indeed, by placing divine scripture as the *Grundnorm*[53] not just for a nation but for the entire *ummah*, such an argument is grist for the mill for fundamentalists: The *Sharīʿah* is the unifying and ultimate criterion for Muslims as the bulwark against "the variety of legal systems which would be the inevitable result if law were the product of human reason based upon the local circumstances and the particular needs of a given community."[54]

Reverting to the issue of "the totality of man's acts in all its aspects" being the concern of the *Sharī'ah*, there is the view that the *maqāṣid al-Sharī'ah* (the higher objectives of the *Sharī'ah*) warrant that a comprehensive definition of the *Sharī'ah* must go beyond mere law to incorporate society, the economy and political philosophy. Towards this end, the *Sharī'ah* must mean "all those systems legislated by God, or whose sources are legislated by God, for the purpose of organizing man's relationship with God, with the Muslim community, with the human community, and life in general."[55] While such a catholic approach towards the definition of *Sharī'ah* would make Schacht's earlier formulation of "*Sharī'ah* as law" look rather myopic, it also puts everyone on notice that the discourse of the *Sharī'ah* must go beyond the confines of *fiqh* jurisprudence to include *kalām* as well as *siyāsah* jurisprudence, entering the domain of political Islam and the Islamic state. We will deal with *kalām* as well as *siyāsah al-shar'iyyah*, two concepts that are highly misunderstood and controversial, but we will have to defer entering into the discourse on political Islam and the Islamic state to another forum.

Those who subscribe to the position that the *Sharī'ah* is all-embracing are prone to cite chapter and verse on the immutability of God's law and the perfection and completeness of the *Sharī'ah* upon the demise of the Prophet. The *āyah* that readily comes to mind is

> "... This day I have perfected for you your religion and completed My favour upon you and have approved for you Islam as religion ..."[56]

Well documented as having been revealed at 'Arafah on the 9th of Dhū al-Ḥijjah, 10 AH, that is, just about 80 days before the passing of the Prophet, this *ayāh* may be likened as the last and most definitive passage signifying the end of Qur'ānic legislation because no legal injunction was revealed after this. If the law has been perfected, anything that comes after would, by logical extension, be flawed, that is, less than perfect. Thus, unlike Western law, be it Roman law,

European continental law or English common law, the traditional view is that the *Sharīʻah*—as fully cast and in need of no addition or emendation by that fateful date—moulds the *ummah*, whereas the *ummah* cannot mould the *Sharīʻah*. There is, as it were, no provision for any kind of jurisprudential reverse osmosis. Along these lines, the idea that the *Sharīʻah* can be shaped by juristic reasoning is therefore repugnant to a law based on divine revelation: you are either with the *Sharīʻah* or against the *Sharīʻah*.[57] Indeed, it is clear that notwithstanding its prevalence, such a position does not comport with the historical reality in the development of Islamic law. In this regard, Coulson's contention posited contingently—that multiple legal systems within the Islamic polity would result "if law were the product of human reason" in response to local circumstances and needs—is problematic for precisely the reason that the history of the development of Islamic law clearly shows that multiplicity in *fiqh* systems has been a reality since the word *fiqh* morphed into its technical usage, as we shall see in the next chapter. One is inclined to agree with the view that the approach as subsumed under Coulson's ascription of the *Sharīʻah* as a one-dimensional monolithic legal system would not be conducive to any significant "discretionary judgment, legal innovation, or legal change."[58] It is this cast-iron outlook of the *Sharīʻah* being God's final word on the law that has led to *Sharīʻah* law being seen as a calcified body of law that is unable to respond to the dynamic changes of society. The notion of *Sharīʻah* law seems to be that whatever was good enough to govern the people more than a millennium ago is good enough today without any need to add, subtract or amend the said law, the progress of society and civilization being somehow divorced from the processes of the law. This is, of course, to put it generally for in Islamic jurisprudence, the doctrine of *al-thawābit wa al-mutaghayyirāt* makes it clear that there are rules that are founded on proofs of absolute certainty (*dalīl qaṭʻi*) and on proofs of speculative assumption (*dalīl ẓanni*), the former being unchangeable and the latter being categorised as *mutaghayyirāt* or variables, and are therefore subject to change, new *tafsīr* and expansion. Nevertheless, while there is no fundamental dispute that such a conception is in place—the view that as society advances, flexibility in the rules is needed to allow for adaptation and adjustment—the central problem lies in deciding which rule falls under what. The orthodox position is that in matters pertaining to *'aqāid* (articles of belief), *'ibādah* (rituals of worship) and *akhlaq* (morality and ethics), the rules are permanently fixed. Conventional wisdom suggests that it is only in the area of worldly affairs such as social, economic and political matters (lumped generally as *siyāsah*) that are categorised as the variables. However, that is only the theory while the reality bites hard for till today the great bone of contention remains whether one can legitimately separate moral and ethical concerns from the issues of *siyāsah* pertaining to political systems or matters of governance as well as socio-economic values and models.

Be that as it may, a caveat must be lodged here against the presumption that man has necessarily progressed just because of the passage of time. Social Darwinism, which purports to transpose the working of biological evolution to civilizational evolution, is at best pseudo-science if not fantasy altogether. Indeed, the civilizational history of Islam, particularly during its golden age, is replete with advances and discoveries in science, mathematics and medicine which are making their impact even today, more than a thousand years later. But the golden age of Islam was what it was not because the law had ossified or that the Muslim world had become introverted and exclusivist. On the contrary, this was a period which saw the assimilation of not just the scientific but also the cultural, linguistic and legal influences that percolated from the conquered lands culminating in the classic works being translated from the ancient civilizations from the Greeks to the Phoenicians into Arabic and Persian among other languages. What it means is that the golden age of Islam is clear testimony of the significance of *kalām* (theology), *falsafah* (philosophy), *taṣawwuf* (Sufism) and *Sharī'ah* law being open to the influence of other civilizations be it classical antiquity, Persian civilization, Indian or oriental culture. What should not be lost in this crucial age of Islamic civilization is the fact that this was not just a history of blind imitation or mere recycling of Greek, Sassanian or other Eastern ideas but "rather an original synthesis and therefore a unique achievement."[59] Having said that, it cannot be denied that society does not remain static, and since time immemorial mankind has been making its own processes of reform and renewal with varying degrees of success and failure too.

Coming back to the basic infelicity of Coulson's proposition that the *Sharīʿah* is static and immutable, my argument is that even if we accept that the *Sharīʿah* is "the unifying and ultimate criterion" (as asserted by Coulson), human reason, when exercised within the province of the *Sharīʿah*, will only yield rulings or principles that will blend with and not run counter to it. The fundamental issue of whether the *Sharīʿah*, as divine law, is immutable or that it is indeed capable of evolution and has in fact evolved, will be more substantively answered in due course, but suffice it to say at this juncture that the answer to this conundrum is again a function of the definition of the *Sharīʿah* itself. Meantime, the rendering of *Sharīʿah* as "the way of life as ordained by God" has another primary implication in terms of the province of the law when taken to its logical conclusion, as contended by fundamentalists. The term "fundamentalist" or "Islamic fundamentalism" is subject to various interpretations, particularly in the discourse of the Islamic state. From one perspective, it covers a wide spectrum of enterprises, organisations and movements. While most of them are intolerant and exclusivist, some are manifestly pluralistic and inclusivist. There is a general misconception that fundamentalists are anti-science and that may have some basis in the early phase of Islamic history, where Traditionists condemned rationalists for resorting to reason, as we will be discussing in greater detail in due course. Today, Muslim engineers and technicians have turned to radical fundamentalism to advance their cause. Therefore, no hard and fast rule may be applied to fundamentalism, as some may be purely devotional movements that advocate universal peace and subscribe to democracy. Yet others may be primarily political, some authoritarian and some violent.[60] Yet another view links it to Salafi reformism traceable to Wahhabism and fine-tuned by the likes of Muḥammad 'Abduh and Jamāl al-Dīn al-Afghānī.[61] The Wahhabis were accused of intolerance in creedal terms, in character with their Ḥanbalī roots, but in terms of the specific historical context of their rise in the Arabian Peninsula in the later part of the eighteenth century, they were allegations of brutality in their reformist zeal in the name of Islam. When the Wahhabis overran Mecca and Medina (1220-1221/1805-1806), one of the first acts committed was the desecration of the cemetery where many relatives and Companions of the Prophet were buried.[62]

Their lineage is said to be traceable to Ibn Taymiyyah of the Ḥanbalī school of law, who declared jihad on Shī'ism, Sufism and *falsafah* and inveighed against the purported pernicious innovation in practices such as visiting the grave of the Prophet and the celebration of *mawlid al-Rasūl*, condemning such acts as akin to the aping of the Christian worship of Jesus as God. The general view is that Wahhabism's eponymous founder, Muḥammad ibn 'Abd al-Wahhāb propagated the doctrine of *takfīr*, which is the excommunication of a Muslim from the faith—declaring him or her to be an infidel on account of not subscribing to his brand of Islam. Apart from those already stated, grounds for excommunication included not recognising the sovereignty of the absolute authority of the king, which would have been obviously politically motivated, considering 'Abd al-Wahhāb's alliance with 'Abd al-'Azīz ibn Muḥammad bin Sa'ūd (d. 1217/1803). In any event, as we shall see in Chapter 4 on the discussion of the law of rebellion and usurpation, there appears to be consensus among the *fuqahā'* concerning the primary rule of obedience to those in power. According to a general view, the Salafis of today, being descended from the Wahhabi line, but unlike 'Abduh and his moderate cohorts, often ride on their moral high horse as being "holier than thou" and are in the habit of condemning other Muslims not of their ilk as being practitioners of *bid'ah* in a similar vein as that done by the Wahhabis.[63] That, of course, is the general view concerning the Wahhabis. An alternative discourse, however, sees its founder as the harbinger of reform, preaching an inclusivist Islam which envisages a society comprising Muslims, Christians and Jews living harmoniously and, significantly, where jihad can only be invoked in the name of self-defence of the *ummah.* According to this narrative, it was only after the death of Muḥammad ibn Saʿūd that his successor ʿAbd al-ʿAzīz ibn Muḥammad, took the hard line of *takfīr* ideas of Ibn Taymiyyah. And that was for political expansion and consolidation of power.[64]

Conclusion

In light of the preceding discussion, it may be said that from the prism of fundamentalism, the *Sharīʿah*—as God's commands—would have to incorporate all aspects of human activity—not just the legal and judicial system but the socio-economic and political system as well. This is the approach taken by fundamentalists such as Abū al-Aʿlā al-Mawdūdī, Ḥasan al-Bannā, Sayyid Quṭb, the Taliban among the Sunnis and the Ayatollah Ruhollah Khomeini among the Shīʿites.[65] The question posed is whether the *Sharīʿah* indeed regulates all aspects of the life of every Muslim and by extension the entire Muslim community. The position that the *Sharīʿah* rules, as are derived directly from the Qur'ān and the Sunnah, are "divine" is generally accepted. However, when the legal rules as derived from *ijmāʿ*, that is, the principles derived from the consensus of the *ʿulamāʿ*, as well as the principles derived from *qiyās*, are included as part of the *Sharīʿah*, the question is whether *Sharīʿah* law, so derived, can still be considered divine and immutable. If the answer is in the affirmative, it raises a foundational issue: Allah, it would appear, is ipso facto not the final word on the *Sharīʿah* in as much as *ijmāʿ* and *qiyās* are essentially juristic processes, yelding man-made laws. Would that not dilute the purport of the *Sharīʿah* as immutable and all encompassing, regulating all aspects of the life of the entire Muslim community? Would that not also pose a fundamental contradiction to the doctrine of the perfection of the *Sharīʿah* as underscored in Surāh al-Mā'idah, *āyah* 3, as explicated earlier? The answers to these questions will be unveiled as we proceed in stages with this enquiry in the next chapter.

Notes

1. With regard to the *Sharīʿah* as law, this monograph is essentially focused on Sunni jurisprudence. For a concise introductory treatment of jurisprudence from the *Shī'ī* perspective, see Muḥammad Bāqir al-Ṣadr's *Durūs fī 'Ilm al-Uṣūl*, translated as *Lessons in Islamic Jurisprudence*, with an introduction by Roy Parviz Mottahedeh (Oxford: Oneworld Oxford, 2003). This book explores jurisprudential and theological issues rather than legalistic issues. For *Shī'īsm* in general, see *Shī'īsm Doctrines, Thought, and Spirituality*, edited by Hamid Dabashi and Seyyed Hossein Nasr (SUNY Press, 1988).
2. Sūrah al-Mā'idah, *āyah* 48, tr. Marmaduke Pickthall, *The Glorious Koran.*
3. Sūrah al-Aʿrāf, *āyah* 163; Edward William Lane, *Arabic-English Lexicon.*
4. Seyyed Hossein Nasr et al, *The Study Quran: A New Translation and Commentary* (Harper One, 2015), Kindle, 58790.
5. Pickthall: "For each We have appointed a divine law and a traced-out way ..."
   Asad: "Unto every one of you have We appointed a (different) law and way of life ..."
   Yusuf Ali: "To each among you have We prescribed a Law and an open way ..."
   Zaki: "For each faith-community we have appointed a Divine Law and a way of life ..."
   Nasr: "For each among you, we have appointed a law and a way..."
6. Nasr, *Study Quran*, 15498.
7. Ibid.

8. "*Wa law shā'a Allāhu laja'alakum ummatan wāḥidah...*" According to Ibn Kathīr, this is a general proclamation to all nations informing them of "Allah's mighty ability." Every prophet was given his own distinct law that is later abrogated partially or totally. Again, this interpretation is said to be inconsistent with the grammatical meaning of the entire *āyah*.
9. Nasr, *Study Quran*, 15498.
10. Sūrah al-Shūrā, *āyah* 13: "*Shara'a lakum min al-dīni mā waṣṣā bihi Nūḥan wa alladhī awḥaynā ilayka wa mā waṣṣaynā bihi Ibrāhīma wa Mūsā wa 'Īsā an aqīmū al-dīna wa lā tatafarraqū fīhi kabur ...*"
11. Pickthall; Yusuf Ali: "The same religion has He established for you as that which He enjoined on Noah—which We have sent by inspiration to thee—and that which We enjoined on Abraham Moses and Jesus: Namely that ye should remain steadfast in Religion and make no divisions therein ..."
12. Sūrah Fāṭir, *āyah* 24.
13. Sūrah Ibrāhīm, *āyah* 4 (Pickthall).
14. Sūrah al-Naḥl, *āyah* 36. See Asad's commentary. *Cf.* Pickthall: "And verily We have raised in every nation a messenger, (proclaiming): Serve Allah and shun false gods."
15. Wael Hallaq, *The Origins and Evolution of Islamic Law* (Cambridge University Press, 2005), 21.
16. Jacob Neusner and Tamara Sonn, *Comparing Religions through Law: Judaism and Islam* (London: Routledge, 1999), 5.
17. Asad, *The Message of the Qur'ān*, 8.
18. William Chittick, *The Sufi Path of Knowledge: Ibn Al-Arabi's Metaphysics of Imagination* (State University of New York Press, 1989), 171.
19. Sūrah al-Anbiyā', *āyah* 25 (Pickthall).
20. Sūrah al-Jāthiyah, *āyah* 18: "*Thumma ja'alnāka 'alā sharī'atin min al-amri fa attabi'hā wa lā tattabi' ahwā'a alladhīna lā ya'lamūn*"

(Pickthall).

21. Nasr, *Study Quran,* 58817.
22. As in Yusuf Ali's translation with annotation.
23. "And, finally, (O Muhammad,) We have set thee on a way by which the purpose (of faith) may be fulfilled: so follow thou this (way), and follow not the likes and dislikes of those who do not know (the truth)."
24. Syed Muhammad Naquib al-Attas, *Prolegomena to the Metaphysics of Islām—An Exposition of the Fundamental Elements of the World View of Islām* (International Institute of Islamic Thought and Civilization, 1995), 42.
25. Ibid., 52.
26. Presumably al-Attas's own translation since no attribution is made to any authority, just as his analyses of the various semantic attributes of key Qur'ānic terms where, after acknowledging that his interpretation of the basic connotations of the term *dīn* is based on Ibn Manẓur's classic *Lisān al-'Arab* (Beyrouth, 1968), he says, on page 41, that "the formulation and conceptualization of the meaning of religion (*dīn*), as well as the explanation of key concepts in meaningful order are, however, my own."
27. Sūrah Āl 'Imrān, *āyah* 83.
28. Joseph Lumbard, "The Qur'ānic View of Sacred History and Other Religions," in *Study Quran.*
29. Sūrah al-Ḥajj, *āyahs* 67-69.
30. Asad, in *The Message of the Qur'ān,* says, "The Sabians were a monotheistic group occupying an intermediate position between Judaism and Christianity". Asad contends that their name (probably derived from the Aramaic verb *tsebha* ('he immersed himself [in water]') would suggest they were followers of John the Baptist. In this regard, they could be identified with the Mandaeans, a community still existing in Iraq. They are not to be confused with the so-called 'Sabians of Harran,' a gnostic sect

which still existed in the early centuries of Islam."

31. Lumbard, *op. cit.*, citing al-Baqarah, *āyah* 62.
32. Abū Jaʿfar Muḥammad ibn Jarīr al-Ṭabarī; see infra, n.38 for anecdotal accounts.
33. Lumbard, *op. cit.*
34. Sūrah Āl ʿImrān, *āyah* 95.
35. Lumbard, *op. cit.*
36. Sūrah al-Ḥūjarāt, *āyah* 13.
37. Therefore, the rendering of "the straight course of a Divine Law," in Zaki's translation as well as similar ones should be read to go beyond "mere formal rites and legal provisions" pertaining to Muslims and in a more comprehensive sense as God's laws governing the entire cosmos.
38. *Tafsīr al- Ṭabarī al-Musammā Jāmiʿ al-Bayān fī Ta'wīl al-Qur'ān* (lit. "Al-Ṭabarī's Commentary Called 'The Known Manifest Compilation in Qur'ānic Hermeneutics'"). His monumental *Tārīkh al-Rusul wa al-Mulūk*, (History of the Prophets and the Kings) chronicles the history of the ancient world, the prophets (a complete recension of Ibn Isḥāq's *Sīrah Rasūl Allāh*) and the Rightly Guided Caliphate in the Arabian Peninsula to the Umayyad caliphate's shift to Damascus and its overthrow by the Abbasid caliphate in 132/750 right down to 302/915. Apart from being an exegete and historian, he was also an accomplished *faqīh* who founded his own school—the Jarīrī *madhhab*—and true to the Islamic tradition, his views on the Ḥanbalī interpretation of Surāh al-Isrā', *āyah* 81, flew straight in the cross hairs of the followers of the Ḥanbalī school which led to his house being often pelted with stones. On the *tafsīr*, there is the famous anecdote related by Abū al-Qāsim ibn ʿAqīl al-Warrāq: "Imam Ibn Jarīr once said to his students, 'Are you prepared to write down my lesson on the *tafsīr* of the Holy Qur'ān?' When they asked how long that would be, he said, '30,000 pages!' They expressed their

reservation on the ground that the task could not be accomplished in one life time. He therefore scaled it down to only 3,000 pages!" Actually, the popular twelve-volume edition by Dār al-Kutub al-ʿIlmiyyah, Beirut, 1997, stocked in most libraries today, comprises more than 8,000 pages.

39. Bernard G. Weiss, *The Search for God's Law: Islamic Jurisprudence in the Writings of Sayf al-Dīn al-Āmidī* (Salt Lake City: University of Utah Press, 1992), 1.
40. Weiss, *God's Law*, 2.
41. Ibid., 3.
42. Ibid.
43. John Austin, *The Province of Jurisprudence Determined* (1832) (The Lawbook Exchange, Ltd., 2012).
44. Brian Bix, "John Austin," *The Stanford Encyclopedia of Philosophy* (Spring, 2015 Edition), edited by Edward N. Zalta; accessed August, 2015; http://plato.stanford.edu/archives/spr2015/entries/austin-john.
45. Ibid. Austin was the first writer in English jurisprudence to approach the theory of law through the analysis of key concepts in what has become known as analytical jurisprudence.
46. Joseph Schacht, *An Introduction to Islamic Law* (Oxford: Clarendon Press, 1964), 1.
47. Ibid.
48. In early Islam, these terms—*dīn*, *kalām* and *qawāʿid*—were interchangeable, as discussed further in chapter 3.
49. Ibn Khaldūn, *The Muqaddimāh—An Introduction to History*, translated by F. Rosenthal, 3 vols (New York: Pantheon Books, 1958): 3:27.
50. Ibid., 28
51. N.J. Coulson, *A History of Islamic Law* (Edinburgh: Edinburgh University Press, 1964), 1-2.
52. Ibid., 2.

53. In the sense of Hans Kelsen's Grundnorm—the highest fundamental norm, assumed as an initial hypothesis. However, unlike Kelsen's pure theory of law, which is morality-neutral, the *Sharīʿah* as Grundnorm is the ultimate moral criterion.
54. Coulson, *History,* 5.
55. Maḥmūd Shaltūt, *Al-Islām: ʿAqīdah wa Sharīʿah* (Cairo: Dār al-Shurūq, 1986), 10, quoted by Ibrahim M. Abu Rabi', *Contemporary Arab Thought—Studies in Post-1967 Arab Intellectual History* (Pluto Press, 2004), 206.
56. Surāh al-Māʾidah, *āyah* 3: "*Al-yawma akmaltu lakum dīnakum wa atmamtu ʿalaykum niʿmatī wa raḍītu lakum al-Islāma dīnā …*"
57. Coulson, *History,* 85; this is, admittedly, a subjective paraphrasing of Coulson's position on the general definition of *Sharīʿah.*
58. Anver M. Emon, "Conceiving Islamic Law in a Pluralist Society: History, Politics and Multicultural Jurisprudence," *Singapore Journal of Legal Studies* [2006]: 350-1.
59. Franz Rosenthal, Emile Marmorstein, *The Classical Heritage in Islam* (Psychology Press, 1992).
60. *Islam, Politics, and Social Movements,* edited by Edmund Burke III and Ira M. Lapidus (University of California Press, 1990).
61. Olivier Roy, *The Failure of Political Islam* (Harvard University Press, 1994), 30-33.
62. Thus, in 1343 AH/1924 AD, they demolished more grave sites, and in 1413 AH/1993, they also demolished the house of Khadījah as well as the house where the Prophet had been born, turning both of them into public bathrooms.
63. See generally Hamid Algar, *Wahhabism: A Critical Essay,* (Islamic Publications International, 2002). ʿAbduh's ideological compatriot Rashīd Riḍā, however, has been accused of being pro-Wahhabi on account of his public defence of the sect and his relationship with King ʿAbd al-ʿAzīz. See *Al-Rāfiḍah wa al-Wahhābiyyah,* ed. *ʿAbd al-Raḥmān ibn ʿAbd al-Jabbār al-Furaywāʾī* (Cairo: Maktabah al-

Nāfidhah, 2007) and Muḥammad ibn ʿAbdullāh al-Salmān, *Rashīd Riḍā wa Daʿwah: al-Shaykh Muḥammad ʿAbd al-Wahhāb* (Kuwait: Maktabath al-Muʿallā, 1988). Both citations are from Khaled Abou El-Fadl, *Reasoning with God: Reclaiming Shariʿah in the Modern Age* (Rowman and Littlefield, 2014).

64. Natana J. DeLong-Bas, *Wahhabi Islam: From Revival and Reform to Global Jihad* (I.B. Tauris, 2007).

65. Many may object to the Taliban being included in this category on the grounds that this is essentially an anti-Western terrorist organization populated by a preponderance of suicide bombers and notorious for the imposition of *ḥudūd* law, floggings, beheadings and its treatment of women as chattels. While that may be true, it does not detract from the fact that theirs is, like the other conservative groups, based on the view of the *Sharīʿah* being the be-all and end-all of the *ummah.*

Chapter 2

Fiqh

Fiqh in the Qur'ān and beyond

The general understanding of "*fiqh*" today is that it is the same as "*Sharī'ah*" as far as it appertains to law. Thus, references to "*fiqh* law" and "*Sharī'ah* law" are synonymous at least in general discourse. Hence, *uṣūl al-fiqh*, literally the sources of the law or jurisprudence, is also said to be synonymous with *uṣūl al-Sharī'ah*.[1] However, the position taken by this study as well as in the treatises and works on *uṣūl al-fiqh*, is that they are not the same. This is not to say that the term "*uṣūl al-Sharī'ah*" is a misnomer but that its usage is intended to be constrained to just the two primary sources of the divine law, that is, the Qur'ān and the Sunnah. This may be illustrated by reference to Ibn Rushd's (d. 595/1198) treatment of the term. According to him, it is not permissible for the *'ulamā'* to explain to the general public the demonstrative proofs or allegorical understanding pertaining to the sources of the Law (*uṣūl al-Sharī'ah*) because that might destroy their apparent understanding and leave them in a state of unbelief (*kufr*). This is on account of the fact that of the three categories of people in respect of the *Sharī'ah*, the class known as the "rhetorical people" (*al-khiṭābiyyūn*) who are the overwhelming multitude (*al-jumhūr al-ghālib*) are incapable of understanding beyond the apparent meaning or interpretation of the Qur'ān/*ḥadīth*.[2] Ibn Rushd's usage of *uṣūl al-Sharī'ah* in this context appertains only to the primary sources—the Qur'ān and the Sunnah—and not other sources derived from *fiqh* which as we shall see appertains to the law in a more technical and nuanced context. Indeed, it has been said that the genuine *Sharīʿah* as derived from the Qur'ān and the Sunnah has been so obscured that the concept of *fiqh* has become "twisted" and regarded as part of the *Sharīʿah* itself.[3] At this juncture these terms are used in a liberal, even loose sense but as the discourse progresses more layers of meaning and connotations will be unveiled and the provinces of both will be more clearly delineated. To begin with, "*fiqh*" explained thus is not good enough to solve the conundrum concerning the first question raised in Chapter 1, that is, the definition of "*Sharīʿah*." The similarity between *Sharīʿah* and *fiqh* has its limits and one must again fall back on the etymology and review its usage first in the literal sense.

In the Qur'ān, "*fiqh*" is used essentially to signify "understanding" in a general sense, with no particular bearing to law or legal ruling, as some examples will demonstrate.[4] With reference to the jinn and mankind doomed to Hell, it is said,

> "... They have hearts with which they do not understand, (*lā yafqahūn*) they have eyes with which they do not see, and they have ears with which they do not hear ..."[5]

Muslim children are taught a common prayer asking God to facilitate their speech and free them from impediment and stuttering. This is from the Qur'ān and the context is the Prophet Moses supplicating to God to mend his speech impediment so that people would understand him:

> "My Lord, expand me, from my breast (with assurance), and ease for me my task, and untie for me the knot from my tongue, that they may understand my speech (*yafqahū qawlī*)."[6]

In Sūrah al-Tawbah, *āyah* 122, the phrase "*li yatafaqqahū fī al-dīn*" (to learn the religion) signifies that the objective of learning is to gain understanding.[7] According to Ibn Kathīr, al-Rāzī and al-Ṭabarī, this *āyah* does not refer to battle but to religious instruction as a whole. When the Meccans converted to Islam only a small group needed to go to Medina and take instruction from the Prophet regarding the religion after which they should return to teach the others. If all were to descend on Medina, it would overwhelm the accommodations available.[8] Qur'ānic usage also talks of those who are known as "*al-rāsikhūn fī al-'ilm*," that is, those who are well grounded in knowledge or of sound instruction and the "*ulū al-albāb*," that is, men of understanding.[9] There are at least two key concepts in that short phrase which warrant amplification: grounding in knowledge and attainment of understanding. Depending on one's spiritual calling or station, these terms are of wide and variable application.[10]

Sufis, for instance, have an interpretation of the terms which departs in material ways from that of the *fuqahā'*.[11] Ibn al-'Arabī speaks of three levels of knowledge. First, there is *'ilm al-'aql*, that is, rational knowledge, which can be acquired by the use of reason. Second, there is *'ilm al-ahwāl*, which is knowledge (*dhawq*/taste) of states, which is what we experience. And finally, there is *'ilm al-asrār*, which is knowledge of the mysteries, intuitive or esoteric knowledge. Such knowledge is innate, beyond reason and manifests itself only in whom that God chooses. This forms the kernel of Ibn al-'Arabī's philosophy of knowledge, which four centuries later finds some expression in Spinoza's *scientia intuitiva*.[12]

In respect of the term "*Sharī'ah*," the Sufis see it as the whole outward dimension (the road of exoteric canon) of Islam as opposed to the *ṭarīqah* (the narrower spiritual path) and the *ḥaqīqah* (the esoteric reality), which makes up its inward dimension.[13] They consider the *Sharī'ah*, as used in the sense of *fiqh* by the scholars of jurisprudence, excludes Islamic intellectuality, leaving out key matters in the pursuit of knowledge such as metaphysics, cosmology, psychology, anthropology, prophetology, eschatology and so on. On the other hand, to the Sufi masters such as Ibn al-'Arabī, *Sharī'ah* or *shar'* means the "wide road" of Islam. Going beyond law in the sense of *fiqh* which is just the legal rules that guide activity, the wide road encompasses "all the teachings on every level that can properly be called Islamic" and also "the intellectual principles which determine correct knowledge and the moral principles and practical guidelines which give birth to noble character traits."[14] One common fallacy attributed to Sufis is that they believe they can attain the ultimate truth by outwardly abandoning the *Sharīʿah* for the sake of profound and intense remembrance of God (*dhikr Allāh*). Nothing could be further from the truth for it is a central doctrine in Sufism that neither mystical experience nor God's saving mercy can be realized without the *Sharīʿah*.[15]

From the perspective of *kalām*, (which will be discussed more fully in the next chapter) knowledge (*ʿilm*), as expounded by the Muʿtazilī ʿAbd al-Jabbār (d. 415/1024) in his *al-Mughnī fī Abwāb al-Tawḥīd wa al-ʿadl* "is an entitative ground (*maʿnā*) which necessitates (*yaqtaḍī*) tranquillity in the self (*sukūn al-nafs*) of the knower in regard to what he has considered (*mā tanāwalah*)."[16] While the Sufis use *maʿrifah* to refer specifically to experiential knowledge of the divine, for the Muʿtazilī, there is no substantive difference between *ʿilm* and *maʿrifah* which are used synonymously by ʿAbd al-Jabbār.[17] His definition of knowledge ontologically relates the world outside of humans to internal experiences of "conviction" and "tranquillity of the self." While *maʿnā* literally signifies "meaning," ʿAbd al-Jabbār's conception, as representative of the Muʿtazilī position, regards it as "the intrinsic causal determinant of a thing being-so," and, as suggested by George Hourani, *maʿnā* implies a "ground" or an "entitative ground" for the attributes and characteristics of a thing.[18] The *maʿnā* of a thing corresponds to the thing "as it really is" and through this notion, ʿAbd al-Jabbār ontologically universalizes as knowledge an individual's subjective perception or conviction as regards a thing "to the point of feeling tranquil and self-assured."[19]

How the Muʿtazilī conceptualization of knowledge relates to *fiqh* becomes clearer when we consider, in Chapter 3, the issues of theodicy and the questions of free will, causality and volition in human actions. These considerations are also pertinent when subjected to the distinction between *fiqh* and *kalām* as regards the approaches towards the categorizations of human acts. At this juncture, suffice it to say that while in *fiqh*, intuition/intellect (*'aql*) and perception (*idrāk*) may not necessarily bind humans in terms of their obligation to obey God (*taklīf*) in as much as there is no certainty or conviction (*i'tiqād*) of knowledge, Mu'tazilī epistemology posits God as the creator of both (perception and intuition) by virtue of which their validity as knowledge is certified.[20]

The Province of Fiqh as Law

For the usage of *fiqh* outside the Qur'ān, there is again a difference in terminology similar to that mentioned about *Sharī'ah*. As alluded to earlier, the early scholars of Islam would use *fiqh* to mean the knowledge and the understanding of the guidance in respect of matters of the faith. Imam Abu Ḥanīfah, in his rather short book about *'aqidah* (belief) titled *al-Fiqh al-Akbar* (The Great *Fiqh*), declared, "As for those relating to His essence, they are life, power, knowledge, speech, hearing, sight, and will. As for those relating to His acts, they are creativity, sustenance, originating and fashioning *ex nihilo*, making, and other active attributes ... Our uttering of the Qur'ān is created, and our recitation of the Qur'ān is created, but the Qur'ān itself is uncreated."[21]

It is clear that the description above about the attributes of God and the "uncreatedness" of the Qur'ān is the concern of *kalām* and not *fiqh* as we understand it today. This is underscored by his description of *fiqh* itself: "*Fiqh* is knowledge of the beliefs and practices which are permitted and which are obligatory in both. What relates to beliefs is called *al-fiqh al-akbar* and what relates to practices is simply *al-fiqh*,"[22] which is self-explanatory. There is the stereotypical impression that *fiqh*—as law—is the overarching concern of Islam, and that the Qur'ān was sent down to mankind as a Book of Commandments. But that is not true and going by the Qur'ān itself, of the six thousand or so *āyahs*, there are only about five hundred that are concerned with law—as in rules and regulations. Even then, out of this, no more than eighty of them may be considered "law" in the positive sense of being implementable in governing society. We will discuss this further in Chapter 7 but suffice it to say at this juncture that the *Sharīʿah* as it pertains to Islam as religion is much more than just law. Indeed, the rest of the *āyahs* in the Qur'ān predominantly deal with the divine nature of God, theological themes on monotheism, eschatology, stories and parables concerning the prophets, fundamental dogmas on belief and mankind's position in the universal scheme of things. However, over the passage of time, these matters became identified within the domain of *dīn* and studied under the discipline of *ʿuṣūl al-dīn* from which *kalām* formally emerged.

Eventually, *fiqh* standing alone concerned only matters of practice or conduct and its study came to be known as *ʿilm al-fiqh* as encapsulated in the classical technical definition given by Imām al-Shāfiʿī (d. 204/820): "*Al-ʿilmu bi al-aḥkāmi al-sharʿīyyati al-ʿamaliyyati al-muktasabati min adillatihā al-tafṣīliyyah*," rendered as "the science of the *Sharīʿah* rules that concern conduct acquired from their specific proofs."[23] *Fiqh* in this sense is, therefore, not *Sharīʿah* in totality but only "*Sharīʿah* rules that concern conduct" with its meaning formally distinguished from the Qur'ān's literal sense. Imām al-Ghazālī (d. 505/1111) confined the usage of *fiqh* to the knowledge and understanding of the guidance, the rulings and the way of life regarding actions only, excluding the areas of belief and moral character.

Fiqh deals with the observance of rituals, morals and legislation in Islam and in this sense of the technical usage, *fiqh* is therefore "practical Islamic jurisprudence."[24] *Fiqh* may be implemented in a variety of ways but historically it was legislated via the rulings given in the form of *fatāwā* by the *fuqahā'*, in their capacities as muftis on questions presented to them. We shall see in Chapter 6 how *fiqh* can become public and in particular, constitutional and administrative law, via the doctrine of *siyāsah al-sharʿīyyah*, when we deal with the controversy as to whether the latter is in fact part of the *Sharīʿah*.

According to the Ottoman Civil Code, popularly known as the Majelle, *fiqh* is about God's rules governing "human affairs" both spiritual and temporal.[25] With the categorizations laid out, it is appropriate to go deeper into the technical definition as given earlier by examining the exposition given by al-Āmidī[26] that *fiqh* is "the knowledge, resulting from reasoning and demonstration, of those divine categorizations of human acts that are mediated to us through revealed or divinely sanctioned indicators and thus constitute the *Sharī'ah*."[27] Following al-Shāfi'ī in defining *fiqh* as "knowledge," al-Āmidī sets the stage for separating it from the ordinary usage of understanding, placing "knowledge" here as a specific kind of understanding acquired by scholars through rational inquiry. *Fiqh* is therefore an "understanding of the *Sharī'ah* in an elevated sense" and those who possessed such understanding were the real *fuqahā'* in being both knowledgeable and learned.[28]

Would opinion, *ra'y*, as typified by the method adopted by Abū Ḥanīfah, be thereby excluded from the purport of *fiqh*—as constituting a legitimate source of legal ruling or principle? It would appear to be so according to the Shāfi'ī school, where *ra'y* is considered to be "subjective opinion" and unworthy of deriving *Sharī'ah* rules.[29] Al-Āmidī, however, does not categorically rule out *ra'y* from the *fiqh* matrix: "*Fiqh* is knowledge of the divine categorizations, or knowledge, based on incontestable perception, of what constitutes conformity to those categorizations *even though the categorizations themselves are a matter of opinion.*"[30] (Emphasis provided). Paraphrased: Even though opinion by itself cannot be equivalent to *fiqh*, opinion is valid in so far as it is used as a basis for informing the categorizations. (Indeed, opinion here is not that of the laity but of the scholars.) Again, this appears to be slouching towards equivocation. In fact, it is not, and if we recall the *kalām* approach to knowledge as discussed in the preceding section, it is said that by virtue of this position taken on the part of al-Āmidī (that *ra'y* may constitute a basis for incontestable perception), there is the view that he might have been a closet Mu'tazilī. That might be taking it too far in the absence of any substantive proof but there is no doubt that al-Āmidī, unlike the typical Ash'arī, worked extensively for a convergence of *ʿuṣūl al-fiqh* with *kalām*. In his partiality towards the use of the Aristotelian method in theological discourse, he blurred the lines between *kalām* and *falsafah*, his professed Ashʿarī creed notwithstanding.

It is worth noting that al-Āmidī's extant works of *kalām* include *Abkār al-Afkār fī Uṣūl al-Dīn*, and *Ghāyat al-Marām fī ʿIlm al-Kalām*. His works of *falsafah* include *al-Nūr al-Bāhir fī al-Ḥikam al-Zawāhir* and a critical commentary exposing the flaws in al-Rāzī's commentary on Ibn Sīnā's *Kitāb al-Ishārāt wa al-Tanbīhāt* (Pointers and Reminders).[31] In Chapter 3, we shall explore a little more the ramifications of his straddling between the two domains of *kalām* and *falsafah* but for now suffice it to say that, for him, *kalām* is the first proper concern of the human intellect in relation to which all other sciences occupy a subordinate position. In this regard, "Knowledge is an attribute through which the mind of one who possesses this attribute is able to distinguish between the essences of universals (*haqāʿiq al-maʿānī al-kulliyyah*) in a manner that does not admit of the possibility of contradiction."[32] In any event, there is method in this attempt to put us on a semantic slope. Al-Āmidī is, in fact, retreating from the rather rigid definition of *fiqh* as given earlier. This is a doctrine central to his jurisprudence: considered opinion is normative in matters of law (*al-ẓannu wājibu al-ittibāʿi fī al-sharʿ*). A considered opinion is a conviction about a probability which is to say that everything is tentative, nothing is absolute and disagreement is tolerated. (It should be noted that *al-ẓann* is also sometimes translated as "speculation" as well as "hypothetical opinion," as opposed to *al-qaṭʿi*, which is rendered as "decisiveness" or "certainty.") Al-Āmidī posits that if something is the probable occasioning factor behind a rule of law then any further rule derived from it by way of *qiyās* can only constitute a probable rule of law. There are significant implications particularly in terms of the prospect of *ijtihād* in future circumstances if one accepts that "the articulations of the divine categorizations by human scholars, no matter how fallible and tentative, must be accepted as a valid reference point for human conduct."[33]

Now, if *fiqh* is the articulation by jurists of the categorizations, the *Sharīʿah* may, therefore, be considered the categorizations themselves, the former being procedural and the latter substantive. Or to put it in plainer terms, *fiqh* is the process by which the *Sharīʿah* rules are established. Nevertheless, the distinction is blurred in conventional usage and, as stated earlier, unless one is engaged in intense jurisprudential discourse where even minor semantic variations have substantive differences in connotation, both terms are used interchangeably even in the academic circles. The question that remains from the procedural-substantive bifurcation is by what process and from where did these "substantive" categories come about?

Uṣūl Al-Fiqh

The answer lies in *ʿilm uṣūl al-fiqh*, that is, the science of the sources of *fiqh* or the science of constructing rules on the basis of the indicators. Works such as Imām Shāfiʿī's *al-Risālah* or Imām al-Ghazālī's *al-Mustaṣfā* or al-Āmidī's *Kitāb al-Iḥkām fī Uṣūl al-Aḥkām* are treatises of theoretical jurisprudence, not books on the substantive Islamic law per se. For the latter, another process is needed, known as *ʿilm al-fiqh*, which is concerned with the articulation of the specific rules of law. To differentiate it from the theoretical, this science may be regarded as practical jurisprudence.[34] In other words, if one wants to find out whether a particular a transaction is valid or invalid, or if a particular act or omission is forbidden or permissible then one would be better off looking up *fiqh* books for which there are *fiqh* manuals according to the respective *madhāhib* (schools of law).

By contrast, *uṣūl al-fiqh* is, in a manner of speaking, "amorphous" and may be likened to "an ocean on whose bottom one has to search, at the price of very great efforts, for the pearls which are hidden there."[35] Mastering this science requires not just a long process of scholarship but the inculcation of fundamental ethical, moral and religious values which may only be realised with experience. In relation to *fiqh*, the term *uṣūl* designates all those things that are required for the emergence of *fiqh*, that is, the foundations. According to al-Āmidī, "*Fa uṣūlu al-fiqhi wa jihāti dalālātihā ʿalā al-aḥkāmi al-sharʿiyyati wa kayfiyyati hāli al-mustadilli bihā min jihati al-jumlah lā min jihati al-tafṣīl.*"[36] The term *uṣūl al-fiqh*, therefore, refers to the indicators upon which the articulation of the law is based, the ways in which they function as indicators of the rules of law, and the considerations that pertain to the role of the scholar who employs those indicators in attempting to articulate the law. To this we may add the definition given by Shaykh Ṭāhā Jābir al-Alwānī: "The aggregate of legal proofs and evidence that, when studied properly, will lead either to certain knowledge of a *Sharīʿah* ruling or to at least a reasonable assumption concerning the same; the manner by which such proofs are adduced, and the status of the adducer."[37] As stated earlier, these matters are treated in a purely theoretical manner as opposed to the specific rules appertaining to the science of *fiqh*. Hence the science dealing with this is aptly translated as "theoretical jurisprudence" while the former—*ʿilm al-fiqh*—should be seen as "practical jurisprudence."[38] To avoid needless repetition *ʿilm uṣūl al-fiqh* is hereafter referred to as just *uṣūl al-fiqh.*

Al-Āmidī's methodology, based on the Aristotelian paradigm of inquiry, warrants that any science encapsulates four essentials: *mawḍūʿ* (subject matter), *ghāyah* (an end), *masāʾil* (an agenda of issues) and *mabādiʾ* (the first principles). The *mawḍūʿ* of any science is the thing whose accidental characteristics (*aḥwāl*) are under investigation in that science. These and these alone may be investigated. Essential characteristics are by definition embodied in the very conceptualization of the *mawḍūʿ* and hence are not fit for investigation because conceptualization precedes investigation or to put it metaphorically, the horse must precede the cart. The accidental characteristics that may be inquired into make up the *masāʾil* or issues in as much as they are *ab initio* open to question and must be ascertained through demonstration. In the case of *uṣūl al-fiqh*, the *mawḍūʿ* comprises the indicators upon which the articulation of the law is premised, namely, the indicators of "the rules of law" (*aḥkām al-shar'iyyah*). The accidental characteristics of these indicators constitute the *masā'il* of the science. This answers the question posed at the outset concerning the province of the *Sharī'ah*. The end of this entire inquiry is the attainment of knowledge of the rules of law, which constitutes a benefit in that it leads to happiness both in this world and the hereafter. According to al-Āmidī, the *mabādi'* of this science is all-encompassing covering propositions drawn from *kalām*, *fiqh* and *lughah* (linguistic science).[39]

As for *kalām*, the methodology for *fiqh* rests in particular on its use of Aristotelian logic (*al-manṭiq*)—at which al-Āmidī, as we have seen, was adept—which is the systematic approach of reasoning, established through formative rules of definition, argumentation, validity and fallacies. Developed in the Stagirite's *Organon* (circa. 340 BC) and introduced into Islamic philosophy by al-Kindī (d. 262/873), being the first Muslim philosopher to translate major tracts of the *Organon* into Arabic[40] to be followed by other great Muslim philosophers such as al-Fārābī (d. 339/950).[41] Al-Fārābī also introduced the concept of poetic syllogism in a commentary on Aristotle's *Poetics* and crafted, *sui generis*, a doctrine of inductive syllogism based on human experience, foreshadowing Kant whose transcendental idealism and increasingly speculative metaphysics appeared as a counter trend to the preponderance of empirical sciences as inspired by Hume's radical empiricism. Departing from the classical view of *al-manṭiq* being only good for analysis of foreign grammar, al-Fārābī transposed the *manṭiq* methodology onto the doctrine of *qiyās* thereby strengthening it further as a procedural tool in *uṣūl al-fiqh*.

Experts in the discipline of *uṣūl al-fiqh* spend a significant length of time trying to fathom what the sources of law should be apart from the Qur'ān and the Sunnah. For example, is the Sunnah of the people of Medina a good source of law? At which point can the jurists agree that there is *ijmā'* on a particular issue to render it as binding on all? Can there be *ijmā'* on theoretical matters? To what extent can *qiyās* be used to make new law? Or as mentioned earlier, can a rule extrapolated from a hypothetical opinion be used for derivative extrapolations?

A practical point of contrast that may be singled out between *fiqh* and *kalām* is the restriction, in *fiqh*, of the usage to *al-aḥkām al-ʿāmaliyyah*, that is, orthopraxy comprising rules of conduct or practical matters, physical acts, acts of the heart or intention, and speech. Orthodoxy, on the other hand, which pertains to correct belief, creeds, and strict adherence to prescribed rites or rituals became the central concern of *kalām*. By constraining *fiqh* to mean the extracting of religious rulings on practical matters from the main sources of Islam, that is, the Qur'ān and Sunnah, and from other sources as well and by limiting it to these and these alone, the province of the *Sharīʿah* became narrowed down. The religious rulings given in consequence of this life-time pursuit by the *fuqahā'* therefore formed the bulk of *Sharīʿah* law.

To sum up the comparison between *Sharīʿah* and *fiqh*, it may be pointed out that since *fiqh* is the result of derivative efforts, that is, the rules are derived (*al-aḥkām al-muktasabah*) from specific sources, *fiqh* cannot be regarded as being cast in stone. The suggestion that *fiqh* is for all time and unchangeable, is by this reasoning alone, untenable if not altogether sacrilegious because infallibility belongs only to God. Now, just because *fiqh* rules are derivative, it does not mean that it can be stripped of the strict rules governing its genesis. The idea that anyone can cite chapter and verse from the Qur'ān or spout sayings of the Prophet and thereby purport to establish *fiqh* rulings is completely illegitimate even though in modern times, this seems to be a phenomenon that is becoming widespread. We will explore this further in Chapter 7.

Fiqh as Islamic law is adaptable though it does not arise from whims and fancies but is to be based on the sound and vigorous methodology required for the exercise of *ijtihād*. As far as this overriding feature of adaptability is concerned, the *Sharīʿah* as used in a general sense when referring to law is synonymous with *fiqh*. But

Sharīʿah is not coterminous with *fiqh* if we are referring only to the Divine will and *Sharīʿah* as *dīn*, that is, as defined in chapter 1, the "way of religion," wider than the mere formal rites and legal provisions. But the two meet again in the context of Man's spiritual relationship with God which would translate into *ʿibādat* and the meaning of *fiqh* here is not Islamic law, that is, not law in the positive law sense. Where the *Sharīʿah* refers to normative social interaction, it corresponds directly with *fiqh* in as far as the latter is concerned with *muʿāmalāt* rules, that is, rules which govern commerce, custom and other social practices.[42] What rules may come within the rubric of positive law and what may not is not easy to delineate but the picture may become clearer by first looking into the discourse concerning the separation doctrines of morality and law on the one hand and church and state on the other. Before we venture into that terrain in Chapter 4, a quick survey of the canonical schools of law within the Sunni denomination followed by a detour into the subject of *kalām*, in Chapter 3, is in order so as to attain a more holistic perspective of *Sharīʿah*.

The Madhāhib and Juristic Law

In light of the above exposition, the *Sharīʿah* as law, is but the canonical law laid down broadly in its pristine form in the Qur'ān and the Sunnah that had been expounded by the *madhāhib*, that is, the four Sunni orthodox schools of law, namely, the Ḥanafī, Mālikīi, Shāfiʿī and Ḥanbalī. Here the term *madhhab* is used in the general sense of it being an institution representing the *corpus juris* of the leading *mujtahids*. However, it could be used in another sense of merely referring to the opinion of a jurist not in an institutional sense but as a situational pronouncement germane to a particular case presented for deliberation. In this doctrinal sense, it meant the opinion adopted as the most authoritative in the school which is then applied widely by the courts and in *fatāwā*. Being normative, such an opinion traverses the gap of legality between a *fatwā* and *madhhab*-opinion.[43] Otherwise, a mere *fatwā* has no force of law. It is said that, in theory, when a mufti adjudicates a question, hermeneutical (*ta'wīl*) presuppositions are employed alongside the standard *tafsīr* paradigm developed throughout the centuries of refinement. This is too general an observation and may be countered as incorrect even for the four Sunni schools, in particular the Ḥanbalī *madhhab* which as a rule will not tolerate hermeneutical exegesis. On the other hand, the other schools, particularly the Ḥanafī *madhhab*, as noted at the outset of this chapter, did not consider the predilection towards *aql* over *naql* as being in violation of the faith. Then again, Imām al-Juwaynī initially engaged in *ta'wīl* but later rendered it unlawful. We will go deeper into this in the next chapter but it is fair to say that, in matters of *fiqh*, the opinions issued forth from *uṣūl al-fiqh* and its attendant rigorous process and methodology could form the basis of positive law once they were received by the *fuqahā'* within the *madhhab*.

In the formative period, *madhhab* also meant the doctrine adopted by a founder and by those of his followers, this doctrine being considered cumulative and accretive. Concomitant with this, if not somewhat earlier, the notion of *madhhab* as a corporate entity appeared in the sense of an integral school to which individual jurists aligned themselves. This was the personal meaning of the *madhhab*, in contrast to its purely doctrinal meaning, which was expressed as loyalty to a general body of doctrine.[44] These *madhāhib* emerged in the course of Islamic history with one or more being predominant in particular geographical areas—Ḥanafī (Turkey, Central Asia, the Balkans, Iraq, Afghanistan and the Indian-subcontinent), Mālikī (Algeria, Tunis, Morocco, Mauritania, Libya, Kuwait, Bahrain, Dubai and Abu Dhabi), Shāfiʿī (Egypt, East Africa and Southeast Asia) and Ḥanbalī (Saudi Arabia, Qatar, North East of Oman and the rest of the Arab Emirates). While they vary on certain rituals and practices, the *madhāhib* are often perceived as complementary rather than mutually exclusive, but this is not to say that the differences are inconsequential, or indeed that the existence of different *madhāhib* did not lead to intra-religious clashes. It will be seen that with the rise of modernity in Muslim societies, new and more "purist" schools emerged with their now familiar labels such as Salafi and Wahhabi and the various shades in between and seen invariably as having some common nexus with the 'modern' Islamic state.

Still, it is clear that such a definition (by identification through the various schools of jurisprudence) though more substantive, and more inclusive, tells us more about the shades of differences of the *Sharī'ah* than the *Sharī'ah* itself. It may be likened to attempting to answer the question of what is law (in Western jurisprudence) by reference to the Common law, or Continental law or even Roman law, which is really just an effort to identify the different systems of law in the West. There is also the presumption that we know what these four Sunni schools represent in a definitive sense as in the common reference to them as representative of *Ahl al-Sunnah wa al-Jamā'ah*. It would be reasonable to expect that one's conception of a school would involve some degree of institutionalization with its adherents conforming to clear principles and doctrines and conducting its affairs in a civilized manner. It is, after all, a school of law. While there is no question of civilized discourse being the rule rather than the exception, the reality was that the disputes were not pertaining at all times to just cold statements of law articulated by stoically inclined men of learning. In their legal disputations, these advocates and adherents of particular schools were not bookish pacifists. On the contrary, they took their law as fervently as they took their religion and were prepared to lay down their lives for their jurisprudence.[45] And of the founders of these four Sunni schools, at least one was killed on account of the differences of opinions, another refused to recant his beliefs in spite of torture and prolonged incarceration and yet another was poisoned while put in prison by the caliph for refusing to accept the position of chief judge. This bears testimony less of their intransigence as some would characterize it than their passion for their creeds and their level of *taqwā*—God-consciousness —that fortified their courage of conviction for the rewards of the hereafter than the material happiness of the temporal world. As for their respective disciples, countless chronicles of their trials and tribulations fill their biographies again, as proof that the men (and women) of learning of the glorious days of Islam were driven by a zeal for ultimate spiritual deliverance in remaining faithful to their juristic as well as creedal allegiances.

That said, it must be added that the *madhhab*-centric definition of *fiqh* that we have managed to patch together is also somewhat narrow being confined only to the four Sunni *madhāhib*, leaving out others, such as the Ẓāhirī school, founded by Imām Abū Dāwūd.[i] During its glory days, the Ẓāhirī school had adherents in a majority of the Muslims in Iraq, Iran, the Iberian Peninsula and North Africa. Their bare-bones, dry-as-dust literalist approach has had a natural appeal to the adherents of the Salafi movement, who as we know make it their crusade to "cleanse" Islamic orthopraxy of what it regards as "pernicious innovation."

Among the champions of the Ẓāhirīs, Ibn Ḥazm (d. 456/1064) is the most famous by far, and his works represent the theological literature of the school, with him leading the opposition against the orthodoxy of his time not just in matters of *fiqh* but in *kalām* as well. In his *Kitāb al-Ibṭāl*, he fervently rejects all forms of speculative *fiqh*, such as *qiyās, ra'y, istiḥsan, taqlīd,* and *ta'līl* (causal interpretation), repudiating all concessions made to hermeneutics and the methodologies of both the Mālikī and Ḥanafī schools.[46] Ibn Ḥazm's criticism of Imām Mālik, as reflected in an account concerning a purported death-bed confession and self-reproach by the great Imām is acutely indicative of the Ẓāhirī intransigence towards the traditional Mālikīs: "When Imām Mālik felt that death was approaching, he said, 'I wish, now, that I could be punished with one lash for each question that I decided on the basis of my own *ra'y*, and that I would not have to appear before the Prophet of God with things that I added to his laws on my own account, or with cases in which I decided against the literal meaning of his law.'"[47]

---

[i] He should not to be mistaken for the Persian *ḥadith* compiler Abū Dāwūd as-Sijistani whose *Sunan Abī Dāwūd* is ranked as number four in strength of the six major *ḥadīth* collections regarded as canonical among Sunnis. He collected half a million *aḥādīth* over a period of twenty years, of which only 4,800 were included in the *Sunan*, *infra* p. 254.

Then there is the question of the 'Ibādīs or 'Ibādī movement. Being neither Sunni nor Shī'ā, and founded hardly two decades after the death of the Prophet, it predates the latter schools, although the claim that it is a reformed sect of the Khawārij has been denied.[48] Furthermore, a definition of the *Sharī'ah* purporting to include the *fiqh* of Sunni and Shī'ā denominations may well lead to the clashing rocks. It is, *strictu sensu*, a contradiction in terms. Twelve-imām (*ithnā 'ashariyyah*) Shī'ā jurisprudence, or what is often referred to as the Ja'farī school, does have substantially common ground in the primary sources of law with the Sunni schools, that is, the Qur'ān and the Sunnah. Nevertheless, there is a significant degree of divergence in the interpretation of these sources, and this has much to do with the fact that Shī'ās also regard the practices of the twelve imāms as independent sources. In fact, in Shī'ism any religious doctrine to be regarded as authentic has to be referred back to the authority of one of the imāms.[49] But by far, the greatest difference is that in Shī'ā law, the views and practices of three of the Rightly Guided Caliphs (*al-khulafā' al-rāshidūn*) are rejected. Under this doctrine of *rafḍ* (rejection), the earlier caliphs are castigated as usurpers of the rightful position of 'Alī, their only recognized successor to the Prophet. Thus, whatever *Sharī'ah* principles that may be derived from the caliphate of Abu Bakr, 'Umar and 'Uthman, and subsequent juristic law flowing from these caliphal principles, cannot, in the eyes of Shī'ā jurists, be part of their definition of the *Sharī'ah*. After the Prophet, the task of defining and interpreting the *fiqh* is the sole prerogative and duty of the twelve *imāms*. However, on account of the last imām being in occultation, this duty has fallen on the *'ulamā'*. This is *ijtihād*, and in this capacity of being the referent, each of them is also known as a *marja'*.

Apart from that, the use of the term canonical law (*qānūn*) poses some difficulties, particularly for one-dimensional viewpoints which reject the comparison of *Sharī'ah* with any form of Judeo-Christian conception of law. This is not about the puritanical Wahhabi approach but just plain orthodoxy which itself will tolerate no extraneous influence creeping into its jurisprudential body politic. But this too is unfounded fear on the part of those *'ulamā'* who seem to think that the greatness of a religion lies in its exclusiveness. As will be made clear in due course, the phenomenon of *qānūn* law is very much an established part of the jurisprudence of Muslim countries. Therefore, steering clear of confessional, denominational or contextually laden language, the *Sharī'ah* may alternatively be said to comprise prescriptions which may be grouped into regulations regarding worship and ritual duties on the one hand, and regulations of a legal/juridical nature on the other. These prescriptions are applicable regardless of denominational persuasions. Again, some difficulties are fairly apparent even with this clinical definition. The *Sharī'ah* no doubt would encompass regulations governing worship and ritual duties but in respect of regulations of a legal/juridical nature the difficulty lies in defining the province of this conception. This is more an epistemological rather than a jurisprudential issue. Is it the province that defines the conception or the definition that determines the province? As Wittgenstein, the great anti-metaphysician once said, all philosophical problems boil down to the language and what we believe it encapsulates. That such regulations would encompass the law of personal status, the law of succession as well as the law of commercial transactions is clear enough in as much as a large corpus of jurisprudence has developed in this area. That certainly is part of the province.

By the second half of the third/ninth century, *Sharī'ah* law was overwhelmingly juristic law, that is, law as expounded by the muftis, *fuqahā'* and *mujtahid*s which are binding in their respective *madhāhib*. Juristic law is to be distinguished from judicial decisions which were those made by *qāḍī*s. They set no precedents in as much as the law of binding precedents has no direct application in the Islamic judicial system. Apart from *taqlīd* (general principle of being bound) applicable within the respective *madhāhib*, the only legal ruling that binds in terms of juristic law is when all jurists have agreed there is *ijmā'* on a particular issue, a matter we shall explore later. Nevertheless, it has been said that next to the Romans, there is no other nation besides the Arabs which could call its own a system of law so carefully worked out.[50]

By the *dhimmī* treaty,[51] which may find some parallel in the notion of *fides* in Roman law, the Jewish and Christian communities as well as other non-Muslim peoples such as the Zoroastrians in Bahrain paid a poll tax (*jizyah*) in return for the guarantee of protection and the preservation of their rights under their own personal law administered by their rabbinical, ecclesiastical and priestly tribunals. It must be stressed that they were not forced to pay the *jizyah*. This was a treaty for protection in lieu of providing military support to the Muslim polity. Nevertheless, there is the view that *jizyah* is discriminatory in nature in typecasting a group as *dhimmī*s within a country rendering them as second-class citizens. Historically, the *jizyah* could well be rationalized as a payment for protection pursuant to a treaty voluntarily entered into between the Muslim state and non-Muslim polities. Today, however, in an age of nation-states and democracies, the institution of the *jizyah* would indeed be anachronistic and is rejected by an overwhelming majority of moderate Muslims.[52]

Apart from the *jizyah*, the Umayyads also elaborated and systematized the tax laws introduced by 'Umar.[53] As for the business of divining the law on matters not governed by the Qur'ān and the Sunnah, the learned among the Companions and the immediate successors exercised *ijtihād*. Meanwhile, disputes amongst the Arabs over business transactions and affairs of the community were resolved either by customary law by their tribal chiefs or by the Caliph or his deputies based on the opinions of the *'ulamā'*. Soon they exercised their own judgment[54] which led to the development of a lacuna between the *Sharī'ah* as expounded by the *'ulamā'* during the first generations, and the political reality brought about by the coming into existence of the new empire. This saw them losing their positions of authority in the face of the ascendancy of the Caliphs in the dispensation of the law. But rather than withdrawing into a cocoon of hermitic existence and fading into oblivion, the *'ulamā'* persisted in their juridical endeavour, drinking deeper from the fountain of the Qur'ān and the Sunnah and exerting their minds in *ijtihād.*

In due course, their opinions and responses to questions on law that had to be voiced de novo (because no clear answers could be found in the revealed text) became the *ijmā'* (the consensus of opinion) of the *ummah.* This is to state it generally because there still remained alternative views about how the *ijmā'* could be known and what it really validated.[55] Be that as it may, the *ijmā'* and the development of the *'ulamā'*s rulings and *fatāwā* constituted the juristic law. Those who were engaged predominantly in *fiqh* were therefore called *fuqahā'* while those who were engaged in the pursuit of *kalām* were called *mutakallimūn.*[56] We have already alluded to the fact that many wore two hats and some even three. By 132 AH/750 AD, the opinions of the *'ulamā'* became the last word on questions of law and theology regardless of who the political masters were. But, paradoxically, the last word was not the only word because even if the *ijmā'* could be likened to the *vox populi,* its components were really the product of the exercise of human reasoning, which meant that differences of opinion were bound to occur. This, however, did not prevent the *'ulamā'* from playing the role of the "pious opposition" to the Umayyads, giving opinions not as magistrates sitting in judgment but as jurists recognized by the community as well as their peers.

Muftis and Shaykh Al-Islam

Typically, the Muslim jurisconsult in his capacity as a mufti (that is, one who is authorized to give a *fatwā* or an opinion) would consult a wide range of sources particularly the *aḥādīth* (traditions). Reference to the Qur'ān would be rather otiose in as much as if the matter were covered no dispute would arise in the first place. Not so with the *aḥādīth* because one claimant may cite one particular *ḥadīth* while the other may cite another which may contradict his opponent's source. If both the *aḥādīth* cited are found to be of weak authority or based on questionable antecedents in their narration, the mufti would have every reason to regard the case before him as not being provided for by the *Sharī'ah* and would thereby be at liberty to exercise *ijtihād*, and make an independent ruling. By definition alone, an "independent" ruling arrived at by way of *ijtihād*, no matter how vigorous and intense the process might have been, cannot be elevated to the realm of the divine. However, that should not detract from the fact that it forms part of the corpus of *Sharī'ah* principles derived from juristic reasoning by these muftis. In the absence of state sanction, their findings or *fatāwā* could not be enforced but were of moral impact to work on the disputants' conscience. But if officially appointed, their *fatāwā* became law as part of the statutory or municipal legal corpus and might be used by *qāḍīs* in their adjudicative role. Initially, the muftis were not employed by the State which meant that they could exercise greater independence and could arrive at an opinion without fear or favour as they did not have to answer to the State.

To be sure, the powers that be did not let the grass grow under their feet as evidenced by the Umayyads' stratagem in appointing muftis, ostensibly to play the role of independent scholars and interpreters of the *Sharī'ah* but in reality to serve as the counterpoint to the pious opposition of juristic independence. Fortunately, authority could not be that easily bought as there were muftis who earned the respect of their people by establishing a reputation for independence, fairness and integrity and not by virtue of their hierarchy in the State. Nevertheless, as the institution spread, prominent jurists began to be recognized as the leading muftis of their cities, eventually bearing the title of Shaykh al-Islam in recognition of their superior competence in the field of law and the religion. This phenomenon is generally traced to tenth-century Khurāsān where the position began rather informally by peer recognition as well as public acceptance. Later, it became a state appointment and under the Ottomans, Safavids, Uzbeks and Mughals, the position became synonymous with Grand Mufti and was regarded as the highest legal authority in the realm. Apart from issuing *fatāwā* to the myriad legal petitions, he also took on the administrative role of overseeing all those bearing the title of Shaykh al-Islām in the empire and, perhaps, even more significantly, the role of giving the stamp of religious approval for the ruler's *siyāsah al-sharʿiyyah.*[57]

During the rule of the Abbasids, the *ʿulamāʾ* wielded a substantive degree of influence over the people in more ways than the term *ʿulamāʾ* is normally understood, that is, not just as scholars or even the pious but a central role in the moulding and development of the *fiqh* and the exercise of *ijtihād* in response to new situations and problems. The overarching concern was in reality more political than legal, namely, the question of giving due *Sharīʿah*-sanctioned recognition to the various caliphal authorities. And we shall see how the problem of the controversy surrounding the createdness of the Qur'ān led to the imposition of the *miḥnah* under the caliph al-Ma'mūn, which lasted through the reigns of his successors till several years of al-Mutawakkil before being finally abolished in 236/850. The ensuing schism saw the fault lines drawn which have remained even today within the Sunni world.

Apart from the fault lines in terms of creed, a central issue was in the area of the recognition of caliphal authority and the *fiqh* concerning legitimacy of rule, the command to obey and the general principles of Islamic governance It is to be noted that while the *madhāhib* that emerged in the ninth century as discussed above had covered substantive ground in all the traditional areas of *fiqh*, the basic rules of government which would come under the rubric of constitutional law, however, were essentially not articulated or formulated as such, that is, as *fiqh* ground rules for state governance. This was to be left eventually to the *fuqahāʾ* of the tenth and eleventh centuries to develop under the paradigm of *siyāsah al-sharʿiyyah* which is strictly speaking not *fiqh* in the sense as contextualised here. Various models of government were developed and advanced to justify Abbasid rule in the face of competing claims to sovereignty by the emerging class of warlord-turned-Sultans. This subject will be examined in greater detail in Chapters 4 and 5 from the prism of *siyāsah al-sharʿiyyah*. Meanwhile, we shall now move on to another substantive part of the *Sharīʿah*-based *fiqh* which collectively denotes much more than the general label "the Islamic law of crimes" would suggest.

Ḥudūd, Qiṣāṣ and Ta'zīr

While legal principles pertaining to marriage and divorce, inheritance, wills and gifts, contracts, mortgages, as alluded to earlier, are part of the *Sharī'ah* governed under *fiqh al-mu'āmalāt*, the definition of the *Sharī'ah* as law needs expansion in order to extend its province with the inclusion of *fiqh al-'ibādāt* and *fiqh al-'uqūbāt*, the former appertaining to matters of worship and rituals and the latter concerning a jurisprudence of punishments or more appropriately Islamic criminal jurisprudence. Our approach here is from the jurisprudential perspective, that is, to examine the foundational notions of the criminal law as may be discerned from the Qur'ān, the Sunnah and the secondary sources. We will not be concerned with the specific crimes or criminal offences and their punishment which should be appropriately studied in a monograph on crimes. Hence, topical and interesting as it may be, we will not get into the discourse whether adultery is or should be punishable by incarceration alone or flogging or death by stoning or whether apostasy is indeed a *ḥadd* crime or a crime at all or whether the law of *qiṣāṣ* in respect of murder is irrelevant as being impossible to implement. We will instead focus on the foundational issues of *Sharī'ah* criminal jurisprudence and begin by examining the concept of *ḥadd* offences (referred indiscriminately as *ḥudūd* laws)—as punishments said to be prescribed by the Qur'ān and the Sunnah in respect of specific crimes.

One startling fact that one discovers, at the outset, is that the word "*ḥadd*" is nowhere to be found in the Qur'ān and when it occurs it is only found in its plural form *ḥudūd* meaning limits which have nothing to do with crimes at all. A classic example is the oft-quoted

> "These are the limits imposed by Allah (*ḥudūd Allāh*), so approach them not. Thus, Allah expoundeth His revelations to mankind that they may ward off (evil)."[58]

In fact, *ḥudūd* appears in this sense of prescribing the bounds of God fourteen times in several other *āyahs* dealing with legal provisions governing matters of *ʿibādāt* and *muʿāmalāt*. In the verse just cited, God's injunction is to observe the limits, that is, the prohibition of conjugal relations with one's wife during the period of *iʿtikāf* during Ramaḍān. As for *muʿāmalāt,* such as divorce, the *ḥudūd* is imposed in respect of the limits to be observed attendant upon the process of *ṭalāq* (pronouncement of divorce), as in Sūrah al-Baqarah, *āyah* 217, which for purposes of clarity is quoted in full:

> A divorce may be [revoked] twice, whereupon the marriage must either be resumed in fairness or dissolved in a goodly manner. And it is not lawful for you to take back anything of what you have ever given to your wives unless both [partners] have cause to fear that they may not be able to keep within **the bounds set by God:** hence, if you have cause to fear that the two may not be able to keep within **the bounds set by God**, there shall be no sin upon either of them for what the wife may give up [to her husband] in order to free herself. These are **the bounds set by God;** do not, then, transgress them: for they who transgress **the bounds set by God**—it is they, they who are evildoers!

Again, this verse, where *ḥudūd Allāh* is mentioned four times, has nothing to do with *fiqh al-ʿuqūbāt* but rather sets the foundation for the exposition of a foundational doctrine on Islamic divorce, about which there is much misunderstanding. According to Asad, there is *ijmāʿ* that this *āyah* confers an unconditional right to the wife to obtain a divorce from her husband in a process known as *khulʿ*, and this is substantiated by several highly-authenticated *aḥādīth.*[59] In accordance with these *aḥādīth, Sharīʿah* law stipulates that whenever a marriage is dissolved at the wife's behest, the husband not having committed any breaches of his marital obligations, the wife, being the party in breach, must return the marriage dower, and in this event "there shall be no sin upon either of them" if the husband takes back the dower which the wife gives up of her own free will.[60] As it is clear from the Qur'ān, God's limits *(ḥudūd Allāh)* therefore are set—not as normative crimes as expounded by some *fuqahā'*—but as limits in respect of conduct and action on the part of parties or individuals. However, these limits are set in passages which may or may not contain legal provisions but regardless of that, the term *ḥudūd* has no reference to punishment for crimes committed. As can be seen with reference to the *āyah* on divorce, the *ḥudūd* is concerned with a moral situation where the Qur'ān demands "good conduct" or an act "done in a goodly manner" or "in accord with good custom" as the phrase *bi al-ma'rūf* may be understood according to the various commentators.[61] It is not spelt out what these limits are but one view suggests that "good custom" by definition varies according to cultural and possibly geographical factors and its content cannot be straitjacketed into the "idea of a fixed and invariable provision." As such, according to Fazlur Rahman, *ḥudūd Allāh* has more to do with prescribing the general parameters of virtuous behaviour. This means that the content of *ḥudūd Allāh* is not static but conceptually dynamic, particularly so as the *Sharī'ah,* as canvassed in chapter 1, is not just about law, let alone merely crime and punishment.[62] On the contrary, certain transgressions of even legal provisions do not necessarily incur any temporal retribution but rather only punishment in the hereafter (*e.g.* Sūrah al-Nisā', *āyah*s 12-13). Rahman points out that this is indicative of "how little concerned the Qur'ān is with the purely legal side and how much more with the setting of the moral tone of the community."[63]

Does that mean that *ḥudūd* laws as in punishments prescribed by the Qur'ān do not exist? Strictly speaking, the answer is in the affirmative. It is contended that while there are, undoubtedly, punishments prescribed by the Qur'ān for certain specific crimes or acts deemed to be criminal, they are not "*ḥudūd* crimes in the Qur'ānic sense" simply because *ḥudūd* as it occurs in the Qur'ān does not deal with crime. The *ḥudūd Allāh* that are embedded in various *āyah*s of the Qur'ān, as discussed, are not linked either contextually or linguistically to the crimes so stipulated. The argument is that while the so-called "*ḥudūd* crimes" that form the main subject matter of *ḥudūd* law—such as wine-drinking (*shurb al-khamr*), theft (*sariqah*), highway robbery (*qaṭ' al-ṭarīq*), illicit sexual intercourse (*zinā'*), false accusation of *zinā'* (*qadhf*), apostasy (*irtidād* or *riddah*)—are indeed prescribed in the Qur'ān, there is absolutely nothing in the Qur'ān itself to support the claim that they constitute *ḥudūd* prescriptions. The reality is that in *fiqh al-'uqūbāt*, the concept of *ḥudūd Allāh*—God's limits—has been transformed and transposed onto the law of crimes by the *fuqahā'* by arbitrarily labelling them as *ḥadd* crimes, signifying an unalterable punishment. This state of "immutability" is justified on the grounds that the said punishments belong to God as *ḥuqūq Allāh* (sing. *ḥaqq*)—God's entitlements or rights. Therefore, *Ḥudūd* crimes, according to the *fuqahā'*, are crimes "against God." What exactly does it mean to talk about "crimes against God"? Conceptually, at the level of *kalām*, it sounds counter-intuitive in as much as God is not an entity that may be so circumscribed that the criminal acts perpetrated by humans can have any bearing. And upon what is the doctrine of *ḥuqūq Allāh* founded? Allah is *al-Ḥaqq*, the only True Reality, the Master, the Lord Supreme, the Absolute. To speak of the rights of God is also incongruent to the concept of God's absolute sovereignty ("Blessed is He in Whose hand is the Sovereignty, and He is Able to do all things"—Surāh al-Mulk, *āyah* 1), for in the language of jurisprudence, for every right there is also a corresponding duty. Man owes duties to his Maker, but it is inconceivable that God owes any duty to His creatures. *Ḥuqūq Allāh,* therefore, cannot be taken literally and indeed is just a metaphorical expression for those rights that appertain to the community and are to serve the public welfare such as peace and security, economic well-being, social cohesion and standard of living. These rights are established in order to stamp out evil from the world *(ikhlā' al-'ālam 'an al-fasād).* The preservation of these rights is incumbent on the State or imām (as leader of a polity). These are indeed logical and rational reasons for the imposition of laws and under the general doctrine of *maṣlaḥah* (public interest) and the concept fits in snugly within the overarching doctrine of the *maqāṣid al-Sharī'ah.* But the crimes cannot be said to be *ḥudūd* crimes within the context of the Qur'ān. The concept of rights of the individual or private rights known as *ḥuqūq al-'ibād* or *al-nās* is a rationally sound doctrine and, as we know, has been extended into the realm of human rights. When creating these principles, the *fuqahā'* had to fall back on this legal conception, that is, the bifurcation between *ḥuqūq Allāh* and *ḥuqūq al-'ibād* when the issue of the clash between state and private interests arose.[64] While *ḥuqūq Allāh* is none other than the rights of the *ummah*, which have a direct bearing on its vital interests, security and welfare, *ḥuqūq al-'ibād* constitutes the conceptual protection against an overbearing state and provides the private individual consolation and compensation for wrongs committed against it.[65] How is this bifurcation helpful for the *ḥudūd* conundrum and why is it necessary to formulate such rights? Is there scriptural authority for the promulgation of such a doctrine?

There is the view that the legal conception of rights is borne by necessity and constitutes a legal heuristic employed by the *fuqahā'* to ensure that the *Sharī'ah* as a rule of law system balances both rights—public and private—which warranted their determination. The heuristic is the basis for a natural rights regime and by definition, as such, it is clear that the *fuqahā'* did not have scriptural authority to formulate such principles, opting instead to rely on implicit naturalistic presumptions.[66] From the viewpoint of the *maqāṣid al-Sharī'ah*, in order to protect the *maṣlaḥah* of the *ummah*, the *ḥadd* offences must by necessity be defined as unalterable punishments (*'uqūbāt muqaddarāt*) where neither pardon nor reduction of punishment is allowed. However, these crimes and punishments as prescribed in the Qur'ān and the Sunnah are not the only constituents of the *Sharī'ah* law of crimes. Two other distinct categories known as *qiṣāṣ* and *ta'zīr* must be briefly mentioned with a possible fourth category roped in under the label of *siyāsah* crimes.

Qiṣāṣ is the law of "retaliation in kind" generally equated as "eye for an eye" law or *Lex Talionis* which is just Latin for the same thing—retaliation.[67] As a biblical law, *Lex Talionis* is retributive justice based on the principle of proportionate punishment[68]but it goes back even further to the twentieth century BC as found in the Code of Hammurabi which, inter alia, prescribes that "if a man has shattered the limb of a man of rank, let his own limb be broken." In Judaic law, the Torah provides the rationale for retaliation as the elimination of evil from the community akin to the justification for *ḥudūd* as mentioned earlier (*ikhlāʿ al-ʿālam ʿan al-fasād*) by way of deterrence.[69]

Qiṣāṣ is available against the accused, to the victim or victim's heirs, when a Muslim is murdered, or suffers any of the wrongs that in common law would be constituted as a tort. The injury applies to the self as well as to one's property in which case compensation may avail thus fulfilling the demands of reciprocal justice.[70] In the case of murder, known as *qiṣāṣ fī al-nafs*, the doctrine confers the right of a murder victim's nearest kin or *walī* (legal guardian) to inflict the same act on the perpetrator in line with the injunction "a life for a life," as the Qur'ān proclaims,

> "And We ordained for them in that [Torah]: A life for a life, and an eye for an eye, and a nose for a nose, and an ear for an ear, and a tooth for a tooth, and a [similar] retribution for wounds; but he who shall forgo it out of charity will atone thereby for some of his past sins ..."[71]

While retaliation appears to be the first principle in *qiṣāṣ*, there is, however, an underlying concept aimed at promoting compensatory justice rather than corrective punishment. Hence, *Sharīʿah* law therefore also treats homicide and other torts as a civil dispute by conferring the right of prosecution on the victim or the victim's heir.[72] Thus, the option is open to the aggrieved parties to press for punitive prosecution or to demand for monetary compensation known as *diyah* or so-called "blood money." As is made clear in the latter part of the *āyah*, there is a third option, which is to forfeit the right of *qiṣāṣ* altogether without demanding the *diyah*, which would be tantamount to an act of *ṣadaqah* (charity) as *kaffārah* (atonement) for past sins

> *fa man taṣaddaqa bihi fa huwa kaffāratun lah* (But he who shall forgo it out of charity will atone thereby for some of his past sins).[73]

Where the culpable acts or wrongs do not fit under the description of *huḍūd* or *qiṣāṣ*, they may be categorised under the doctrine of *ta'zīr* offences which may be defined as punishments applied to the other offences for which no punishment is specified in the Qur'ān or the Sunnah.[74] There is a general perception that *ta'zīr* is reserved for lesser crimes which may be punished by the imposition of fines or short terms of imprisonment. That is simply unfounded. What is true is that because they cannot be pigeon-holed in either of the two primary categories, the punishment may be at the discretion of the court. Secondly, the rules of evidence such as evidentiary burden, onus of proof and admissibility of confessions are not subject to the same level of rigidity and strictness as those required for *ḥadd* and *qiṣāṣ* crimes. The defining feature about *ta'zīr* offences is the considerable discretion given to the court in passing sentence including a non-custodial non-punitive sentence.[75] The obvious question then is under what circumstances would an act be made a *ta'zīr* offence? What criteria should a judge apply in determining the punishment? The short answer is that while historically the question of ascertaining a punishment for a crime that did not fit into the established pigeon-holes was a somewhat ad-hoc affair, over time this task was taken over by the state through the process of legislation, and under these circumstances an entire corpus of *ta'zīr* offences was legislated de novo. In other cases, where crimes are identified or extractable from the Qur'ān bereft of a prescribed punishment, the *'ulamā'* employed exegesis by way of *qiyās* or *al-ra'y* to formulate a rule of discretionary punishment. *Ta'zīr* offences may be inchoate offences, that is, those offences that are considered preparatory or attempts to commit *ḥudūd* crimes. *Ta'zīr* offences may also arise from acts committed that violate the moral strictures enjoined in the

Qur'ān and the Sunnah such as usurious practices in money-lending, failure to observe the fast in public in the month of Ramaḍān or even failure to observe the Friday congregation prayers without valid reason. *Taʿzīr* offences may also be legislated in respect of acts that are considered detrimental to public order and security, such as sedition, causing dissention, or incitement to religious hatred or violence in which case they are said to fall within the category of *siyāsah* offences.

The categories of offences that may be legislated under the *taʿzīr* rubric are virtually limitless and this is not the appropriate forum to go further than what is already discussed. What remains to be said in conjunction with this category is the concept in Western jurisprudence concerning crimes that are *mala in se* and *mala prohibita*. The former refers to acts inherently criminal while the latter comprises acts which have been criminalized by the law. At common law, murder may be presumed to be criminal as it is anywhere in the world but smoking marijuana may not. Likewise, with robbery as compared to intellectual theft such as copyright infringement or plagiarism. And so on. But it is said that these difficulties arise only from the complex workings of modernity which in the West has given rise to so-called liberal societies where absolutes are rejected and everything becomes relative. On the other hand, it is contended, classical Islamic jurisprudence has expounded clearly that the *Sharīʿah* is all-inclusive and there is no area of human activity that cannot be legislated by it. While that may be true, it remains a major bone of contention as to what final criterion should be used when pursuing new legislation.

According to one perspective, because of Islamic revivalism, Muslim intellectuals of variegated persuasions have now taken the exposition of the *Sharīʿah* along a different path, which allows for a multiplicity of views. It would, however, be a mistake to imagine that modernity equals secularity. Coming back to the past, that is, after the formative years of Islam, new situations had arisen to which the existing legal corpus had no answer. Would the outcome of attempts to deal with those situations mentioned above constitute *Sharīʿah* or *siyāsah al-Shar'iyyah?* Or should there be any material difference in the first place?

There are strong views which suggest that these are not part of the *Sharī'ah* which means that they are not eternal and can be altered. For example, Muhammad Asad[76] takes a narrow view of the *Sharī'ah* as far as its definition is concerned. For him, only those clear texts (*nuṣūs*) of the Qur'ān and the Sunnah which constitute ordinances expressed in positive terms of laws, which are not subject to conflicting interpretations, and these alone, constitute the real, eternal *Sharī'ah* of Islam. We may compare this with the approach adopted by Western jurists in attempting to limit the province of their jurisprudence by offering a philosophical explanation of the difference between positive law and natural law.[77] According to Asad, the *Sharī'ah* cannot be changed because it is a Divine Law and it need not be changed, because all its ordinances are so formulated that none of them ever conflicts with the real nature of man and the genuine requirements of society. The legitimate field of the community's law-making activity comprises the details in cases and situations where the *Sharī'ah* provides a general principle, and principles with regard to matters which are *mubāḥ*, that is, matters not covered by the *Sharī'ah* at all. One way of interpreting the *āyah* "For every one of you, We have ordained a Divine Law and an open road," is to view it as a method ordained by God to resolve the issues of the *ummah* as they arise. Thus, while the *Sharī'ah* outlines the area within which Muslim life may develop, the Law-Giver has conceded to us, within this area, an "open road" (*minhāj*) for temporal legislation which would cover the contingencies deliberately left untouched.[78]

Asad's approach appeals to our common sense in so far as it seems to say that whatever that has not been stipulated by the Law-Giver may therefore be stipulated by other than the Lawgiver. This is effectively a summation of the principle of *ijtihād* based on the textual authority of a well-known *ḥadīth* commonly cited by jurists. We will discuss that later when we get to the subject of *ijtihād*. But although there is no problem in principle with the approach taken by Asad in advocating the "open road" doctrine, suggesting therefore that political rules are not part of the *Sharīʿah*, there are equally strong views which say that these matters are part of the *Sharīʿah*. One is inclined towards the latter view though for reasons which are entirely different from those of fundamentalists and at this juncture, it suffices to say that political rules should be incorporated within the province of the *Sharīʿah*.

According to the Traditionists' viewpoint, the five categorizations of human acts attain greater significance for rules of worship and ritual, generically under the rubric of *fiqh al-ibādāt* covering matters such as ablution, prayers, fasting, charities, and the performance of the *ḥajj*. Differences of views begin to become more pronounced in respect of the other categories of acts. These include human interactive activities governed under *fiqh al-muʿāmalāt*, such as commercial and financial transactions, and matters generally under the law of personal status as outlined earlier. And the differences become even more pronounced as one wades into the shifting waters of different forms of sanctions for criminal offences governed under *fiqh al-ʿuqūbāt*, as just discussed, jurisdiction and powers of judges, and finally the conduct of state. Nevertheless, an even more profound schism of ideas began to take shape as the *ummah* grew in numbers across the Islamic world's geographical immensity brewing discord and exposing fundamental fissures in creed and world views, a subject we shall explore next.

Notes

1. *Shorter Encyclopaedia*, 524.
2. Ibn Rushd, *Kitāb Faṣl Al-Maqāl wa Taqrīr Mā Bayn al-Sharīʿah wa al-Ḥikmah min al-Ittiṣāl*, translated as *The Book of the Decisive Treatise—Determining the Connection between the Law and Wisdom*, by Charles Butterworth (Brigham Young University

Press, 2001), 26; Rushd and this treatise will be given greater treatment in Chapter 3.

3. Muhammad Asad, *This Law of Ours and Other Essays* (Islamic Book Trust, 1987), 47.
4. As used in the Qur'ān: *yafqahūna* (they understand); *yafqahūhu* (they understand it); *yafqahū* (they understand); *nafqahu* (we understand); *tafqahūna* (you understand); *liyatafaqqahū* (in order to understand or simply to study).
5. In Sūrah al-A'rāf: 179; in Sūrah al-An'ām: 65: "Say [O Muhammad!]: "It is He who is able to send on you chastisement from above you or from under your feet, or to confuse you in sects, and to make some of you taste the violence of others." See how We handle the signs that they may understand (*la'allahum yafqahūn*)."
6. *Rabbi ishraḥ lī ṣadrī wa yassir lī amrī wa uḥlul uqdatan min lisānī yafqahū qawlī* (Tāhā: 25-28). *Cf.* Exodus 4:10-12, King James Version (KJV): "And Moses said unto the Lord, O my Lord, I am not eloquent, neither heretofore, nor since thou hast spoken unto thy servant: but I am slow of speech, and of a slow tongue. And the Lord said unto him, Who hath made man's mouth? or who maketh the dumb, or deaf, or the seeing, or the blind? Have not I the Lord? Now therefore go, and I will be with thy mouth, and teach thee what thou shalt say."
7. "And it is not for the believers to go forth all at once. For there should separate from every division of them a group [remaining] to learn the religion (*liyatafaqqahū fī al-dīn*) and warn their people when they return to them that they might be cautious."
8. Nasr, *Study Quran*, 25977.
9. Āl 'Imrān: 7 and al-Nisā': 162.
10. For a concise treatment of the literal and technical usage of the term see: Imran Ahsan Khan Nyazee, *Theories of Islamic Law: The*

Methodology of Ijtihad (The International Institute of Islamic Thought, Islamabad, 1994), 20-26.

11. Weiss, *God's Law,* 13-16.
12. A.E. Affifi, *The Mystical Philosophy of Muhyid Din Ibnul Arabi* (Cambridge at the University Press, 1939), 105-106.
13. Chittick, *The Sufi Path of Knowledge,* 171.
14. Ibid., 170.
15. The Amman Message, a detailed statement issued by 200 leading Islamic scholars in 2005 specifically recognized the validity of Sufism as a part of Islam.
16. Kambiz Ghaneabasseri, "The Epistemological Foundation of Conceptions of Justice in Classical *Kalām*: A Study of 'Abd al-Jabbār's *al-Mughnī* and *Ibn al-Bāqillānī's al-Tamhīd,*" *Journal of Islamic Studies* 19:1 (2008), 80 doi:10.1093/jis/etm058.
17. *al-Mughnī,* xii. 16.
18. Ghaneabasseri, *op. cit.,* 81; Richard M. Frank, 'Al-Ma'nā: "Some Reflections on the Technical Meaning of the Term in the *Kalām* and Its Use in the Physics of Mu'ammar," *Journal of the American Oriental Society,* 87 (1967), 250; George Hourani, *Islamic Rationalism: The Ethics of 'Abd al-Jabbār* (Oxford: Clarendon Press, 1971), 37-128.
19. Ghaneabasseri, *op. cit.,* 81-82.
20. Ibid.
21. See Abu 'l-Muntaha al-Maghnisawi, *Imām Abu Hanīfa's Al-Fiqh al-Akbar Explained,* Compiled and Translated with an Introduction by Abdur-Rahman ibn Yusuf (White Thread Press, 2007).
22. M. Abdel Haleem, "Chapter 5—Early *kalām,*" in *History of Islamic Philosophy,* Edited by Seyyed Hossein Nasr and Oliver Leaman (London & New York: Routledge, 2001), 75 citing K.A. al-Bayadi,

Ishārat al-marām min ibārat al-imām (Cairo, 1949): 28-9; also Nyazee, *Islamic Jurisprudence,* 20; Nyazee, *Theories,* 23-26.

23. Mohamed Abu Zahrah, *Usūl al-Fiqh;* Nyazee, *Islamic Jurisprudence—Usūl al-Fiqh* (Adam Publishers & Distributors, New Delhi, 2004), 20; Nyazee, *Theories,* 22: The knowledge of the legal rules pertaining to conduct that have been derived from their specific evidences.
24. Mahmassani Subhi, *The Philosophy of Jurisprudence in Islam* (Falsāfat Al-Tashri' Fi Al-Islām), translated by Farhat Ziadeh (Leiden, E.J. Brill, 1961); Fred Reinhard Dallmayr, *Border Crossings: Toward a Comparative Political Theory* (Lexington Books, 1999).
25. "The science of Islamic jurisprudence consists of knowledge of the precepts of the Divine Legislator in their relation to human affairs. The questions of Islamic jurisprudence either concern the next world, being known as rules relating to worship, or to this world, being divided into sections dealing with domestic relations, civil obligations and punishments ..." Introduction to the *Majelle* (Ottoman Civil Code).
26. Indeed, the writings of the great thirteenth century *faqīh* and *mutakallim* (jurisprudent cum theologian) Sayf al-Dīn al-Āmidī (d. 631/1233) on the subject are unparalleled. According to Weiss, al-Amidī's magnum opus *Kitāb al-iḥkām fī uṣūl al-aḥkām* (the *Ihkām* for short) remains unsurpassed in its comprehensiveness, not even by the great Fakhr al-Dīn al-Rāzī whose *Kitāb al-Mahsūl* towers over the landscape of theoretical Islamic jurisprudence: *Al-Mahsūl fī 'Ilm Usūl al-Fiqh* (6 volumes), edited by Ṭāhā Jabir al-Alwānī (Beirut: Mu'assasat al-Risala, 1992). The edition of the *Ikhām* referred to is a two-volume publication of Dar al-Kitāb al-'ālamīyya, Beirut, 1985/1405.

27. *Al-fiqhu makhsūsun bi'l-'ilmi 'l-hāsīli bi-jumlatin min al-ahkāmi 'l-shar'īyati 'l-furū'iyāti bi'l-nazāri wa'l-istidlālī*—translation rendered by Weiss, *God's Law*, 24.
28. Weiss, *God's Law*, 25
29. Muhammad Shafiq, "The Meaning of *Ra'y* and Nature of its Usage in Islamic Law (An Examination of Select cases of the Legal Reasoning in the Period of 'Umar, the Second Caliph)," *Islamic Studies*, 23, no. 1 (1984): 21-32.
30. *Al-fiqhu 'l-ilmu bi-ha awi 'l-'ilmu bi'l-'āmali bi-hā banā'an 'ala 'l-idrāki 'l-qat'i, Ihkām*, 1:7, quoted by Weiss, *God's Law*, 25.
31. Laura Hassan, "The Encounter of *Falsafa* and *Kalām* in Sayf al-Dīn al-Āmidī's Discussion of the Atom: Asserting Traditional Boundaries, Questioning Traditional Doctrines," The *SOAS Journal of Postgraduate Research*, Vol. 6 (2014), 78.
32. Weiss, *God's Law*, 35-36: *Al-'ilmu 'ibāratun 'an sifatin yahsulu bihā li-nafsi 'l-muttasifi bihā'l-tamyīzu bayna haqā'iqi 'l-ma'ānī 'l-kullīya, Ihkām*, 1:15.
33. Ibid., 624-625, 25.
34. *'Ilm al-fiqh* is literally the knowledge of the *Sharī'ah* rulings.
35. Wael Hallaq, "Can the *Sharī'ah* be Restored?" *Islamic Law and the Challenges of Modernity*, edited by Yvonne Y. Haddad and Barbara F. Stowasser (Walnut Creek: Altamira Press, 2004), 21-53. Accessed on June 21, 2013; available at http://globalwebpost.com/farooqm/study_res/islam/fiqh/hallaq_shariah.html.
36. Ibid., 8, al-Āmidī: "The indicators (*adillah*) upon which the understanding of the *Sharī'ah* is based, the ways in which those indicators function as indications of the divine categorizations, and the considerations which pertain to the role of the scholar who employs those indicators in the actual formulation of the

divine categorizations all of which matters are treated in a general way, not in relation to specific instances": Weiss, *God's Law*, 26.

37. Ṭāhā Jābir al-Alwānī, *Usūl al Fiqh al Islāmī—Source Methodology in Islamic Jurisprudence: Methodology for Research and Knowledge* (Herndon: The International Institute of Islamic Thought, 1990).
38. Weiss, *God's Law*, 27.
39. Ibid., 24-27.
40. Abū Yūsuf Ya'qūb ibn 'Isḥāq as-Ṣabah al-Kindī. *Rasā'il al-Kindī al-Falsafiyyah* (The Philosophical Treatises of al-Kindi), ed. M.A.H. Abu Ridah (Cairo: Dar al-fikr al-'arabi), 2 volumes in 1, 1953.
41. Abū Naṣr Muḥammad ibn Muḥammad al-Fārābī. His commentary and translation of the *Organon* inspired Maimonides to write his famous Treatise on logic, *Maqālah fī ṣinā'ah al-manṭiq*, expounding the essentials of Aristotelian logic.
42. Kerr, M.H. *Islamic Reform: The Legal and Political Theories of Muhammad 'Abduh and Rashid Reda* (Berkeley: University of California Press, 1966), 56. The author includes a fourth level of correspondence between normative relationship between man and nature and habits and social behaviour *'ādāt*/social change.
43. Waniel Hallaq, "From Fatwas to Furu': Growth and Change in Islamic Substantive Law," *Islamic Law and Society* (1994):17-56, at 31-38.
44. Ibid.
45. Glasse, *Concise Encyclopaedia of Islam*, 361.
46. Ignaz Goldziher, *The Zahiris: Their Doctrine and Their History, a Contribution to the History of Islamic Theology,* Translated and edited by Wolfgang Behn first published as *Die Zahiriten, ihr lehrsystem und ihre geschichte: beitrag zur geschichte der Muhammedanischen theologie.* (Leiden: E.J. Brill, 1971), 110-111.
47. Ibid., 111, citing Ibḥāl, fol. 12b; al-Sha'rānī, I, p. 65.

48. Valerie Jon Hoffman, *The Essentials of Ibadi Islam* (Syracuse: Syracuse University Press, 2012), 3.
49. Ignaz Goldziher, *Vorlesungen uber den Islam* (Heidelberg: C. Winter 1910, reprint 1958), 215; translated by A. Hamori and R. Hamori, *Introduction to Islamic Theology and Law* (Princeton University Press, 1981), 191.
50. Muhammad Iqbal, *The Reconstruction of Religious Thought in Islam* (Institute of Islamic Culture: Lahore, 1986), 133.
51. See Sūrah al-Tawbah: 8, 28 and the commentary in Nasr, *Study Qur'an*, 24907-24958.
52. Khaled Abou El Fadl, *The Great Theft: Wrestling Islam from the Extremists* (HarperOne, 2007), 214.
53. Coulson, *History*, 27.
54. H.A.R. Gibb, *Mohammedanism: An Historical Survey* (London: Oxford University Press, 1950), 72-84.
55. On the rejection of *ijmāʿ* as advanced by ʿAli Abd. Rāziq see Leonard Binder, *Islamic Liberalism: A Critique of Development Ideologies* (University of Chicago Press, 1988), 135-140.
56. Hashim Kamali, *Principles of Islamic Jurisprudence* (Cambridge: Islamic Texts Society, 1989), 8-9.
57. *The Princeton Encyclopedia of Islamic Political Thought*, edited by Gerhard Bowering (Princeton University Press, 2013), 501.
58. Sūrah al-Baqarah, *āyah* 187 (Pickthall).
59. Asad says: "The Traditions are to the effect that the wife of Thābit ibn Qays, Jamīlah, came to the Prophet and demanded a divorce from her husband on the ground that, in spite of his irreproachable character and behaviour, she "disliked him as she would dislike falling into unbelief after having accepted Islam." Thereupon the Prophet ordained that she should return to Thābit the garden which he has given her as her dower (*mahr*) at the time of their wedding, and decreed that the marriage should be

dissolved. (Several variants of this Tradition have been recorded by Bukhārī, Nasā'ī, Tirmidhī, Ibn Mājah and Bayhaqī, on the authority of Ibn 'Abbās.) Similar Traditions, handed down on the authority of 'A'īshah and relating to a woman called Hubaybah bint Saḥl, are to be found in the *Muwatta'* of Imām Mālik, in the *Musnad* of Imām Ahmad, and in the compilations of Nasā'i and Abu Dā'ūd (in one variant, the latter gives the woman's name as Hafsah bint Saḥl)." (*The Message of the Qur'ān*).

60. Asad adds: "An exhaustive discussion of all these Traditions and their legal implications is found in *Nayl al-Awtar* VII, pp. 34-41. For a summary of the relevant views of the various schools of Islamic jurisprudence, see *Bidayat al-Mujtahid* II, pp. 54-57."
61. Hashim Kamali, *Punishment in Islamic Law: An Enquiry into the Hudud Bill of Kelantan* (Institut Kajian Dasar, 1995), 48. For a laconic explanation of *ḥudūd* and its context in the Qur'ān, see 45-50.
62. Ibid., 49; Fazlur Rahman, "The Concept of *ḥadd* in Islamic Law," *Islamic Studies* 4 (1965), 237.
63. Rahman, 240.
64. Anver M. Emon, "*Huqūq Allāh* and *Huqūq al-'Ibād*: A Legal Heuristic for a Natural Rights Regime," *Islamic Law and Society*, 13 (2006): 326-327.
65. Kamali, *op. cit.*, 72-73.
66. Emon, *op. cit.*, 328.
67. Mohamed S. El-Awa, *Punishment in Islamic Law*, American Trust Publications (1993); Shahid M. Shahidullah, *Comparative Criminal Justice Systems: Global and Local Perspectives* (Jones & Bartlett Publishers, 2012), 370-372.
68. Exodus xxi, 23 ff, Leviticus 24:18-20, and Deuteronomy 19:21.
69. Yohanan Friedmann, *Tolerance and Coercion in Islam: Interfaith Relations in the Muslim Tradition* (Cambridge University Press, 2006), 42-50.

70. This is the majority position with the exception of the Hanafite: Majid Khadduri and Herbert J. Liebesny, *Law in the Middle East: Origin and Development of Islamic Law,* 2nd Edition (Lawbook Exchange, 2008), 337-345.
71. Sūrah al-Māidah, *āyah* 45; For comparison, even a cursory glance at Exodus xxi, 23 ff. (as cited earlier) will present an impression of a harsh Mosaic law. Consider, for instance, the verses (28 and 29) on the punishment for death caused by an ox: "If an ox gore a man or a woman, that they die: then the ox shall be surely stoned, and his flesh shall not be eaten; but the owner of the ox shall be quit; But if the ox were wont to push with his horn in time past, and it hath been testified to his owner, and he hath not kept him in, but that he hath killed a man or a woman; the ox shall be stoned, and his owner also shall be put to death." However, compensation is allowed: "If there be laid on him a sum of money, then he shall give for the ransom of his life whatsoever is laid upon him."
72. Tahir Wasti, *The Application of Islamic Criminal Law in Pakistan: Sharia in Practice* (Brill Academic, 2009), 283-288.
73. Asad: "The Pentateuch does not contain this call to forgiveness which is brought out with great clarity not only in the Qur'ān but also in the teachings of Jesus, especially in the Sermon on the Mount: and this, read in conjunction with the following verses, would seem to be an allusion to the time-bound quality of Mosaic Law."
74. Wael Hallaq, *Sharī'a: Theory, Practice, Transformations* (Cambridge University Press, 2009), 551-558.
75. El-Awa, *Punishment in Islamic Law,* 1-68.
76. A Jewish-born convert to Islam, Asad was a staunch opponent of the Zionist Movement and spent a considerable amount of time living with Bedouins. He befriended the poet-philosopher Muhammad Iqbal and partly at his behest, wrote his short but

laconic treatise on the Islamic State. His magnum opus, as referred to earlier: *The Message of the Qur'an*—an English translation and commentary of the Qur'ān—continues to be both a great source of Qur'ānic research as well as exegetic controversy.

77. See Austin's *The Province of Jurisprudence Determined*, by which the title of this monograph was inspired.
78. As explicated at the outset: *Li kullin ja'alnā minkum shir'atan wa minhājā* (Sūrah al-Mā'idah 5:48); Asad, *Principles of State*, 12-15, Asad's translation; see earlier discussion on the etymology of "*Sharī'ah*," 2-6, n.3.

Chapter 3

Kalām and Falsafah

Kalām[1]

In light of the previous discussion on the bifurcation between *fiqh* and *kalām*, it may be said that what *fiqh* abandoned or was forced to forsake, *kalām* picked up while *falsafah*, perched atop the intellectual heights of the Academy and Lyceum, swooped in to carry aloft the thinkers and scientists of the Muslim world. It should be remembered that *kalām* arose from the generic science of *uṣūl al-dīn* which studies the basic doctrines of the faith based on the revealed text. In conventional terms, it may be difficult to differentiate *'ilm al-kalām* from *uṣūl al-dīn* as both may be defined as "the science of the basic doctrines of the religion." However, the distinction becomes clear once we reclassify *kalām* as scholastic/dialectic theology and *uṣūl al-dīn* as descriptive/normative theology.

Kalām in this regard is the science of identifying the basic doctrines of faith and seeking to prove their validity. While the term *kalām* was already pervasive in the classical Islamic tradition, it gained particular importance only within the scope of religious dogma. First, as a broad conceptual platform for the rational synthesis of the array of religious dogmas, including those beyond the confines of orthopraxy, *kalām* would fit into the matrix of scholastic theology. Secondly, within a more restricted framework, it is dialectic theology in as much as it connotes a sophisticated dialectical technique in theological discourse.[2] In Qur'ānic hermeneutics, therefore, *kalām* proved to be far superior to *fiqh* which, as a rule, employed an absolutist approach to revelation in contrast to the temporal relativism of *kalām*.[3]

As alluded to earlier, Abū Ḥanīfah extended the province of the *Sharī'ah* inquiry by defining *fiqh* jurisprudence to include the concern of *kalām*. It bears stressing the point that Abū Ḥanīfah was among the first of the *mutakallimūn* before both the terms gained currency and pejorative connotations. We have noted how his *al-Fiqh al-Akbar* was in fact more *dīn/kalām* than *fiqh*, representing the formative expositions on the Divine attributes and the uncreatedness of the Qur'ān. In this regard, the Ḥanafī *madhhab* may be regarded as the first of the orthodox[4] Sunni schools to employ rational enquiry in their *ijtihād*. The rationalist approach was adopted in *kalām* and articulated more formally later via the school of al-Māturīdī, named after its founder Abū Manṣūr al-Māturīdī (d. 333/944) who started by following in the footsteps of Abū Ḥanīfah in affirming that whereas man had his own capacity and will to act, God was the creator of man's acts. By then, *kalām* was already clearly distinguished from *fiqh* and considered a special area in *uṣūl al-dīn*.

The *kalām* disputes started some time at the end of the first century after *Hijrah* and eventually covered an entire spectrum of issues that occupied the *ummah* including *fiqh*, *dīn*, the physical sciences and sociology. The fundamental problematique arose from the nature of God and His Attributes centering on the twin concepts of God's Speech and God's Will. While the former relates to the belief in the uncreatedness of the Qur'ān, the latter pertains to the createdness of the world.[5] The discourse is articulated through the Aristotelian methodology of logical proofs, fine-tuned eventually as *al-Manṭiq*. Those who deny a reality for the attributes, the uncreatedness of the Qur'ān and God's Will were the Mu'tazilites and those on the other side were generally the Ash'arites, subject to some qualifications. The Traditionists—*aḥl al-ḥadīth*—as we shall see, had no truck with the *mutakallimūn* because of their antipathy towards the exercise of *kalām* though in sum, their harshest criticism was reserved for the Mu'tazilites. It is therefore appropriate to dwell a little more into these controversies from which the two major creeds—the Mu'tazilī and the Ash'arī—have come to dominate the discourse of the *Sharī'ah* at a higher plane, beyond the more down-to-earth disputations on *fiqh*.

The adherents of the school of al-Māturīdī, being largely Ḥanafis, took a position largely similar to the Ash'arites. They parted ways on the nature of belief and the place of human reason. In his *Kitāb al-Tawḥīd*, al-Māturīdī, perched on the Ḥanafi *madhhab*, states categorically that *īmān* consists in "conviction in the heart and affirmation by the tongue," which according to the other three *madhāhib* of Mālik, al-Shāfi'ī and Aḥmad ibn Ḥanbal is insufficient without including the proviso "practice with the limbs."[6] While *īmān* remains static, *taqwā* (piety/God-consciousness) may ebb or rise. On the pre-eminence of the '*aql*, the Māturīdīs contend that even without *naql* (revealed texts) the intellect is capable of discernment of the major vices and transgressions, indicative no doubt of the Ḥanafi preponderance for *al-ra'y* in matters of *fiqh*. This position is rejected by the Ash'arites.

Mu'tazilī Creed

According to a well-known anecdote, the genesis of the Mu'tazilī creed was occasioned when Wāṣil ibn 'Aṭā' (d. 131/748) "withdrew" from the *ḥalaqah* (learning circle) of Ḥasan al-Baṣrī (d. 111/728) over the question concerning *al-Manzilah bayn al-Manzilatayn* (lit. the position between two positions—effectively, the intermediate position between two extreme positions).[7] This concept is best elucidated by Ibn Ḥazm:

> "In case what has been committed happens to be a grave sin, the man is a *fāsiq* (grave sinner), neither a believer nor a *kāfir*, nor, indeed, a *munāfiq*."[8]

This has significant implication in terms of the *fiqh* of *ḥalāl* and *ḥarām*. The Mu'tazilī position therefore implies that the normal relations of marriage and inheritance are licit between such a man and other Muslims and the animal slaughtered by him is *ḥalāl*. According to Izutsu, what is of crucial importance is that the Mu'tazilites made out of the *fāsiq* an independent category between the believer-Muslim and the *kāfir* whereas hitherto the orthodox position was disjunctive, that is, one is either a believer (*i.e.* believer-*fāsiq*) or *kāfir* (*i.e. fāsiq-kāfir*).[9]

At the risk of oversimplification, Mu'tazilī precepts may be abridged as comprising the following core five principles[10]: *tawḥīd*, justice, free will, the intermediate position (as just related) and commanding good and forbidding evil. The appellations of "*Ahl al-tawḥīd wa al-'adl*" (People of Unity and Justice) or *Aṣḥāb al-'adl wa al-tawḥīd* (Companions of Justice and Unity) are ascribed to the Mu'tazilites (more by themselves than others) as reflected in the title to the monumental work of al-Qāḍī 'Abd al-Jabbār (d. 415/1024), *al-Mughnī fī Abwāb al-Tawḥīd wa al-'Adl*. As one of the foremost exponents of the creed, 'Abd al-Jabbār presented Mu'tazilī doctrines under the twin banner of unity and justice. To avoid repetition, we will defer discussion on justice to a separate section together with the Ash'arī position by offering a comparative discourse on the epistemological frameworks of both creeds.

The doctrine of *tawḥīd* is taken for granted by most Muslims the comprehension of which, however, may at times be described as superficial. Indeed, the doctrine is encapsulated in Sūrah al-Ikhlāṣ which is also known as "the Reminder" because it reminds us of Divine Unity "in a pure and simple form." As regards the *asbāb al-nuzūl* (the reasons or occasions for revelation), according to at least two accounts, this was in relation to the question posed by Jews and Christians to the Prophet concerning the "lineage of his Lord." With Sūrah al-Kāfirūn, the two are considered as the most complete statement on Divine Unity, al-Ikhlāṣ being the affirmation of truth and al-Kāfirūn the categorical rejection of falsehood.[11]

Much has been made out of the fact that the term *tawḥīd* is not mentioned in the Qur'ān but considering that the theme of Divine

Unity, that is, the Oneness of God is prevalent throughout the Qur'ān and the Sunnah, that is a non-issue. The commentators generally agree that while *wāḥid* and *aḥad* are semantic cognates, their exact meaning differs. *Wāḥid* is used as a numerical quality as in "one" in relation to other numbers and the divine name *al-Wāḥid* is to signify the attribute of God, as one. *Aḥad*, as it occurs in the first *āyah* of al-Ikhlāṣ, refers to "Absolute Oneness that is unique and cannot take a second or be divided" without any consideration of the multiplicity of creation.[12] This is best expressed conceptually as *tanzīh* meaning God's transcendence, that is, "declaring incomparability," or affirming God's transcendent distance from humanity. *Wāḥid* conveys the Oneness of the Divine Being in relation to the Divine Attributes, that is, conceptually *tashbīh*—the Divine Immanence, closeness, affirming similarity and "nearness."[13]

It is, however, in the area of ascription of attributes and the question of God's Essence that the Muʿtazilī doctrine is diagonally opposed to the other schools of *kalām*, and is used in their defence of divine unity against Dualists and Trinitarians.[14] The Muʿtazilī position would exclude the qualities and assert that Allah is Oneness in Himself, the only Being with Absolute existence, all other beings having merely a contingent existence.[15] They assert that any association of the Divine names, the *asmā' al-ḥusnā* (generally translated as the Beautiful Names of Allah) with His Essence is *shirk*. Asad's translation of *asmā' al-ḥusnā* as it occurs in al-Aʿrāf, 180 as "the attributes of perfection" is clearly indicative of a broader meaning as compared with the more literal rendering by Yusuf Ali and generally others as "the most beautiful names."[16]

God comprises all the attributes of perfection and represents, therefore, the Ultimate Reality. Among these attributes, seven are often singled out as particularly pertinent to the *kalām* discourse, namely, the Knowing, the Powerful, the Willing, the Living, the Hearing, the Seeing, and the Speaking. The Literalists and the Ashʿarites hold that God had certain attributes corresponding to these names. The Muʿtazilites, however, see this as violating the principle of the Divine Essence. Contextually in the historic discourse, the Mu'tazilī position is that in as far as God knew, He knew by Himself or his Essence, and not by any hypostatic Knowledge,[17] as in the shared existence of spiritual and corporal entities such as that in Neoplatonism where the Soul, Intellect (nous) and the One are merged or in Christian theology, where hypostasis is one of the three elements of the Holy Trinity.

'Aḍud al-Dīn al-Ījī (d. 756/1355) reports that the Mu'tazilites accused those who believed in the reality of divine attributes of having fallen into the error of the Christian belief in the Trinity.[18] It may be recalled that 'Aḍud had notably launched ad hominem attacks on the Shaykh al-Akbar Muḥyī al-Dīn Ibn al-'Arabī and had advised his students not to learn about Mecca from the book—*Fuṣūṣ al-Ḥikam*—of "the Maghribī of that dry temperament" (*yābis al-mizāj*), who "apart from being an infidel, was also a hashish-eater."[19] Among his followers was Sa'd al-Dīn al-Taftāzānī who wrote a commentary on the *'Aqāid al-Nasāfī*, which remains a major testament of the Ash'ariyyah creed.

It should be noted that disputations on the theological conceptions of Christianity such as the doctrine of the Logos necessitated more sophisticated arguments on the part of the Muslim scholars. Indeed, when it came to such discourses with the older religions, it was obvious that the Traditionists were simply not equipped to engage in meaningful intellectual combat with the Christians (namely, the Monophysites, Jacobites, Nestorians, Malkites), the Manichaeans, Zoroastrians, Magians and others. The Ash'arites in theory would have been suitably equipped to counter this issue but because of their committed stance on the uncreatedness of the Qur'ān, found themselves hamstrung and "boxed-in," as it were. For example, on the references in the Qur'ān to Jesus as *kalimatin minhu* (a Word from Him) and *kalimatuhu* (His Word)[20] and the argument that these passages support the dogma of the divinity of Christ, the position of the 'Ash'arites and the Ḥanbalites on the uncreatedness of the Qur'ān actually lent weight to the Christian claim. The Traditionists led by Imām Aḥmad ibn Ḥanbal (d. 245/855) argued that God has an eternal Attribute of Speech and the Qur'ān was a part of this as evidenced by the verses which state that God spoke to Moses. While the words of the Qur'ān as uttered and written by people are not eternal, the Qur'ān is part of God's eternal Attribute of Speech.[21] It is noteworthy that most of the different versions of the Bible in English proffer a literal rendering in the *Gospel of John* as: "In the beginning was the Word, and the Word was with God, and the Word was God. The same was in the beginning with God." (King James). On the other hand, the Today's English Version (TEV) takes a translation clearly intended to assert not just the divinity of Christ as the Word but the doctrine that Christ, being uncreated, is one and the same as God: "Before the world was created, the Word already existed; he was with God, and he was the same as God." On the divinity issue, scholars point to the influence of the Manichaeans on early Christianity and how this claim so provoked Muslims that they had to find more sophisticated means to counter the Christian polemic. With the Muʿtazilī position that the Qur'ān was created, the claim that the divinity of Christ was supported by the Qur'ānic reference to "His Word" therefore had no leg to stand on.

On *ya'murūna bi al-maʿrūfi wa yanhawna ʿan al-munkar* (enjoining good and forbidding evil),[22] the Muʿtazilī position, notwithstanding their doctrine of free will, regards compulsion as permissible in order to enforce the imperative. On this rationale, the notorious *miḥnah* (on the createdness of the Qur'ān) was instituted by the caliph al-Ma'mūn though a closer analysis of the historical circumstances would show that it was political necessity rather than doctrinal imperative that provided the main impetus. As for *āyah* 7, Sūrah Āl ʿImrān, cited by the Traditionists as a categorical prohibition against the use of allegorical interpretation, a brief review is in order. Let us look at the *tafsīr* and translation of Asad's which is largely based on al-Zamakhsharī, which for the sake of completeness, is reproduced *in toto*:

"He it is who has bestowed upon thee from on high this

> divine writ, containing messages that are clear in and by themselves—and these are the essence of the divine writ—as well as others that are allegorical. Now those whose hearts are given to swerving from the truth go after that part of the divine writ which has been expressed in allegory, seeking out [what is bound to create] confusion, and seeking [to arrive at] its final meaning [in an arbitrary manner]; but none save God knows its final meaning. Hence, those who are deeply rooted in knowledge say: 'We believe in it; the whole [of the divine writ] is from our Sustainer—albeit none takes this to heart save those who are endowed with insight."

According to Asad, al-Ṭabarī identifies the *āyāt muḥkamāt* ("messages that are clear in and by themselves") with what the philologists and jurists describe as *nuṣūṣ*—namely, ordinances or statements which are self-evident (*ẓāhir*) by virtue of their wording. *Āyāt muḥkamāt* are therefore only those statements of the Qur'ān which do not admit of more than one interpretation. These are described as the "essence of the divine writ" (*umm al-kitāb*) because they comprise the fundamental principles underlying its message and, in particular, its ethical and social teachings. The *āyāt mutashābihāt* may be defined as those passages of the Qur'ān which are expressed in a figurative manner, with a meaning that is metaphorically implied but not directly stated. Nevertheless, Asad says that it would be too dogmatic to regard any passage of the Qur'ān which does not conform to the definition of *āyāt muḥkamāt* as *mutashābih.* A distinction is made between allegorical statements and statements that may be open to multiple interpretations. Asad contends that there are many statements in the Qur'ān which are liable to more than one interpretation but are, nevertheless, not allegorical.

As for "seeking out confusion," according to al-Zamakhshari, it is not the consequence of *ta'wīl* per se but of "those whose hearts are given to swerving from the truth" in interpreting allegorical passages in an "arbitrary manner." As for the oft-quoted "*wa mā ya'lamu ta'wīlahū illā Allāh*" (none save God knows its final meaning), most of the early commentators say it refers to the interpretation of allegorical passages which deal with metaphysical subjects: God's attributes, the ultimate meaning of time and eternity, the resurrection of the dead, the Day of Judgment, paradise and hell, the nature of the beings or forces described as angels, and so forth—all of which fall within the category of *al-ghayb*, *i.e.*, that sector of reality which is beyond the reach of human perception and imagination and cannot, therefore, be conveyed to man in other than allegorical terms. Asad contends that one cannot arrive at a correct understanding of the above passage without paying due attention to the nature and function of allegory as such. A true allegory—in contrast with a mere pictorial paraphrase of something that could equally well be stated in direct terms—is always meant to express in a figurative manner something which, because of its complexity, cannot be adequately expressed in direct terms and, because of this very complexity, can be grasped only intuitively, as a general mental image, and not as a series of detailed "statements": and this seems to be the meaning of the phrase, "none save God knows its final meaning."[23]

As al-Zamakhshaī phrases it in his commentary on Surāh al-Ra'd: 35, it is

> "through a parabolic illustration, by means of something which we know from our experience, of something that is beyond the reach of our perception" (*tamhīlan li mā ghāba 'annā bi mā nushāhid*).

And this is the innermost purport of the term and concept of *al-mutashābihāt* as used in the Qur'ān. This gives rise to the fundamental question: Why are there *āyāt mutashābihāt* if all the verses in the Qur'an are to be interpreted only literally? According to Asad, the Qur'ān tells us clearly that many of its passages and expressions must be understood in an allegorical sense for the simple reason that, being intended for human understanding, they could not have been conveyed to us in any other way. It follows, therefore, that if we were to take every Qur'ānic passage, statement or expression in its outward, literal sense and disregard the possibility of its being an allegory, a metaphor or a parable, we would be offending against the very spirit of the divine writ.

Ash'arī Creed

As for the genesis of the Ash'arites, its founder Abū al-Hasan al-Ash'arī (d. 330/941) was initially an adherent of the Mu'tazilī creed before his change of heart brought on by a dream, as anecdotal accounts tell us. Be that as it may, among the theological writings, his rather short tract entitled *Risālah fī Istiḥsān al-Khawḍ fī al-Kalām* synthesizes the Ash'arite doctrine and answers the objections against the use of *kalām*. His *al-Maqālāt al Islāmiyyīn wa Ikhtilāf al Muṣallīn* is an excellent and comprehensive treatise on the variant positions of the different schools concerning dogmas and doctrines, foreshadowing in fact, great works such as al-Shahrastānī's *Kitāb al-Milal wa al-Niḥal* and Ibn Ḥazm's *al-Fasl fī al-Milal wa al-Ahwā' wa al-Niḥal.*

God's transcendence is a central aspect in the Qur'ān which, in this regard, departs significantly and prominently from the Bible. For example, we are told in *Genesis* 2:2 that God created the heavens and the earth in six days,

> "... and on the seventh day God ended his work which he had made; and he rested on the seventh day ..."[24]

The Qur'ān (Sūrah al-A'raf, *āyah* 54), on the other hand, states that God

> "created the heavens and the earth in six days and is firmly established on the throne"

leaving no room for any interpretation that might suggest that God would need "to rest." Again, where there is the oft-cited saying taken from Genesis 1:27 that "God created man in His own image," no parallel statement is to be found in the Qur'ān. Similarly, the conception of the Holy Trinity is challenged on the basis that God's transcendence would logically rule out the need to have a son.[25] In other words, God cannot be conceived of in human terms. But then such a proposition immediately brings forth the question: why then are anthropomorphic terms used in the Qur'ān and the *aḥādīth*?

On this matter concerning God's attributes, we have already made clear the Muʿtazilī position which is that such passages are subject to *ta'wīl* interpretations while the Ḥanbālis insist on a literal position. The Ashʿarites take a medial position between the anthropomorphism of the Literalists and the rationalist hermeneutics of the Muʿtazilīs. The Literalists is just a generic term for a mixed group comprising the Ẓāhirites, the Mujassimites (anthropomorphists), the Muḥaddīthīn (Traditionists), and the *fuqahā'* (jurists) particularly the Ḥanbalites, all of whom were united in opposition to the use of *kalām* in religious discourse. The Ashʿarites were caught between Scylla and Charybdis. If God is essence (*māhiyyah*), then there should be no attributes (*ṣifāt*). To assert the eternal attributes of God as being identical with His essence is to deny the physical or corporeal attributes and to end up at the Muʿtazilī pole. On the other hand, if God is composed of attributes, then He is not essence. To assert that they are wholly different from His essence would be to posit the multiplicity of eternals and that would be siding with the Literalists. So, the Ashʿarites came up with a brilliant solution: God possesses attributes in general, both *ṣifāt al-salbiyyah* (negative attributes) and *ṣifāt al-wujūdiyyah* (existential/positive attributes.) These positive attributes appertain to *ʿaqliyyah* (intellectual) faculties such as knowledge, power, will, life, hearing, seeing, and speech. Under the doctrine of *mukhālafāt* or absolute differences, Muslims should just believe in God's anthropomorphic attributes without questioning how and without making comparisons with man's attributes—*bi lā kayf wa bi lā tashbīh*.[26] In one sense, the attributes are included in God's essence and, in another, they are excluded. The proposition that essence and attributes are two distinct categories can be explained semantically: God's essence differs from God's attributes, the latter being supplementary to the former.

However, in terms of the *ḥaqīqah* (ultimate reality), the attributes are inherent in the essence. To the Muʿtazilites, the Ashʿarī position on this was equivocation, plain and simple. For them, God is one, eternal, unique and absolute and "There is none like unto Him" and hence all anthropomorphic references in the Qur'ān must be subjected to the hermeneutics of *ta'wīl*, that is, allegorical interpretation.

On free will versus pre-determination, the Ashʿarites again took a middle ground between the Muʿtazilites and the Qadarites on the one hand and the Jabarites on the other. The Muʿtazilites and the Qadarites held that man has full power over his actions and has absolute freedom of choice, while the Jabarites maintained a purely fatalistic view. Human actions are predetermined and predestined by God. Man has no power to will any action. God has power over all things as manifest in the oft-recurrent phrase in the Qur'an: *wa 'ala kulli shay'in qadīr.* The Ashʿarites distinguished between God the Creator (*al-Khāliq*) of human actions and man, and God the Acquisitor (*al-Muktasib*). Because human beings are created (*makhlūq*), their actions are also His creation. God has original power (*qudrah qadīmah*) while man only has power derived from God (*ḥadīthah*). God creates in man the power and the ability to perform an act. He also creates in him the power to make a free choice (*ikhtiyār*) between two alternatives, that is, between right and wrong. But man is free only in making the choice and intending to do the particular action and has no power whatsoever to determine the trajectory and outcome of his decision. Because he has no real and effective power, he, therefore, has no free will in the Muʿtazilite sense.

According to Ibn Rushd, the Ashʿarites have tried to adopt a mean between the two extreme views.

> "They say that man can do action, but the deeds done, and the power of doing it, are both created by God. But this is quite meaningless. For if the deed and the power of doing it be both created by God, then man is necessarily compelled to do the act."[27]

However, he does not agree with the Mu'tazilites either and posits his answer to the conundrum from the prism of *falsafah*, to where we shall go in due course in this chapter when we discuss the *falāsifah* of Islam.

Coming back to the *mutakallimūn*, the point about acquisition of reward for good deeds and retribution for bad deeds is spelt out in the Qur'an:

> "... every soul shall be paid what it earned and none shall be dealt with unjustly"; "On no soul doth Allah place a burden greater than it can bear. It gets every good that it earns and it suffers every ill that it earns."[28]

Everything depends on God's will (*irādah*) and power. Flowing from the theory of acquisition (*kasb*) there is, therefore, only an illusion of free will, for man, being merely the agency upon which the accidents of atoms are created, cannot actually be the cause of any of his own 'actions'.[29] God's omnipotence and omniscience would by necessity translate into knowledge and power over all particulars for

> "He is the Knower of the Unseen. Not an atom's weight, or less than that or greater, escapeth Him in the heavens or in the earth, but it is in a clear Record."[30]

As for man, the completion of the act is partially due to his intention: He is to be rewarded or punished according to his intention—which indeed harks back to the famous *ḥadīth* of the Prophet on *niyyah*. But man's free choice is just to occasion the action by God. Hence, this doctrine is essentially occasionalism as there is no real causality. God creates and completes the action. For the majority of Sunnis this is the accepted orthodox position as in generally all the other key aspects of Ash'arī theology.

For the central problem of causality, in the Ash'arite scheme of things, God's acts in the world are *mubashshir*, that is, direct. But, what about man's acts? On this question a very interesting scenario was put forth in discussing the concept of *tawallud* (the generation of acts), that is, to what extent an act is said to be responsible for leading to other acts. For instance, if *A* shoots an arrow, and *B* diverts it thereby killing *C*, who would be morally responsible for his death?[31] This type of scenario is in fact discussed in English criminal law when considering criminal culpability in respect of the nexus between *mens rea* and *actus reus*, that is, between the intention of committing a criminal act and the physical act that must be executed for the intention to be realised thus constituting a punishable crime. An act that is criminally intended but is not accompanied by any physical act towards its commission can never be a crime. That is the legal position. Likewise, in the case of a physical act that causes injury or death but is not preceded or accompanied by criminal intention. This broad doctrine is summed up in the maxim *actus non facit reum nisi mens sit rea*. Thus, in the scenario mentioned in the *kalām* discourse, even if *A* had intended to kill *C* but had shot the arrow in such a way that would have been physically impossible for it to reach its target *C* if not for *B*'s intervention no crime of homicide would be constituted. It would not even constitute an attempt under these circumstances. On the other hand, where *A* had no intention whatsoever of killing anyone in the first place but had nevertheless shot the said arrow which because of *B*'s intervention ended up killing *C*, *A* might well be guilty of manslaughter or involuntary homicide by sheer negligence or recklessness, if it could be shown that *A*'s act could foreseeably lead to anyone being killed regardless of who the intended target was.

On the subject of being taken to account for one's inward and outward actions, a *ḥadīth* states,

> "Whosoever intends a good deed but does not do it, God records a completed good deed for him. If he intends it and does it, God records ten good deeds and up to seven hundred times more or even greater than that. If he intends to commit an evil deed but does not do it, God records a good deed for him. If he intends to do it and does it, God records a single evil deed for him."

As foreshadowed in the *ḥadīth*, a line exists between the psychological state and the executed choice, that is the *mens rea* and the *actus reus*.

The best defence of occasionalism comes from al-Ghazālī in his *Tahāfut al-falāsifah* (The Incoherence of the Philosophers) where he employed Aristotelian and Neo-Platonist arguments to buttress the doctrine as pioneered by al-Ash'arī against the positions taken by the *falāsifah*, particularly, Ibn Sīnā (d. 980–1037).[32] Ibn Sīnā's view on causality was diametrically opposed to traditional beliefs in miracles for they are by definition nothing but divine interruptions of the ordinary course of events in nature. The Mu'tazilite conception of free will and causality would imply that natural causes will actually prevail over divine intervention which of course is anathema to the belief (held by all creeds including the Mu'tazilites themselves) of God's omnipotence.[33]

A common fallacy concerning the Ash'arites is their purported aversion to reason over revelation as the basis of truth. This is incorrect as there is no such aversion though comparatively they place less weight than the Mu'tazilites would on reason in the event of a conflict. In fact, for the Mu'tazilites, revelation must give way to reason when such a conflict arises. For the Ash'arites, revelation always takes precedence over reason in ascertaining the ultimate truth. The use of reason is but to confirm what is given by revelation. It is on this distinction that one can speak of the rationalist *kalām* of the Mu'tazilites as compared to the orthodox *kalām* of the Ash'arites. It is somewhat coterminous with the polar positions on *fiqh* between the *ahl al-ra'y* and the *ahl al-ḥadīth* summed up, as mentioned earlier, as *'aql* (reason/intellect) and *naql* (revelation). But even the *kalām* bifurcation does give rise to the fallacy of the Mu'tazilites being adepts at pure reason or analytic thought to such a degree that they treat it as the sole source of the truth. That is incorrect. The Mu'tazilites consider that the purpose of reason is to rationalize faith and not to question it but only to question the purported bases or suppositions.

On the problem of the eternity of the Qur'ān, we have dealt with under the discussion on the Mu'tazilī position and the need to engage in discourse with the adherents of Christianity—Monophysites,

Jacobites, Nestorians and Malkites—and the followers of Manichaeism, the main rival to Christianity. Some of them employed Aristotelian syllogism and Neoplatonic principles in their polemics. Here, what remains is to deal with the related question whether speech is one of God's attributes. To the Ḥanbalites and Ẓāhirites, the answer is in the affirmative and because God's attributes are eternal, the Qur'ān, being Divine speech, must be eternal. Against the Mu'tazilites, the Ash'arites contended that the Qur'ān in its meanings is uncreated and eternal but against the Ḥanbalites and Ẓāhirites, they held that the Qur'ān, as expressed in words and sounds, is temporal. They conceded that the reasons given by the Mu'tazilites in support of the createdness of the Qur'ān were acceptable but only in respect of "the expressed Qur'ān" but not the internal and latent meaning of the Qur'ān.[34]

Justice from the Kalām standpoint

Let us outline the general understanding concerning the different positions of the two main creeds *vis-à-vis* the central concern of justice. We approach this first by looking at the issue of good and evil (*ḥusn wa qubḥ*) which is conceptually linked to the doctrine of *al-qaḍā' wa al-qadr* (the divine decree and predestination). We will then consider in greater detail the epistemological conceptions of justice as represented by the two luminaries of *kalām* of Basra at the turn of the fifth/eleventh century: the Mu'tazilī 'Abd al-Jabbār (d. 415/1024–5) and the Ash'arī Ibn Al-Bāqillānī (d. 403/1013). On the same issue, we will look briefly into a third voice through Ibn Ḥazm who, while appearing to lean towards the Ash'arī position, is actually against all the conventional schools and creeds. At this, while we have caveated at the outset of this study that Shī'ī doctrines will be out of our purview to prevent the discourse from biting off more than it can chew, a short side bar touching this particular aspect of *kalām* from the Twelver Imāmī perspective is in order considering the importance given to the role of reason or rationality (*al-'aql*) in their *uṣūl al-fiqh* and *kalām*. The Shī'ī approach to the issue of good and evil is via the doctrine of independent rationality (*al-mustaqillāt al-ʿaqliyya*). This stands in contrast to the Ashʿarī "theological voluntarism" which posits that good and evil acts are predicated on God's subjective command that may be known only via revelation. The Shīʿī approach which is based on a substantive notion of justice may thus be described as a rationalist moral jurisprudence concerning the praiseworthiness and blameworthiness of acts (*al-ḥusn wa al-qubḥ al-ʿaqliyyān*)—as opposed to the legal positivism of Ashʿarī meta-ethics. The Muʿtazilī position, known as "rationalist objectivism," is essentially parallel with the Shīʿī approach.[35]

On the question of the divine decree, the Muʿtazilī position is that God's *qudrah* (power) cannot include the power to will something that is evil. Every suffering can find recompense because good and evil are intrinsic properties and when evil is committed blame cannot be attributed to God. The Ashʿarī and literalist position sees this argument as limiting God's power and it is the height of audacity to suggest that human intellect can impose such a limitation. The Muʿtazilī rejoinder would be that ascribing culpability on a man's action by mere intention while denying him any power over the outcome of such an action manifestly offends against our sense of rationality and our innate sense of justice. While no one is disputing the crucial role of intention, the Ashʿarī position makes it impossible to differentiate between *ikhtiyar* and *niyyah* because in the case of the former, volition seems to be the only act within man's control, the consequential sequence of actions leading to the final result being completely beyond his control, which effectively leads to fatalism. This utter absence of power over individual acts is thus seen by Muʿtazilites as anathema to their conception of Divine justice as manifested in the Qur'ān.

The Muʿtazilites subscribe to absolute free will and reject predestination. They believe in the causality of actions and that a man's actions ought to be judged as evil or good. To reiterate, the conception of God directly creating man's actions having deprived him of free will and then punishing him for those actions, was simply repugnant to our inherent idea of justice. The only logical conclusion to be drawn therefore is that God cannot be the creator of man's actions.[36] Man created his own actions with the power that God had given him. Decisions are to be made independently and each and every one is to be accountable for his or her actions on the Day of Reckoning according to the scale of Divine justice. To the Ash'arīs, this line of reasoning was without Divine foundation. It should be remembered that they considered *naql* and not *'aql* as the criterion. Acts become good or evil only by dint of Divine ascription in the Qur'ān and the Sunnah. Thus, what is enjoined by the *Sharī'ah* is good, and what is forbidden is evil. That is the absolute criterion set by God. As there is no inherent good or evil, resorting to reason to determine it would not only be an exercise in futility but an act of arrogance towards the Almighty.

As for the epistemological discourse, for both 'Abd al-Jabbār and Ibn al-Bāqillānī, justice was not defined as an abstraction but in accordance with the way in which humans interpret the intuitions and internal experiences that God created in them and this was not germane only to the individual but applicable to the community at large.[37] But that was about all that they agreed on and the rest was open season. 'Abd al-Jabbār defines justice by looking at the intention of an act and the purpose that is meant to be served. An act which is *'adl* (just) is "every act that is done either to benefit (*yantafi'*) or harm (*yaḍurr*) the recipient of the act in a way (*wajh*) that is good (*yaḥsun*)." An act to benefit oneself or to discharge a religious obligation (*wājib*) would not count as such. As for a judge, acting justly between the adversaries means being good and equitable (*inṣāf*) in bringing either a benefit or detriment.[38] For 'Abd al-Jabbār, the goodness and badness of acts, their praiseworthiness or blameworthiness, are all matters known necessarily (*bi 'ilm ḍarūrī*) through intuition.

A conception of justice according to *kalām* is predicated on a conception of knowledge, which 'Abd al-Jabbār divides into two broad categories: necessary (*ḍarūrī*) and acquired (*muktasab*).

Necessary knowledge is knowledge that is indisputable and immediately known by all *compos mentis* individuals either by a means (*ṭarīq*) or without it. The former appertains to knowledge of particulars (*mufaṣṣal*) gained through perception (*idrāk*), either through the senses or by finding ourselves (*wujida anfusanā*) in a particular state at a particular time. The latter (knowledge gained without a means) is perceived by way of intuition (*ʿaql*), and it is generalizable (*mujmal*). Examples are knowledge of the rules of logic (*e.g.*, two contradictory statements cannot both be true) and knowledge of ethical attributes of acts (*e.g.*, injustice (*ẓulm*) and lying are bad).[39] The categorization of ethical knowledge as intuitive knowledge is significant to ʿAbd al-Jabbār's conception of justice for he posits that intuition (*ʿaql*) and perception (*idrāk*) are creations of God in humans that obligate them to God (*taklīf*). To say that one intuitively knows the goodness or badness of an act is to ascribe divine validation to individual intuitions, and, according to GhaneaBassiri, in this way ʿAbd al-Jabbār "universalizes his personal intuitions of the nature of the God-human relationship."[40] Another key point is ʿAbd al-Jabbār's definition of knowledge (*ʿilm*) as an entitative ground (*maʿnā*) which necessitates tranquillity in the knower about what has been considered. *Maʿnā* as knowledge has to be at the level of a conviction (*iʿtiqād*), that is, one must be convinced with what it actually is *(ʿalā mā huwa bihi wāqiʿ*).[41] Through this notion, an individual's subjective experience of certainty and tranquillity is ontologically universalized. In ʿAbd al-Jabbār's epistemology, God is therefore the creator of perception and intuition, which guarantees the validity of these personal experiences as generalizable sources of knowledge.[42] Unlike the conventional understanding, in Muʿtazilī theology, *ʿaql* does not correspond to the intellect or reason. Nor is it a substance (*jawhar*) or a faculty (*quwwah*) or an instrument (*ālah*) nor a sense (*ḥiss*).[43] *ʿAql* is a set of *a priori* known things that are found in *compos mentis* persons that allow them to discern and thus become subject to religious obligations. According ʿAbd al-Jabbār, it refers to "an aggregate of specific knowledges (*al-'ulūm al-makhṣūṣah*)" and in a religiously obligated individual (*mukallaf*), "his reflections, reason, and undertaking what he has been religiously obligated to do are sound (*ṣaḥḥa minhu al-naẓar wa al-istidlāl wa al-qiyām bi adā' mā kullifa*).[44]

In this regard, as a passing remark, it may be said that rather than mere 'intuition' or 'common sense', as has been suggested, the more proximate linkage that one is reminded of is Immanuel Kant's *a priori* cognition which is transcendental. But unlike the rationalists of his time, Kant posits that *a priori* knowledge is "knowledge that is absolutely independent of all experience" and *a priori* cognition, in its pure form, is seated in one's cognitive faculties, and are not provided by experience in general or any experience in particular. Space, time and causality are considered pure *a priori* intuitions under Kant's transcendental deduction and this constitutes the central argument in his magnum opus, *Critique of Pure Reason.*[45]

Representing the Ash'arī position, Ibn al-Bāqillānī condemns "most fervently" the Mu'tazilī notions that justice is known intuitively and that the *'aql* by itself is a way to knowledge of the badness or goodness of an act or whether it is prohibited, permissible, or mandatory. Ibn al-Bāqillānī posits that these *aḥkām* are all only proven by the *Sharī'ah* without any consideration of the *'aql* and that justice and goodness, therefore, can only be determined through the divine commands.[46] In keeping with the Ash'arī overarching position where *naql* prevails over *'aql,* Ibn al-Bāqillānī's conception of justice rests on the assertion, unlike 'Abd al-Jabbār's, that justice is an attribute ascribed to acts by divine commandments and prohibitions. His conception of justice is also founded upon his understanding of necessary knowledge and intuition but the nexus between divine creation and humans is understood differently. Rejecting 'Abd al-Jabbār's contention that necessary knowledge is proof that God has created in humans the innate ability to know and reflect, Ibn al-Bāqillānī argues that necessary knowledge is testimony to man's utter dependence on God: we cannot know anything, much less make sound ethical assessments, without the direct involvement of God.[47]

The difference between Mu'tazilī and Ash'arī epistemology is that while the former posits humans as existentially obligated to God (*mukallaf*), the latter regards humans as existentially dependent subjects of a divine master. The Mu'tazilī conception of justice is deontological, focused on the nature of acts rather than consequences. We intuitively know that an act that unduly harms another is unjust, and as made clear earlier, because the *ma'nā* of our knowledge evinces a conviction experienced as 'tranquillity of the self', we attain certainty. Ash'arī conception, on the other hand, rejects deontological ethics by denying that ethical knowledge of acts is intuitive. Ibn al-Bāqillānī states that justice and injustice cannot be known through *'aql* alone because it is empirically demonstrable that people disagree about what is good and just.[48]

Whereas Mu'tazilī justice appeals to our ingrained sense of good and evil, Ash'arī justice places divine subjectivism over deontological ethics, and as the following passage of Ibn al-Bāqillānī demonstrates, comes off as rather brutal in its cold-and-clinical declaration of the Divine decree:

> If someone says, 'Is it possible for God to inflict pain on children without any compensation, to command the killing and the infliction of pain on animals for no beneficial reason, to make some animals subordinate to others, to impose continual punishment for discontinuous crimes, to make obligatory for His servants what they cannot bear, to create in them that for which they shall be punished, and other such things?', it is said to him, 'Certainly! That is just when it is one of His actions. It is permissible and commendable according to His wisdom.' If he says, 'How could that be permissible and good from Him and all of it bad when issued from us?', it is said to him, 'That is bad and considered unjust when issued from us only because the Lord of living and non-living entities forbade us from doing it. If He had not deemed it bad and forbidden it, it would not have been bad when it occurs from us.'[49]

Detractors find the apparent heartlessness of the statement concerning children and suffering too hard to swallow and the logic difficult to fathom. How could inflicting pain on children without any compensation be just and commendable? Now, even if it is conceded that only God can determine what is good and bad, just and unjust, why would God want to cause so much pain and suffering? Man may not be the arbiter of right and wrong but pain and suffering are certainly not abstractions and can be experienced. To this, Ibn al-Bāqillānī says that internal experiences should not limit God's revelation and cannot set the criterion for the justness of divine acts.[50] Justice is, therefore, whatever God commands.

On a similar vein, Ibn Ḥazm contends that if God so wills, He could reward evil and punish good and that left to its own devices, the human emotional soul would counsel towards evil, and that there is no salvation through reason alone without the aid of revelation.[51] God's actions are based on His wisdom and justice which are beyond our comprehension. Contrary to Mu'tazilite claims, Ibn Ḥazm holds that humanity is in need of God's favour to attain good behaviour and reward, and reason alone will leave us in doubt. Each person's destiny is dependent on God's mercy. All things come from God. Thus, any evil that befalls us comes from God, and "we deserve punishment for the moral evil that proceeds from us as His subjects."[52]

It should not be forgotten that as a staunch Ẓāhirite, Ibn Ḥazm also rejected other attempts at interpretative reasoning apart from *kalām* and *falsafah* such as the *madhāhib*, questioning the validity of their moral teachings and calling instead for strict adherence to the literal contents of the revealed texts.[53] The role of the mind (*'aql*) is first and foremost to receive God's revealed communication. The mind cannot determine what God permits and prohibits or even the reasons why He permits what He permits and prohibits what He prohibits. But Ibn Ḥazm does not doubt the mind's capacity for knowledge. He distinguishes between "our knowledge of the *meanings* of value terms [such as "good" and "evil"], which is given to us by our intellectual understanding of language, prior to revelation (although confirmed by it), and our knowledge of the specific *contents* of ethical value, such as virtues and obligations, which is given to us only through revelation."[54] God's communication establishes legal norms wherein are context and content and here is the rub: whereas one would expect that the natural corollary to a literalist and exoteric approach to textual exegesis would yield a legalistic conception of the religion, Ibn Ḥazm takes a significant turn here by stressing that context is not the application of *Sharī'ah* rulings. In fact, the context is not even the *Sharī'ah* at all but the moral precepts for righteous living *vis-à-vis* the vagaries and challenges of life in society.

The Traditionists

It should be noted that both Mu'tazilites and Ash'arites were opposed by the Traditionists led by Aḥmad ibn Ḥanbal, fundamentally on the methodology employed as well as the conclusions drawn.[55] But pedants may want to split hair here by differentiating a smaller and more specific group from the Traditionists whose adherents are known as the Athariyyah or Atharīs, who reject *kalām* altogether regardless of the method employed in the discourse. Comprising *'ulamā'* from the Ḥanbalī and Shāfi'ī *madhāhib*, they are defined by a steadfast and fundamental antipathy against *kalām* in favour of strict textualism even well after Ash'arism had percolated into mainstream Sunni Islam.[56] In this study, we treat both—Traditionists and Atharīs—as synonymous *vis-à-vis* their positions on *kalām*.

They condemned its use on the authority of *āyah* 7 of Sūrah Āl 'Imrān, in diagonal opposition to the Mu'tazilī interpretation as best summed up by Asad referred to earlier.[57] Even though the Mu'tazilites placed their justification of rational argumentation primarily on the Qur'ān and secondarily on the Sunnah, every attempt at independent and original interpretation was regarded as heresy. In a well-known refutation,[58] Ḥanbalī theologian Muwaffaq al-Dīn Ibn Qudāmah (d. 620/1220) attacked the rationalist views of a fellow Ḥanbalite Ibn 'Aqīl (d. 119/737) and the hostility against *kalām* and in particular Mu'tazilism took on such a venomous hue that the discourse was essentially *argumentum ad hominem.* After recounting Ibn 'Aqil's purported recantation of his heretical views upon having been adjudged a *kāfir* and that his blood is lawful to be shed, Ibn Qudāmah then accuses him of religious hypocrisy for the public retraction was just a mere farce. He says that it is not his custom to talk ill or mention the faults of "our (Ḥanbalī) companions" and he would have "preferred to hide his defects," but the call of duty mandates that he "exposes him for having deceived the people with his doctrines and a group of our companions have followed the heretical innovation of this *zindīq* ..." According to him, the *mutakallimūn* are the "most ignorant of men with regard to the traditions of the Companions, the least possessed of knowledge with regard to those of the Successors and the most neglectful of their transmission." The sole possessions of these people "consist in forgery, falsehood, and false witness." The primary assertion was that *aḥadīth* pertaining to the attributes of Allah must not be interpreted.

Beatific Vision

What remains to be said concerns the question of the Beatific Vision, an issue in the *kalām* polemics that goes to the root of the debate on attributes and anthropomorphism concerning which space constraints only permit a cursory examination. Can normal mortals see God? That is the question. And where would God be? Does God sit on a throne in the sky? These apparently naïve questions are pregnant with ontological significance and they are questions usually asked by children who, as we know, in their naiveté often ask the most profound questions. And these questions are not germane to Islam but apply to all religions. To the Ẓāhirites and certain sections of the Traditionists, the recompense for righteous living and good deeds is the vision of God who will be "seated" above His Throne (*'Arsh*), which is said to be the greatest of all things that God has created. It has pillars and is carried by bearers who are angels of immense size. Then there is the *Kursī*, which is the Footstool of God. Where exactly is the Throne and is it found together with the Footstool and if not how much are they separated by time and space? Whether or not these are frivolous questions, the fact is they were asked and answered. And no one need be surprised that they remain to be asked even today.

It has been narrated that ʿAbd Allāh ibn Masʿūd[59] (d. 32/653), a Companion of the Prophet, said,

> "Between the Seventh Heaven and the Footstool is five hundred years. Between the Footstool and the water is five hundred years, and the Throne is above the water. Allah is above the Throne, and nothing whatsoever of your deeds is hidden from Him."[60]

On this phrase, Ibn Kathīr said, "He is the Sovereign and Creator of all things, because He is the Lord of the Mighty Throne which is the roof of creation. All created things, the heavens and the earth and all that is in them and in between them are beneath the Throne of Allah and are subject to His power. His knowledge encompasses all things and His power controls all things, and He is Watcher over all things."[61] As a ruler's throne is the symbol of wealth and sovereignty, *ʿarsh* has also been used to mean wealth and sovereignty in metaphor.[62]

The Ashʿarites held that it is possible to see God but could not reconcile with the conception of God as corporeal and temporal as was the logical extension of the belief as held generally by the Traditionists. To get round this conundrum, they postulated that seeing an object did not require physical presence before the perceiver. As the Muʿtazilī position was clearly a rejection of anthropomorphism, beatific vision would be counter-intuitive. The anthropomorphic references in the revealed text are to be read hermeneutically as allegorical expositions, not literally. For example, references to "Owner of the Throne, the Glorious" and "Lord of the Throne Supreme" (*wa huwa rabb al-ʿarsh al-ʿaẓīm*) is conceived of as the summit of the created order, not a temporal object in a spatial locus.[63] There is, of course, the well-known and often cited *āyah al-*

Kursī (255) in Sūrah al-Baqarah: "*wasi'a kursiyyuhu al-samāwāti wa al-arḍa wa lā ya'ūduhu hifẓuhumā wa huwa al-'aliyyu al-aẓīmu.*" While most of the conventional translations render *Kursī* as "throne" or "footstool," as alluded to earlier, the one by Asad speaks volumes: "His *eternal power* overspreads the heavens and the earth, and their upholding wearies Him not. And He alone is truly exalted, tremendous." According to Asad, some of the commentators (*e.g.* al-Zamakhsharī) interpret this as "His sovereignty" or "His dominion," while others such as Muḥammad 'Abduh take it to mean "His knowledge" (*al-Manar* III, 33). Al-Rāzī inclines to the view that it denotes God's majesty and indescribable, eternal glory.

Taking these phrases literally would imply that God is limited in space and this would contradict the concept of an Infinite Being. Thus, Asad maintains that according to allegorical hermeneutics, references to the "heavens," the "throne," and God being "established" on it must be seen as linguistic vehicles meant to convey an idea which is outside all human experience or even comprehension. Likewise, descriptions of God's omnipotence and omniscience in terms of being "all-seeing," "all-hearing" or "all-aware" have nothing to do with the phenomena of vision with eyes, hearing with ears but are allusions to God's eternal omnipresence for the Qur'ān mentions that "No human vision can encompass Him, whereas He encompasses all human vision for He alone is unfathomable, all-aware" (*La tudrikuhu al-abṣāru wa huwa yudriku al-abṣāra wa huwa al-Laṭīfu al-Khabīru.*)[64] Asad posits that the term *laṭīf* denotes something that is extremely subtle in quality, and therefore intangible and unfathomable. Whenever this term occurs in the Qur'ān with reference to God in conjunction with the adjective *khabīr*, it is invariably used to express the idea of His inaccessibility to human perception or comprehension.

As for "No soul knoweth what is kept hid from them of joy, as a reward for what they used to do," clearly indicative of the impossibility of man's comprehension of paradise, no one can offer a better *tafsīr* than the Prophet himself:

> "God says: 'I have readied for My righteous servants what no eye has ever seen, and no ear has ever heard, and no heart of man has ever conceived.'"[65]

The use of anthropomorphic expressions such as God's "wrath" (*ghaḍab*) or "condemnation," "pleasure" at good deeds or "love" for His creatures is a mode of verbal translation of God's activity into human terminology.[66]

On the Traditions which relate that

> "God will be seen, that He descends to the Heaven closest to the earth, and that He sets His foot down,"

Ibn Qudāmah, in his refutation, asserts that the credo taught by the masters (led by Imām Aḥmad ibn Ḥanbal) is: "we believe in them and accept as true ... God should not be described in excess of His own description of Himself, boundless and immeasurable, nor do we remove from Him any of His attributes." One searches to discern some grounded discourse on the refutation of the *mutakallimūn* but what we get is only one diatribe after another. It is a polemic peppered with exhortations of fire and brimstone for the "partisans of *kalām*."[67] As for the nine points enumerated in his refutation, most are traceable to his first in *āyah* 7 of Sūrah Āl 'Imrān, as explicated earlier, citing it as God's clear condemnation of those who resort to *ta'wīl* (allegorical interpretation) as those who seek trouble and go astray because "*wa mā ya'lamu ta'wīlahū illā Allāh*" (and no one knows its interpretation except Allah). Ibn Qudāmah takes this as a clear *naṣṣ* against *kalām*, equating it with *ta'wīl*. The rest are essentially arguments in support of the prohibition against *kalām*, for example, citing the fact that the Prophet never prescribed it nor did the Companions ever resort to it, that it was *bid'ah*, and so on. We will come back to this subject when we revisit the *Sharī'ah* sources.

It must be stressed that the Traditionists were also not enamoured of the Ash'arites in as much as the latter also resorted to *'aql* in their methodology of discourse even though in terms of basic doctrine they had similar affinities. Nevertheless, their vitriol was reserved for the Mu'tazilites. For that matter, all attempts at trying to rationalise the clear texts were branded as pernicious innovation and all Muslims must believe, without question, all the principles of faith. This also accounts for the Ḥanbalī opposition to logic and philosophy as well. Other great Ḥanbalites such as Ibn Taymiyyah and Jalāl al-Dīn al-Suyūṭī were similarly opposed to it. Even today, in less well informed gatherings and discourses in Sunni circles, the Mu'tazilites are the most convenient punching bag as being among those who would lead astray the *ummah* by virtue of their insistent recourse to allegorical interpretations using methods of Greek philosophers.

Falāsifah

The notion which subsists till today among the general *ummah* that *kalām* and *mutakallimūn* should be avoided like the plague because of their "Aristotelian" proclivities is rather ironical when we consider that the *falāsifah* (Muslim philosophers) themselves generally did not approve of *kalām*.[68] Abū Naṣr Muḥammad al-Fārābī (d. 339/950) distinguished between *kalām* and *fiqh* defining the former as "a science which enables a person to support specific beliefs and actions laid down by the Legislators of the religion and to refute all opinions contradicting them."[69] While not neglecting *naqlī* proofs, al-Fārābī, widely known as the Second Teacher (after Aristotle), naturally resorted often to *'aqli* proofs. Renowned for having, inter alia, influenced many prominent philosophers like Ibn Sīnā and Maimonides and perhaps more significantly, for preserving the original Greek texts because of his commentaries and treaties, al-Fārābī also wrote on political philosophy leaving for posterity his *Al-Madīnah al-Faḍīlah* (The Virtuous City) where he posited the ideal Islamic state modelled on Plato's *The Republic*. Al-Fārābī theorized that the "Virtuous City" was the city-state of Medina under the governance of the Prophet who was in direct communion with God whose *Sharī'ah* was revealed to him. As for scholastic theology, it is said, rather incorrectly, that al-Fārābī regarded *kalām* as a Christian invention foisted on Judaism and Islam.[70] German orientalist Carl

Heinrich Becker contended that the dependence of Mu'tazilite philosophy on Christian philosophy was well known and that the whole method of *kalām* was derived from Christianity: "Die Abhangigkeit der Mu'tazilitischen Philosophie von der christlichen ist eine lang bekannte Tatsache ... Dass die ganze Methode des *kalām* aus dem Christentum stammt, ist bekannt...."[71]

That is only partially correct as our discussion on the need to engage in *kalām* discourse with the Christians and the older religions shows. But to make the overarching claim that the entire method of *kalām* was essentially learnt from Christianity is far-fetched. Firstly, the three renowned speculative thinkers in classical Islamic history, namely, al-Kindī (d. 259/873), al-Fārābī and Ibn Sīnā (d. 429/1037) combined Aristotelianism and Neoplatonism with other ideas introduced through Islam. Ibn Sīnā, well known as Avicenna in the Latin West, remains much misunderstood in terms of his purported preponderance and reliance on Greek learning and the thinking is that he should thus be studied merely as a side chapter in Western philosophy along with other Muslim philosophers. This is nonsense. Suffice it to say that there can be no meaningful discourse of the thought of Ibn Sīnā without studying his *al-Ḥikmah al-Mashriqiyyah* (Oriental Philosophy), which "belongs to the same world as that of Suhrawardī's *Ishrāq*" and acknowledged as such by the likes of Mullā Ṣadrā and Sabzwārī.[72] Islamic philosophy is a distinct and intellectual tradition that should not be treated as a side bar in the history of Western philosophy or seen by many in the Muslim world itself as the aberrant development of heretic or heresy-leaning "Aristotelian" scholars. In his short treatise *Manṭiq al-Mashriqiyyīn*, Ibn Sīnā distances himself from the Peripatetic works and articulates certain logical views different from those of Aristotle's.[73] Almost two centuries earlier, al-Kindī had initiated the systematic process of drinking from the well of the peripatetic philosophers, and in doing so acquired the title of "father of Islamic philosophy" for his synthesis of Greek philosophy paving the way for al-Fārābī to take Islamic philosophy to the next level. There were early studies that suggested that al-Kindī was a Mu'tazilī but this has since been convincingly refuted.[74] Nevertheless, al-Kindī's commentaries and views concerning the "First Cause," which was similar to Plotinus' "First Agent," employing the Aristotelian method to deal with issues of *dīn*, added fuel to the fire already raging in the debate between the Mu'tazilites and Ash'arites and sowed the seeds of the subsequent intellectual debates among the various groups: Traditionists versus rationalists; Traditionists versus *mutakallimūn, mutakallimūn* versus *mutakallimūn; mutakallimūn* versus *falāsifah*, and so on.[75]

However, the claim that the Mu'tazilites gave undue credence to Aristotelian and Neoplatonic paradigms is not correct though it may be partially justified on account of their position, as aforementioned, concerning the doctrine of creation *ex nihilo* as opposed to the eternity of the world. It was in fact the *falāsifah* in particular al-Fārābī and Ibn Sīnā who had applied Greek philosophy to issues of Islamic cosmology and the prototypical worldview culminating in Ibn Rushd purging the Aristotelian precepts of what he had considered to be "Neoplatonic adulteration." Following Ibn Rushd, *falsafah* was distinguished from *kalām*, dismissively, as the difference between Platonic philosophy and sophistry (of the sophists) of Plato's time. In his *Kitāb Kashf 'an Manāhij al-Adillah,* Ibn Rushd criticized the method of the *mutakallimūn* in proving God's existence as being inaccessible to the masses while failing to reach a real demonstration, about which more later. He castigated them for attempting to resolve the possible ambiguities of revelation through allegorical interpretation for it will only lead to confusing truth with *al-ra'y* (personal opinion). Contending that the false logical implications of *kalām* would only serve to trouble the spirit, he singled out al-Ghazālī as the heir of all these *agents provocateurs* as much theologians creating false problems as Sufi creating false solutions.[76] He criticized the *mutakallimūn*, as headed by al-Ghazālī, as posing a danger to the purity of Islam and appealed to the powers that be to forbid the *mutakallimūn* of his time from spreading heresy, schism, and unbelief. Typical of the exuberance that went with such polemics on both sides of the ideological divide, Ibn Rushd charged al-Ghazālī with deliberate deception of the masses. "In that way, one group came to slander wisdom (*ḥikmah*), another group to slander the Law (*Sharī'ah*), and another group to reconcile the two." He further charged that al-Ghazālī "wished thereby to alert people's minds (*tanbīh al-fiṭar*)" as if "he adhered to no single doctrine in his books. Rather with the Ash'arites he was an Ash'arite, with the Sufis a Sufi, and with the philosophers a philosopher."[77]

Interestingly, as between the Ash'arites and Mu'tazilites, Ibn Rushd appears to grant the latter more benefit of the doubt in terms of their rationality in respect of their *ta'wīl* interpretations regarding the duty that is incumbent on the *'ulamā'* or "those whose reflective powers reach that of dialectic."[78] He says, "To this sort belong some of the interpretations of the Ash'arites and Mu'tazilites, although for the most part the statements of the Mu'tazilites are more reliable." Ibn Rushd reiterates the point that these interpretations are only meant for the initiated and not the laymen: "The duty of the masses (*al-jumhūr*), who are incapable of more than rhetorical statements (*al-aqāwīl al-khiṭābiyyah*) is to let them stand in their apparent sense (*'alā ẓāhirihā*), and it is not permissible for them to know that interpretation at all."[79]

As an Aristotelian philosopher who was also holding high judicial office, Ibn Rushd was very conscious of the attitude of the *fuqahā'* towards *falsafah*. The full title of the treatise itself is indicative of the tenor and purport of Ibn Rushd's enterprise in writing it[80] which is to demonstrate that *ḥikmah* as in wisdom which is used synonymously with *falsafah* is not only compatible with the *Sharī'ah* as in Law but that its pursuit is a religious obligation. Thus in launching the strident attacks on *kalām*, and al-Ghazālī, he was in reality "baiting" the *fuqahā'*, particularly the *naqlī*-centric conservative-minded jurists by way of reverse psychology. It is tantamount to telling them that the *falāsifah* and the *fuqahā'* are on the same boat with a common adversary and that they should not be opposed to philosophy or philosophical interpretation of Scripture.

Essentially, it is: Let us join hands in focussing on the theologians instead and their erroneous *kalām* peregrinations. Ibn Rushd first makes the case for the use of syllogistic reasoning (*qiyās*) founded on the *Sharīʿah* obligation to reflect on existing things by means of the intellect (*al-naẓaru bi al-ʿaqli fī al-mawjūdāt*). An essential method of *falsafah*, therefore, is *qiyās*, which many *fuqahā'* themselves use. But not all *qiyās* or reasoning is the same or of the same level of significance. In Chapter 7, we will look into *qiyās* in greater detail as a source of law. Suffice it here to state that in *falsafah, qiyās* is synonymous with intellectual exertion employing a syllogistic method. The most basic is *qiyās khiṭābī* (rhetorical). Next is *qiyās jadalī* (dialectical), which is generally employed by the *mutakallimūn*, who explore the truth through rational analysis and argumentation. The highest, *qiyās burhānī* (demonstrative) is the preserve of the philosophers who use this mode in conjunction with *ta'wīl* to get to the origin (*awwal*) of an issue going beyond the obvious or the apparent.[81]

While *qiyās* did not exist among the first generation of the Muslim community, it was nevertheless later accepted as a proper *fiqh* method and was not considered to be *bidʿah* by the *fuqahā'*, save an insignificant group of Literalists—*al-hashwiyyah*. Now, if reasoning (which is what *qiyās* is effectively) was so widely used by the *fuqahā'*, then they must have had a legitimate ground to practise it. Since there is nothing explicit about the use of such a method in the *Sharīʿah*, then they must have applied inference. Ergo, acquisition of legal reasoning cannot be objected to on religious grounds. Where it is appropriate for the *fuqahā'* to use reasoning based on opinion to infer legal matters, a fortiori for the *falāsifah* for their *ta'wīl* and syllogism may command stronger legitimacy, yielding reconciliation between text and syllogism (*qiyās yaqīnī*).[82]

Finally, Ibn Rushd employs the theory of Double Truth to establish that the *Sharīʿah* does not and cannot conflict with philosophical conclusions: Truth does not contradict truth; Truth attained by demonstration cannot contradict the truth that Scripture gives us; therefore, any contradiction between them must only be in appearance. Thus, he asserts that in as much as the "truth does not oppose truth but accords with it and bears witness to it" the demonstrative science does not lead to conclusions conflicting with what Scripture teaches.[83] He then goes on to illustrate the question of the difference between the *muḥkamāt* and the *mutashābihāt* with which we have already dealt concerning the implications of the pivotal Sūrah Āl-Imrān, *āyah* 7.

In *Faṣl al-Maqāl*, Ibn Rushd says that "many of the roots upon which the Ashʿarites make their cognizance are sophistical (*sūfisṭāiyyah*) for they deny many necessary things, such as the stability of accidents, the influence of some things upon others, the existence of necessary reasons for what is made to occur (*wujūd al-asbāb al-ḍarūriyyah li al-musabbabāt*), substantial forms and intermediates."[84] In likening the Ashʿarites to Plato's sophists, Ibn Rushd was essentially targeting al-Ghazālī as evidenced in his *Tahāfut al-Tahāfut* (*The Incoherence of the Incoherence*), a point-by-point refutation of the arguments posited by al-Ghazālī in his *Tahāfut al-Falāsifah*. Space constraints do not permit further excursion into this debate. Suffice it to say that much misunderstanding both in the Muslim world but more so in the West has been generated concerning the polemics on this subject including the general supposition that al-Ghazālī was somehow responsible for the "death of science" in the Islamic world on account of his apparently devastating assault on Greek philosophy and that even the refutation by Ibn Rushd, known widely as Averroes in the West, the so-called father of secularism, could not provide the necessary impetus to take the Islamic world out of its darkness. Indeed, these are suppositions based not on facts but distortion of the truth and represent a devious attempt at articulating a counterfactual narrative skewed towards portraying Muslims and the Muslim world as a backward civilization that prizes irrationality over science.

Only three points need to be stated as regards this. First, concerning al-Ghazālī's anti-philosophy, thus anti-science position, nothing could be further from the truth as exemplified, among other things, in the second introduction to his *Tahāfut* where al-Ghazālī responds to the matter raised by the philosophers concerning the solar and lunar eclipses: "The solar eclipse means the presence of the lunar orb between the observer and the sun. This occurs when the sun and the moon are both at the two nodes at one degree." Al-Ghazālī makes it clear that not only is there no religious obligation to refute such a theory but on the contrary, doing so would actually be harmful to religion. This is because "these matters rest on demonstrations, geometrical and arithmetical, that leave no room for doubt" and to attack matters that are proven with certainty constitutes not an attack on science but on religion itself.[85]

Secondly, the supposition that Ibn Rushd was the defender of "Greek godlessness" and a purveyor of secularism is yet another classic instance of factual contortion. Being a chief *qāḍī* himself, Ibn Rushd had during his career stated that religious laws are necessary political arts, the principles of which are taken from natural reason and inspiration. He made it clear that general religious matters concerning ontology of God's existence or the true aims of happiness must not be objected to. Referring not just to Islam but all religions, he asserted that they are obligatory, "since they lead towards wisdom in a way universal to all human beings." The charge that he prioritized philosophy over religion is nullified by his statement that "philosophy only leads a certain number of intelligent people to the knowledge of happiness, and they therefore have to learn wisdom, whereas religions seek the instruction of the masses generally." There is no doubt that Ibn Rushd considered philosophy as an elitist pursuit but that in no way is testimony of any aversion to religion.[86]

Thirdly, on the supposed descent into darkness from science, there are two related issues here. One, there is no descent as such. On the contrary, the Golden Age of Islam[87] flourished between the second/eighth and seventh/thirteenth centuries. That means it continued for another two hundred years after al-Ghazālī's so-called devastating critique on science. There is a multiplicity of reasons for this scientific golden age too numerous to go into but suffice it to say that Islam's approach to knowledge has always been founded on the principle of unity between reason and revelation and not reason *against* revelation. Two, it is well and good to talk about the importance of science for human progress but science is not the be-all and the end-all of civilization. Particularly in this day and age when atheists and other detractors donning the hat of scientism tend to go overboard in their condemnation of faith, their arrogance knowing no bounds as they readily consign to the dustbin of pseudoscience or non-science every statement—of metaphysics, ethics, theology, literary criticism, and indeed daily life—that does not meet the Western criterion of falsifiability.[88] As it is, the three areas of inquiry—metaphysics, epistemology, and ethics—traditionally within the domain of philosophy, are now appropriated as suitable only for scientific enquiry, no doubt in a great part arising from the positivist tradition in philosophy. Today, scientists, particularly the proponents of scientism, arrogate to themselves the exclusive mantle of rationality, frequently equating science with reason itself, claiming that science has already resolved questions that are inherently beyond the ability of religion to answer.[89]

According to Nasr, most philosophers in the West since Immanuel Kant "have become the handmaid of physics" and from the "scientistic" perspective, the scientific view of nature is "absolutized as being the only view of nature and everything other than that is rejected in total as being false."[90] Kant, it will be recalled, is generally regarded as having singlehandedly synthesized the school of rationalism on the one hand (as expounded by René Descartes, Baruch Spinoza,[91] and G. W. Leibniz) and the school of empiricism on the other (as advocated by John Locke, George Berkeley, and David Hume). Their major bone of contention was whether all concepts are derived from experience and whether humans can have any substantive *a priori* knowledge, whether of the corporeal world, or of the metaphysical world. Kant, who was neither an empiricist nor a rationalist, is said to have resolved this conundrum in his new critical philosophy.[92] In this regard, we would just add the rider that the assertion should be that most philosophers—after Kant, that is excluding him as well as a few other exceptions such as Hegel and Schleiermacher—have become the servants of physics.

In any event, from the prism of Western science, the notions of mass, force, and energy are usually ideas arising from "the Cartesian bifurcation of the world into measurable and subjective knowledge, then Galileo's uniformity of the universal laws, and finally Newton's brilliant synthesis."[93] As Western scientists embarked on their reductionist foray of the physical world, the purveyors of scientism in the garb of philosophers set off on their evangelical mission to spread "the gospel of truth" via mathematical analysis. But we know that the latter-day studies and advances in the scientific field itself have exposed the fallacy of Cartesian bifurcation and the purported superiority of quantitative knowledge, betraying philosophical scientism and exposing its limitations.[94]

It is, however, true that within the Muslim world today, there is resistance to intellectual progress as manifested in the opposition in various circles in spite of the millennial span of its history of the development of the intellect. While the great tragedy of the West is the death of intellect (as opposed to mere reason), the even greater tragedy is that the Muslim world is bending backwards in aping it, making the worship of science and technology as the new religion, as it were. We are now a passive civilization vis-à-vis the various "isms" of the West.[95] According to Nasr, the response to scientism has to be holistic from the perspective of Islamic philosophy as in *ḥikmah*, not just purely *falsafah*—as a translation of Greek philosophy.[96]

Coming back to the charge of sophism on the part of the *mutakallimūn*, it is true indeed that in his refutation, Ibn Rushd does resort to name-calling under the overarching indictment of al-Ghazālī employing "the highest form of *kalām* dialectics" which, however, "fails as demonstrative proof" (*al-qiyās al-burhānī*)—a key criterion for the philosophical method. He accuses al-Ghazālī of deception and subterfuge and in many instances he attempts to counter his proofs by starting with the statement that "this is an example of sophism." For example, in respect of the first point of contention concerning the eternity of the world, Ibn Rushd says: "To treat what is in reality a plurality of questions as one problem is one of the well-known seven sophisms, and a mistake in one of these principles becomes a great error by the end of the examination of reality."[97]

As for Sophists, there are mixed views concerning who they really were though the preponderant position arising from the negative light cast by Plato and Aristotle sees them as intellectual charlatans who, on the pretext of teaching virtue, were really propagating immoral doctrines.[98] This is indeed an oversimplification because in reality they did contribute to Western philosophy although under the shadow of the three giants—Socrates, Plato and Aristotle—Sophistry is said to represent a choice for a certain way of life, embodied in a particular attitude towards knowledge. Plato's[99] distinction between philosophy and sophistry is based upon a fundamental difference in ethical orientation, in terms of the choice for a way of life that is oriented by the pursuit of knowledge as a good in itself.[100] On the other hand, the utilitarian classicist George Grote (d. 1904) regarded them as "progressive thinkers who placed in question the prevailing morality of their time" while certain writings by Jacques Derrida (d. 1981) and Jean Francois-Lyotard (d. 1985) point towards linkages between them and postmodernism.[101]

A side note on the "ghost of Averroism" is perhaps pertinent at this juncture before we conclude. As a philosopher who synthesised Aristotelianism with Islam, Ibn Rushd stood out as the leader in its exposition. His influence became so pervasive that it engendered a new school of thought under the name of Averroism adopted by 13th century scholastic philosophers in the Latin Christian and Jewish intellectual traditions. He cast a major influence on such theological luminaries of Christendom as Albertus Magnus (Albert the Great), his *magister studentium*, St. Thomas Aquinas, and John Duns Scotus who, while adopting the Averroist style of exposition, vehemently opposed his doctrines. This was understandable on account of his commentaries on Aristotle which were being propagated by his followers among the Western philosophers (the "Averroists"), ideas that were opposed to the ontological precepts being expounded by these Christian theologians. The fact was that in the Latin West, Ibn Rushd's commentaries on Aristotle spawned the development of scholastic theology subjecting Christianity to the discourse of reasoning and intellectual analysis.[102] Though vigorously condemned in 1277[103], these ideas saw a renaissance in the 16th century as percolated through the works of Giordano Bruno, Pico della Mirandola, and Cesare Cremonini centering on the elitist status and intellectual superiority of philosophers over the masses and the affinities between the intellect and human dignity as guided by the divine wisdom.

But there is a need to break away from the judgment-laden paradigm of referring to Ibn Rushd's philosophy as "Averroism" which carries the presumption that all he had to contribute was mere recycling of Aristotelian precepts. It bears repeating that while Europe was still hibernating in the Medieval Ages, the Islamic world was experiencing its golden age of philosophy and science. But the 19th-century French philologist and historian Ernest Renan (d. 1892), for example, considered Ibn Rushd to be a pure rationalist and saw absolutely no originality in him in connection with Aristotle apart from being a commentator.[104] However, it is said that Renan took that strict rationalist angle in order to advance the theme of philosophy's oppression by religious orthodoxy: within Islam and within the Christian Church.[105] That seems rather apologetic and does not hide the reality of Renan being unquestionably one of the earliest purveyors of Islamophobia and anti-Semitism. In his *Orientalism*, Edward Said points out Renan's view of "Semitic" as "a phenomenon of arrested development" as against "the mature languages and cultures of the Indo-European group." By virtue of his European ethnocentrism, oriental languages and Semitic languages, for Renan, "are inorganic, arrested, totally ossified, incapable of self-regeneration," and not only is Semitic not a live language, "neither are

Semites live creatures."[106] In any event, although Renan's discourse of Averroism and Medieval Renaissance inadvertently revived the theme of the Islamic tradition's contributions to the Western world, some of his arguments have also been used by detractors and Islamophobes in their attempt to deconstruct the intellectual achievements of Islam and advance a narrative of "Christian Europe" being the saviour of Greek rationalism.[107]

The truth is that Ibn Rushd's differences with Aristotle are more than superficial. To begin with, as asserted by Dominique Urvoy, "if one can speak of 'Rushdian thought' in order to describe the unity of the three philosophical/theological texts, *Kitāb Faṣl al-Maqāl*, *Kitāb Kashf ʿan Manāhij al-Adillah* and *Tahāfut al-Tahāfut*, which express a specific synthesis of Almohād Islam and Aristotelianism," then what good reason is there to speak of his commentaries on Aristotle as "Averroism"?[108]

Apparently, one of the reasons—according to certain proponents—is that Averroism is something distinct from the philosophy of Ibn Rushd. It is supposed to be a set of philosophical views associated with "Averroes" who is not really Ibn Rushd the Islamic philosopher but merely his "literary incarnation in translations and philosophical treatises of the Latin West."[109] In other words, Averroism is the intellectual phantom of Ibn Rushd as conjured by the Latin West. Because of his being so well acquainted with the ancient Greek commentators on Aristotle such as Alexander of Aphrodisias and Themistius, it is also said that Ibn Rushd—as Averroes—was seen as important to the Latin West but only as a second-hand source of knowledge. There were those such as the prominent Renaissance Platonist Marsilio Ficino (d. 1499) who attacked Averroism based on the works of Aquinas who, for example, in the matter of the principle of the universal intellect of humankind, regarded it as "the most shameful error."[110] Hence, Ficino ridicules the doctrine as "a monstrous octopus with a giant head and countless tentacles." In fact, Ficino has an entire book of his *Platonic Theology*[111] devoted to the refutation of Averroes using largely polemics employed by Aquinas.[112]

As stated earlier, Ibn Rushd's differences with Aristotle go beyond the surface as can be discerned, for instance, in his responses to the fundamental issue raised by al-Ghazālī in *Tahāfut al-Falāsifah* concerning the question of divine causality. For al-Ghazālī, the doctrine of an eternal world—as advanced by Ibn Sīnā, and, according to al-Ghazālī, entirely founded on Aristotelian and Neoplatonist principles—means the negation of the attribute of the Divine will. It was through the choice of the Divine will that the world and time were created simultaneously at a finite point in the past.[113] In response, Ibn Rushd, while maintaining Aristotle's position concerning the Prime Mover being unmoved, posits that God yet moves the world for "The Originator is He of the heavens and the earth: and when He wills a thing to be, He but says unto it, 'Be' and it is—*kun fa yakūn*."[114] "*Amr*" as it occurs in the *āyah* may be translated as "will" (as in Asad) or "command or decree" (as in Pickthall and Yusuf Ali) but regardless of that, at the highest semantic level it is the equivalent of the Word or *Logos*. There is therefore no real creation *ex nihilo* because nothingness is secondary to existence. Ibn Rushd's position is that God creates from matter and from form the metaphysical building blocks "on which the secondary causes act in order to instantiate what was only potential."[115]

He posits a three-stage cosmology beginning with God originating the kinetic energy of the first heaven. Then, through contemplation and circular motion, the celestial spheres imitated this before finally setting off the physical processes of the sublunary world.[116] Unlike Aristotle who posits that the Prime Mover causes the movement of other things as only a final cause, Ibn Rushd construes it not only as a final but effective cause. These causations cooperate to govern the movements of both celestial and sublunary bodies. In metaphysical terms, celestial souls are utterly immaterial and as such utterly indistinguishable from the Prime Mover.[117] That is no longer mere commentary but original exposition, not just moving away but against the Master himself.

Conclusion

The ascendency of the Mu'tazilī creed should be understood contextually as a response to political circumstances, namely, the continued suzerainty of the Abbasid caliphate against any likely revival of the Umayyad caliphate. It was warranted, from the caliphal vantage point, as a counterfoil to the growing influence of the *'ulamā'* who were being increasingly cast by the *ummah* as the rightful guardians of religious knowledge and the Prophet's traditions. As at the start of the 4th/10th century, the Mu'tazilī creed reigned supreme, challenged unsuccessfully by the *ahl al-ḥadīth/Atharī*s until the emergence of al-'Ash'arī. Unlike other Traditionists, he did not subscribe to Aḥmad Ḥanbal's *fatwā* that *kalām* was unlawful, himself having been initially an avowed Mu'tazilī adherent before his conversion. On the contrary, in his *Risālah fī Istiḥsān al-Khawḍ fī 'Ilm al-Kalām* he contended, citing scriptural authority, that not only was it not unlawful but there was a duty to defend the doctrines of the religion including employing the tools of logic in order to do so.[118] Whether or not one agrees with him, he started a creed that eventually comprised a pantheon of luminaries that included Imām al-Ḥaramayn al-Juwaynī, Imām al-Ghazālī and Imām Fakhr al-Dīn al-Rāzī (d. 606/1209).

The success of Ash'arism may be attributed to several key factors not the least of which was the incremental unpopularity of Mu'tazilism as it came under the incessant politicization of the Abbasid caliphs. Among the black spots of their reign was their adoption of the doctrine as the State credo in a manner and to such a degree that could be rivalled only by the Inquisition of the Roman Catholic Church, bearing in mind what the latter did to heretics or those perceived as such. Likewise, in 212/827, Caliph al-Ma'mūn (d. 218/833) proclaimed his adherence to the credo of the "created Qur'ān" and shortly before he died raised the Mu'tazilī theology to the level of a *confessio fidei* with the imposition of the *Miḥna*, turning it into a weapon of mass oppression. During this dark phase, *'ulamā'* who would not unequivocally profess the "creation of the Qur'ān" doctrine were incarcerated, tortured and even executed. The *Miḥna* continued through the reigns of al-Mu'tāṣim and al-Wāthiq, and several years of al-Mutawakkil before he finally abolished it in 236/850.[119]

Another key factor for the decline of the Mu'tazilī creed was the ascendancy of the Saljūq Turks in Iran replacing the Būyīds during whose time Mu'tazilism along with Shī'ism with its innate rationalist leanings had flourished. Opposition against Mu'tazilism also came from other leading medieval Sunni *'ulamā'* such as Ibn Ḥazm, al-Juwaynī and al-Ghazālī. From al-Juwayni onward, there was a tendency among the *mutakallimūn* to mould Islamic jurisprudence into a highly formalised science on the Aristotelian model,[120] but no other Ash'arite exponent did this better than al-Juwayni's pupil, al-Ghazālī who vehemently defended this doctrine on logical and epistemological grounds. Thus, by the close of the 11th century, Ash'arism had become the dominant creed. It espoused a metaphysics of transient atoms and accidents in material bodies and regarded all temporal existents as God's direct creation, decreed by His eternal Attribute of will.[121] In this regard, it is more pertinent to say that the Christian dialectical method and the *kalām* technique shared a common ancestry in the Platonic and Aristotelian paradigm.

Even though he himself had mastered Aristotelian logic and was an adept at *kalām*, al-Ghazālī did not encourage the masses to engage in it as expressed in his *Iljām al-'awāmm 'an 'Ilm al-Kalām.*[122] Suffice it to say that according to al-Ghazālī, if a community lacks a *faqīh* and a *mutakallim*, and there is someone who can master only one of these arts, he should study *fiqh* and not *kalām*, for "only the few who are troubled by doubts need *kalām* while everyone needs the decrees of *fiqh*." When the populace asks about anthropomorphic verses, al-Ghazālī advises that they should be rebuked and told: "This is not your pursuit, so stay clear of it." He says that when asked about God's sitting on the throne, the answer to be given is that employed by the earlier scholars that "the sitting is known, the modality is unknown, to ask about it is a heresy, and to believe in it is a duty." Al-Ghazālī explains that "the minds of the populace are inadequate to receive the intelligibles, and their knowledge of the language is not broad enough to understand the Arab's expansive use of metaphors."[123]

As we have seen, *falsafah* as Islamic philosophy in its own right, not as an appendix to Western philosophy, is advocated by the *falāsifah* as not merely *mandūb* (recommended) for the intellectual elite but *wājib* (obligatory). Contrary to the view of the detractors, *falsafah* and the *Sharī'ah* are said to be in perfect harmony as the former infuses the law with wisdom. *Falsafah* staked its claim in the theological polemics by rejecting both the Ash'arite and Mu'tazilite positions. As exemplified by the assault led by Ibn Rushd, *kalām* is dismissed as sophistry, its dialectical method denigrated as being incapable of producing the requisite demonstrative proof of God's existence and other cosmological and ontological issues.

Notes

1. This is a brief review of the classical discourse. For a modern assessment see, inter alia, Richard C. Martin and Mark R. Woodward, *Defenders of Reason in Islam: Mu'tazilism from Medieval School to Modern Symbol* (Oxford 1997). T. Bauer, *Die Kultur der Ambiguität* (Berlin 2011) 385–87, points out that Mu'tazilism has not been exempt from dogmatism. See also the writings of Abdulkarim Soroush a self-declared neo-Mu'tazilite, and *A History of Muslim Philosophy,* edited and introduced by M.M Sharif (Islamic Book Trust, 2016), two-volume set; see chapters 10 to 13 for a concise but broad survey of the main creeds.
2. Mustafa Shah, "Trajectories in the Development of Islamic Theological Thought: the Synthesis of *Kalām*," *Religion Compass* 1/4 (2007): 430–431. Accessed on November 18, 2014

10.1111/j.1749-8171.2007.00026.x.

3. Murtaḍā Muṭahharī, *An Introduction to 'Ilm al-Kalām*, translated from the Persian by 'Ali Quli Qara'i, Vol. II No. 2, 1985; accessed on June 19, 2014; available at http://www.muslimphilosophy.com/ip/kalam.htm.
4. Orthodox has various connotations and a caveat here is in order so that we do not confuse ourselves with the usage in either the Christian sense or the Judaic sense as in a college of cardinals via the magisterium teaching of the precepts or the teachings of the halakha of the Judaic practice. Orthodox in Islam here is with reference to the *Aḥl al-Sunnah wa al-Jamā'āh.*
5. James Pavlin, "Sunni *kalām* and theological controversies," in Nasr, Seyyed Hossein & Leaman, Oliver. Ed. *History of Islamic Philosophy* (London & New York: Routledge, 2001), 105.
6. Al-Māturīdī, *Kitāb al-Tawḥīd*, 471-73; also al-Ṭaḥāwī, *'Aqīdah*, 62: "Belief consists in affirmation by the tongue and acceptance by the heart." See Ibn Abī al-'Izz, *Sharḥ al-'Aqīdah al-Taḥāwiyyah* (4th ed. 373-374).
7. S'ad al-Dīn al-Taftāzānī, *Sharḥ 'Aqaid al-Nasafī: A Commentary on the Creed of Islam* (ScribeDigital.com); He and his followers, including 'Amr ibn 'Ubayd (d. 144/761), were labelled "Mu'tazilī" stemming from Hasan's remark, "Wāṣil has withdrawn from us," where *i'tazala* means "to separate (oneself); to withdraw from."
8. Ibn Ḥazm, *al-Faṣl fī al-Milal wa al-Ahwā' wa al-Niḥal* (Treatise on Religions and Schools of Thought), Cairo: Maktabat al-Khanji, no date; IV, 229.
9. Toshihiko Izutsu, *The Concept of Belief in Islamic Theology* (The Other Press, 2006): 58-60.
10. For a broader but still laconic account of Mu'tazilism, see Volume 1, Book 3, Part 1, Chapter 10 of Sharif, *A History of Muslim Philosophy.*

11. Shihāb al-Dīn al-Alūsī, *Rūḥ al-Ma'ānī fī Tafsīr al-Qur'ān al-'Aẓim wa al-Sab' al-Mathānī*, as cited in Nasr, *Study Quran.*
12. 'Abd al-Razzāq al-Kāshānī, *Tafsīr al-Qur'ān al-Karīm* (2 vols. Beirut: Dar al-Yaqzah al-'Arabiyya, 1387/1967) as cited in Nasr, *Study Quran.* See also *Tafsīr al-Qur'ān al-Karīm* [*Tafsīr Ibn 'Arabī* on cover], 2 vols. Beirut: Dār al-Kutub al-'Ilmiyyah, 1422/2001. On this work see Pierre Lory, *Les Commentaires ésotériques du Coran d'aprés 'Abd al Razzaq al Qashani* (Paris: Les Deux Océans. 1980).
13. Sachiko Murata & William C. Chittick, *The Vision of Islam* (I.B. Tauris, 2000), 267–282
14. To appreciate better the difference, we may first look at nontrinitarianism which refers to monotheistic belief systems, which reject the Christian doctrine of the Trinity, namely, that God is three distinct hypostases who are coeternal, coequal, and indivisibly united in one being or ousia. Jews and Muslims are therefore Nontrinitarians together with a minority of Christians whereas Trinitarians comprise the overwhelming majority of Christians who subscribe to the creed as definitively declared by the First Councils of Nicaea and Constantinople. See Dale Tuggy, "Trinity," *The Stanford Encyclopedia of Philosophy,* edited by Edward N. Zalta <http://plato.stanford.edu/archives/sum2016/entries/trinity/>. On Dualism, see Monk of the West & Alvin Moore Jr., *Christianity and the Doctrine of Non-Dualism* (Sophia Perennis, 2004)
15. *Shorter Encyclopedia.*
16. "And God's [alone] are the attributes of perfection; invoke Him, then, by these, and stand aloof from all who distort the meaning of His attributes ..." (Asad); "The most beautiful names belong to Allah: so call on Him by them; but shun such men as use profanity in His names ..." (Yusuf Ali)

17. W. Montgomery Watt, *Islamic Philosophy and Theology* (Aldine Transaction, 1962), 63.
18. Harry Austryn Wolfson, *The Philosophy of the Kalām* (Harvard University Press, 1976), 112-113.
19. Alexander D. Knysh, *Ibn 'Arabi in the Later Islamic Tradition: The Making of a Polemical Image in Medieval Islam* (SUNY Press, 1999), 148.
20. Āl 'Imrān, *āyah* 45: "Behold! the angels said 'O Mary! Allah giveth thee glad tidings of a Word from Him: his name will be Christ Jesus the son of Mary held in honour in this world and the Hereafter and of (the company of) those nearest to Allah.'" (Yusuf Ali); al-Nisā', *āyah* 171: "O People of the Book! Commit no excesses in your religion: Nor say of Allah aught but the truth. Christ Jesus the son of Mary was (no more than) a messenger of Allah, and His Word, which He bestowed on Mary, and a spirit proceeding from Him ..." (Yusuf Ali).
21. Pavlin, "Sunni *kalām*," 106-107.
22. See Sūrah Āl 'Imrān, *āyah* 110; also al-Tawbah: 71, 112; Luqmān: 17.
23. Asad, *The Message of the Qur'ān*, quoted almost verbatim save for some minor paraphrasing.
24. See also Exodus 16:22-36; Hebrews 4:1-11.
25. Devin J. Stewart, "God," in *The Princeton Encyclopedia of Islamic Political Thought*, edited by Gerhard Bowering (Princeton University Press, 2013), 196; Toshihiko Izutsu, *God and Man in the Qur'an* (Ayer Co Pub, 1980).
26. Al-Ash'arī, *al-Ibānah 'an Uṣūl al-Diyānah* (The Elucidation of the Principles of Religion) (al-Riyād Dār al-Faḍīlah, 2011), 47.
27. Ibn Rushd, *Kitāb Faṣl al-Maqāl wa Taqrīr Mā bayn al-Sharī'ah wa al-Ḥikmah min al-Ittiṣāl* (Manshārāt al-Jamal, Beirut-Baghdad, 2009); Averroes, *On the Harmony of Religion and Philosophy*, A Translation, with Introduction and Notes, of Ibn

Rushd's *Kitāb Faṣl al-Maqāl*, With Its Appendix (*ḍamīmah*) and an Extract from *Kitāb al-Kashf ʿan Manāhij al-Adillah* by George F. Hourani (Messrs. Luzac & Co. 1976); This quote is from the section: "On the Third Problem—Of Fate and Predestination."; It should be noted that I have resorted to two translations of this major Rushdian work, the other being the later version done by Charles Butterworth, as cited previously.

28. Sūrah al-Baqarah, *āyah* 281, 286.
29. W. Montgomery Watt, *The Formative Period of Islamic Thought* (Oneworld Publications, 1998), 355.
30. Sūrah Saba', *āyah* 3.
31. al-Ashʿarī, *Maqālāt*, 408-10.
32. Recent studies contend that al-Ghazālī did not personally subscribe fully to this doctrine (of occasionalism) but proffered these arguments as essential to counter the polemics of the Mu'tazilites and the philosophers and therefore it would be incorrect to deny totally al-Ghazālī's belief in genuine causality in creatures: Frank Griffel, "Al-Ghazālī," *The Stanford Encyclopedia of Philosophy* (Fall 2007 Edition), Edward N. Zalta (ed.), URL = <http://plato.stanford.edu/archives/fall2007/entries/al-ghazali/>.
33. Ibid.
34. M. Abdul Hye, Ash'arism, accessed 8 July 2014; available at: http://www.muslimphilosophy.com/hmp/14.htm#_ftn28.
35. Ali-Reza Bhojani, *Moral Rationalism and Shariʿah: Independent Rationality in Modern Shiʿi Usul Al-Fiqh* (Routledge, 2015), 1-2.
36. *al-Mughnī*, vol. 6, 26, 30-34.
37. Kambiz GhaneaBassiri, "The Epistemological Foundation of Conceptions of Justice in Classical *Kalām*: A Study of ʿAbdal-Jabbār's *Al-Mughni* and Ibn Al-Bāqillāni's *Al-Tamhid*," *Journal of Islamic Studies* 19, 1 (2008), 95-96; doi:10.1093/jis/etm058.
38. Abū al-Ḥasan ʿAbd al-Jabbār, *al-Mughnī fī Abwāb al-Tawḥīd wa al-ʿAdl* (Cairo: Mu'assasāt al-Miṣriyyah al-ʿĀmmah lī al-Ta'līf wa

al-Tarjamah wa al-Ṭibā'ah wa al-Nashr, 1960–68), vi. I. 48; GhaneaBassiri, *op. cit.*, 79.
39. *al-Mughnī,* xii. 66; GhaneaBassiri, 88.
40. GhaneaBassiri, 80.
41. Ibid.
42. Ibid., 81
43. *al-Mughnī,* xi. 375-9; GhaneaBassiri, 82.
44. Ibid.
45. Immanuel Kant, 1787, *Critique of Pure Reason*, [*Kritik der reinen Vernunft*] (Norman Kemp Smith (transl.), New York: St. Martin's Press, 1965), 43.
46. *al-Tamhīd*, 105; GhaneaBassiri 86.
47. Ibid.
48. Ibid, *al-Tamhīd*, 342, GhaneaBassiri 87.
49. Ibid, *al-Tamhīd*, 341, GhaneaBassiri, 88-89.
50. GhaneaBassiri, 89.
51. James Pavlin, "Sunni *Kalām* and Theological Controversies," in *History of Islamic Philosophy,* edited by Seyyed Hossein Nasr & Leaman Oliver (London & New York: Routledge, 2001), 109.
52. Ibid.
53. Paul L. Heck, "Human Experience As Source of Moral Insight: Ibn Ḥazm's *Ṭawq Al-Ḥamāma,*" *Islamochristiana* 39 (2013), 95.
54. Hourani, "Reason and Revelation in Ibn Ḥazm's Ethical Thought," in *Islamic Philosophical Theology*, ed. Parviz Morewedge. (Albany, 1979), 145.
55. Pavlin, "Sunni *Kalām* and Theological Controversies," 105.
56. Jeffry R. Halverson, *Theology and Creed in Sunni Islam: The Muslim Brotherhood, Ash'arism, and Political Sunnism* (Palgrave Macmillan, 2010), 36.
57. A non-*kalām* translation, as opposed to the one given by Asad, is as follows: "He it is Who has sent down to thee the Book: In it are verses basic or fundamental (of established meaning); they are

the foundation of the Book: others are allegorical. But those in whose hearts is perversity follow the part thereof that is allegorical, seeking discord, and searching for its hidden meanings, but no one knows its hidden meanings except God. And those who are firmly grounded in knowledge say: "We believe in the Book; the whole of it is from our Lord:" and none will grasp the Message except men of understanding." (Yusuf Ali)

58. *Taḥrīm al-Naẓar fī Kutub Ahl al-Kalām* (*The Censure of Speculative Theology of Ibn Qudama*), translated and edited by George Makdisi (Gibb Memorial Trust, 1985).
59. It is well known that the Prophet recognised 'Abd Allāh ibn Mas'ūd as one of the four foremost experts on the Qur'ān. According to a very moving account as narrated in Muslim 4:1752, the Prophet once asked Ibn Mas'ūd to recite and he replied, "Should I recite it to you when you are the one to whom it was sent down and revealed?" The Prophet said, "I love to hear it from someone else." Ibn Mas'ūd then recited it until the Prophet wept.
60. Narrated by Ibn Khuzaymah in *al-Tawḥīd*, p. 105; also al-Bayhāqī in *al-Asmā' wa al-Ṣifāt*, 401.
61. *Tafsīr Ibn Kathīr*, 2/405
62. *Cf.* Psalm 47:8 "God reigneth over the heathen: God sitteth upon the throne of his holiness." King James Bible.
63. Respectively, Sūrah al-Burūj, *āyah* 15 and Sūrah al-Tawbah, *āyah* 129.
64. Sūrah al-An'ām, *āyah,* 103.
65. Sūrah al-Sajdah, *āyah* 17; al-Bukhārī and Muslim, on the authority of Abū Hurayrah; also al-Tirmidhī. *Fatḥ al-Bārī* VIII, 418 f.
66. Asad, *The Message of the Qur'ān.* Appendix 1.
67. *Taḥrīm al-Naẓar, op. cit.*

68. See Volume 1, Book 3, Part 3 of Sharif, *A History of Muslim Philosophy.*
69. Abū Naṣr Muḥammad ibn Muḥammad al-Fārābī (known in the West as Alpharabius), *Fī Iḥṣā al-'Ulūm*, edited by 'Uthman Amin (Cairo, 1968): 69-70 as cited in Haleem, "Chapter 5—Early *kalam*," 75.
70. Moritz Steinschneider, *al-Farabi (Alpharibius) des Arabischen Philosophen Leben und Schriften* (1869): 211-13; http://www.archive.org/details/alfarabialphara00steigoog.
71. C. H. Becker, "Christliche Polemik und islamische Dogmenbildung," Festschrift fur Ignaz Goldziher, Herausgegeben von Carl Bezold, *Zeitschrift fur Assyriologie und Verwandte Gebiete* (Strassburg: Karl J. Trubner, 1912): 190.
72. Seyyed Hossein Nasr, "Ibn Sīnā's 'Oriental Philosophy'," *History of Islamic Philosophy*, edited by Seyyed Hossein Nasr & Oliver Leaman (London & New York: Routledge, 2001), 247.
73. Ibid., 248.
74. Felix Klein-Frank, "Al-Kindi," in *History of Islamic Philosophy. London*, 165-169.
75. Majid Fakhry, *A History of Islamic Philosophy* (Columbia University Press, New York, 1983), 69-90.
76. Dominque Urvoy, "Ibn Rushd," in *History of Islamic Philosophy*, 338.
77. Ibn Rushd, *Kitāb Faṣl Al-Maqāl*, Butterworth, 22.
78. Ibid., 26
79. Ibid.
80. It should be noted that Hourani's translation renders *Sharī'ah* as Religion for the title but Law for the content, reflecting the variant shades of the term as we have discussed in Chapter 1. The translation by the Indian authors, Hamid Nassem Rafiabadi and Aadil Amin Kak consistently renders *Sharī'ah* as "the Divine Law": *The Attitude of Islam Towards Science and Philosophy: A*

Translation of Ibn Rushd's (Averroës) Famous Treatise Faṣl al-Maqāl (Sarup & Sons, 2003). This is a commendable effort though admittedly far from satisfactory in terms of fidelity to the English language.

81. Vincent J. Cornell, *Voices of Islam: Voices of Change* (Greenwood Publishing Group, 2007), 36.
82. Fehrullah Terkan "Ibn Rushd – *Faṣl al-Maqāl* and the Theory of Double Truth," İstanbul Üniversitesi İlahiyat Fakültesi Dergisi Sayı: 13, Yıl: 2006, 117-118.
83. Ibid. Terkan, however, argues against this Double Truth theory.
84. *Kitāb Faṣl al-Maqāl*, Butterworth, 30.
85. Marmura, *The Incoherence of the Philosophers: Tahāfut al-falāsifah: A parallel English-Arabic text* (Provo: Brigham Young University Press, 1997), 6.
86. Nevertheless, Ibn Rushd was targeted by the orthodox Mālikī *fuqahā'* in an intellectual climate that was generally unsympathetic to *falsafah*. Being engaged in a war against the Christians in Spain, political expediency prevailed over intellectual considerations necessitating al-Mansūr to withdraw his patronage of Ibn Rushd. He needed all the support he could get from the orthodox *fuqahā'* to help him propagate the message of *jiḥād* against the Christians. Ibn Rushd was tried for heresy and condemned into exile. His books were ordered to be burned.
87. The Islamic golden age, signified by great advances in scientific, cultural, and religious matters, is said to have started from the reign of Harun al-Rashid (d. 193/809) with the establishment of the *Bayt al-Ḥikmah* (House of Wisdom) in Baghdad. In 656/1258, the marauding Mongols under Hulagu invaded Baghdad and razed the House to the ground unleashing destruction of genocidal proportions, marking the end of the age. Of course, there are variant narratives concerning the span of the period. This is the predominant view.

88. Austin L. Hughes, "The Folly of Scientism," *The New Atlantis* (Fall, 2012), 34-36. See Karl Popper, *The Logic of Scientific Discovery,* Second edition (Routledge, 2002).
89. Ibid., 38-46.
90. Seyyed Hossein Nasr, "In the Beginning Was Consciousness" accessed 22 October 2015, available at https://www.youtube.com/watch?v=oJbASTsjxE8.
91. As we noted in Chapter 1, notwithstanding being lumped as among the three Rationalists, Spinoza must be seen in a way as *sui generis* particularly on account of his preponderance towards ethics. As his summa *Ethics* would readily testify, Spinoza remained grounded firmly on an ethical vision resting on a monistic metaphysics—where knowledge of God is the mind's greatest good and the greatest virtue is to know God.
92. Alberto Vanzo, "Kant on Empiricism and Rationalism," *History of Philosophy Quarterly*, 30, no. 1 (2013), 55, 69-70; According to this contrarian study, Kant did not regard most or all early modern philosophers as empiricists or rationalists. Nor did he see his own philosophy as an alternative to empiricism and rationalism as such but, rather, as a form of rationalism. Although he regarded his philosophy as a synthesis of dogmatism and scepticism, he did not regard it as a synthesis of empiricism and rationalism as such. Nevertheless, he employed a pattern of argument based on the rejection, unification, and overcoming of dichotomies into a third viewpoint. Accessed on November 17, 2014; available at http://wrap.warwick.ac.uk/59913.
93. Caner K. Dagli, "The Time of Science and the Sufi Science of Time," accessed on 28 November 2014; available at: http://www.ibnarabisociety.org/articles/timeofscience.html.
94. Ibid.
95. RIS Talks: Seyyed Hossein Nasr, "Philosophy Matters" at RIS

2012; accessed on 17 April, 2015; available at https://www.youtube.com/watch?v=qAgGB407FHs.

96. Ibid.
97. Ibn Rushd, *Tahāfut al-Tahāfut* (The Incoherence of The Incoherence), translated from the Arabic, with Introduction and Notes by Simon Van Den Bergh (The Trustees of The "E. J. W. Gibb Memorial").
98. G.B. Kerferd, *The Sophistic Movement* (New York: Cambridge University Press, 2009).
99. For Plato's later dialogue, "The Sophist" see Martin Heidegger, *Plato's Sophist*, Translated by Richard Rojcewicz and Andre Schuwer (Indiana University Press, 2003); in this treatise, Heidegger devotes the first part of his exposition of Plato via Aristotle's *Nicomachean Ethics* before proceeding to discourse the ontological issues.
100. George Duke, "The Sophists (Ancient Greek)," *Internet Encyclopedia of Philosophy*, accessed on 27, June, 2014; http://www.iep.utm.edu/sophists.
101. Ibid.
102. Liz Sonneborn, *Averroes (Ibn Rushd): Muslim Scholar, Philosopher, and Physician of the Twelfth Century* (The Rosen Publishing Group, 2006), 89.
103. In *De unitate intellectus contra Averroistas*, Thomas Aquinas attacked the doctrine of monopsychism and panpsychism.
104. Ernest Renan, *Averroès et l'averoïsme: essai historique* (Paris: Augusta Durand, 1852.)
105. John Marenbon, "Ernest Renan and Averroism: The Story of a Misinterpretation," in Anna Akasoy & Guido Giglioni (eds.): *Renaissance Averroism and Its Aftermath: Arabic Philosophy in Early Modern Europe* (Springer Science & Business Media, 2012), 276.
106. Edward W. Said, *Orientalism* (London and Henley: Routledge

and Kegan Paul, 1978), 145-146.

107. Marenbon, "Ernest Renan and Averroism," 283; As reflected in the writings of Sylvain Gouguenheim, *Aristotle au Mont Saint-Michel: Les racines grecques de l'Europe chrétienne* (Paris: Seuil, 2008); *cf.* Djamel Eddine Kouloughli, "Langues sémitiques et traduction. Critique de quelques vieux mythes," in *Les Grecs, les Arabes et nous: Enquête sur l'islamophobie savant* edited by Philippe Büttgen et al. (Paris: Fayard, 2009), 79–118.
108. Urvoy, "Ibn Rushd," 340-343.
109. Akasoy & Giglioni, *Renaissance Averroism and Its Aftermath,* Introductory Chapter.
110. Urvoy, op cit., 340.
111. Marsilio Ficino, *Theologia Platonica de immortalitate animorum* (Olms; Nachdr. d. Ausg. Paris, 1559 edition) (1975)
112. James G. Snyder, "Marsilio Ficino (1433-1499)," *Internet Encyclopaedia of Philosophy*; accessed 12 June, 2014; http://www.iep.utm.edu/ficino.
113. Marmura, *The Incoherence of the Philosophers,* xvi-xvii.
114. Al-Baqarah, *āyah* 117.
115. Urvoy, "Ibn Rushd," 339.
116. Ibn Rushd, *Tafsir ma ba'd at-tabi'at*: Vol. 3, 1606; Averroes, *Grand Commentaire de la Metaphysique* (Edition : Paris : les Belles Lettres, 1984.)
117. Matteo di Giovanni, "Averroes's Reading of the Metaphysics," in Fabrizio Amerini & Gabriele Galluzzo, Ed. *A Companion to the Latin Medieval Commentaries on Aristotle's Metaphysics.* (Brill, 2013), 75-76.
118. Abu al-Hasan 'Ali al-'Ash'ari, *Kitab al-Luma'*, edited by Father McCarthy (Beirut, 1953) *Risalah fi Istihsan al-khawd fi al-kalam,* see for English translation *The Theology of al-'Ash'ari: The Arabic Text of al-'Ash'ari's "Kitab al-Luma'" and "Risalat fi Istihsan al-khawd fi 'Ilm al-Kalam,"* with annotated translations and

appendices by Richard J. McCarthy (Beirut: Impremerie Catholique, 1953). It is also included in Abd Al-Rahman Badawi, *Madhahib al-Islamiyyin: al-Muktazilah* (Beirut, Dar al-Ilm li al-Malayin, 1970), Volume 1.

119. For a colourful and spirited account of the *Miḥna*, see Reza Aslan, *No god but God—The Origins, Evolution, and Future of Islam* (New York: Random House Trade Paperbacks, 2011), 142-146.
120. Weiss, *God's Law*, 21.
121. Marmura, *The Incoherence of the Philosophers*, xvi-xvii.
122. Haleem, "Chapter 5—Early *kalam*," 81.
123. Al-Ghazālī's *Moderation in Belief (Al-Iqtisad Fi Al-I'tiqad)*, translated, with an Interpretive Essay and Notes by Aladdin M. Yaqub (The University of Chicago Press, Chicago and London, 2013), 56. Al-Ghazālī is also known as "*Ḥujjah al-Islām*," usually translated as "the proof of Islam" though more appropriately, should be "the very embodiment of Islam."

Chapter 4

Morality and Sharīʿah Law

God's Law

Sharīʿah law is often referred to as God's law, used in a broad sense. This includes on the one hand, positive law derived from revelation which concerns the duties of religion (*fiqh al-ʿibādāt*), the legal rules governing transactions (*fiqh al-muʿāmalāt*), and the principles governing the law of crimes (*fiqh al-jināyāt*) and on the other hand, positive law derived by way of reason, namely, *siyāsah al-Sharʿiyyah.* The former category is often referred to as *naqliyyah*-centric law, while the latter is referred to as *ʿaqliyyah*-centric law. We will have occasion in chapter 6 to discourse on the latter as to whether it is proper to classify that under *ʿaqliyyah* law rather than *naqliyyah* but at this juncture we are only dealing with the usage of the term "God's law" as a contrast to its usage in Western jurisprudence. It is said that religions that venture beyond individual conviction into the realm of collective conscience will frame public policy through laws and "will enforce those laws in God's name."[1] It is recognised that generally, native speakers of English (who are not Muslims) at least since the 16th Century Reformation may have some trouble associating the term with positive law because of its separation from morality and religion.[2] This is a foundational issue on the treatment of the definition of law itself about which many tomes have been written. Hence, a slight elaboration suffices to put the discussion in its modern context.

By positive law as known in modern jurisprudence is meant law that compels or stipulates an action as well as establishes specific rights and prescribes duties for an individual or group. Etymologically, it stems from the verb "to posit." Hence, *ius positum*. Unlike what we have just ascribed to the term God's law for the *Sharīʿah*, the western conception of positive law generally equates it with secular law as opposed to law based on religious or moral precepts.[3] But this was not always so. The history of the Abrahamic religious systems manifest a universal aspiration to legislate religion and morality for the whole of society without setting a wall between religious and secular norms of behaviour. Theological conviction about God and His demands on human beings will translate into rules that regulate conduct in all aspects, no matter how trivial it may seem.[4]

From the view point of a traditional or conservative Muslim, an Evangelist, a fundamentalist Christian, or a Haredi Jew, there is no reason why positive law cannot include God's law. Haredi Judaism, unlike mainstream Orthodox Judaism, rejects modernism and secularism and to a certain extent, Haredi Jews resemble conservative fundamentalist Muslims who are similarly opposed to the values of the Enlightenment, liberalism and other forms of modernity. In terms of lifestyle, they are, among other things, defined by their strict adherence to a particular mode of dressing and the use of headgear that includes Homburg hats and black skull caps. More significantly, they adhere strictly to Jewish religious law. For Hindus, God's law, as a generic term is easily understood though in British India, the colonial masters used the term "Hindu law" to cover laws applicable to not just Hindus but Buddhists, Jains and Sikhs as well.[5] However, in modern usage, the concept of Hindu law as God's law is restored and the law is expressed via the ancient term *Dharma*, as a subset that includes, inter alia, rights, laws, conduct and virtues.[6]

In sum, apart from the generally Western aversion to allowing God's law the force of positive law, there is no doctrinal reason why positive law should not be based on religion or moral precepts. In any event, according to St. Thomas Aquinas, positive law does not have to be secular law because "... if, however, the law has been divinely placed, it can be done by divine authority."[7] Seen in this light, the use of the term 'God's law' need not give anyone sleepless nights.[8] This conception of God's law in a jurisprudential sense is not to be confused with the Muslim fundamentalist conception of the *Sharī'ah* as all-encompassing, governing every aspect of the life of a Muslim including his polity, a term associated with the rise of such luminaries (or radicals depending on which side of the divide one is on) as Sayyid Quṭb and Abū al-A'lā Mawdūdī as noted earlier.

The label "fundamentalist Christian" in a broad sense refers more to religious orientation or reaction to the liberalism and moral relativism of modernity rather than any particular movement. Nevertheless, some British and American Protestant churches took on a combative and confrontational position in defence of certain "fundamentals" concerning the faith such as biblical infallibility, Immaculate Conception and the doctrine of atonement and resurrection of Christ. Orthodox and Haredi Jews trace their religion to Moses, regarded by Muslims as not just a Prophet but a Messenger of God as well. The Torah given to Moses on Mount Sinai is none other than the *Tawrāh* ordained upon all Muslims as one of the books that constitute one of their articles of faith. The Torah is also known as the Five Books of Moses or the Pentateuch—Greek for "five containers," which refers to the scroll cases in which books were kept.[9] As for Muslims, even apart from the aspects pertaining to worship and ritual, which are necessarily within the spiritual and moral domain, Islamic law as it governs society in all its other aspects cannot be unwoven from its moral and religious fabric. As Coulson puts it: "The Islamic *Sharī'ah* is, in our terminology, both a code of law and a code of morals. It is a comprehensive scheme of human behaviour which derives from the one ultimate authority of the will of Allah; so that the dividing line between law and morality is by no means so clearly drawn as it is in Western societies generally."[10]

While Coulson's summation of the Islamic position is correct, it is contended that this "dividing line" is not as clearly drawn as generally supposed even in Western jurisprudence. It is a subject of intense debate whether it is the purpose of positive law to enforce standards of morality and in so doing cross the jurisprudential Rubicon from the realm of the secular to the religious. Though much water has flown under the bridge since the landmark decision of the House of Lords in the "Ladies' Directory" case where it was decided that conspiracy to corrupt public morals is a crime known to the law of England, the basic inquiry into the nature and function of law remains relevant even today.[11] In any event, the law-morality bifurcation is untenable when subjected to Kantian ethics which regards human interaction from the prism of the cardinal "categorical imperative" postulated as: "I ought never to act except in such a way that I could also will that my maxim should become a universal law."[12]

Church/State Separation

On balance, it seems correct to say that Western legal systems have steadfastly attempted to draw the line between the Church as representing morality and religion, and the State as representing positive law, in order to give them a distinct secular orientation.[13] In the 16th century, separation of ecclesiastical authority from civil power was advocated as a manifestation of the Protestant Reformation as exemplified in the Calvinistic doctrine that

> "he who knows to distinguish between the body and the soul, between the present fleeting life and that which is future and eternal, will have no difficulty in understanding that the spiritual kingdom of Christ and civil government are things very widely separated."

According to Calvin "it is a Jewish vanity to seek and include the kingdom of Christ under the elements of this world" and because the blessings we derive from Christ are spiritual, we should "remember to confine the liberty which is promised and offered to us in him within its proper limits."[14]

Unlike the Reformation diatribes, the argument for separation that was advanced by John Locke (d. 1704) had less vitriol and more persuasive substance though it was nevertheless very much motivated by political considerations predisposed towards the partisan interests of the Whigs. Locke refuted the doctrine that secular law was or ought to be subordinate to religion. As an empiricist, Locke, amidst the concern of an imminent Catholic domination over England, posited a doctrine advocating toleration for various Christian denominations. Unlike Hobbes, who was inclined towards totalitarian virtues in religion as well as in government, Locke contended that freedom of conscience and plurality of religious groups was essential to the proper functioning of civil society. State intolerance would only serve to breed civil unrest. There was a need to distinguish between the business of civil government and the business of religion. He advanced the proposition of the bifurcation of the key roles, namely, that the government's province concerned life, liberty, and general welfare, while the *raison d'etre* of the church was to ensure the salvation of the human soul. Locke asserted that the "bounds of the church" cannot be extended to civil affairs "because the church itself is a thing absolutely separate and distinct from the commonwealth and civil affairs. The boundaries of both sides are fixed and immovable."[15] The central function of the state is to preserve civil interests against attack and it may use whatever force needed to do so but such authority does not extend to regulating religious concerns with salvation. Locke argues that there is no Biblical injunction for the compulsion of faith in people. Nor could there be any consent from them even if such a purpose was ordained on the government.

In this regard, it may be postulated that when Jesus said, "Render therefore unto Caesar the things which are Caesar's; and unto God the things that are God's,"[16] he conferred on the State secular sovereignty but expeditiously stripped Caesar of any pretension to the throne of divinity. With respect, Jesus is essentially saying: "You can't have your cake and eat it too. Take your empire and your law but religion belongs to me." Caesar's temporal realm is therefore different from

Jesus' spiritual realm.

The church-state dichotomy is said to give the broad rationale why Jesus made no effort to introduce political or social reform let alone interfere with the running of the State even though the government of his time was tyrannical and corrupt. Conjectural as it may be, the explanation that has been offered for this benign indifference is that Jesus saw through the hearts of men and knew that corruption and tyranny was but a manifestation of man's innate evil whose remedy was not to be found in material prescriptions such as improved juristic or political systems. These attempts would be an exercise in futility. Just as sins may be expiated by atonement and repentance, man's only remedy for his innate evil lies in the Holy Spirit, devoid of which man is but an animal moved only by the dictates of the flesh. Nothing short of the implanting of Christ's nature in humanity would suffice: "But as many as received him, to them gave the power to become the sons of God, even to them that believe on his name; which were born, not of blood, nor of the will of the flesh, nor of the will of man, but of God."[17] According to St. Thomas Aquinas, "the Father loves us because he sees his own Son in us; only Christ can justify and save us."[18]

According to another interpretation, using the Christianity paradigm, the differentiation doctrine is really not a secular view but simply one borne out by historical reality. The Roman State had already established itself when Christianity arrived and just as Rome was not built in a day, the development of a legal system from infancy to maturity would take time. Nevertheless, according to Bernard Lewis, in the context of linking Christian theocracy to the Islamic paradigm on polity, there was de facto separation warranted by the dictates of political wisdom, and not by a deep seated conviction that society must be governed by a duality of powers, that is, *sacerdotium* and *regnum* or church and state.[19] This "Doctrine of the Two Swords" (i.e., the spiritual sword and the temporal sword) theoretically laid the ground rules for separation but at the end of the day, the church would not yield on the question of "God's law" being supreme to the laws of men. The argument is something that would resonate perfectly with proponents of the *Sharīʿah* being the be-all and end-all: the laws of the Church were fixed and immutable and all man-made laws inconsistent with it were null and void. The principle is *Roma locuta sit, cause finita sit* (Rome has Spoken, the Case is Concluded) as generally attributed to St. Augustine of Hippo (d. 430) whose writings had a profound impact on Western Christianity and philosophy. What he had actually said at the famous sermon against Pelagianism was: *Causa finita est, utinam aliquando finiatur error.* (The case is concluded; would that the error would soon cease also.)[20] While the point here is not to get embroiled in the polemics of whether the dogma was decided for good, or whether Pelagius was a victim of calumny, the point is that there is a general misconception that secularism is accepted across the board in the West. The existence of the Bible Belt in the United States of America and the role of the Evangelicals in determining which Republican candidate would be the Presidential candidate is a case in point even without going into the debate concerning America's "culture war" over issues such as abortion and homosexuality. Of course the difference is that when God's law is advocated by Christians as being supreme to Man's law in the West, it is regarded as a renaissance of religiosity while a similar call by Muslims concerning the *Sharīʿah* being likewise supreme will be seen as "fundamentalism and terrorism raising its ugly head." Nevertheless, note the decision in *Wallace (Governor of Alabama) v. Jaffree*, discussed later.

Indeed, two centuries before the advent of Islam, St. Augustine posited that while the authority and duties of the "city of God" and "the earthly city" were separate, it was the work of the "temporal city" to make it possible for a "heavenly city" to be established on earth: "Anyone, however, who lives this earthly life in such a way as to orient his use of it towards an end which is the end of the heavenly life—loving the heavenly life ardently, and loyally hoping for it—anyone who lives like that can without absurdity be called blessedly happy even now: happy in the heavenly hope rather than in the earthly reality."[21] In his monumental, *A Study of History*, Arnold Toynbee observes that the problem of the relations between "the Kingdom of God" and "the Society of This World" is a thread that runs right through the texture of the *De Civitate Dei*.[22] What is the essential difference between the two commonwealths? St. Augustine says that "... in the one the love of God comes first, in the other the love of Self ... Indeed, the two commonwealths have been created by the two loves—the earthly commonwealth by a love of Self that goes to the length of contemning God; the heavenly commonwealth by a love of God that goes to the length of contemning Self. The one glories in itself, the other in the Lord. The one seeks glory from men; the other finds its greatest glory in God as the witness to its own good conscience."[23]

Today, the separation view is a key doctrine in Western jurisprudence, particularly on constitutional issues.[24] Western democracies virtually thrive on it as part of their belief in fundamental rights. The United States Constitution, for example, is emphatic on this.[25] The doctrine is said to be embedded in the First Amendment to the United States Constitution which provides that "no religious Test shall ever be required as a Qualification to any Office or public Trust under the United States." While, as discussed earlier, the modern conception of a secular government goes further back to John Locke, the phrase "separation of church and state" is traceable to Thomas Jefferson's letter (January 1, 1802) to the Danbury Baptist Association in Connecticut: "I contemplate with sovereign reverence that act of the whole American people which declared that their legislature should 'make no law respecting an establishment of religion, or prohibiting the free exercise thereof,' thus building a wall of separation between Church and State."[26] In *Reynolds v. United States* (1878)[27] the Supreme Court declared that Jefferson's comments "may be accepted almost as an authoritative declaration of the scope and effect of the [First] Amendment."[28]

However, since the 1940s, there has been criticism of the separationist doctrine which, in the United States, has since become increasingly vocal because of the ascendancy of a conservative Supreme Court. An approach based on the Church/State bifurcation is said to be no longer religion-neutral but anti-religion by imposing secularism, that is, advancing "a culture of disbelief," creating a religiously "naked public square."[29] The justification of separationism on the ground of advancing the liberal agenda as enjoined by the spirit of the U.S. Constitution is also being challenged with the claim that, historically, its genesis can be linked to the Protestant zeal to lord over Catholics, Jews and Muslims, as could be discerned from the writings of Calvin and Martin Luther.[30] Even in the 19th century, separation was advocated not for the protection of the state but in order to secure the independence of the church. Nothing can be more explicit than the assertion by Supreme Court Justice Joseph Story's 1833 treatise on constitutional law: "… the real object of the [First] amendment was not to countenance, much less to advance, Mahometanism, or Judaism, or infidelity, by prostrating Christianity: but to exclude all rivalry among Christian sects, and to prevent any national ecclesiastical establishment which should give to a hierarchy the exclusive patronage of the national government."[31]

As alluded to earlier, in the landmark case of *Wallace (Governor of Alabama) v. Jaffree*, 472 U.S. 38 (1985), the appellants challenged the constitutionality of a 1981 Alabama Statute authorizing a one-minute period of silence in all public schools "for meditation or voluntary prayer." Ishmael Jaffree, a Muslim, had repeatedly but unsuccessfully requested that the prayers in the school where his three children were attending be stopped. He complained that his youngest son was being made fun of by peers because he refused to say the prayers. His other two children had been subjected to various acts of religious indoctrination and the school teachers had led their classes in saying certain prayers in unison on a daily basis. Because they refused to participate in the prayers on religious grounds his minor children had been exposed to ostracism from their peers.

At the trial level, the District Court held that the Establishment Clause of the First Amendment does not prohibit a State from establishing a religion. The Court of Appeals reversed the decision and held that Section 16-1-20.1 of the statute "is a law respecting the establishment of religion, and thus violates the First Amendment" which was "adopted to curtail Congress' power to interfere with the individual's freedom to believe, to worship, and to express himself in accordance with the dictates of his own conscience…." It was stressed that individual freedom of conscience incorporates "the right to select any religious faith or none at all."

This holding was affirmed by the U.S. Supreme Court in a 6/3 majority decision wherein was cited the unanimous decision in *Cantwell v. Connecticut*, 310 U. S. 296, 303 (1940) and the key principles enunciated by Justice Roberts. First, freedom of conscience and freedom to adhere to a religious organization or form of worship of choice cannot be restricted by law. On the other hand, the free exercise of the chosen form of religion is constitutionally protected. Quoting Justice Jackson in *West Virginia Board of Education v. Barnette*, 319 U. S. 624, 319 U. S. 642 (1943), the Supreme Court said: "If there is any fixed star in our constitutional constellation, it is that no official, high or petty, can prescribe what shall be orthodox in politics, nationalism, religion, or other matters of opinion or force citizens to confess by word or act their faith therein."

Chief Justice Burger, dissenting, said that the decision is not simply a manifestation of "non-interference" and "non-involvement" but of a "brooding and pervasive dedication to the secular and a passive, or even active, hostility to the religious." William Rehnquist, also dissenting, opined: "The "wall of separation between church and State" is a metaphor based on bad history, a metaphor which has proved useless as a guide to judging. It should be frankly and explicitly abandoned."

The outcome of this case is most revealing both of the significance of the separation doctrine as well as the profound practical consequences of constitutionalism. First, not all who advocate separation are secular-minded or irreligious. As this case shows, it is to protect his and his children's Islamic faith that Jaffree had resorted to the principles of separation. In other words, subscribing to the separation doctrine is not an endorsement of depravity, licentiousness or immorality. Indeed, separation is not a postulate for the abandonment of religiosity in as much as among its ardent advocates there are those, as in this case, who believe that separation is absolutely necessary in order to safeguard the freedom of religion.

Secondly, the decision is testimony of the triumph of constitutionalism and how steadfastly it is espoused and protected by the United States Supreme Court, its occasionally aberrant decisions notwithstanding. Were we to reverse the scenario and set the situation in a Muslim-majority country substituting the appellants for non-Muslim parents filing a similar action against the school authorities, it would take a great leap of the imagination to conclude that a similar outcome would be arrived at by its Supreme Court. Conversely, a glaring example lies in the case of Muslims getting sanctuary in today's Western world while back home (in their Muslim-majority countries), they themselves may be hounded for holding on to certain convictions not in line with the 'official dogma.' This is particularly so for an establishment that prides itself as 'holding on fast to God's law'. The intolerance that still prevails in the Muslim world across the board in this regard is manifested in myriad ways. One of the best examples is what may be termed as the "separation heresy."

Separation Heresy

It is said that conceptual questions of the age that are most poignant should as a rule be addressed in the most circumspect manner because of the stakes for broaching them and the even higher price of settling them in the "wrong way."[32] When the separation of the religion and state doctrine is transposed on Islam, the response by certain segments of the *ummah* is extraordinary. Woe betide the Muslim who attempts to deny the role of the Prophet as the political head of state. Fire and brimstone await him who insists that the Prophet of Islam's mission was but to appeal to man's heart only spiritually and not to his political nature.

That, in fact, was precisely what 'Alī 'Abd al-Rāziq (d. 1386/1966) did in 1925 when he asserted that Islam was a religion and not a state, and had nothing to do with either government or politics.[33] According to him, the Prophet created an *ummah*, not a state because forms of government are of no concern to the divine will. Advocating absolute separation between church and state, he contended that whereas religion is an act of faith, politics demands the exercise of human reason.[34] Any prescription for the *Sharī'ah* as the foundation for the governance of the State is therefore completely out of keeping with the Prophetic role. Religion and politics must be separated altogether. Al-Rāziq argued that the *ummah al-Islāmiyyah* was not a unitary Islamic state and the Prophet's leadership role ended with his death. The caliphate was purely a creature of custom and not an integral part of Islam or the *Sharī'ah*. On the contrary, history had shown that the caliphate had caused more damage than good to the *ummah*.

Al-Rāziq was no ghettoised leftist with extreme socialist angst screaming for expression. Born into a wealthy landowning family identified with the Liberal Constitutionalist Party (*al-Aḥrār al-Dustūriyyūn*), he was educated at the top universities in Egypt as well as at Oxford. The family home in Cairo hosted prominent intellectuals such as Muḥammad 'Abduh (d. 1322/1905), Rashīd Riḍā (1865/1935), and Aḥmad Luṭfī al-Sayyid (d. 1353/1963).[35] All indications suggested the emergence of an Egyptian John Locke or a 20th century al-Māwardī, a modernist Egyptian whose writings are anchored on a solid foundation of the Qur'ān, moored on Khaldūnian social epistemology and manifesting the Western political philosophy of Aristotle, Plato, Hobbes, Locke and Thomas Arnold.[36] The gist of al-Rāziq's contentions may be summarised as follows: What is the source of caliphal power? God or the *ummah*? In the absence of substantive textual evidence to support the conception of the *khilāfah* (caliphate), a separation between political and religious governance was warranted. The *'ulamā' al-siyāsah* (political scientists) posited that power was needed to govern any *ummah*, be it secular or religious and the mode of governance may be *dustūriyyah* (constitutional), *istibdādiyyah* (tyrannical), *jumhūriyyah* (republican), or *al-Bāshafiyyah* (Bolshevik). The caliphate developed historically with the emergence of the Islamic state during the time of Abu Bakr and not before. What this means is that the Prophet was not a political leader in the fullest sense of the word but rather a messenger on a religious mission (*rasūl da'wah dīniyyah*) in similar fashion as that of the other great messengers before him. It is true that the Prophet of Islam did establish an entity that had elements of governance and traces of power and even *jiḥād* invoked for preaching the new faith but the missionary enterprise was for all intents and purposes accomplished by spiritual and peaceful means. It should be remembered that the prophetic state (*al-mamlakah al-nabawiyyah*) was but a state in the formative stages of development (*ḥukūmah al-fiṭrah*) led by a man who loved simplicity and was close to the people. The Muslims obeyed the Prophet unquestioningly because his authority was ordained by God. His rule should never be equated with that after him. Islam was not a political prescription but a call to mankind for *iṣlāḥ* and *tajdīd* (reform and renewal) and a means for the attainment of happiness (*taḥṣīl al-sa'ādah*). In respect of the Pan-Arabism that was gaining currency, al-Rāziq said that Islam was neither an Arab religion nor a manifestation of Arab unity. Islam privileged not one nation, language, or historical period over another but was a global and humanistic mission.[37]

The backlash against this "separation heresy" was fast and furious. After the publication of *al-Islām wa Uṣūl al-Ḥukm*, he was dismissed from al-Azhar University in 1925. The assertion that the Prophet was sent only to preach a spiritual message but not to establish a nation built on the precepts of the Qur'ān and the Sunnah was seen as a fundamental assault on Islam's legitimacy as a religion and the first systematic challenge to the advocates of the Islamic state.[38] The doctrine of the separation of religion and law in Islam was, therefore, and still is, predominantly seen as heresy against the very foundations of Islam as a complete way of life. As a matter of principle, Islamic law recognizes no distinction between morals and positive law and this is traceable to the view that in classical Islam the question of separation between religion and state never arose because *de jure* there were no two separate powers—at least, not in the sense as the separation between Church and state in medieval Europe where there was the power of the Christian church on the one hand and the various monarchical powers on the other.

Nevertheless, it has been argued that in the history of the caliphate, there was a *de facto* separation between the temporal power of the caliph and the spiritual authority of the *ʿulamā'*. This is a correct statement but contextually *non-sequitur* on the issue of the church-state dichotomy. In the case of the Caliphate, temporal power was never ceded to the *ʿulamā'* in as much as what the latter wanted was not to substitute secular rule of the caliphs or sultans with theocratic rule. On the other hand, during the heyday of the Papacy, the church laid claim to temporal as well as spiritual supremacy and even intervened in foreign affairs because it "is necessary for salvation that every living creature be under submission to the Roman pontiff."[39]

Separation of law and morals and separation of state and church are closely related concepts but are two separate issues and this is a point that cannot be overstated. To talk of the separation of law and morals is to inquire into the fundamentals of law itself, the consequence of such a separation being positive law on the one hand and personal law over a wide spectrum of matters on the other. To talk of the separation of religion and state is to inquire into the foundations of a judicial, legal and political system the consequence of which is secularism as best exemplified in the American model as discussed at the outset.

This distinction applies more to Western jurisprudence than Islamic jurisprudence but that is only at a theoretical level. In fact that would be the only logical conclusion in light of our discussion on the *Sharīʿah* and *fiqh*, apart from the obvious ascription of Islamic law as "God's law." This is because the *Sharīʿah* is based on the Qur'ān and the Sunnah and it is inconceivable to have a definition of law in the Islamic sense without taking into account the question of morality. While it is true that even under *Sharī'ah* law, certain acts would only be judged in the hereafter (and not constituted as positive law) it does not negate the proposition that the *Sharī'ah* in its broad sense, does not discriminate between matters in the spiritual realm and those in the temporal. Indeed, the two are not two distinct domains and, according to Iqbal, there is no truth in the suggestion that Church and State are two facets of the same thing, the fallacy arising from the bifurcation of the unity of man into two distinct and separate realities. Matter is spirit in space-time reference. Man is body when acting in regard to the external world. He is soul when acting in regard to the ultimate aim and ideal of such acting.[40] The merely material has no substance until rooted in the spiritual and all is holy ground as in the Prophetic saying, "The whole of this earth is a mosque" (*al-arḍu kulluhā masjidan*).[41] Iqbal asserts that seen within such a paradigm, the state in Islam is a theocracy but not in the sense conventionally understood, as a polity led by a *khalīfah Allāh fī al-arḍ* (God's representative on earth) or one headed by a despot ever ready to hide behind the veil of infallibility. The state is only an effort to realize the spiritual in a human organization. But in this sense all states, not based on mere domination but aiming at the realization of ideal principles, are theocratic.[42] In Iqbal's estimation, Christianity revolted against the legalism in Judaism and established an ideal of "other worldliness" attaching no value to temporal affairs but Islam struck a balance between "religion and state, ethics and politics in a single revelation much in the same way as Plato does in his *Republic*."[43]

Alas, between the ideal and the reality falls the shadow of unrealised expectations for while the ideal might have been arguably attained during the time of the Prophet and the Rightfully Guided Caliphs, from the Umayyads onwards, through to the Abbasid caliphate and beyond, separationism had been the order of the day. Nevertheless, the bifurcation arose from political expediency rather than doctrinal imperatives, resulting in a diarchy with two coterminous centres of power. Religious authority was vested in the caliph while secular power belonged to the *sulṭān*. The two had been separate, bifurcated not in the sense of the Western model of secularism but in the widespread phenomenon of *siyāsah al-Shar'īyyah*. For the moderate position, there is, therefore, no heresy as such when one talks about Islam not enjoining the establishment of a polity purely founded on the revealed texts as long as one steers clear of treading on blasphemous waters by relegating the role of the Prophet of Islam to no more than just a messenger of a revealed book whose sole purpose ends upon his demise. In Chapter 6 we will see that even this is not conceded by the ideological inheritors of Ibn Taymiyyah in particular Sayyid Quṭb and his cohorts. According to Ibn Taymiyyah, state and religion are inseparable as the *Sharī'ah* requires the exercise of temporal rule (*sulṭān*) and the expenditure of the revenues (*māl*) of the state in the path of God. This would benefit not just the *dīn* of the *ummah* but the world at large. However, if temporal power was separated from religion or vice versa, discord and disorder would prevail in the affairs of men.[44]

Sharī'ah and Greco-Roman Law

At the time of the passing of the Prophet, the *Sharī'ah* while retaining certain past traditions and customs manifested a distinct law based on the Qur'ān and the Sunnah administered over the Arabian Peninsula. But contrary to general perception, the peninsula, particularly the cradle of Islam, the Hejaz, was not comprised of impoverished backward settlements populated by nomadic and primitive tribes with a low culture and generally isolated from the rest of the world. The populations in Mecca and Medina were in fact largely sedentary with Mecca having an established system of commercial law and Medina an agrarian law that was anything but primitive. The Arab Bedouins living outside the cities had an extensive system of commerce and trade.

Thus, as the nascent state began its imperial expeditions against the Sasanian Empire eastwards and the Byzantine Empire (Palestine and Syria) northwards, the Arab armies were not uncivilised marauding tribes led by uncouth leaders hailing from lawless lands. As Hallaq puts it, they did not go in "empty-handed desperately in search of new cultural forms or an identity." Mounting scientific evidence shows that the Arabian Peninsula was "part and parcel of the general culture that pervaded the entire Near East since the time of Hammurabi."[45]

Therefore, the notion about an early Islamic civilization, including the *Sharīʿah*, being nothing but largely borrowings from the high culture of Byzantium has no leg to stand on. Indeed there were cross-influences in the early period of Islamic history after the death of the Prophet. But the upshot was not a *Sharīʿah* with foreign law superimposed on it, much less borrowed, but a legal system firmly based on the Qur'ān and the Sunnah that at the same time syncretized the various components of the laws of the empire particularly the customs and usages (*al-ʿurf wa al-ʿādah*) that were not fundamentally in violation of the revealed texts.

In this regard, there is the issue of the supposed borrowing of Greco-Roman law as well as Judaic and Christian law by the *Sharīʿah*. Traditional *ʿulamā'* will cringe, if not react with righteous indignation altogether, at the suggestion that any aspect of the *Sharīʿah*, no matter how minor, could in fact be derived from "pagan" Greco-Roman or Judeo-Christian sources. As long as we are unable to break free from the mind-set that *Sharīʿah* law must be pure and "unadulterated by extraneous influences," such a suggestion might well be taken as sacrilegious. But such a response is unwarranted. In our preliminary discussion on the need to separate the *Sharīʿah* from the *fiqh*, it was asserted that the while the *Sharīʿah* as *dīn* is indeed divine, the *fiqh* as law is human. *Sharīʿah* law here must, therefore, be understood as having a sacred component on the one hand and a profane component on the other. It is in the domain of the latter that the affinities with other legal systems and principles may be seen.

As for the debate on the issue, there is at one end of the spectrum the suggestion that "Islamic law is Roman law in Arab dress,"[46] which is nonsensical. At the other end, Islamist or fundamentalist writers reject any suggestion of such a borrowing because Islamic law is the last word of God and any suggestion of pagan origins or even Judeo-Christian antecedents is blasphemous.[47]

The secular-religious dichotomy is often applied in the argument against any such borrowing. However, the insistence that Roman law is purely pagan betrays the deep-seated prejudice of the *ʿulamāʾ* as well as a failure to recognise the influence of the College of Pontiffs on the development of juristic reason in early Roman law. The codification of the Twelve Tables notwithstanding, they were rather limited in scope.[48] In any event, the College of Pontiffs, being the sole body permitted to interpret them, gave a religious hue to legal interpretation.[49] The Latin maxim *ratio est radius divini luminis*[50] (reason is a ray of divine light) should come to mind before one starts casting the stone of outright godlessness on Roman law.

However, no one in his right mind would suggest that *Sharīʿah* law is Roman law in Arab attire. Even the so-called percolation of Roman law into Islamic law is not conclusively proven granted that echoes of a number of principal Roman law axioms can be heard in *Sharīʿah* law. But as Patricia Crone puts it: "A couple of lines do not suffice to establish Roman influence on the laws regarding hire, security and theft, particularly when theft is a subject in which there are manifest Jewish elements."[51] The two systems being entirely unrelated in terms of foundational principles and the spirit of application, it would be more correct to say that similarities were the result of the common conclusions of developed law.[52]

According to Schacht, however, Islamic law owes an enormous debt to Roman law. Following Goldziher, he claims that the maxim "*al-walad li al-firāsh*" is the *Sharīʿah* version of the Roman *pater est quem (iustae) nuptiae demonstrant* (he is the father whom the marriage indicates to be so), flowing from which the presumption of legitimacy and paternity arises for children born in wedlock. This suggestion is baseless in as much as it is an axiom that can be directly traced to the Prophet who said: "*al-walad li al-firāsh wa li al-ʿāhir al-*

ḥajar" (the child belongs to the bed and to the one who engaged in illicit sexual relations belongs nothing).[53] To suggest that the maxim had passed to the Arabs because it was "familiar to all persons trained in Greco-Roman rhetoric" is therefore wild speculation.[54] According to Crone, not a single item of Goldziher's and Schacht's list of Roman elements in Islamic law "has been proved while several are clearly wrong." For example, contrary to their claim, there was no such thing as *opinio prudentium* and while the Romans had *interpretatio prudentium* and *responsa prudentium*, both these doctrines are not associated with either *ra'y* or *ijmāʿ*.

Likewise, the *Sharīʿah* principle of *maṣlaḥah* or *istiṣlāḥ* (public interest/to deem proper) which features prominently in the doctrine of *maqāṣid al-Sharīʿah* cannot be equated with *utilitas publica.* Whereas the Roman doctrine was generally invoked as a rationale for the ruler or the prince to subjugate the private liberties and rights of the individual (on the ground of public interest),[55] the *maqāṣid* is a tool to expand the *ummah*'s welfare in a wide spectrum of affairs while circumventing the rigour of *Sharīʿah* strictures. A closer comparison, therefore, should be in the area of *aequum et bonum* (right and just) which is said to be a characteristic not just of Greco-Roman law but also Judeo-Christian laws brilliantly "refurbished" by the Italian philosopher Giambattista Vico whose works bear the influence of none other than one of the leading advocates of *maqāṣid al-Sharīʿah* himself, Abū Isḥāq al-Shāṭibī.

It should be remembered that when the Umayyads came to power, their basic policy was the preservation of the existing administrative structure in the provinces. Whenever applicable, institutions of foreign origin were absorbed and the legal status of non-Muslim subjects in Islam was both modeled in form on the position of the non-citizen groups in the Eastern Roman empire while in spirit was informed by Qur'ānic imperatives. Hence, the linkage of the treaty of *dhimmah* and the *jizyah* tax.

There may be some parallels between the role of the *'ulamā'* in giving opinions with the *responsa prudentium* of the Roman jurists who were similarly authorized to render opinions on questions of law referred to them and these *responsa* constituted one of the most important sources of the earlier Roman law, holding much the same place of authorities as the modern precedents and law reports of English common law.[56]

To be sure, the phenomenon of transforming what is essentially *lex divina* into *lex juridica* by private specialists is not alien to the sociology of law. In this regard, there are significant parallels between the function of such specialists in *Sharī'ah* law and Roman law not so much in their similarities but in their differences and it would be a grave misperception to imagine that the *fiqh* of the *fuqahā'* would admit of the reduction of divine law into secular law. In the case of the *Sharī'ah*, what was divine as ordained in clear textual evidence remained sacral but what was derived therefrom would be merely juristic though not necessarily conjectural. There was never any real threat or danger of God's law being reduced to man-made law whereas there was too often a tendency to sacralize juristic law—even till today.

So, while Roman law grew out of the exigencies of commercial life, *Sharī'ah* law was informed by a spiritual drive that warranted the application of religious norms to all problems of behaviour. Hence, the saying that while marriages are but contracts, all contracts are sacred for God enjoins that promises must be fulfilled. It is thus said that the formation of Islamic law took place neither under the impetus of the needs of practice, nor under that of judicial technique, but under that of religious and ethical ideas.[57] That is true if by judicial technique we are referring to *uṣūl al-fiqh* for no such discipline had ever been heard of during the time of the Prophet or his companions. The *'ulamā'* studied the Qur'ān and the Sunnah deriving *fiqh* therefrom and expressed opinions long before Imām al-Shāfi'ī penned his *al-Risālah* and articulated the doctrine of the *uṣūl*. Imām Abū Ḥanīfah made pronouncements on about half a million issues which were learnt and passed on but the legal principles were never transmitted.[58] According to one view, expressed in rather hyperbolic terms, Islamic society did not give birth to the law. It was the *Sharīʿah* itself which gave birth to Islamic society.[59] Perhaps, we should meet these two polarities half-way. To suggest that the *Sharīʿah* law is nothing but the product of the *ummah* is to deny the existence of a body of about 500 *āyah*s in the Qur'ān concerning legal matters, granted that only 80 or so of that may be extracted as positive law. But to say that Islamic society is borne of the *Sharīʿah* law alone is to misunderstand the concept of the law itself as well as to fail to consider fully the diverse cultural, geographical and societal influences of the Muslim communities in shaping the *Sharīʿah* law.

Sharīʿah influence on Western Jurisprudence

A major source of the confusion surrounding the nature of *Sharīʿah* law and the misconception concerning its origins as well as the actual influence of non-Islamic law stems in part from the twin affiliation of the Common law with Roman law and Islamic law. Studies have shown that these points of convergence particularly in various areas of law such as agrarian law and the law of inheritance are indicative more of the influence of Islamic law on English law which in turn is caught under the influence of Roman law.[60]

The similarity of the principle of *istiḥsān* with the English doctrine of equity is so strong that it cannot escape comparison. *Istiḥsān,* generally translated as juristic preference, is a procedural principle of *uṣūl al-fiqh* which allows for the application of exceptions to the strict or literal interpretation of an existing *ḥukm* (legal rule) on the ground of *maṣlaḥah.* For it to be operative, there must first be at least more than one possible outcome arising from a multiplicity of apparent authorities of differential weightage in which case jurists may decide to "prefer" a weaker authority over one that is stronger if choosing the latter (such as following *qiyās*) might lead to apparent injustice or hardship. While there is no *qaṭʿī* (definitive) authority for it, the doctrine is guided by the overarching principle in the Qur'ān: *wa qaddarnā fīhā al-sayr* (and We made the stage between them easy); *wa ittabiʿū aḥsana mā unzila ilaykum min rabbikum* (And follow the better (guidance) of that which is revealed unto you from your Lord)[61]; and the Sunnah via the *ḥadīth* "*Lā ḍarara wa lā ḍirāra fī al-Islām*" (There shall be neither harm nor retribution in Islam).

Understandably, *istiḥsān* was favored by the Ḥanafīs and rejected by the Shāfi'īs. We will revisit this doctrine in Chapter 6 and go deeper into its modern ramifications. Suffice it to say that in English law, justice is dispensed strictly according to established rules of common law, which under certain circumstances may be harsh on certain parties. To circumvent these rigidities so as to avoid undue hardship, a body of principles evolved alongside these common law rules to enable decisions to be decided according to equity and good conscience.[62] Thus, equity in English law and *istiḥsān* in the *Sharī'ah* converge along the road to justice, and it is indeed to the credit of the early *fuqahā'* of Islam that more than a thousand years ago, such a system of jurisprudence was already in place as pioneered and expounded by the Ḥanafī jurists and reinforced by the Mālikīs and Ḥanbālīs. But it would be a misperception to imagine that equity as a concept in Western jurisprudence did not exist until its formulation by the English Court of Chancery.

As alluded to earlier, a significant convergence can be seen in the approach of Giambattista Vico[63] towards natural law and the method of al-Shāṭibī and his *maqāṣid* doctrine. For example, the foundation of the public sphere in the Jewish and Christian traditions as well as Greek philosophy and Roman law rests on the concept of the common good, the *aequum et bonum*, "the just and the fair," or justice. This was brilliantly recast by Vico bringing it closer to al-Shāṭibī's doctrine of *maṣlaḥah* subsumed under his *maqāṣid* framework. There are several other apparent and latent similarities between the two and the convergence is more than a theoretical affinity. It is traceable to the two Thomist Christian Spanish theorists of the law, Francisco Victoria and Francisco Suarez, who were clearly influenced by fellow Spaniard, al-Shāṭibī as manifested in both content and methods.[64] According to Vico, the father of natural law Hugo Grotius (d. 1645) laboured under the fallacy of reconstructing the "essence" of man founded on the quintessential European white male and the idea that nature had conferred a natural right to Western maritime powers to pillage and plunder the rest of the world.

In debunking Grotius' contention that justice may be simply derived on a rational minimalist conception of human sociability, Vico argued that the pursuit of the common good must take into account the inherent risks and complexities of managing society. As aptly described by Edward Said, Vico saw the interdependence of human history and cultures that are organically bound together.[65] Natural law could not be treated in isolation from the historical development of customs and of the rules, usages and legal principles emanating from those customs. Natural law should be simultaneously understood as an ideal for a universal eternal truth and as a historical development of the customs and traditions of society.[66]

This approach manifests the influence of al-Shāṭibī's treatment of custom as part of the foundational principles of the *Sharīʿah*. This has a close nexus with reason and revelation on the issue of moral epistemology.[67] While other jurists contend that the foundations of the *Sharīʿah* are definitive because of its divinity, al-Shāṭibī reversed the order. The definitiveness of the foundations stems from multiple rational, customary and textual indicators. It is in this linkage that Vico's jurisprudence bears the conceptual footprints of al-Shāṭibī's *ʿurf* doctrine. Custom is employed with reference to practical wisdom which does not confer certainty of sound opinion through absolute rational deduction if it is bereft of divine guidance. To al-Shāṭibī, reason alone did not stop nations from committing errors. Revelation, therefore, remains the ultimate source of guidance even when reason fails.[68]

As we move closer to modernity, again the principle of *istiṣlāḥ* is echoed in the philosophy of Jeremy Bentham and the theory of justice as expounded by John Rawls.[69] In the former, which has come down in Western jurisprudence as utilitarianism, the purpose of law is to ensure that the outcome is the maximization of the overall level of welfare of the people ("the greatest happiness of the greatest number"). Nevertheless, the similitude cannot be taken too far as it may slouch towards *utilitas publica* rather than *aequum et bonum* or *bonum publica*. The problem is that while defending liberty and political rights, utilitarians at the same time have no objection to constraining them, provided that doing so would promote greater welfare. That, of course, is a time-honoured dubious argument commonly employed by the autocrats and tyrants of today, reminiscent of the emperors and rulers of yore.

A stronger affinity may be found in the case of Rawls where *istiṣlāḥ* reverberates as a distant echo in his conceptions of justice and liberalism.[70] Very much linked to *maṣlaḥah*, and sometimes used interchangeably, the concept of *istiṣlāh* enables the jurist to consider the *maqāṣid al-Sharī'ah* (objects and purposes of the *Sharī'ah*) in the determination of a juristic problem as well as the formulation of legal rules and principles. Favoured by the Ḥanbalīs, its application is, however, limited to a case by case basis as well as to situations of the utmost necessity concerning matters which are not linked to *'ibādat* (religious observances). Again, it is not recognised by the Shāfi'ī *madhḥab* on account of the latter's strictures against reliance on *ra'y* as well as the subjective nature of what constitutes "public interests." The doctrine therefore bears affinity with Western jurisprudence, first in terms of the natural law tradition as represented by the precepts of Thomas Aquinas and later with greater relevance to contemporary jurisprudence, in particular Rawlsian liberalism. The Islamic antecedents for this linkage go back first to the modern interpretation of the doctrine by Muhammad 'Abduh and Rashīd Riḍā where the Qur'ānic declaration "*yurīdu Allāhu bikum al-yusra wa lā yurīdu bikum al-'usr*" (Allah desires for you ease; He desires not hardship for you) and the prophetic dictum "*Lā ḍarara wa lā dirāra*" (neither harm nor retribution), as alluded to earlier, are given a much wider berth and greater significance in the articulation of the *istiṣlāḥ* doctrine.[71] A liberal construction would enable the doctrine to validate legislation to protect fundamental human rights and to secure distributive and other forms of justice. In this regard, this approach finds a clear nexus with Rawls' first principle (the equal maximum liberty principle) which posits that there are some rights such as freedom of speech and association, the right to vote and stand for public office, liberty of conscience and freedom of thought, and freedom from arbitrary arrest which every system must respect. These are rights which may not be sacrificed on the altar of aggregate welfare. Utilitarianism benefits are concerned with welfare while Rawls defines benefits in terms of primary goods and uses a remodeled version of the social contract argument to establish his principles of justice including of course distributive justice.[72]

Forum Externum/Internum

To understand the conceptual background and significance of the *Sharīʿah* and the scope of its application in positive law as well as private law, let us consider briefly the doctrines of *forum externum* and *forum internum.* One primary question that is raised concerning the enforcement and scope of *Sharīʿah* law is whether all transgressions against the *Sharīʿah* are punishable by law. The general view is that transgressions in respect of obligatory and forbidden acts as are under the rubric of "religious practice pertaining to the private individual" are not enforced by the *Sharīʿah* courts even though they are unquestionably part and parcel of the *Sharīʿah*—as understood in the broad sense. This is the logical conclusion of the fundamental view that "the *Sharīʿah*, as *forum externum*, regulates only the external relations of the subject to Allah and his fellow men and ignores his inner consciousness, that is, his attitude to the *forum internum.*"[73] Briefly stated, in canonical law, *forum internum* refers to matters usually associated with the concept of freedom of conscience whereas *forum externum* concerns the manifestations of conscience. Likewise, the point here is that the *Sharīʿah* is not concerned with one's subjective beliefs as it is positive law in the sense of regulating the externalization of one's beliefs. By way of example, the *Sharīʿah*, as municipal law, can punish a Muslim for failure to observe the fast—in public—in the month of Ramaḍān but it is not concerned with enquiring whether he or she actually observes the fast in the privacy of the home. For that matter, the *Sharī‘ah* will not regulate a Muslim's subjective belief in the Five Pillars of Islam. That is a matter beyond the purview of the *Sharī‘ah*, and just as in *forum internum*, that is a matter between the individual and his or her Maker, if the individual actually believes in one in the first place. However, if the said individual publicly proclaims that he does not subscribe to the Five Pillars but insists that he is still a Muslim by religion, the *Sharī‘ah* can deal with him under *ta‘zīr* laws of spreading sedition or causing public dissention. Since these are not *ḥudūd* crimes—in the sense as generally understood—there is discretion for the legislative body to prescribe the appropriate penalties deemed fit to deal with the mischief to be punished and deterred. Indeed it is debatable whether he can be tried for apostasy considering that he maintains that he is a Muslim even though it could be argued that repudiation of the Five Pillars would automatically lead to apostasy.

Nevertheless, in theory, a Muslim living in a country where Islam is the dominant religion, or even in an Islamic state, would not expect the moral police to come barging into his house in the middle of the night to apprehend him for having failed to perform the obligatory '*Isha*' prayers before he retired or for having failed to observe the strictures of fasting at home in the month of Ramaḍān. It is also generally viewed that the real sanction for any omission of obligatory religious practice in private or the commission of forbidden acts in private as between individuals lies not in the temporal courts but in the spiritual court of the Hereafter. To commit transgressions in respect of those acts is to invoke divine displeasure or retribution, and Providence is in no hurry to execute its judgment, a belief which is not unique in Islam. But sometimes deferred judgment for transgressions of the religion of such a kind is preceded by acts of penance, not just mere contrition to be internally felt but carried out by overt acts of atonement (*kaffārah*) in order to expiate one's sins. The *Sharī‘ah*—as a complete system but not as *Qānūn* law—provides clearly for this by stipulating the requirement for alms giving, feeding the poor and generally the performance of acts of charity as well as supererogatory prayers. The point is that for transgressions against God committed in private, temporal punishment is generally not envisaged. This may seem academic but when the other aspects of activities such as *al-muʻamalāt*, in particular, issues of Islamic criminal law are discussed (as in Chapter 2) difficulties will arise over the definition of what constitutes transgressions against God and what constitutes transgressions against society.

This raises the question: If the individual publicly renounces his faith, would the *Sharīʻah* be applicable as *forum externum*? The answer to this is peppered with many permutations. Firstly, it is still unresolved among scholars whether apostasy is a *ḥadd* offence. If it is, then it becomes subject to the *Sharīʻah*. If not, the question is whether it can be made a *taʻzīr* offence—essentially *mala prohibita*—in which case it becomes punishable according to the legislation. Then, there is the argument that on account of the *forum internum* arising from a clear *āyah* in the Qur'ān that there shall be no compulsion in matters of faith, making apostasy a *ḥadd* offence is not only without foundation but runs counter to the spirit of the Qur'ān.

There is also the question of the *niyyah* or intention which is required in the performance of religious rituals and acts of worship as made obligatory by the *Sharīʻah*. When a person is compelled to believe in Islam and does so under such compulsion, apart from the said *āyah*, it also runs counter to the well-known saying of the Prophet concerning the paramount importance of intention accompanying all acts of worship. In fact, the general view is that it governs all acts. ʻUmar narrated that the Prophet said: Indeed, deeds are only of the intentions and an individual is [rewarded] only according to that which he intends.[74] Nevertheless, it should be noted that there is a counter argument to that line of reasoning. The principle derived from the *niyyah ḥadīth*, it is contended, applies only in respect of reward for deeds but does not absolve one from punishment in respect of the performance of mandatory acts. This is a long standing issue that remains unresolved. It becomes even weightier when subsumed under the discourse on free will and determination which was discussed in Chapter 3 on *kalām*.

Notes

1. Jacob Neusner & Tamara Sonn *Comparing Religions through Law: Judaism and Islam* (London: Routledge, 1999), vii.
2. According to Weiss, speakers of English do not ordinarily understand the term "law of God" to be a reference to positive law. English speaking societies presuppose a separation of substance between positive law and morality so that if the latter is to be called the law of God, the former may not: Weiss, *God's Law*, 5.
3. It should be noted that while Aquinas espoused a sovereignty divided in the spiritual and temporal realms, Austin, following Hobbes, sought a single sovereign as the ultimate font of the law which leaves him with no choice but to deny the existence of divine positive law. Sovereignty is vested in man subject, however, to divine natural law.
4. Neusner & Sonn *Comparing Religions through Law, op. cit.*, ibid.
5. Donald Davis Jr, "A Realist View of Hindu Law," *Ratio Juris*, 19, no. 3 (2006): 287-313.
6. Richard W. Lariviere, "Law and Religion in India," in *Law, Morality, and Religion: Global Perspectives*, edited by Alan Watson (Berkeley: University of California, 1996).
7. Translating Aquinas's "*si autem lex sit divinitus posita, auctoritate divina dispensatio fieri potest.*" (Summa contra Gentiles, lb. 3 cap. 125): Kevin Flannery, *Acts Amid Precepts: The Logical Structure of Thomas Aquinas's Moral Theology* (Continuum International Publishing Group, 2007), 73.
8. For a more elaborate discussion on the differences see Weiss, *God's Law*, 6-11.
9. Cyril Glasse, *The Concise Encyclopedia of Islam* (Rowman & Littlefield Publishers, 2008), 72. See King James Bible—all biblical

references are from this version of the bible.

10. Noel J. Coulson, *Conflicts and Tensions in Islamic Jurisprudence* (Chicago: University of Chicago Press, 1969), 79.
11. *Shaw v Director of Public Prosecutions*, [1962] AC 220. See also H.L.A Hart, *Law, Liberty, and Morality* (London: Oxford University Press, 1963).
12. Kant's *Groundwork of the Metaphysic of Morals*; "Kant's Moral Philosophy" section 3, in *Stanford Encyclopedia of Philosophy* accessed on October 23, 2014, http://plato.stanford.edu/entries/kant-moral.
13. Coulson, *Conflicts and Tensions,* 79-81.
14. John Calvin, *Institutes of the Christian Religion,* Book IV, Chapter 20—"Of Civil Government," (1559), 899. Calvin earlier attacks the priests as serving not God but the Devil: "When Scripture plainly testifies that it is the duty of a presbyter to rule his own church (Acts 20:28), is it not impious profanation to transfer it to another purpose, nay, altogether to change the sacred institution of God? ... I briefly say, that if it is the office of a presbyter ... to feed the Church, and administer the spiritual kingdom of Christ, all those priests who have no work or stipend, save in the traffic of masses, not only fail in their office, but have no lawful office to discharge. No place is given them to teach, they have no people to govern. In short, nothing is left them but an altar on which to sacrifice Christ; this is to sacrifice not to God but to demons ..." Book IV, Chapter 5,—The Ancient Form of Government utterly corrupted by the tyranny of the Papacy, 671.
15. John Locke, *A Letter Concerning Toleration,* originally written in Latin as *Epistola de Tolerantia.* Translated by William Popple (1638 -1708).
16. Matt. 22: 21.
17. John 1: 12, 13.
18. Thomas Aquinas, *Commentary on St. Paul's Epistle to the*

Ephesians, translated and introduced by Matthew L. Lamb (Magi Books Inc, New York, 1966), 30, 51-55.

19. Bernard Lewis, *The Political Language of Islam* (Chicago: University of Chicago Press, 1988), 2; W. Montgomery Watt, *Islamic Political Thought* (Edinburgh at the University Press, 1968), 26-7.
20. Sermon 131, 10, vol. v, p. 734; http://www.biblicalcatholic.com/apologetics/num16.htm.
21. St. Augustine, *De Civitate Dei*, Book XV, Chapter 1; Book XIX, Chapter 17.
22. Arnold J. Toynbee, *A Study of History*, Vol VI: *The Disintegrations of Civilizations* (Oxford University Press 1939), 365-368.
23. St. Augustine, *De Civitate Dei*, Book XIV, Chapter 13; *De Civitate Dei contra Paganos*, translated in English as The City of God Against the Pagans and popularly as The City of God, St. Augustine's magnum opus which cast a profound influence on not just Christian but Western philosophy.
24. Going further back into Western history, separation was more the exception than the rule. Julius Caesar was Pontifex Maximus before he was Consul of Rome. The Edict of Thessalonica, also known as Cunctos populous, propounded in 380 AD, made Nicene Christianity the state religion of the Roman Empire: Sidney Zdeneck Ehler & John B. Morrall, *Church and State Through the Centuries: A Collection of Historic Documents with Commentaries* (Biblo & Tannen Publishers, 1967), 6; Apart from being accused of "corrupting the youth of Athens," Socrates was also charged with "failing to acknowledge the gods that the city acknowledges" and sentenced to death, indicative no doubt of the union of state and religion: Plato. *Apology*, 24–27.
25. See the Virginia Bill for Religious Freedom submitted by Thomas Jefferson in 1779 which was one of the only three accomplishments he had put on his epitaph.

26. Philip Hamburger, *Separation of Church and State* (Cambridge, MA: Harvard University Press, 2002); Daniel L. Dreisbach, *Thomas Jefferson and the Wall of Separation of Church and State* (New York: New York University Press, 2002).
27. 98 U.S. (8 Otto.) 145 (1878).
28. The case itself concerned the legality of the practice of polygamy or to be precise, a constitutional challenge to the law purporting to prohibit and criminalize bigamy, namely, the Morrill Anti-Bigamy Act. Inter alia, the defence raised was that it was the accused's religious duty to practise polygamy and that the said statute was ultra vires the Constitution. It was argued that the First Amendment protected his practice of his religion as a Mormon. While the Court agreed that constitutionally, Congress could not legislate to outlaw the free exercise of religion, it held that the impugned statute prohibiting bigamy did not amount to interference with the free exercise of religion. Monogamy was a time honoured principle in English law since the reign of King James I of England. The court reasoned that if polygamy was allowed, someone might eventually argue that human sacrifice was a necessary part of their religion, and "to permit this would be to make the professed doctrines of religious belief superior to the law of the land, and in effect to permit every citizen to become a law unto himself." The First Amendment only forbade legislating against opinion, but not against action.
29. Stephen L. Carter, *The Culture of Disbelief: How American Law and Politics Trivialize Religious Devotion* (New York: Basic Books, 1993); Richard John Neuhaus, *The Naked Public Square: Religion and Democracy in America* (Grand Rapids, MI: William B. Eerdmans, 1984).
30. See, for example, Luther's *On the Jews and Their Lies* (*Von den Juden und ihren Lügen*) written in 1543 and *Of the Unknowable Name and the Generations of Christ* (*Vom Schem Hamphoras und*

vom Geschlecht Christi) published a few months later.

31. Joseph Story, *Commentaries on the Constitution of the United States* (Boston: Hilliard, Gray, and Co., 1833).
32. A.K. Reinhart, *Before Revelation: The Boundaries of Muslim Moral Thought* (SUNY Press, 1995), 5.
33. ʿAli ʿAbd al-Raziq, *Al-Islam wa usul al-Hukm* (Islam and the Bases of Political Authority) 2nd edition (Cairo: 1925). Albert Hourani, *Arabic Thought in the Liberal Age—1798-1939* (Cambridge University Press, 1983), 183-4.
34. Hourani, *Arabic Thought*, 186-187.
35. The political writings and ideas of Luṭfi al-Sayyid, his journal al-Jarīda, and Ḥizb al-Umma (the "Party of the Nation") laid the groundwork for the emergence of a liberal democratic Weltanschauung from 1907-15. This was an elitist conception of democracy built on the assumption of the role of intellectuals as Plato's philosopher-kings on account of the ignorance and irrationality of the masses. With time, many of the intellectuals schooled on Luṭfian ideas would migrate to a more inclusive liberal democracy. Prominent among them were ʿAbbas Mahmud al-ʿAqqad, Ahmad Amin, Salama Musa, Taufiq al-Hakim, ʿAli ʿAbd al-Rāziq, and ʿAbd al-Razzaq al-Sanhuri and of the intellectual voices of women were Huda Shaʿarawi, Nabawiyya Musa, and Labiba Ahmad. All were born at the end of the nineteenth century and were active as public intellectuals. Two of them were most exceptional: Taha Husayn (d. 1392/1973) and Muhammad Husayn Haykal (1375/1956) who were considered representative Arab thinkers of the day and the most authoritative proponents of a liberal democracy: Israel Gershoni, "Liberal Democratic Legacies in Modern Egypt: The Role of the Intellectuals, 1900-1950," *Institute for Advanced Study* (Summer 2012); accessed 23 March, 2014; available at https://www.ias.edu/about/publications/ias-letter/articles/2012-

summer/democratic-legacies-egypt.

36. *The Princeton Encyclopedia of Islamic Political Thought*, edited by Gerhard Bowering (Princeton University Press, 2013), 5 (Hereafter *PE*).
37. ʿAbd al-Rāziq, *al-Islām wa Uṣūl al-Ḥukm*, passim; *PE*, 5-7; Hourani, *Arabic Thought in the Liberal Age*, passim.
38. There was the knee-jerk reaction and vitriol that ʿAlī Rāziq was yet another lackey of the West tasked to divide the *ummah* for the cause of Western colonialism. Unfortunately, Rashīd Riḍā joined in the condemnation. Pressure was brought to bear by the conservative *ʿulamāʾ* on al-Azhar to have ʿAlī Rāziq sacked as Qādī with his name being struck off the roll of *ʿulamāʾ*. And for a while, he became a pariah among the Egypt's political elite.
39. For example, Pope Boniface VIII fought with Philip the Fair of France on account of staking out both temporal and spiritual power and excommunicated him in 1303. In the case of England, King Henry II wanted to extend his authority over the Church via the Constitutions of Clarendon and this was condemned by the Archbishop of Canterbury Thomas Becket and the Pope.
40. Iqbal, *Reconstruction*, 122.
41. Ibid., 123.
42. Ibid.
43. Ibid., 132.
44. Ibn Taymiyyah, *al-Siyāsah al-Sharʿiyyah fī Iṣlāḥ al-Rāʿī wa al-Raʿiyyah*, ed. Muḥammad Mubārak, Beirut 1386/1966. (The Book of Governance According to the Sharīʿah), 142; Ann K. S. Lambton, *State and Government in Medieval Islam: An Introduction to the Study of Islamic Political Theory: the Jurists* (Psychology Press, 1981), 145.
45. Hallaq, *The Origins and Evolution of Islamic Law*, 25-26.
46. Ayman Daher, "The Shari'a: Roman Law Wearing an Islamic Veil?" *Hirundo: The McGill Journal of Classical Studies*, Volume

III (2004): 92.

47. R. Mottahedeh, "Some Islamic views of the pre-Islamic past," *Harvard Middle Eastern and Islamic Review* 1 (1994): 17.
48. George Mousourakis, *Roman Law and the Origins of the Civil Law Tradition* (Springer, 2014).
49. Daher, "The Shari'a: Roman Law Wearing an Islamic Veil?" 95.
50. Co. Litt. 232.
51. Patricia Crone, *Roman, Provincial and Islamic Law: The Origins of the Islamic Patronate* (Cambridge University Press, 2002), 11.
52. *Shorter Encyclopaedia*, 612.
53. Harald Motzki, *The Origins of Islamic Jurisprudence: Meccan Fiqh Before the Classical Schools* (Brill, 2002), 126.
54. Crone, *Roman, Provincial and Islamic Law,* 10.
55. Kenneth Pennington, *The Prince and the Law, 1200-1600: Sovereignty and Rights in the Western Legal Tradition* (University of California Press, 1993), 233-236.
56. *Black's Law Dictionary* (St. Paul: West Publishing Co., 1990); J. Wellhausen, *The Arab Kingdom and Its Fall* (Calcutta: University of Calcutta, 1927).
57. Schacht, *Introduction,* 209.
58. Tahā Jabīr al-Alwāni, *Uṣūl al-Fiqh al-Islāmi—Source Methodology in Islamic Jurisprudence: Methodology for Research and Knowledge* (Herndon: The International Institute of Islamic Thought, 1990), 60-63.
59. Hunt Janin, André Kahlmeyer, *Islamic Law: The Sharia from Muhammad's Time to the Present* (McFarland, 2007), 31.
60. See John Makdisi's essay: "An Inquiry into Islamic Influences during the Formative period of the Common Law" in *Islamic Law and Jurisprudence*, edited by Nicholas Heer (University of Washington Press, Seattle and London, 1990), 135-46.
61. Respectively, *Sūrah Sabā', ayāh* 18 and *Sūrah al-Zumar, ayāh* 55.
62. See Heydon, Leeming & Turner, *Equity Doctrines & Remedies*, 5th

edition (LexisNexis, 2014); *Black's Law Dictionary.*

63. Giambattista Vico, *Universal Right* (Diritto universale). Translated from the Latin and edited by Giorgio Pinton and Margaret Diehl (Amsterdam/New York, Rodopi, 2000); also his magnum opus, *Scienza Nuova:* Vico, *The New Science of Giambattista Vico* (1744). Translated by Thomas G. Bergin and Max H. Fisch (Ithaca: Cornell University Press, 1968).
64. Armando Salvatore, "Public Religion, Ethics and Cultural Dialogue," in *Contemporary Islam: Dynamic, Not Static,* Edited by Abdul Aziz Said, Mohammed Abu-Nimer, Meena Sharify-Funk (Routledge, 2006), 92-97.
65. Edward Said, *Orientalism* (Vintage Books, 1978).
66. Salvatore, "Public Religion, Ethics and Cultural Dialogue," 92-97.
67. Ayman Shabana, *Custom in Islamic Law and Legal Theory: The Development of the Concepts of 'Urf and 'Adah in the Islamic Legal Tradition* (Palgrave Macmillan, 2010), 114.
68. Ibid., 128.
69. See in particular Jeremy Bentham, *An Introduction to the Principles of Morals and Legislation*, edited by J.H. Burns and H.L.A Hart (Clarendon Press, 1996), and John Rawls, *Political Liberalism* (New York: Columbia University Press, 1993).
70. Rawls, *Political Liberalism.*
71. *Al-Baqarah, ayāh* 185; Knut S. Vikør, *Between God and the Sultan: A History of Islamic Law* (Oxford University Press, 2005), 234–35.
72. Freeman, *Lloyd's Introduction*, 357.
73. *Shorter Encyclopaedia*, 525.
74. "*Innamā al-a'māl bi al-niyyāt wa innamā li kulli imri'in mā nawā.*" This *ḥadīth* has only one path to 'Umar: Yaḥyā ibn Sa'īd al-Anṣārī on the authority of Muḥammad ibn Ibrāhīm al-Taymī, on the authority of 'Alqamah ibn Abī Waqqāṣ al-Laythī, who narrated it from 'Umar ibn al-Khaṭṭāb. Large numbers of people

narrated this *ḥadīth* on the authority of Yaḥyā b. Saʿīd, including Imām Mālik, al-Thawrī, al-Awzāʿī, Ibn al-Mubārak, al-Layth ibn Saʿd, Ḥammād ibn Zayd, Shuʿbah, Ibn ʿUyaynah and others. Accessed on August 7, 2015; available at http://www.sunnah.org/ibadaat/alamal_bilniyyat.htm.

Chapter 5

Concepts of Authority in the Sharīʿah

In the preceding discussion what remains unanswered is a more fundamental question: what authority do the *ʿulamāʾ* (the *fuqahāʾ/muftīs/mujtahids*) have for their rulings to be deemed effective? The answer lies in the typification of authority, the first being legislative and the second being interpretive or declarative. The former belongs to God and is concretized as the authority of the foundational texts while the latter belongs to the jurists. In Roman law, the *auctoritas prudentium* of private jurists was deemed to be derived from societal recognition and respect accorded to them and it is this kind of authority that Joseph Schacht attributed to the *fuqahāʾ* except that the latter, according to him, was "an extreme case of jurists' law," that is, the authority was more pervasive, supreme and always fiercely independent of state control or interference. That may be true to a point but as we shall see when *fiqh* meets temporal sovereignty, the *fuqahāʾ* particularly those appointed as *muftis* by the state, tend to defer to the powers that be. Thus, it may be more correct to say that theirs is an "exclusively declarative authority" based on "an intentionalist interpretation of foundational texts."[1]

During Umayyad rule, Islam was used to legitimize the wars of expansion and conquests with the Caliphs purporting to play the role of protectors and defenders of the faith. But there was hardly anything Islamic about transforming the principle of succession by selection or election during the rule of the Rightly-Guided Caliphs to hereditary rule and the establishment and perpetuation of an Arab military aristocracy. In the process, the relative Islamic egalitarianism was replaced by an Arab-centric caste system which marginalized non-Arab Muslims (*mawālin*) as well as non-Muslims. Among other things, it gave rise to the ascendancy of the *'ulamā'* who became increasingly disenchanted with the deviant innovations of the caliphs, their court intrigue and the elitist power politics taking the *ummah* further away from Islam.

The *Sharī'ah* was seen as being gradually sacrificed on the altar of secular rule and the command of the caliph appeared to prevail over the command of God. For the rising class of *fuqahā'* and *mujtahids* their interpretive or declarative authority was gaining little traction. On the contrary, the caliphal powers that would have had the legitimacy to initiate greater implementation of the *Sharī'ah* were instead more enamoured with the diversity of cultures, customs and laws. We have already seen how juristic law developed in tandem with the expansion of the Muslim empire but to some, at least at this stage of the caliphal history of Islam, the latitude with which legal disputes and *fiqh* issues were resolved also meant that the upshot was a confused and often contradictory *corpus juris*. Eventually, the rise of the *'ulamā'* led to a coalescence of a "pious opposition" from the *ummah* with Muslims committing themselves to the conceptualization and exposition of the *Sharī'ah*.

Under these circumstances, the seizure of power by the Abbasids could easily be legitimized under the banner of Islam with which they took great pains to align their continued reign even though it was by hereditary succession. The *'ulamā'* were given pride of place as the Abbasid caliphs attempted to bridge the gap between the *Sharī'ah* and the *siyāsah* (political reality), by making *Sharī'ah* law, ostensibly at least, the only law of the land. The idea here was to cloak the exercise of political power with the sanction and sanctity of sacral law, a feature that was glaringly wanting under the Umayyads. With the mantle of sacral authority endorsed by the *'ulamā'*, delusions of grandeur prompted the Abbasid caliphs to ascribe to themselves the title of *Khalīfah Allāh* or God's Vicegerent in place of the humbler

Amīr al-Mu'minīn while the designation of *Khalīfah al-Nabī* was seen as not being grand enough to match their sublime status in the Muslim empire. To embellish the towering position, subjects had to kiss the ground before them in the servile ritual of the old Persian court. Higher officials or more favoured dignitaries were allowed either to kiss the Caliph's hand or foot, or the edge of his robe.[2] This was, however, judiciously balanced by the promotion, ostensibly at least, of Islamic egalitarianism with the introduction of reform in the system of military and civil appointments where non-Arabs, particularly Persians, were given a greater role.

Be that as it may, historians are generally agreed that it was because of the Abbasids that the *Sharīʿah* was actively promoted and received its greatest impetus in terms of the development of *uṣūl al-fiqh* with the *ʿulamā'* given not just free rein in articulating the law via the *mujtahids* but also authoritative recognition via the appointment of *qāḍī*s and *muftis* and the dissemination of *fatāwā* (juristic opinions). As we saw in Chapter 2, the early *madhāhib* which had arisen towards the latter part of Umayyad rule, were allowed to flourish under the Abbasids which finally led to the establishment of the four main Sunni schools of law with the authority of the *ʿulamā'* in matters of *fiqh* virtually being unquestionable.

Eventually, even as the caliphs were wielding absolute power, at the same time, a bureaucratic class of middle-level 'Caesars' emerged whose contribution to the administration of the Abbasid caliphate was signified by their hostility towards the *ʿulamā'*. Perhaps middle-level Caesarism is an understatement as they actually wielded much of the caliph's power and, together with other elements, constituted the autocratic bloc in the power struggle under the rule of the first Abbasids. Even tyrants want to be seen to have legitimacy as evidenced even in this day and age, and some have actually been able to snatch "divine victory" from the jaws of their autocratic defeat. Some of the *ʿulamā'*, however, in this case purportedly obeyed the autocratic rulers but continued with their practice of issuing *fatāwā* independent of the views of the establishment. In theory, they retained full liberty to exercise *ijtihād* and to censure the actions of the rulers. In reality, some "sold out" for personal gain, some capitulated under the domineering influence of certain Abbasid rulers and yet some stood their ground but paid a heavy price, sacrificing their freedoms, even their lives, on the altar of moral integrity and the courage of their ideological convictions.

The notion of authority itself, as explicated earlier, needs to be re-examined including the expression "*wa ūlī al-amri minkum*" contained in the injunction:

> "O you who have believed, obey Allah and obey the Messenger and those in authority among you...."[3]

One view suggests that the phrase "those in authority" refers to leaders of expeditions or delegations rather than experts in legal or religious knowledge. This rules out the *ʿulamāʾ*, and, ipso facto, the declarative or interpretive authority as referred to earlier is said to be not entirely sanctioned by the Qur'ān. The expression is said to point to a political leader. Another view suggests that the more significant subtext of the phrase is indicative of the "egalitarian spirit of Qur'ānic injunctions" in respect of matters concerning the *ummah* and reinforces the argument that the government of a Muslim state must be democratically elected.[4] The more prevalent view, however, is that the expression represents a clear *naṣṣ* (scriptural text; textual authority) enjoining obedience to those in power. While we do not want to stray too far into this important concept lest we get lost in the labyrinth of political discourse on the Islamic state (which no doubt warrants treatment in another monograph), it is nevertheless necessary to add a few more remarks concerning the issue of what may be seen as an apparent clash between two Qur'ānic imperatives: one that commands the believers to obey those in authority and the other that calls on them to enjoin good and forbid evil. In the remaining pages of this chapter we shall look at the position of the leading Shāfiʿī jurists on the question of obedience to the rulers vis-à-vis the legality of rebellion or usurpation of power which is the old paradigm of framing the discourse. In today's parlance perhaps, terms like people's uprising, revolution or regime change might set the contextual reference in more realistic terms. Nevertheless, we will stick to the traditional phrases as used by the jurists who were discussing them in the context of the political and social circumstances they were in. For comparison, we will look at Ibn Taymiyyah's position as well.

The Shāfiʿī Positions

To begin with, the conventional understanding that the traditional *fuqahā'* advocated total obedience to the rulers needs to re-examined.[5] While it is true that the classical Shāfiʿī jurists argued that as a general rule, the ruler must be obeyed, at the same time, they also accepted that there was a duty to obey the usurper as well.[6] To the cynics this is a non-starter and indicative of a classic case of blowing hot and blowing cold. But once we get past the apparent contradiction and start examining the underlying rationale for the ruling, it becomes clear that the *ḥikmah*, and not the devil, is in the details. The general principle was in favour of a system of basic order. The fundamental argument as advanced by al-Māwardī, al-Juwaynī and al-Ghazālī was that bereft of a foundation of order the possibility of justice would be denied but, contrary to what much contemporary scholarship assumes, this rule was not cast in stone. There was a countervailing principle that allows for rebellion under specified circumstances and for various reasons with different yardsticks of applicability according to different classes of the *ummah*—whether they belong to the laity, to the *ʿulamā'* or to those categorised as *ahl al-ḥall wa al-ʿaqd* (literally, "the people who loosen and bind") a metaphor for those who possess power in society. Through these doctrines, it may be said that the juristic thinking, according to the Shāfiʿī *madhhab* in particular, "does not grant the state an absolute, unmitigated right to obedience."[7]

Al-Māwardī

Such a discourse often begins with some insight into the art and policy of government as advocated by al-Māwardī (d. 450 /1058)[8] in his *Kitāb al-Aḥkām al-Sulṭāniyyah wa al-Wilāyāt al-Dīniyyah* ("The Principles of Governance and the Province of Religion" usually shortened as "The Ordinances") where the caliphate is portrayed as a holistic system governing the political and religious affairs of the *ummah*. There was no doubt that during his time, *Aḥkām* provided the prevailing mantra on the duty to obey and was endorsed by the majority of Sunni jurists. With *Aḥkām,* al-Māwardī became the first *'ālim* to gather and arrange all the *Sharī'ah* principles pertaining to public law into a single treatise and expound them in a systematic manner.[9] It was also the first in attempting to formulate a theory of the Imamate within the matrix of actual political circumstances rather than the earlier works, including his own, which were written in the Persian genre of "Mirrors for Princes" which tended to be more academic rather than practical. *Aḥkām* is therefore said to be the definitive authority on political theory not only in respect of the Imamate but also *fiqh* matters governing public and constitutional law.

It should be borne in mind that the advent of the Abbasid caliphate ushered in a fresh set of political circumstances that soon warranted a reassessment of the position and role of the Imamate for the purpose of legitimization set on by the fact that eventually the caliphal authority of the Abbasid started to dissipate. This disintegration began as early as the late 2nd/8th century when the Abbasid leaders began to lose their grip on the different states across the empire and autonomous dynasties started springing up from Spain and Morocco right across to Persia so that by the 4th/10th century the authority of the Abbasid caliph hardly extended beyond Baghdad, and even there the caliph himself was powerless to manage his own affairs.[10] What happened and what were the causes of this break-up are worth looking into but for our purposes suffice it to say that after the initial rise and accumulation of power by the caliphs, eventually their failure or neglect to fortify their positions with military capabilities led to a decline in authority and saw the emergence of provincial war lords. Backed by their powerful armies,[11] they wasted no time in asserting their spheres of dominance by carving out their own territories to rule as independent heads or *amīrs* such as the Shī'ī Būyid al-Mustakfī who captured Baghdad in 334/945, and established the Būyid dynastic rule over Iraq and certain adjacent provinces for more than a century. Thenceforth, a new epoch in Islamic history unfolded when almost all of the temporal authority of the caliphs moved into the hands of a Shī'ī dynasty.

What then was the role, if any, of the caliph after taking into account the overriding authority of the sultans? The Būyids, however, were not reckless in their statecraft. While the caliphate was entirely subordinated to the powerful and independent dynasty and almost all state affairs came under its control,[12] the Sunni caliph was retained as a symbol of religious and political unity. He still possessed vestigial temporal authority in respect of the appointment of *qāḍīs* and *imāms* of mosques[13] but for all intents and purposes the supreme ruler was a Shī'ite. This created a rather diabolical situation as yet unprecedented with a Sunni caliphate being dominated by Shī'ite powers that be. Working under this anomaly within the structure of Islamic government required political adroitness, a penchant for diplomacy as well as a profound familiarity with the ways of the world. The fact that al-Māwardī', being a Shāfi'ī *'ālim*, was able to hold on to his *madhhab* even as he was constantly advising his Būyid overlords therefore speaks volumes about both his extraordinary abilities as a *faqīh* and scholar as well as his role as a diplomat. But too much might be read into the work as if it were a definitive treatise of political philosophy whereas there is in fact not much theory in that regard. After all, he was not writing political theory but elucidating rules of *fiqh* embodying competing and conflicting values with many assertions being hide-bound by the *taqlīd* to the Shāfi'ī *madhhab*.[14]

And that is because it was not intended to be a book on political theory *per se* as there are other works written by him dealing with politics and government such as *Adab al-Dunyā wa al-Dīn* (A Primer on Worldly and Spiritual Conduct), *Kitāb Naṣīḥah al-Mulūk* (Advice to Kings) and *Qawānīn al-Wazārah* (Laws of the Ministry) or its variant known as *Kitāb al-Wizārah* or *Adab al-Wazīr* which as the titles suggest deal with governance. While these three treatises were essentially guides written in the "Mirror for Princes" tradition, it is significant that his less publicised work *Tashīl al-Naẓar wa Ta'jīl al-Ẓafar* (Facilitating Administration and Accelerating Victory) manifests a different side of his political thinking which warrants a review of the conventional understanding of al-Māwardī.[15] It is said that Plato composed *The Laws* to serve as a preamble that explains the aims of the legislation and "the reasons why its enactments are what they are and why the transgressions are what they are"[16] which would explain the need for *Tashīl al-Naẓar*. It is contended that this treatise manifests the philosophical side of al-Māwardī seldom presented in the discourse on statecraft which tends to lean towards the legalistic aspects of governance where *Aḥkām* tends to eclipse his other works. In *Tashīl al-Naẓar*, al-Māwardī is in no hurry to discuss the nuts and bolts of government but chooses instead to cover the ethical groundwork of sovereignty of man over man. This showcases al-Māwardī as political philosopher expounding an ethical doctrine towards securing not just an efficient government but one that is morally justifiable. It is significant that al-Mawārdī leans on the side of kingship (*mulk*) rather than imamate (*imāmiyyah*) or sultanate (*sulṭāniyyah*) signifying the Persian cultural-ethical antecedents of his exposition on the categorizations and origins of ethical foundations of kingship and the process of the acquisition of sovereignty. Nevertheless, to get a better perspective of al-Māwardī's political philosophy, a brief excursion to his initial doctrine on statecraft for kings as can be gleaned from *Naṣīḥah al-Mulūk* is in order.

This tractate, which posits a theory on the formation and disintegration of a state, was addressed to the Būyid *amīr* Jalāl al-Dawlah who, coming from the line of Būyids, was not averse to claiming the title of *mālik*, the Arabic cognate to the Persian Shah. One could put it down to sycophancy as the motive for al-Māwardī's writing this primer (as some commentators tend to) but we should take his word for it instead and in his own terms, it was a religious obligation (pursuant to the Qur'ānic commandment to the *'ulamā'* to obey their commander) on his part to advise the king on how best to govern his subjects. The paramount consideration was justice and happiness.[17]

One fact that should not be glossed over was that al-Māwardī was a Shāfi'īte but there was nothing hypocritical about his advising a Shī'ī leader. In today's Muslim world, however, it would be inconceivable to have a Sunni *'ālim* taking on the official duty of advisor to a Shī'ī leader but al-Māwardī did not see anything fundamentally wrong with that. It was the duty of every Muslim, particularly from the *'ulamā'* (and this point would be reiterated later by Imām al-Ghazālī) to advise the sovereign for the belief was that his righteousness in character and soundness in governance would determine the fate of his subjects or his *ummah.* [18] According to al-Māwardī, obedience to the sovereign is founded on the doctrine of man's position in a divinely ordained hierarchy where God "raised some among them above others in ranks that some of them may serve others."[19] Needless to say, the king occupies the highest rank as he is His shadow on earth and while he is the shepherd the subjects will be his flock. Or to vary the metaphor, the sovereign is the head while the people are the organs with society being the corpus which cannot survive without the head which in turn must be kept alive and well by the organs. His rule is therefore absolute for who are we to dispute what has been written in the scripture?[20] While that would secure integration, the reverse would naturally be a sure-fire formula for disintegration which was inevitable on account of *fasād al-dawlah* (state corruption) brought on by power struggle in which case it would be art imitating reality or theory reflecting practice.[21] Indeed, the internecine conflict within the Būyid dynasty was tearing it apart and, treading on eggshells, al-Māwardī had to get the message across while attempting his best to evade getting into the crossfire. Avoiding any reference to the pink camel in the tent, he launched into the lessons of history about how the Islamic polity of the early years fell apart at the seams on account of the conflict over succession upon the demise of the Prophet. Al-Māwardī then attacked the corruption attendant on the practice of hereditary rule where kingship was passed on to sons and relatives purely on account of blood ties. In *Naṣīḥah al-Mulūk*, the criticism was directed only towards the pre-Abbasid caliphate and particular care was taken to avoid ascription of any error, fault or blemish to the Būyid rulers, who, as is well known, were no strangers to the practice of nepotism but, as we shall see later in *Tashīl al-Naẓar*, he upped the ante, as it were, by taking a more critical approach towards the Abbasids. Al-Māwardī also referred to the perpetual sectarian conflict between the Sunnis and the Shīʿites which often flared into bloodshed as contributing to state decay. Another factor is the circle of sycophants—court jesters of all persuasions such as the viziers and the scribes—whose chief mission, in return for material gain and advancement in office, was to satisfy the king's worldly desires and to feed his ego and ensure that men of piety and religiosity be kept out of the circle.

On the management of the populace or government of the people in general (*siyāsah al-ʿāmmah*),[22] justice is the overarching consideration as ordained in the Qur'ān:

> "Be just. This is closest to being God-conscious" (*iʿdilū huwa aqrabu li al-taqwā*); "(that) whenever you judge between people, judge with justice" (*idhā ḥakamtum bayna al-nāsi an taḥkumū bi al-ʿadl*).[23]

Al-Māwardī is therefore extracting a principle that will find its recompense in the hereafter on to a temporal setting—that the ebb and flow of societies is dependent on the existence of a just sphere. Therefore, justice must dominate all aspects of life, a fortiori, the life of the subjects (*al-raʿiyyah*). Tyranny would spell destruction and a despotic king rules not over his *ummah* except one that is in ruins.

The attainment of justice, however, was preconditioned on four basic prerequisites: absolute fidelity of the subjects, pledge not to revolt, sincere support, and respect for their king.[24] Reciprocal obligations on the part of the sovereign include defending the *dīn* against *bidʿah*, eradicating the *ummah* of vices such as wine-drinking and gambling and other forms of immorality, and protecting their security and prosperity. There was also an unstated fifth precondition which could be extrapolated from al-Māwardī's doctrine of societal stratification, as mentioned earlier, again purportedly on textual evidence: "... and raised some of them by degrees above others ..." (*wa rafaʿnā baʿḍahum fawqa baʿdin darajāt*) and this refrain is repeated in various other verses.[25] It is understandable why these verses have been interpreted by al-Māwardī to signify inherent inequality of status of humanity. This is needed to lend scriptural foundation for his societal stratification paradigm which in turn was not an unrealistic representation of the reality of Baghdad society as it was then. Under the reign of the Būyids, the Baghdad community was divided into three social classes: first, the royalty and aristocracy, then bourgeoisie and landowning class and finally, the populace.[26] Not unlike other socially stratified societies, the wealth and economic differences were so stark and woven into the social fabric that these classes continued in their distinct categories for ages regardless of who the rulers were. Needless to say, while the masses would be content to just make ends meet if not preoccupied with the struggle against hunger and poverty, the rich and the powerful were living the high life, awash in luxury and opulence. According to Ibn Kathīr, in 373/983 many inhabitants perished because food was priced out of the reach and "the roads were littered with the corpses of those who had died of starvation."[27] And in the midst of such disasters, hundreds of thousands of dinars were being spent to celebrate the wedding of the Būyid Prince Muliyad al-Dawlah. The point about this is that the call for justice therefore rings totally hollow in the face of such hypocrisy and double standards for the people. To attempt to justify such discrimination with supposed Qur'ānic evidence is therefore even more repugnant. The fact is that in spite of the multiplicity of interpretations from the established commentators, it is contended there is no solid basis for taking al-Māwardī's inequality position if that view is used to justify discrimination of treatment of citizens by the state as represented by the sovereign. Al-Rāzī gives it at least three layers of meaning as in differing degrees of worldly provision and goods (shared by al-Ṭabarī and al-Zamakhsharī), nobility (also al-Zamakhsharī), or intellect. In all these three semantic shades, the nexus is God's test of generosity and kindness of man towards others and of the humility and trust of those given little, to inspire them to emulate those who are nobler[28] but there is no suggestion by any that it is a basis for *siyāsah al-'āmmah* to practise a policy of discrimination. Such a policy is implicit in al-Māwardī's assertion that the sovereign should treat each person according to his social rank while the elite (*al-khāṣṣah*) should be accorded special treatment.[29] In this regard, his interpretation is not just minoritarian but *sui generis* and as a matter of academic discourse may be rejected on that score alone. Nevertheless, there is also a fundamental contradiction in the call to judge according to justice (which indeed is well founded scripturally) while advocating at the same time a socially stratified non-egalitarian society which is inherently unjust, and hence against the Qur'ān.

In *Tashīl al-Naẓar*, he continues the theorizing but there is a subtle shift in focus and emphasis and one gets the impression that he wants to lay a doctrinal foundation for kingship along a more philosophical line that, to my mind, foreshadows Hobbes' *Leviathan* and even arguably Kant's *Groundwork of the Metaphysic of Morals.*[30] I will take up this contention later but first, a run-through of the main points. What is significant is al-Māwardī's position as regards not just power politics but the very foundation of power itself. Do we expect the requisite "those in power" mantra and hence the invocation of complete obedience to authority and if so, what is the theory behind it? Or does al-Māwardī go beyond where no *faqīh*, *'ālim* or palace advisor had hitherto gone in sanctioning rebellion or, in modern parlance, regime change?

At the outset in *Tashīl al-Naẓar*, al-Māwardī bemoans the state of society and considers that on account of its multifaceted nature and the community's preponderance towards divisiveness, authority is therefore necessary. Hence, subjects must entrust their affairs collectively to their Sultan in as much as people must be compelled to live together as a community because reason (*al-'aql*) alone is incapable of uniting the masses for the attainment of justice.[31] Heralding a divine-right-of-kings paradigm, al-Māwardī posits that subjects have no inherent right to question the sovereign *qua* his acts of kingship for such a right vests only in God almighty.[32] This divine right therefore warrants absolute recognition of the king's authority to be requited by total obedience to do what is commanded and refrain from what is prohibited. There is, however, the rider that such absolute fidelity to the monarch is not unconditional in that transgression on the latter's part against the religion would nullify such a duty.[33] While the paramount importance of obedience to the king and the latter's reciprocal obligations finds some common nexus with the position asserted in *Naṣīḥah al-Mulūk*, it is clear that it is only in *Tashīl al-Naẓar* that he argues from a more foundational perspective which forms the basis of a social contract between the sovereign and the people in the sense that would be adopted by—or reflected in, shall we say less contentiously—Hobbes' *Leviathan*, that celebrated classic western opus on statecraft written six centuries after *Tashīl al-Naẓar*.

Al-Māwardī posits the divine right of kings on the authority of his interpretation of textual evidence:

> "O David! Behold, We have made thee a vicegerent on earth: judge, then, between men with justice, and do not follow vain desire, lest it lead thee astray from the path of God …"[34]

However, this term "vicegerent on earth" (*khalīfah fī al-arḍi*) has received variant interpretations and depending on the contextual paradigm has been rendered to refer to prophethood (as in the general understanding), or kingship (as in al-Māwardī's here) or even just to humanity. It is also used in its plural form *khalā'if al-arḍi* as in "He it is Who appointed you vicegerents upon the earth ..."[35] *Khalā'if* as plural for *khalīfah* is also synonymous with the usual plural *khulafā'* generally meaning "representatives" or "successors". We know that in the language of political Islam, the term *khalīfah* has attained a technical meaning referring exclusively to the titular head of a unified Islamic state. So, al-Māwardī is not stretching the contextual reference of the Prophet David unrealistically as it would appear to be at first blush when he interprets the earlier verse on David—who was king after all—to substantiate a theory of the divine right of kings. While space does not permit too long an excursion on this point, it must be said that David, or Dāwūd, is recognized in Islam as a prophet and a messenger who brought the *Zabūr* (Psalms of David) and as *khalīfah*, he was king of the Israelites. Upon his demise, his son, Solomon (Prophet Sulayman), succeeded as king and also was called to the mission of prophecy. There is, however, some controversy concerning the biblical stories attributing the transgressions of adultery and murder to David which are categorically rejected by Muslims who believe generally that the prophets are *ma'ṣūm*—infallible. And, as far as the Qur'ānic narrative is concerned, even if infallibility may not apply to all the prophets in terms of imparting the *Sharī'ah*, it offends our common sense that they—as God's chosen few—would be capable of committing such grave sins.

Coming back to the different exegesis on the term *khalīfah*, the first vicegerent appointed was Adam and, according to Nasr, in as much as Adam represents humanity as a whole, all human beings can therefore be understood to be God's vicegerents on earth. The Qur'ān also uses the term in the plural to refer to new communities that succeed older ones that have been destroyed for their wrongdoing.[36] In respect of this particular verse, commentators such as al-Ṭabarī view the term to refer primarily to the Muslim community having succeeded earlier religious communities. Al-Rāzī and al-Zamakhsharī give it a slightly broader berth to relate to generations of Muslims succeeding one another or that they have inherited the position of

God's representatives on earth. There is then again the more universal idea of human vicegerency.[37] But all these seem to be not within the contemplation of al-Māwardī in his divine-right and authoritarian doctrine which finds closer affinity with the ideas of Persian kingship. Where military power is neglected the king's rule becomes weak and becomes vulnerable to usurpation particularly if it is rule by tyranny and despotism, grounds which may justify revolution. This therefore goes beyond the traditional juristic position against regime change for al-Māwardī takes a softer line against revolt and rebels by pronouncing on its legitimacy or otherwise only *ex post facto*. If and when it happens, regime change seems to be accepted as *fait accompli*, which is not the issue but what happens after, is. If revolution is followed by tyrannical rule, that is, rule by brute force, it is unacceptable. If post-revolution rule is just with the position of the king or Imām safeguarded, it is deemed a legitimate power under the hitherto formative concept of authority by delegation.[38] This doctrine constitutes the precursor to his theory of "emirate by seizure" which as we shall see is advanced more substantively in *Aḥkām*. While the theory is quite straightforward, it nonetheless is indicative of al-Māwardī's perceptiveness of the political undercurrents fomenting within the Abbasid caliphate which eventually led to its disintegration even as he was attempting to cloak it with legitimacy—for the Būyids though and not for the Abbāsids. Still, in a manner of speaking, he rushed in where the *'ulamā'* feared to tread.

Al-Mawārdī counselled against the accumulation of excessive wealth in the hands of the king's retinue in order to discourage revolt as wealth leads to covetousness. Unreliable men and those with a penchant for material possessions should be kept away from administrative positions and the state becomes particularly susceptible to ruin "when the king becomes weak and his followers are corrupted by temporal pleasures."[39] Hence, the paramount importance of coercive power in establishing social order and security for the state. He states that the state starts with roughness and violence so that people hurry to give their obedience. Then and after establishing it on firm foundations, tenderness and righteousness are required for managing state affairs. Finally, the state ends with a diffusion of injustice and weakness.[40] In describing the rise and fall of a state, al-Māwardī says that states do not just appear overnight like mushroom. They have a genesis and by stages reach apotheosis before eventually declining and finally meeting its nadir and at every step, the force of circumstances is brought to bear. It is contended that his position on this issue does not depart significantly from that already enunciated in *Naṣīḥah al-Mulūk*.

In the latter part of the discourse, al-Māwardī deals with the art of government or the policies of governance or statecraft (*siyāsah al-mulk*). First, al-Māwardī stresses that leadership that is not based on religion can only be based on tribal lineage, that is, *'aṣabiyyah*—a concept that would be borrowed by Ibn Khaldūn three centuries later and popularized beyond recognition.[41] While it is conceded that this is *mulku qahrin* (rule of coercion) such a regime "can transform itself, through justice and good conduct of public affairs, into a rule of law thus attaining the confidence and consent of the people." This position constitutes legal endorsement of usurpation with negative implications as regards the "those in authority" doctrine.[42] Nevertheless, such a position is understandable once we factor in the prevailing political scenario that al-Māwardī was in—an Abbasid political empire that was in self-destruct mode and the emergence of local dynasties such as the Tahirids, the Salarids, the Samandis and the Ghaznavids staking out their territories of independence while notionally recognising the authority of the caliph. Elevated to the rank of *aqḍā al-quḍāh* (the most eminent judge) by the Abbasid caliph al-Qā'im bi-Amr Allāh and a political adviser, al-Māwardī was in the thick of the power politics that was being played out but, detractors notwithstanding, he did not compromise his principles.[43] While, as argued by Gibb, it might well be true that he wrote the treatise to buttress moral support for the caliphs against the Būyid princes, as an astute strategist, he had also opted for engagement rather than confrontation with the dissident groups. Theory and practice merged:

the rise of discontent and its attendant generation of causes for rebellion or regime change was the inevitable consequence of the failure of governance of the caliphate—the injustice, inefficiency and corruption within the corridors of power. The answer becomes self-evident: Where a corrupt ruling elite is deposed and replaced by one which turns out to be fair and just, what justification is there to oppose it? Furthermore, no regime can secure its prolonged existence by sheer power alone because power must be transferred to authority. Al-Māwardī is therefore killing two birds with one stone: persuading those in power to mend their errant ways while reminding usurpers of the imperatives of governing according to justice and equity.[44]

Speaking of imperatives and what I had said earlier about the al-Māwardī-Kant affinities, however remote, it is perhaps opportune to mention now that in his *Groundwork of the Metaphysic of Morals*, Immanuel Kant posits a definitive moral doctrine that would inform the ethical foundations of the modern West, paving the path for future research. Just as al-Māwardī had posited 700 years earlier in *Tashīl al-Naẓar*, the doyen of Western philosophy and the prime mover of European Enlightenment argued that concepts and principles of moral theory need not be confined to the realm of the metaphysical but are indeed normative for rational agents, *i.e.* man. In doing so, Kant laid bare the fundamental principle of morality and expounded with devastating rational force its direct application to us. While al-Māwardī's theory is doctrinally constrained by the circumstantial matrix he was working in, being intended to address the philosophical—and hence, moral—foundation of kingship, Kant's motivation, if indeed that was ever needed, was to challenge the prevailing teleological dogma of moral philosophy. In this regard, there is no doubt that Kant's opus takes on a far more universalistic dimension than al-Māwardī's. Inter alia, Kant posited the brilliant—though now rather clichéd—idea of the categorical imperative, that one must act only according to that precept which one would will to become a universal law. I say clichéd not because it has outlived its relevance—it certainly has not—but because it has been appropriated by all and sundry to provide a stamp of respectability to otherwise insubstantial arguments.

Coming back to the academic discourse, it should be noted therefore that al-Māwardī's personal position on the larger issue of why and how a legitimate central rule is to be overthrown is not expounded in *Ahkām* but in *Tashīl al-Naẓar* where, as alluded to earlier, he takes a more critical position *vis-à-vis* the Abbasid rulers. "Rulers," he says, "are like the sea out of which small rivers flow if the water of the sea is sweet, rivers will also be sweet, and if the water of the sea is salty then rivers will also become salty."[45] The ruler must therefore start by purifying and restraining himself before instructing others to do so for reform can hardly be effected by someone who himself is not in the right set up: "*ba'īdun an yaḥdutha al-ṣalaḥu 'amman laysa fīhi ṣalāh.*"[46] As alluded to earlier, al-Māwardī also talks about the inner circle and those who occupy the corridors of power who cast huge influence on the caliph referring to them as the "army of hypocrites who capitalise on the *Khalifah's* weakness towards flattery, and manage to alienate him from sincere advisers and true supporters."[47]

Now, a brief exposition on what I said earlier concerning the nexus between *Tashīl al-Naẓar* and generally al-Māwardī's doctrine of kingship on the one hand and *Leviathan* and generally Hobbes' doctrine on the other hand. In *Leviathan,*[48] Hobbes theorized on the structure of society and the legitimacy of the sovereign as government in a social contract where absolute monarchy is not only to be tolerated but argued as the best of three choices of government. Reminiscent of the introduction in *Tashīl al-Naẓar*, Hobbes wrote that civil war and the brute situation of a state of nature could only be avoided by strong undivided government. Interestingly, just as the *'ulamā'* of al-Māwardī's time were prone to attacking the *mutakallimūn*, Hobbes partook of his fair share of savaging the scholastic theologians—these were men of religion trained in the use of dialectic reasoning in similar fashion as the *mutakallimūn* were accustomed to centuries earlier with both finding their common nexus in Aristotelian syllogism. We mentioned in Chapter 3 the likes of St. Thomas Aquinas who was no doubt the greatest of the scholastics in the thirteenth century, and as far as Christian speculation is concerned, Thomistic scholasticism is supposed to have resolved the issue of the compatibility of philosophy with religion in much the same way as Ibn Rushd had much earlier resolved *falsafah* with *Sharī'ah* but we do not have sufficient space to pursue this further. Suffice it to say that detractors have tried to disassociate Averroism from scholasticism on the ground that the former purportedly was too grounded on rationalism while the latter never left its roots in faith and that Aquinas maintained that the mysteries of faith could not be proved by reason alone.

Coming back to Hobbes, he attacks various views associated with the Aristotelian method as employed by the scholastics including the issue of "incorporeal substances" which he brushes off as nonsense. The following passage is much cited:

> "Another, when men make a name of two names, whose significations are contradictory and inconsistent; as this name, an incorporeal body, or (which is all one) an incorporeal substance, and a great number more. For whensoever any affirmation is false, the two names of which it is composed, put together and made one, signify nothing at all…."[49]

As an ardent believer in materialism, Hobbes claims that the Aristotelian concept of "the human soul, separated from man, subsists by itself", is nonsensical and that scholastics like Peter Lombard and John Duns Scotus are writing like "two of the most egregious blockheads in the world".[50]

These attacks take us back to the rancourous debates in Islamic history—as we have described in Chapter 3—where the Literalists attacked the *Mutakallimūn* charging them with importing Aristotelian ideas to corrupt and confuse ordinary Muslims. Likewise, Hobbes' doctrinal offensive against the scholastics has a similar refrain: that the philosophical view is counter-intuitive, that some philosophers were out to obfuscate simple issues in order to create confusion, and that—and this is reminiscent of the charge against the Sophists—they were motivated by a desire to exploit the public for pecuniary advantage.

Coming back to *Leviathan's* affinity with *Tashīl al-Naẓar*, Hobbes posits that the state of nature of man is anarchy, one that is inherently violent and awash with fear. Given the multiplicity of human desires and the scarcity of resources to fulfil them, there is a perpetual "war of every man against every man." This state is so horrible that human beings naturally seek peace, and the best way to achieve peace is to construct the Leviathan through social contract. Who or what exactly is this Leviathan? It has, strictly speaking, nothing to do with the leviathan—sea-monster, giant whale *etc.*—of the Bible but rather, as portrayed by Hobbes in the introduction, it is an "artificial person" signifying a political entity or commonwealth that mimics the human body. Graphically, it is represented as a gigantic human form built out of the bodies of its citizens with the head representing the sovereign. We may recall the metaphor used by al-Māwardī in *Naṣīḥah al-Mulūk* in depicting the ideal state or government as one where the sovereign is the head while the people are the organs with society being the corpus. Just as al-Māwardī posits the head as absolute ruler and indispensable in maintaining peace and security, both in *Naṣīḥah al-Mulūk* and *Tashīl al-Naẓar*, Hobbes postulates that the Leviathan, as the definitive metaphor for perfect government, is absolutely necessary for the preservation of peace and the prevention of civil war and for this to be secured, the sovereign being the head must wield absolute power over the commonwealth. In his formulation of the commonwealth, however, Hobbes takes his postulations to a higher level with a more structured exposition details of which we do not have the luxury of space to dwell into.[51] What remains to be said is that regarding the three forms of government—monarchy, aristocracy and democracy—Hobbes opts for a hereditary monarchy as the best choice.[52] It must be stressed, however, that absolute monarchy notwithstanding, in Hobbes' formulation, it will be a government of civil laws either promulgated by sovereign decree or endorsed by tacit acceptance and backed by punitive sanctions.[53] Finally, one significant departure from al-Māwardī lies in the treatment of Hobbes towards the question concerning the divine right of kings and the role of religion in government.

The theory of the divine right of kings which posited the king's absolute authority in both political and spiritual matters came to the fore in England under the reign of James I of England (1603-1625). Thirteen years upon the death of James 1, the English Civil War broke out and would only officially end in 1651, two years after Charles 1 was beheaded. Upon the cessation of war, *Leviathan* was published arguing for a social contract and rule by an absolute sovereign. Is obedience to a sovereign authority consistent with obedience to a divine authority? Hobbes contends that the Kingdom of God exists wholly outside the natural world and members of the commonwealth cannot possibly subscribe to a religious authority. The only power that exists for man is sovereign power. Citing chapter and verse, Hobbes rejects the concept of eternal damnation or heavenly recompense, singling out Aristotle's philosophy of essentialism as lending credence to such a belief, albeit a rather odd strategy considering his antipathy towards the Aristotelian method. He concludes that the proper worship of God lies in obedience to civil laws.

Coming back to al-Māwardī, the concept of *imārah al-istīlā'* (emirate by seizure) as expounded in *Ahkām*[54] is not to be confused with a *coup d'état* against "those in authority". In that treatise, he was in fact referring to the phenomenon of territories or regions asserting their autonomy by formally "breaking away" from the central authority. In today's parlance, these movements would be branded "secessionist". It is these unilateral acts of secession that al-Māwardī, after taking into account the history of Islam, concedes as acceptable on condition that the new Imām fulfils seven conditions: First, justice, together with all its conditions; second, knowledge which equips them for *ijtihād* in unforeseen matters and for arriving at relevant judgements; third, good health in their faculties of hearing, sight and speech such that they may arrive at a sound assessment of whatever they perceive; fourth, sound in limb, free of any deficiency which might prevent them from normal movement; fifth, a judgement capable of organising the people and managing the offices of administration; sixth, courage and bravery enabling them to defend the territory of Islam and to mount *jiḥād* against the enemy; and seventh, of the family of the Quraysh, because of the text (of a *ḥadīth*) on the matter and by virtue of *ijmā'*.[55]

Niẓām Al-Mulk

As alluded to earlier, it is rather ironic that the clash between caliphal supremacy and religious sanctity and independence arose not so much from *Sharī'ah* or *fiqh* matters as from *kalām*, as we may recall in our discussion earlier on the Mu'tazilī doctrine and the *Miḥnah* instituted under Caliph al-Ma'mūn and continued by his successors. The *Miḥnah* was finally lifted after the powers that be realised that more benefit could be derived from relying on the *'ulamā'* than on the middle-level Caesars and for the next one hundred years the Sunni *'ulamā'* flourished until the Buyīds took over command of Baghdad and all but eclipsed their role with their brand of Shī'ism. But this was short-lived for by 396/1055, the Saljūqs under Tughril Beg Muhammad (d. 455/1063) wrested the control of Baghdad and they too came to realize that their power could be greatly enhanced by the support of the *'ulamā'*. This was the period of the Niẓām al-Mulk, (d. 485/1092) vizier to the Saljūq sultans Alp Arslan (d. 465/1072) and Mālik Shāh (d. 485/1092), prime minister extraordinaire under whose patronage al-Ghazālī gained prominence. Niẓām al-Mulk wrote *Siyāsat Nāmeh* which is Persian for Book of Government. It was also known as *Siyar al-Mulūk* which is Arabic for The Lives of Kings, scripted in the "Mirror for Princes" tradition much like al-Māwardī's earlier works. After al-Māwardī's *Aḥkām*, *Siyāsat Nāmeh* would count as one of the earliest treatises on constitutional law and government albeit focusing on the monarchical constitution of the Saljūq Empire. But as far as doctrine is concerned, it would have nothing substantive to offer that is not already expounded in the earlier works particularly al-Māwardī's *Naṣīḥat al-Mulūk, Tashīl al-Naẓar* and *Aḥkām.* However, there is greater stress on justice, protection of the weak and the marginalized and the need to give everyone his due. According to the Niẓām al-Mulk, the essential function of the King is to bring order out of chaos and to maintain peace and justice. The ultimate object to which the King must direct his efforts is to create and maintain wholesome conditions so that the people may live with comfort under the shadow of his justice. That of course was the theoretical side of the discourse but he had at the same time a more practical agenda to advance considering the power politics surrounding the caliph whose policy it was his to influence and in many instances to dictate. Just as al-Māwardī had done so with respect to the caliphs, the Niẓām here counselled the Sultans on a wide spectrum of matters including against what in modern parlance would be the hazards of cronyism—irresponsible influence of personal friends on state affairs. To minimise the threat of insurgency as well as to gain the upper hand in palace intrigue, he also urged greater use of secret agents.[56]

He presided over the Saljūq Empire for over three decades and translating ideals into reality, he established lasting structures of governance and administration. Under his rule, Persia and Babylonia regained their past prosperity while his fame was no doubt primarily due to his patronage of the *ʿulamāʾ*. He also founded *madrasahs* throughout from Nishapur to Baghdad which became known as *Niẓāmiyyah.* In 484/1091, Niẓām al-Mulk appointed al-Ghazālī to head the *madrasah* in Baghdad after his initial stint at Nishapur. The upshot of the Niẓām's skilful manoeuvring was a medieval strategic alliance between the rulers and the *ʿulamāʾ*, symbiotic in nature but more apparent than real: both parties believed they were getting the most out from the other without having to give anything in return. On the part of the *ʿulamāʾ*, their side of the bargain was to extol the virtues of the political masters and sacralise their role as keepers of the faith. In return, the powers that be gave due recognition to the force and influence of the *Sharīʿah* wielded by the *ʿulamāʾ* in governing societal structure. In this way, the fabric of the *ummah* as a distinct Islamic society remained intact amid the political convulsions of the next few centuries.[57]

In reality, however, what was the state of the *Sharī'ah* as law? Again, according to his *Siyāsat Nāmeh*, the law was in a state of flux, if not altogether chaotic. He warned against delegating *mamlūk*s (slaves) to adjudicate trials and disputes as this naturally opened the floodgates for abuse of power and corruption. This practice was really an extension of the custom of Turkish princes delegating the administration of law to bureaucrats handpicked by them but the Niẓām himself could not exonerate even the properly trained judges of an inclination to abuse their office. He also cautioned against the rise of a ballooning bureaucracy.[58] This was aimed at taking the institution of the sultanate out of the shadow of caliphal authority which by the eleventh century was already starting to dissipate on account of the increasingly independent posturing of the Saljūq rulers. This treatise was essentially intended to justify institutionalising power under a fair and just ruler guided by religion and the principles of good governance.[59] As against the caliph who represented authority in religion, the sultan was to symbolise the institution of religion itself whose authority was sanctified by divine decree. The Niẓām procured the support and endorsement of Imām al-Ḥaramayn al-Juwaynī and al-Ghazālī with respect to the principles expounded in his *Siyāsat Nāmeh*, ensuring at the same time that they graced his *madrasah*s as principals.

Al-Juwaynī

On the legality of rebellion, al-Juwaynī says that as a general rule, the *ūlī al-amri* must be obeyed while the duty of the individuals among the laity of enjoining good and forbidding evil can still be fulfilled on condition that it does not entail the use of force or that it may lead to violence and *fitan* (plural of *fitnah*—civil strife).[60] The duty, however, only applies to grave sins or matters not involving questions of *fiqh*. In other words, one cannot wage war against the ruler on account of disputations over matters of law. Armed rebellions by individuals or small groups may not be tolerated because it only leads to the spread of violence and lawlessness. Consequently, al-Juwaynī counsels that people should conscientiously weigh the pros and cons of rebellion against the benefits and harm of obeying an unjust ruler. He asserts that in most cases the harm of rebellion outweighs the benefits because it leads to bloodshed and other calamities. The status quo should be maintained where there is only a supposition that greater good may be derived from rebellion. What is certain is that there will be violence and harm inflicted and conjecture cannot displace certainty. Anticipating the argument that it is improper to resort to a balancing of evils in matters of principle as in the case of ʿAlī in his decision to fight Muʿāwiyah without regard to the possible outcomes, al-Juwaynī refutes it by claiming that many Companions in fact did just that—when they refused to rally behind ʿAlī specifically because of the greater harm that might result. ʿAlī himself had not foreseen the extent of the consequential destruction but once it became clear to him, ʿAlī regretted fighting, and sought peace through arbitration.[61] According to al-Juwaynī, ʿAlī's sons, al-Ḥusayn and al-Ḥasan, that is, the Prophet's grandsons, pledged their allegiance to Muʿāwiyah because that was the right thing to do—if a person of considerable strength takes power, it becomes obligatory to obey him. Even a usurper who is *fāsiq* and unjust must be recognized, not as a rightful *imām* but as a *de facto* leader. According to al-Juwaynī's formulations, the prohibition against rebellion and the recognition of a usurper are therefore relative concepts that must be measured against the criterion of necessity to maintain peace and order versus the necessity to maintain rule by a just and morally upright leader. Giving recognition to a successful usurper *ex post facto* is giving recognition to the fruits of rebellion. Thus, where an uprising against an established ruler leads to territorial control as well, acts and adjudications subsequent thereto must also be recognised. Any act or attempt at reversing the status quo would be detrimental to the people and would undermine law and order. It should be remembered that the general prohibition against rebellion has so far been directed against the laity. According to al-Juwaynī, the Qur'ānic injunction to enjoin good and forbid evil takes on a higher degree of priority for a man of piety. If such a person were to rebel in order to uphold the best interests of the *ummah* while possessing enough power to guarantee a fair chance of success, then it is legal for him to do so and "may God aid him to victory."[62] The same principle is enunciated in his *Kitāb al-Irshād* where he contends that the *ahl al-ḥall wa al-ʿaqd*, as alluded to earlier, may rise up and wage war against an unjust and *fāsiq* ruler.[63]

Al-Ghazālī

Al-Ghazālī deals extensively, though not necessarily comprehensively, on the subject of enjoining right and forbidding evil and there is no question that he holds the position that forbidding wrong is an obligation established by the Qur'ān and the Sunnah, apart from consensus (*ijmā' al-ummah*) and common sense (*ishārāt al-ʿuqūl al-salīmah*).[64] The duty is *farḍ kifāyah* (collective obligation) on the authority of the verse: "and that there might grow out of you a community who invite unto all that is good, and enjoin the doing of what is right and forbid the doing of what is wrong: and it is they, they who shall attain to a happy state!"[65] In respect of the actual process of carrying out this duty which al-Ghazālī calls the *nafs al-iḥtisāb*, eight levels (*darajāt*) of performance are spelt out—seeking information (*taʿarruf*), informing (*taʿrīf*), *vis-à-vis* those in authority, exhortation (*waʿẓ, nuṣḥ, takhwīf bi Allāh*), harsh language (*al-sabb wa al-taʿnīf bi al-qawl al-ghalīẓ al-khashin*), physical action (*al-taghyīr bi al-yad*), the threat of violence (*al-tahdīd wa al-takhwīf*), actual violence (*mubāsharah al-ḍarb*), and finally, armed helpers, that is, gathering assistance from those who may be armed in order to enforce the principle. In this matter, there is dispute whether this requires the ruler's consent with one view saying that subjects cannot perform this because it might lead to civil strife and anarchy (*taḥrīk al-fitan wa hayajān al-fasād wa kharāb al-bilād*) and another position maintaining that if the lower levels are permissible, then the matter must be allowed to take its logical course including the formation of armed bands (*tajnīd al-junūd*).[66]

The levels of action as spelt out above are constrained by two major impediments. Firstly, at each level there are pre-conditions and secondly, and more significantly, they do not apply in relation to the rulers save only the first two levels (informing and exhorting). So, in his fourth and final chapter, al-Ghazālī goes one step further than al-Juwaynī in disallowing even speech in enjoining good and forbidding evil if doing so would result in *fitnah* and the spread of strife. Harsh language—expressions such as "You tyrant (*ẓālim*)! You who have no fear of God!"—is not permitted if its use brings harm to others. However, if one fears only for oneself it is permitted, and indeed commendable (*mandūb*). Al-Ghazālī relates that the early Muslims would expose themselves to such risks in the full knowledge that death in such a case was martyrdom. He then quotes a series of seventeen anecdotes to illustrate their courage and plain speaking.[67] It is noteworthy that al-Ghazālī places a heavier obligation on the *'ulamā'* particularly the *fuqahā'* as regards the duty to enjoin good and forbid evil, an obligation that must be discharged even at the cost of persecution or harm. While the early jurists stood up to injustice and were martyred, alas, al-Ghazālī laments, the jurists of his time are silenced by greed, and instead of fearing God, they fear kings and rulers.[68] It takes more than a modicum of effort to resist the surrealistic association of such censure to our present times. Nonetheless, the view is that al-Ghazālī was not as supportive of *aḥkām al-bughāh* as other Shāfi'ī jurists and that he was non-committal on the treatment of rebels although it is also said he does not entirely discount the possibility that under certain circumstances a rebellion might be defensible. By contrast, his contemporary Aḥmad al-Qaffāl (d. 507/1113), who was the head of the Shāfi'ī jurists in Iraq and who also taught in the Niẓāmiyyah school, unequivocally endorses positions which are tolerant of rebels.[69]

Ibn Taymiyyah

A look at the Ḥanbalī position would show up the difference in approach as exemplified by one of the foremost *fuqahā'* of the school, Ibn Taymiyyah (d. 728/1328). As the leading exponent of *siyāsah al-shar'iyyah*, he advocated a proactive role for the *'ulamā'* while taking a near-fatalistic approach towards the concept of rebellion. Juxtaposed against Ibn Taymiyyah's docile acceptance of unjust rule, the Shāfi'ī jurists come off as near revolutionary advocates of rightful usurpation. In his famous tome *al-Siyāsah al-Shar'iyyah fī Iṣlāh al-Rā'ī wa al-Ra'iyyah* (The Political Rules in Assessing the Ruler and the Subjects),[70] written between 709/1309 and 714/1314, he states at the outset that the purpose of his treatise was to reform society and the state by bringing the *Sharī'ah* back to its proper place and influence. He describes it as a treatise on the general principles of divine governance (*siyāsah ilāhiyyah*) and appointment to the vicegerency of the Prophet (*al-inābah al-nubuwiyyah*) that is indispensable for the ruler and his subjects and for those in charge of affairs (*wulāh al-umūr*),[71] of which he categorises as the *'ulamā'* and the *umarā'* (rulers). At first blush, there holds out the promise of a firm juristic exposition that would appeal to our innate sense of right and wrong, and justice and freedom. He warns of the *ummah* sinking into a state of corruption (*fasād*) if and when the sultan fails on the side of the *dīn*, and those in positions of power fail to meet the dictates of true faith and the perfection of religion as ordained by the Qur'ān.

> "If they (the *'ulamā'* and the *umarā'*) are sound, the people are sound, but if they are corrupt, the people are corrupt."[72]

The *dīn* may only be established by the Book of Guidance and by "the mighty power of iron".[73]

The exercise of *ijtihād* is obligatory to seek divine intercession and succour and only then will the cause of the *dīn* be served.[74] Departing from the classical Sunni position on the strict prerequisites for the legitimate ruler, Ibn Taymiyyah sets fidelity to the *Sharī'ah* as the sole criterion and subsumed under this rubric is the ruler's observance of the injunction to enjoin good and forbid evil. Three salient aspects may be singled out. First, the caliphate is not obligatory. Secondly, there is no limit on the number of *imāms* at any one time. In other words, more than one *imām* can rule simultaneously.[75] Thirdly, the concept of election by consensus has no valid precedent for even at the outset of the caliphate, the assumption of the leadership was actually by dint of circumstances, albeit prodded by notional displays of popular support even as the caliph was either designated or imposed. What really mattered was the *mubāyaʿah*, the double oath of allegiance by which the *imām* and the community were joined.[76] The *mubāyaʿah* may be viewed as the ratification of the ruler's assumption of power in a kind of social contract defined by its end which was the common will to obey God and His Prophet binding two parties: the ruler on the one hand and the *ʿulamāʾ* as well as the *ahl al-ḥall wa al-ʿaqd,* on the other, representing the people. In theory, this symbiosis would secure effective power in perpetuity for the ruler and peace, security and constitutional protection for the people.[77]

For check and balance, Ibn Taymiyyah advocated the doctrine of *taʿāwun* which was essentially a broad-based platform for mutual cooperation between rulers and *ʿulamāʾ*.[78] The *ummah* can fulfil its obligations to God only by being united so as to harness the complementary strengths of its members.[79] There is a tinge of Machiavellian opportunism in prescribing that it is better to appoint an army commander who may be impious but strong rather than one who is pious but weak; on the other hand, in the choice of clerical or sedentary appointments, the reverse rule should apply.[80] It is incumbent on all to counsel (*naṣīhah*) the rulers[81] while enjoining good (*maṣlaḥah*) and forbidding evil (*mafsadah*) entails striking the right balance between the two, warranting at times the commission of a prohibited act in order to avoid a greater evil.[82]

So much for the expectation of a juristic doctrine that would appeal to our innate sense of right and wrong, justice and freedom for the overarching theme that runs through Ibn Taymiyyah's *al-Siyāsah* is the paramount importance of maintaining order and stability of the state as a matter of absolute public interest. Hence, the need for coercive power. Sanction is sought in a saying by 'Alī ibn Abī Ṭālib that the authority of an unjust Imām was better than anarchy and through law and order, "the legal penalties were exacted, the roads made safe, holy war carried on against enemies and *fayḍ* distributed."[83] The Qur'ānic injunction on obedience is the *sine qua non* for the wellbeing of the *ummah* and this must be read conjointly with the injunction on enjoining good and forbidding evil which cannot be actualized unless there is authority to carry out the legal penalties of the law. Failure to implement this would result in a breakdown of what would be effectively the rule of law and this would perpetuate oppression by the strong and powerful over the weak and the marginalised.[84] Ibn Taymiyyah's advocacy of obedience to the ruler reaches its apotheosis when he doubles down on the saying, "Sixty years with an unjust *imām* was better than one night without a *sulṭān*" by reminding the readers that the early ancestors including *imām* Aḥmad ibn Ḥanbal used to say "If only one of our prayers is to be answered, our prayers would be for the *sulṭān*."[85]

As alluded to earlier, unlike the stringent rules concerning fitness to rule as laid down by the Shāfi'ī jurists, as far as the Ḥanbalī jurist is concerned, the moral character of the ruler is irrelevant. Thus, even the unjust ruler legitimately demands to be obeyed as this was a right of the sultan. Needless to say, rebellion constitutes a major sin as no Muslim "ought to draw the sword against his brother because a rupture of the public peace is one of the least unforgivable sins."[86] Obedience was the first duty imposed upon the subjects by the *mubāya'ah* which obliges each person to participate actively in the community but there was a caveat that any act of endangerment to the solidarity of the community must be stopped.[87]

Before we rush to pass judgment on what appears to be excessive and slavish deference to the principle of authority, it should be remembered that Ibn Taymiyyah lived during turbulent times, caught between the external threat of the Mongols and internal threat of insurrection by dissident minorities. As a Traditionist, Ibn Taymiyyah was roped in by the Mamlūk sultan al-Malik al-Manṣūr (696/1297) to exhort the faithful to *jiḥād*. Again, during the Mongol invasion of 699/1300, he was commanded to do the same. It would be inconceivable for someone tasked by the sultan to rally the *ummah* to fight to defend his kingdom to be at the same time advocating rebellion.

As a side note, it should be mentioned that he was a robust defender of his faith and his creed. In Cairo, manifesting typically literalist and anti-rationalist positions, he railed against Sufi practitioners accusing them of antinomianism and condemned as heretics, the Rawāfiḍ and others. Fitting the bill as an ardent Ḥanbalī literalist and the precursor to the rise of modern fundamentalism and its characteristic intolerance for other Muslims who take different positions, he was himself accused of anthropomorphism and imprisoned in Cairo. Incarceration, however, appears to have made no difference for he was soon imprisoned again for his virulent attacks against *bidʿah* practices labelling the practitioners as *kuffār*. [88]

Conclusion

It is tempting to dismiss the foregoing discourse as being purely academic because we are now in the 21st century and the paradigm of the ruler and subjects is outmoded and is not reflective of the reality of the times. Rebellions, uprisings and even revolutions in the Muslim countries have happened and, it is contended, the arguments for and against such phenomena are seldom if at all made and if made are hardly taken seriously. Indeed, taking such a position is tempting but the fact is that even in the context of contemporary history, the command to obey "those in authority" is habitually invoked by autocratic rulers, tyrants and dictators to demand obedience and loyalty from their Muslim subjects or citizens. Sham democracies in Muslim-majority countries are particularly prone to using this doctrine as part of their propagandistic effort to cloak their governments with divine sanction and impress upon the people that it is therefore a religious obligation to pledge undivided and absolute loyalty to the government of the day. It is often cited by state-appointed and state-sponsored *ʻulamā'* as a basis for issuing *fatāwā* condemning citizens who resort to street demonstrations or activities of civil disobedience as part of a collective effort to force leaders to give up power. This was particularly evident during the Arab Spring and in the case of Egypt, it was used aggressively to buttress the military coup of a democratically elected government by the use of perverted logic employing both doctrines—that the existing democratically elected government was taking the nation down the path to economic and social ruin (hence, the need for the new regime under military rule) and that the newly installed sham democracy must now be obeyed on account of the imperatives of the Qur'ān and the Sunnah. Now, it is acknowledged that obedience to a democratically elected government is a principle of citizenship recognised as fundamental in all civilised communities whether under an Islamic or a secular state. However, the connotation that comes with the requirement for obedience takes on an entirely different hue in this regard. In states where there is a clear separation of church and state such as the United States of America or the established democracies in Europe, and in Asia such as Japan and India, obedience is pledged to the State as a sovereign nation with a supreme constitution and inter alia the oath of allegiance includes an undertaking to respect the laws of the nation. There is no such thing as a pledge to obey the government of the day if by that is meant the leaders and the ruling political elite who should therefore not be criticised let alone be toppled. Such a pledge would not only be unconstitutional but blatantly unrealistic. The question of "toppling" or "rebelling" against the government is therefore anachronistic and irrelevant in communities where the rule of law is institutionalised and the political system is one that is based on constitutional democracy. In such a system, due electoral processes are also institutionalised to allow for democratic change of government. Whether such a process is, in the doctrinal sense, applicable in an

Islamic state is indeed a point that has to be debated (in another forum) if we hold on to the view that the *Sharī'ah* (with regard to the doctrines on obedience and rebellion including the *aḥkām al-bughāh*) as formulated by the traditional jurists is still relevant. According to Asad, in the context of an Islamic State, the duty to obey those in authority remains a duty only as long as the government does not legalise actions forbidden by the *Sharī'ah* or forbid actions which are enjoined by it in which case "obedience to the government ceases to be binding on the community."[89] This position, Asad asserts, is clearly stated by the Prophet as in the following *ḥadīth* by al-Bukhārī and Muslim on the authority of Ibn 'Umar:

> "Hearing and obeying is binding on a Muslim whether he likes or dislikes the order—so long as he is not ordered to commit a sin, but if he is ordered to commit a sin, then there is no hearing and obeying."

The community's allegiance to those in authority is conditional upon those in authority acting in obedience to God and His Apostle which indeed is central to the interpretation of the *āyah* in Sūrah al-Nisā', which bears repeating:

> "O you who have believed, obey Allah and obey the Messenger and *those in authority* among you ..."

In other words, the command cannot be taken out of context as the imperatives must be read conjunctively. Taken to its logical conclusion, and in the context of an Islamic State, a government rules only by the people's consent—as manifested by way of truly democratic elections—which means that the *ummah* is duty bound to supervise the activities of the powers that be and to withdraw its consent whenever the government deviates from the path of good conduct.[90]

Notes

1. Bernard G. Weiss, *The Spirit of Islamic Law*, (Athens and London: The University of Georgia Press, 1998), 113-115.
2. Thomas. W. Arnold, *The Caliphate*, (Oxford 1924), 29; also reissued T. W. Arnold, *The Caliphate*, (London: Routledge and Kegan Paul, 1965) with an additional chapter by Sylvia G. Haim.
3. Sūrah al-Nisā', *āyah* 59.
4. Ovamir Anjum, *Politics, Law, and Community in Islamic Thought: The Taymiyyan Moment*, (Cambridge University Press, 2012), 52.
5. For a fuller treatment of the subject see Khaled Abou El Fadl, *Rebellion and Violence in Islamic Law*, (Cambridge University Press, 2006), a systematic exposition of the subject of political resistance and rebellion according to the classical *Sharī'ah* texts.
6. Ibid., 164.
7. Ibid.
8. Abū al-Ḥasan 'Alī Ibn Muḥammad Ibn Habīb al-Māwardī (450/1058) served under the Abbasid caliphs al-Qā'im and al-Qādir and, not surprisingly, branded a Mu'tazilī adherent as most officials serving under them were. For a critical study of his political works, see Aḥmad Mubārak al-Baghdādī, "The Political Thought of Abū al-Ḥasan al-Māwardī," PhD thesis, the University of Edinburgh, 1981.
9. D. May, "Al-Māwardī's *al-Aḥkām al-Sulṭāniyyah*," PhD thesis, Indiana University, 1978, 67.
10. W. M. Watt, *Islamic Political Thought*, (Edinburgh University Press, 1968), 99; Baghdādi, 11-13.
11. Watt, *The Formative Period of Islamic Thought*, 254.
12. Arnold, *The Caliphate*, 57-60.
13. H. Siddiqī, "Caliphate and Kingship in Medieval Persia," I. C., (1936), 118-121; Baghdādī, 14.
14. El Fadl, *Rebellion and Violence in Islamic Law*, 180.
15. *Tashīl al-Naẓar wa Ta'jīl al-Ẓafar* (Facilitating Administration

and Accelerating Victory) collected and edited by Muhyi al-Din al-Hilal al-Sarhan, (Beirut: Darul al-Nahda al-Arabiyya, 1981); Eltigani Abdulqadir Hamid, "Al-Māwardī's Theory of State: Some Ignored Dimensions," *The American Journal of Islamic Social Sciences* 18, 4 (2001), 2-4; al-Baghdādī, *Political Thought of al-Māwardī*, 77-90.

16. Alfred Edward Taylor, *Plato: The Man and His Work*, (New York: Meridian Books, 1956), 464 as cited by Hamid, ibid., 5.
17. Al-Baghdādī, *Political Thought of al-Māwardī*, 62.
18. Al-Māwardī, *Naṣīḥah*, fol. 4a; al-Baghdādī, 62.
19. Sūrah XLIII, 32; al-Māwardī, *Naṣīḥah*, fol. 9a.
20. *Naṣīḥah*, 9a.
21. Ibid., 10-11; Baghdādī, 65.
22. *Naṣīḥah*, 57 ff; al-Baghdādī, 70-71.
23. Respectively, al-Māidah, *āyah* 8; al-Nisā', *āyah* 58.
24. *Naṣīḥah*, 58-69; al-Baghdādī, 72.
25. Al-Zukhruf, *āyah* 32; Sūrah al-'Āmm, *āyah* 165.
26. al-Baghdādī, 19, citations omitted.
27. Ibn Kathīr, *Bidāyah*, v. 11, 302; al-Baghdādī, 20.
28. Nasr, et al, *Study Quran*. Kindle Locations 19876-19893.
29. *Naṣīḥah*, 45ff; al-Baghdādī, 72-73.
30. *Grundlegung zur Metaphysik der Sitten*, (Hartnoch, 1785), reprographic reprint (Harald Fischer, 1984); also one edited by Timmermann, (Vandenhoeck & Ruprecht, 2004); *Groundwork of the Metaphysic of Morals*, translated by Thomas K. Abbott revised by Lara Denis, (Broadview, 2005); See also Jens Timmermann, *Kant's Groundwork of the Metaphysics of Morals: A Commentary*, (Cambridge University Press, 2007).
31. *Tashīl*, 2, 3, 31a.
32. Ibid., 30b.
33. Ibid., 31-32.
34. Sūrah Ṣād, *āyah* 26.

35. Sūrah al-An'ām, *āyah* 165; Nasr, *Study Quran*.
36. On Adam, see Sūrah al-Baqarah, *āyah* 30; also Sūrah al-A'rāf, *āyah*s 74, 129 where the term used is *khulafā'* and *yastakhlifakum* respectively, the latter meaning "make you vicegerents"; also Sūrah Yūnus, *āyah*s 14 and 73 which refer to *khalā'if*.
37. Nasr, et al, *Study Quran*. Kindle Locations 19876-19893; 19872-19876.
38. al-Māwardī, *Tashīl*, 31-32; 32b.
39. Ibid., fol. 33a; Baghdādī, 77.
40. Ibid.
41. Hamid, "Al-Māwardī's Theory of State," *op. cit.*, 8.
42. Ibid., citing E. I. J. Rosenthal, *Political Though in Medieval Islam*, (Cambridge: Cambridge University Press, 1962) 33.
43. In this regard, unless my reading is completely off the mark, Baghdādī, in spite of the generally favourable tone of his analysis in his PhD thesis, harbours a certain cynicism towards al-Māwardī particularly in respect of his dealings with the powers that be.
44. Hamid, *op. cit.* Ibid. This is, however, not a faithful paraphrasing of Hamid's view and the variant interpretation—if incorrect—may be attributed to my own misreading or bias.
45. *Tashīl,* op cit., 45; Hamid, *op. cit.*, 9.
46. *Tashīl*, 47; Hamid, *op. cit.*, 9
47. *Tashīl*, 55; Hamid, *op. cit.*, 9
48. Full title: *Leviathan* or *The Matter, Forme and Power of a Common Wealth Ecclesiasticall and Civil* by Thomas Hobbes (d. 1679), published in 1651 (revised Latin edition 1668).
49. Thomas Hobbes, 1655, *De Corpore*, chapter 1, 4.20 in A.P. Martinich (trans.), Part I of *De Corpore*, (New York: Abaris Books, 1981).
50. Hobbes, *Leviathan*, in E. Curley (ed.), *Leviathan*, with selected variants from the Latin edition of 1668, Indianapolis: Hackett,

1994.

51. See *Leviathan* II 17.
52. *Leviathan* II 19.
53. *Leviathan* II 26.
54. Beirut: Dār al-Kutub n.d. 39-40.; translated by Asadullah Yate as *Principles of Islamic Governance*, (Ta-Ha Publishers, 1996), 10-11.
55. Ibid.
56. Carl Brockelmann, *Geschichte der islamischen Völker und Staaten* (Mu̇nchen, Berlin, R. Oldenbourg, 1939) translated by Joel Carmichael and Moshe Perlmami as *History of the Islamic Peoples*, (G. P. Putnam's Sons, New York, 1947), 177.
57. Watt, *Islamic Political Thought*, 73-77.
58. Brockelmann, *History of the Islamic Peoples*, 177.
59. M. A. Faksh, "Theories of State in Islamic Political Thought," *Arab Journal of Social Sciences*, (1987), 4.
60. El Faḍl, *Rebellion and Violence in Islamic Law*, 180-181; for this book's treatment of al-Māwardī's position, see 162-179; al-Juwaynī, *Kitāb*, 312.
61. Faḍl, 181-2; al-Juwaynī, *Ghiyāth al-Umam*, 109-115.
62. Faḍl, 182; al-Juwaynī, *Ghiyāth*, 326-7, 374, 115.
63. Faḍl, 182; al-Juwaynī, *Kitāb*,312
64. *Iḥyā' 'Ulūm al-Dīn* II: 280-326; Michael Cook, *Commanding Right and Forbidding Wrong in Islamic Thought*, (Cambridge University Press, 2000), 427-8.
65. Sūrah Āl ʿImrān, *āyah* 104: "*Wal takun minkum ummatun yadʿūna ilā al-khayri ya'murūna bi al-maʿrūfi wa yanhawna ʿan al-munkar wa ulāika hum al-mufliḥūn.*"
66. Cook, *op. cit.*, 438-441.
67. Ibid., 446.
68. Faḍl, 181, n. 65; al-Ghazālī, *Ihyā'*, II: 243, 357.
69. Faḍl, 186-189.
70. Ibn Taymiyyah, *al-Siyāsah*, 169-172.

71. Lambton, *State and Government in Medieval Islam*, 144.
72. Ibn Taymiyyah, *al-Ḥisbah fī al-Islām*, Cairo, 1318/1900-1,117.
73. Sūrah al-Ḥadīd, *āyah* 25: "We verily sent Our messengers with clear proofs, and revealed with them the Scripture and the Balance, that mankind may observe right measure; and He revealed iron, wherein is mighty power and (many) uses for mankind, and that Allah may know him who helpeth Him and His messengers, though unseen. Lo! Allah is Strong, Almighty."
74. Ibn Taymiyyah, *al-Siyāsah,* 169–172; Frank E. Vogel, *Islamic Law and Legal System: Studies of Saudi Arabia*, (Boston: Brill, 2000), 202.
75. Henri Laoust, *Essai sur les doctrines sociales et politiques de Taki-d-Din Ahmad b. Taimiya.* Le Caire: coll. Mélanges de philologie et d'histoire de l'IFAO, 1939, 282; also *Le Traité de droit public d'Ibn Taimiya, traduction annotée de la Siyâsa shariya*, Beyrouth, Institut français de Damas, 1948.
76. See Andrew Marsham, *Rituals of Islamic Monarchy—Accession and Succession in the First Muslim Empire,* (Edinburgh University Press, 2009); Chapter 8 on "Writing and the Bayʿa in the Marwanid Period".
77. Laoust, *Essai*, 287-8; Lambton, 147-8.
78. Laoust, *Essai*, 293-94; Vogel, 204.
79. Ibn Taymiyyah, *al-Siyāsah*, 47-48, 50–58.
80. Vogel, 204; Ibn Taymiyyah, *al-Siyāsah,* 17-19.
81. Ibn Taymiyyah, *al-Siyāsah*, 16.
82. Ibn Taymiyyah, *Risālah al-Maẓālim*, 334-36; Vogel, 204.
83. Ibn Taymiyyah, *al-Siyāsah*, 57, Lambton, 147.
84. Ibn Taymiyyah, *al-Siyāsah*, 65, 81, 138; Lambton, 145.
85. Ibn Taymiyyah, *al-Siyāsah,* 139; Lambton, 146.
86. Laoust, *Essai,*; *Le Traité,* 315; Lambton, 146.
87. Lambton, 148.
88. Ibid., 144.

89. *The Principles of State and Government in Islam,* (Kuala Lumpur: Islamic Book Trust, 1980), 34-36.
90. Ibid.

Chapter 6

Siyāsah Al-Shar'iyyah[1]

In the preceding chapters, we saw the development of *fiqh* from its earlier semantic moorings as an amorphous term of varying applications to evolve into a corpus of juristic—highly legalistic—rules and regulations derived from the primary sources via the process known as *uṣūl al-fiqh*. We saw how *fiqh* principles were eventually shaped according to the subtle differences in interpretation following the masters from which four—within the Sunni denomination—distinct *madhāhib* have developed and remained the orthodox, as it were, schools of law that define the majority of Muslims today. Indeed, there were other juristic schools most prominent of which was the *Ẓāhirī madhhab* which for various reasons, chief of which being its inherent internal and doctrinal rigidity eventually lapsed into oblivion except for academic study. There is of course the *Shī'ī* Twelvers or *Ithnā'ashariyyah* with its elaborate theology and jurisprudence.

We also considered how the *Sharī'ah* expanded and spread its wings across geographical boundaries while absorbing the various legal and juristic influences that were not anathema to its divine structure. Indeed, the history of the extension of the *Sharī'ah* as the law of the land cannot be separated from the history of the rise and ebb of caliphal dynasties and powers *vis-à-vis* the influence of the *'ulamā'*. As we have tried to show in the preceding chapter, the general rule was that in return for the bestowing of spiritual sanction of their positions as temporal rulers of the *ummāh*, the powers that be in turn recognized the religious law in theory and ostensibly abjured the right of legislation within the *Sharī'ah.* However, when the occasion warranted it, they were not averse to circumventing the *Sharī'ah* by issuing independent regulations on legal matters and instituting administrative courts of laws including matters governing the police, taxation, and criminal justice. The word here is "circumvent" and not going headlong against the *Sharī'ah.* The extra-*Sharī'ah* law-making activity was called *siyāsah al-Shar'iyyah* literally meaning policy of the *Sharī'ah.* It is into this arena that we now venture and attempt to assess its significance, if any, in shaping the *Sharī'ah.* A most pertinent point about *siyāsah al-Shar'iyyah* is the wide discretionary powers given to temporal rulers particularly in criminal law. Using this doctrine, governments may legislate on new offences not covered by the *hudūd* provisions and prescribe punishments deemed appropriate by public policy considerations as determined by the *maqāṣid al-Sharī'ah.* The *ratio legis* of such discretionary punishments is deterrence which accounts for the term "*ta'zīr*" being applied to such offences. Since the overall purpose of *ta'zīr* is to prevent conduct detrimental to the state and the *ummāh*, the state may therefore intervene even in civil cases such as the demand for blood money or *diyah* in cases of culpable homicide and assault and battery. So, in accordance with one of the *maqāṣid al-Sharī'ah* enjoining the sanctity of life, legislation may be passed to provide for punishments even if the victims or their next of kin have opted for monetary compensation.[2] As we shall see, viewed broadly, this doctrine may well be the key to unlocking the *ummah's* treasure trove in the context of law and society that is sorely needed for it to progress in the temporal world. It certainly nails the lie to the *Sharī'ah* detractors' mantra that it is desert law entrenched in an ossified legal system. The significance of the doctrine lies in the fact that there are clear historical precedents to substantiate the advocacy of extra-*Sharī'ah* jurisdictions without rendering them as deviating from the *Sharī'ah* as long as the *ratio legis* falls within the *maqāṣid.*

Siyāsah and Sharī'ah

The etymology of *siyāsah* may be traced to the classical Arabic verb meaning "to train a horse," the majestic animal evoking the symbol of effective power. For the Ottomans, the horsetail was a mark of authority, and being assigned in varying numbers would signify rank in the hierarchy with the largest and most important group of officers of the Sultan designated as "the Agas of the Imperial stirrup (in Turkish: *agāyan-i rikāb-i humāyūn*)."[3] In theory, therefore, *siyāsah al-Shar'iyyah* marked the process of law-making by those occupying the highest rung in the hierarchy of government. In medieval times, this would be none other than the caliphs or the Imāms or later the warlords who eventually took on the title of Sultans. *Siyāsah* may thus be seen as a generic label for actions of rulers relating to law.[4]

According to Coulson, *siyāsah al-Shar'iyyah* may be described as "government in accordance with the revealed law" but "*Shar'iyyah*" here goes further than its technical usage associated with traditional *fiqh* expounded in the manuals of the *madhāhib*.[5] However, it is arguable whether there is justification in ascribing it as being "in accordance with the revealed law" on account of the fact that if it were so, then there is no basis for talking about any circumvention of the *Sharī'ah*, which by logical inference means that it is by definition not in accordance with the revealed law. What is certain is that *siyāsah al-Shar'iyyah* was not a feature of the *Sharī'ah* during the time of the Prophet for whatever that the Prophet might have introduced outside the Qur'ān would become his Sunnah and hence an integral part of the *Sharī'ah* which in such a case would come under the broad definition of "revealed law." This is so notwithstanding the few and far between occasions when, according to certain Traditions, the Prophet exercised *ijtihād*, concerning which Chapter 8 will attempt to elucidate. I would therefore take the more cautious approach by describing it as law or principles of governance that are not against the *Sharī'ah* and that even as they may not be founded on any specific naṣṣ, these principles are nevertheless in accordance with the spirit of the *Sharī'ah.*

Indeed, one may be hard pressed to answer the next question: What does that really mean? What is this spirit or *rūḥ al-Sharī'ah?* How do we ascertain that what is done in the name of *siyāsah al-Shar'iyyah* is indeed in line with the spirit of the *Sharī'ah?* It is submitted that the answer lies in the Qur'ān itself:

"We have sent thee not but as a mercy for the peoples,"[6]

which captures the spirit of the *Sharī'ah* as mercy as well as being a blessing to all of mankind. Yet another manifestation of the spirit of the *Sharī'ah* lies in this short verse:

"And, behold, with every hardship comes ease."[7]

This is the spirit that must inform the *siyāsah al-Shar'iyyah*—that the purpose of the law is to bring facility, not hardship to the *ummah.* In terms of its juristic content, the entire concept of *siyāsah al-Shar'iyyah* means the law pertaining to the principles of state, public administration and other aspects of public law which may be subsumed under the rubric of political, administrative and constitutional rules.

For Ibn Taymiyyah, however, the scepticism concerning *siyāsah* being *Sharī'ah*-based is totally unwarranted. Just as there is no basis for doubting *fiqh* to be part and parcel of the *Sharī'ah,* the same applies to *siyāsah.* Ibn Taymiyyah, at least as interpreted by his protégé, Ibn al-Qayyim,[8] advances the position that *siyāsah* is also part of the divine *Sharī'ah.* Unification, and not bifurcation, of the *Sharī'ah* was the "spirit" of the earliest Muslims. In his estimation, *Sharī'ah,* properly defined, includes the principles of the *dīn,* the *siyāsah* of rulers and treasurers, the judgment of the judge, the leadership of the tribal shaykhs as well as the various policing (*ḥisbah*) authorities as they are obliged to rule by the revealed *Sharī'ah.* Those who would hold that "there is no *siyāsah* but what the *Sharī'ah* enunciates," lack knowledge of the reality of the *Sharī'ah,* and of the harmonization between it and the world of fact.[9] Both hold the position that if *Sharī'ah* is duly observed, the *siyāsah* of rulers cannot come into conflict with scholarly *fiqh*. As regards the views of the Shāfi'ī jurists (al-Māwardī and others) that rulers may legitimately depart from the *fiqh* of the *Sharī'ah* to achieve effective *siyāsah*, Ibn al-Qayyim's response falls back on the unification theme: there were no such deviations as alleged to be practised by the Prophet's companions for *siyāsah* and *fiqh* must agree and if there is an apparent conflict, it is a question of either erroneous interpretation of the *fiqh* or wilful disregard of the divine imperative by an unjust ruler in which case it is *siyāsah ẓālimah*. True *siyāsah* (*siyāsah 'ādilah*) will never deviate from the *Sharī'ah*.[10]

This legislative process pertained only to public law and it was to empower the authorities to determine the manner in which the *Sharī'ah* was to be administered as circumscribed, in theory at least, by the Qur'ān and the Sunnah. The theory was that *siyāsah al-Shar'iyyah*, properly understood, was power derived, albeit indirectly, from the *Sharī'ah* to enable legislation in areas as yet not governed by *fiqh* in detail. In reality, however, the promulgation of laws and regulations by way of *siyāsah* meant the arrogation of judicial and administrative power by the authorities who were considered to be more secular rather than *Sharī'ah* minded. The cumulative effect of *siyāsah al-Shar'iyyah* was that it eventually worked in inverse proportion to the force of the *Sharī'ah*: The more of one, the less of the other. With that, the notion of *siyāsah al-Shar'iyyah* as "governance in accordance with the *Sharī'ah*" flies out the window. In practice, the upshot of the predominance of the *siyāsah* as dictated by temporal expedience rather than religious imperatives meant that the *Sharī'ah* itself—or whatever that remained of it—lost its hold on the *ummah* in terms of its force as positive law. In due course, the *Sharī'ah* lost its status as the supreme law of the land—*lex terrae*—and virtually ceased to demand actual observance. This was because observance of the *Sharī'ah* was dependent on the state apparatus which in turn was governed by the principles of *siyāsah al-Shar'iyyah*. In the absence of uniform state sanctions against its non-observance, on account of the lack of the political will of the powers that be, the

Sharī'ah could not be effectively enforced and fell into desuetude. Of course, there were also extraneous factors such as the eventual emasculation of the powers that be under the onslaught of colonial occupiers but there is a limit beyond which arguments based on victimology hold no water.

However, it is to be noted that in the history of Islam, there was no penal sanction for the omission of most religious duties and even the commission of certain acts or practices which were clearly prohibited. Furthermore, the doctrine of *ḍarūrāt* (necessity) was often invoked so as to render permissible what would have been prohibited, and ingenious measures were devised to evade the rules of the *Sharī'ah* for certain transactions including prohibited dealings involving *ribā* (usury), *waqf* and three-time repudiation *ṭalāq* (divorce) cases through the use of casuistry known as *ḥiyal*, which are effectively legal trickery with the purpose of circumventing an established *Sharī'ah* rule. Again, the word is circumvent and not violate.[11]

In fact, the same observation may be made even today. Traditional scholars will readily warn against falling into the "Weberian trap" of the separation of theory and practice in Islamic law. As mentioned earlier, they see this doctrine as advanced by Western writers, being based on a false parallel with the development of Roman law.[12] While I do not see anything diabolical about the Weberian view, falsifiable as it may be, I believe this theory of the bifurcation between the observance of the *Sharī'ah* and the enforcement of the *siyāsah* by the State cannot be pushed too far and one is inclined to view that the extent and degree of the division is more imagined than real. For example, while it is true that there was a lack of penal sanction for the omissions and commissions, this was only so at the individual, private level. As was advanced earlier concerning the *forum externum*, when the person moves from the private domain into the public realm, failure to observe religious practices could be punishable. For instance, failure to perform the Friday congregation prayers while one is in a public place is punishable in some Muslim countries even though the law of the land is not *Sharī'ah* based. Drinking wine in public has always been a punishable *ḥaḍḍ* offence though the actual punishment to be meted out is rarely followed, being substituted instead with a pecuniary fine or short jail term in which case the punishment is *ta'zīr* and no longer *ḥaḍḍ*. These are basic examples of *siyāsah al-Shar'iyyah* indicative of the wide chasm between the *Sharī'ah* and the *siyāsah*. But a contrarian view says that if the gap had been that wide, it would be difficult to explain the existence of the office of the *qāḍi* which developed when the Umayyads came to power. At first there was no fixed body of law to be applied, so each *qāḍi* decided according to what he thought fit, following Qur'ānic rules and the Sunnah where applicable. In due course, the office of *qāḍi*, as will be elaborated later, became institutionalized and gradually, there began to appear among them some who were also jurists.[13]

Caliphal Authority in Siyāsah

According to one view, the doctrine of *siyāsah Shar'iyyah* confers extensive authority to rulers to legislate within the constitutional framework of the *Sharī'ah*, hence its variant meanings as "government," "administration" or "policy" in accordance with the *Sharī'ah*.[14] At the other end of the spectrum, it is simply the sum of sources of law where there is no text, (*mā lā naṣṣa fīh*). Ibn Taymiyyah and Ibn al-Qayyim declare that where there are no texts on a particular matter, the ruler may make laws in addition to the *Sharī'ah* for the public good *(maslaḥah 'āmmah)*, provided that the *Sharī'ah* is not infringed thereby.[15] This prohibition against legislating in violation of the *Sharī'ah* is itself subject to variant interpretations. One position imposes a blanket prohibition whenever there exists a *fiqh* ruling even if such a ruling is purely a creature of *ijtihād*. A less restrictive view only prohibits legislating on indisputable tenets (*naṣṣ qaṭ'ī*). The most liberal position prohibits only legislation that might conflict with the spirit or the *rūḥ al-Sharī'ah* or with its "principles" (*qawā'id mabādi'*).[16] What this means is that the doctrine cloaks the ruler with vast powers to act for the sake of the public good without having to fall back on textual authority or the need to justify a ruling in the manner that the *'ulamā'* were wont to do in their *fiqh* derivations. In light of this it is said that "*siyāsah Shar'iyyah* (is) the virtual inverse of *fiqh* as a law-making method."[17]

The enormity of the implication in terms of law-making by temporal powers will be easily appreciated once we allow the postulations of Ibn Taymiyyah to sink in. This is a position that confers validity to any action of a ruler that met the two primary conditions of *siyāsah Shar'iyyah*: that it does not expressly transgress the Qur'ān or an authoritative *ḥadīth* or *ijmā'* and that it is done in pursuit of the *maslahāh* (public interest). And this is not merely an academic point for his doctrines on state power have had significant influence on constitutional and administrative matters long after him, paving the way for the emergence of the wholesale legislation and implementation of *siyāsah Shar'iyyah* during the reign of the Ottomans (15th to 20th century).[18] No meaningful discourse of the *siyāsah Shar'iyyah* may be had without an in-depth objective look at the Ottomans and their singular achievement in blending the *Sharī'ah* inherited from their ancestral Seljuqs with the imperatives of *fiqh* and *siyāsah*.[19]

In the early sixteenth century, the Ottoman sultans, Selim I and Suleymān I, applied the *Sharī'ah* in a manner and to an extent that the Abbasids never did. According to Lewis, they "based the whole administration of justice on the *Sharī'ah*," made the smallest unit of their civil administration coextensive with the office of the *qaḍā'* (judiciary) and put the local chief of police answerable to the *qāḍī*. The Grand Muftī, the *muftī* of Istanbul was conferred the title of *Shaykh al-Islām* and tasked with the role as the chief enforcer of the *Sharī'ah* with full jurisdiction over the activity of the *qāḍī*s. He was therefore consulted on all important matters including whether the sultan's decrees on new laws complied with the *Sharī'ah*.[20]

These "new laws" were in fact a singular feature of the rule of the

Ottoman sultans who became actively engaged in enacting them under the rubric of *qānūns* or *qānūn-names.* It is said that notwithstanding the secular sounding labels of these laws, the sultans earnestly believed that they were legislating in the name of the *Sharī'ah* and that they neither abrogated nor contradicted the sacred Law.[21] Nevertheless, such a contention is hard to sustain considering that among the first of the significant laws decreed by Sultan Meḥemmed II (d. 885/1481) were *ta'zīr* laws of a penal nature purporting to substitute certain *ḥadd* punishments with beatings, and/or monetary fines. These were in fact *siyāsah shar'īyyah* laws enacted for the very reason that the existing *Sharī'ah* law was found to be either inadequate or unsuitable to deal with the problems at hand. While we will look deeper into the specific *siyāsah* institutions, suffice it to say at this juncture that concerning penal law, *ta'zīr* punishments were legislated to provide for castration of those convicted of enticement, hanging for certain cases of theft and house-breaking, amputation of the hands of those guilty of what would be in modern parlance commercial crimes such as forgery and counterfeiting. The use of torture to extract confessions was also sanctioned. More elaborate rules and regulations were also decreed dealing with military fiefs, the position of non-Muslim subjects, the police, land law, and, as discussed in some detail in Chapter 5, the law concerning insurrections and rebellions and also war in general. Also notable was the establishment of what would be tantamount to the "moral police" for the supervision of public morals under the jurisdiction of the *qāḍī* and enforced by the *subashi* or police chief who was answerable to the *qāḍī.* The office of the *muḥtasib* supervised trade and industry on their behalf.[22] There is no question that from the prism of a strict definition of the *Sharī'ah*, these laws were not based on the Qur'ān or the Sunnah and going by the literalist approach typical of the Ḥanbālīs would constitute *bid'ah.* Ironically, this argument is essentially neutralised by resort to none other than the chief exponents of the Ḥanbali School on *siyāsah* as outlined earlier—that these measures are completely in consonance with the *Sharī'ah.*

Furthermore, as shall be made clear below, these laws are also justified as being not only *Sharī'ah*-compliant but *Sharī'ah*-warranted as well under the imperatives of the *maqāṣid al-Sharī'ah.*

From the prism of the Ottoman powers, this was a synthesis between the opposed principles of *'ulamā'* and ruler, *fiqh* and *siyāsah*, forged on the anvil of strategic advantages for regime control and preservation. These new laws and modes of administration should not be seen as completely *sui generis* in that the Ottomans by virtue of their ancestral lineage were in a position to reap the benefits of "adapting Turkic and Mongol patterns of statecraft into new forms of *siyāsah* and from the new outlook on *siyāsah* pioneered by Ibn Taymiyyah and others after him."[23] This may be seen as rather odd considering that the Ḥanafī *madhhab*, not the Ḥanbali, was the official law of the empire. As may be recalled, historically during the early development of the *fiqh*, both these schools were at opposing ends of the spectrum. But what it really means is that the dividing lines among the four major schools were not really cast in stone and that in certain areas acceptance of the *fiqh* of another school was not seen as abjuring the main *fiqh* corpus of one's school. This is a testimony to the superiority of the legal order in the Ottoman Empire in the sixteenth century which was far more advanced than that prevailing in contemporary Europe.[24]

Since its genesis, *fiqh*—as *Sharī'ah*-derived juristic law—had over the formative years delineated its respective domains through the articulations of the leading *mujtahids* in formulating principles of law. These crystallized into the established *madhāhib* which while recognisable as distinct schools of law shared a universal feature of being independent of the *siyāsah* of the rulers. If the Ottoman synthesis was indeed so conducive to the influence of the *'ulamā'* in their juristic conceptualizations, the question is at what price—to the *fiqh*—was this synthesis achieved? There is no question that this was a ruler-driven compromise and the price or outcome of the *siyāsah* was that it "nationalized, positivized, and institutionalized *'ulamā'* law" forcing "the *'ulamā'* and society to rigid *taqlīd*, to bureaucratization and routinization of *qāḍī* function, and to ruler legislation."[25]

This was a prolonged process spanning nearly four centuries and might well have gone on even longer but for the seeds of destruction that were sown with the bestowal of such unimpaired and unhindered juristic and adjudicative power to the *'ulamā'*, particularly the *qāḍīs*. Perhaps somewhat overstated but the deleterious effects of this compromise eventually led to the collapse of the *fiqh* columns erected on the *siyāsah* paradigm of the Ottoman rulers, as triggered when the East was confronted with the West or in Huntingtonian terms when the *Sharī'ah* of Islam clashed with European-based modern jurisprudence and buckled, as will be elaborated later. Meanwhile, a closer look at some of the key *siyāsah* institutions is in order.

Siyāsah Institutions

The Qāḍī

While it is true that Ottoman rule had virtually transformed the office of *qāḍī* into a kind of judicial leviathan beholden to none but the Sulṭāns, it would be misconceived to suggest that the institution had nothing to commend itself. The reign of the Umayyads saw a paradigm change in the development of the Islamic judiciary with the institutionalisation of the office of *qāḍi*, heralding the birth of a body of judges who by their decisions laid the basic foundations of *siyāsah al-Shar'iyyah* jurisprudence as a juristic supplement to the existing *fiqh* corpus of the *Sharī'ah*. Under the Umayyads, the governmental institutions in the conquered Byzantine and Persian territories were taken over by the *qāḍīs* in administrative and judicial matters but significantly their jurisdiction extended to Muslims only while non-Muslim subjects maintained their ecclesiastical and rabbinical tribunals and other features of their traditional legal institutions.[26] Unlike the judges of the later Abbasid and Ottoman empires, these earliest *qāḍīs*, in giving their verdicts, were not averse to relying on their rā'y based on customary practice and equity as long as it did not contravene the letter and spirit of the Qur'ān or the Sunnah. In theory, *qāḍīs* were independent in giving judgements. However, being state appointees, they were beholden to the ruler and were often under the pressure of those occupying the corridors of power. Though historically the *qādīs* were generally respected as juristic experts, during the reign of the Umayyads, the *fuqaha'* were marginalised from the judiciary.[27]

As part of state policy, the Abbasids recognized the *Sharī'ah* as the only legitimate norm in Islam. In theory this meant that the *qāḍī*s were to apply nothing but Islamic law free of political interference. Alas, judicial independence was never a hallmark of the rule of the Abbasids, nor of other caliphates and Muslim governments past or present for that matter. As Abbasid rule degenerated from mere authoritarianism to absolutism, the temporal powers became increasingly reluctant to tolerate the existence of any truly independent institution. Consequently the *qāḍī*s were not only subject to dismissal at the whim of the ruler but had to depend on the political authorities for the execution of their judgments, be it in civil or criminal matters.[28]

As alluded to earlier, the early *qāḍis* too could not be said to be "seen to be independent" in cases where the state or the ruler could be a party—and that would apply to criminal cases as well as civil disputes where the ruler or the powers that be could be a litigant. To take up the post of *qāḍī* was to potentially enter into a Faustian bargain because a *qāḍī* often laboured under the Sword of Damocles—one ruling against the ruler could spell the end of one's career, or even one's life. Thus, the *qāḍī* would decide in favour of the ruler in order to enforce his will or justify his actions even if it entailed violating the law. Many prominent scholars therefore declined the position lest they fell into evil doing the ruler's bidding but unfortunately in the process, they might well be signing their death warrants.[29] The best example is that of Imām Abū Ḥanīfa who refused to accept the appointment, no doubt influenced by the belief that if upright men filled this office their principles would be compromised on the altar of obedience to the *ūlū al-amri* or the powers that be and might be compelled to bend the law to suit the will of authority. One story has the Umayyad governor of Kufa, Yazīd ibn ʻUmar ibn Hubayrah meting out the punishment of public flogging on him for refusing to take up the position. In another account, when he again refused the offer later by the Abbasid caliph al-Manṣūr, he was imprisoned and died while incarcerated in 767/1365. Other reports suggest that he was released before he died but in any event he paid a heavy price for refusal. But we are looking at men of such moral uprightness that neither incarceration nor death would deter them from holding fast to their moral high ground. There were also *mujtahid*s and *fuqahā'* who would choose poverty over wealth gained from suspect sources.

On the other hand, there were *qāḍī*s and court officials who did not think twice about using the office to amass personal wealth through dishonest means such as charging fees for hearing cases and processing documents, apart from the blatant acts of taking gratification to influence the outcome of cases. Embezzlement and misappropriation of the funds of orphans and other parties who were wards of the court were not uncommon apart from the standard acceptance of kickbacks in facilitating favourable administrative decisions. The sale of the posts of deputy *qāḍī* for the various sub-jurisdictions within the control of the chief *qāḍī* was the biggest illicit income earner because the initial exorbitant sums paid could be easily recouped once they took office. Elevation or appointment to that position was therefore a passport to more power and wealth. Perhaps "illicit" may be an incorrect ascription of the situation because the corruption was systemic and it was not a case of it being done under the counter as various accounts relate that when the later Fāṭimid caliphs were desperately in need of money, dishing out appointments to the position of chief judge was the tried and tested way of getting fast cash, as it were.[30] In this regard, corruption certainly began at the top.

Is this an indictment against all judges being corrupt to the core? Certainly not as there were always exceptions. After the Abbasids came to power, the Ḥanafīs entered the service of the central government in Baghdād. Abū Yūsuf was made the chief judge (*qāḍī al-quḍāh*) even as his master Abū Ḥanīfa had refused to accept such an office. Though no historian would suggest that he was not among the most eminent of the *'ulamā'* of his time or that his decisions or opinions were anything but the product of great erudition and piety, Abū Yūsuf soon found himself at the mercy of the caliphate court. Nevertheless, by virtue of his office, he was able to secure the caliphate's sanction of his master's teachings as the official doctrine. When the Islamic empire was at the height of its power, Hārūn al-Rashīd commissioned him to write a treatise on taxation and financial issues facing the empire: the outcome was *Kitāb al-Kharāj*, a Ḥanafī magnum opus on taxation and constitutional questions and an advisory on how to appropriately conduct financial policies in accordance with the *Sharī'ah*. While the caliph took some suggestions and ignored others, the overall effect was to place limits on the caliph's discretion over the tax system.[31] In today's parlance, Abū Yūsuf's tax treatise could be used as the basis for enacting legislation on *ex-ante* and *ex-post* principles of accountability and the conferring of parliamentary oversight on spending by the Executive, a process that was set in motion with the institution of the *Muḥtasib*, as discussed below.

The Muḥtasib

Barring political interference of the powers that be, the *siyāsah al-Shar'iyyah* has, nevertheless, produced noteworthy public and administrative institutions considered integral in an Islamic legal system. Among the most significant was the office of the *Muḥtasib*, sometimes crudely described as the "market inspector." Indeed, he was an inspector on account of the fact that he was in charge of matters which in today's parlance would be the equivalent of protector of consumer affairs. This spanned from the inspection of weights and measures, prevention of price rigging and hoarding for essential foodstuff. He was empowered not only to check on complaints of individuals against authorities and oversee proper operation of markets preventing fraud in economic transactions, but was authorised as the enforcer of public morality. As our discussion in Chapter 5 on the divine injunction to enjoin good and forbid evil would have foreshadowed, this institution of the moral police, being clearly *Sharī'ah*-derived, remains a central feature of the forum externum of the Islamic legal paradigm. This aspect is, however, prominently projected, almost circus-like, as a defining feature of a puritanical Islamic state. Hence, the stereotypical enforcement of punishment of male Muslims who fail to attend the Friday congregational prayers, shaming female Muslims who do not dress appropriately, parading unmarried couples caught in "close proximity" and at one time public snipping of the neck-ties worn by men during the height of the Islamic revolution of Iran under Khomeini. Among the more obvious actions were the closure of wine bars, gambling dens, brothels and other places of disrepute.

This is not to trivialize the institution of the *Muḥtasib* but to underscore the fact that beyond the veneer of such stereotypical enforcement of public morality and the wilful imposition of religious practices on the people, the institution plays a more profound role within the bigger picture of Islamic civilization. For when merged with the office of *Dīwān al-Maẓālim*, (court for the redress of injustice, mazālim being "victims of injustice") it exercised judicial functions over those responsible for public administration. The office appears to go back to 'Umar who, according to the Sunnah, had taken on the role as a guardian of public morals and the observance of justice in daily life.[32] So, rather than the embodiment of the menacing phase of intolerant Islam meting out street justice to transgressors of public morality, in practice, the *Muḥtasib* protected people who were victims of injustice, or of discrimination and of unfairness at the hands of public officials.

Rather than referring to it as the "Islamic Ombudsman," it is more appropriate to regard it as the spiritual father of the Swedish Ombudsman, introduced by Parliament in Sweden in 1809, which

English administrative law touts as one of the great institutions for the principles of accountability and judicial review.[33] The jurisdiction of the court of *Dīwān al-Maẓālim* was very wide including that of appellate court from decisions of the *qāḍis*. This system comprised a council for hearing complaints essentially against unfair and unjust acts committed by public officials. Remarkably comprehensive and inclusive so as to be truly representative, it consisted of representatives of five sectors of the community, namely, the police who were to preserve law and order, the *qāḍī*s and *muftī*s who were to be consulted on legal issues, the clerks who were to record the statements of the adversaries and the proceedings of the trial, and, lastly, the witnesses who were to certify the bench's decisions and orders. Only when all these representatives were present would the court sit for hearing.

It is said that the *Dīwān al-Maẓālim* has its roots in the doctrine of intercession (*shafā'ah*) as encapsulated in the Qur'an, where deciding to grant divine or eschatological intervention is God's prerogative as bestowed on the Prophet. Under the Abbasids, the practical implication of intercession was translated into direct justice or setting things aright. The implications of this in the socio-political realm were that those either permanently or temporarily lower in the hierarchy sought intercession from the caliphs through petitions. The premise was that the victims of injustices should have recourse to justice (*'adl*) as directly as possible. When direct access was impracticable, appeal to rulers via intermediaries became the norm, with increasing regimentation and ceremony associated with the process of appeal and *mazālim* justice in general, especially under the Mamluks.[34] The *Dīwān al-Maẓālim* competed directly with the courts of ordinary judges but this was attenuated in the early Abbasid period by the fact that the judges were put in charge of the *maẓālim* process. However, by the late ninth century, the viziers had essentially usurped the role, with a brief reversal under the Būyids. The significance of the system cannot be overstated when we take into account that most victims of injustices

> "are powerless people, paupers and retiring women, most of whom arrive from distant parts of the realm, believing that they are approaching someone who will help them and redress their grievances and assist them against their adversaries."[35]

The only drawback to this excellent paradigm was that while the theory on the *maẓālim* jurisdiction was good, the delivery fell far short of expectations. In reality, it never fully reached out to the masses. Nevertheless, it fit in snugly with the *muḥtasib* system and remained an active but idiosyncratic expression of the ruler's desire to be seen personally as the last resort in the quest for justice. In the religious courts, and sometimes in *maẓālim* courts as well, it was a common procedure to submit a summary of any important case to a qualified jurist for his opinion.[36] It will be recalled that the Parliament of the United Kingdom only established a commission for local administration in 1974 to investigate complaints by the public of injustice suffered through maladministration by local authorities including the police authorities.[37] The local government commissioner is known as the Ombudsman.

Maqāṣid Al-Sharīʿah

Another major aspect of *siyāsah al-Sharʿiyyah* is the conceptual paradigm known as *maqāṣid al-Sharīʿah*, that is, the higher objectives of the *Sharīʿah*, which in the last two decades has seen a revival of interest. Many, particularly politicians, have jumped on the bandwagon waving the *maqāṣid* flag or mouthing the right phrases as sound bites when appealing to a Muslim audience but if their actions are anything to go by, between the idea and the reality, falls the shadow of unfulfilled promises. Between the promise of reform and the delivery to the people, lies a great chasm of insincerity and hypocrisy. This is because the *maqāṣid* doctrine is not just a mantra that is to be pressed into service for embellishing speeches or to be bandied about during electoral campaigns. It is in fact an all-encompassing concept which if implemented with full conviction and understanding may well be the panacea for the recurrent ills of the *ummah* provided always that its formulations remain faithful to the spirit of the Qur'ān and the Sunnah. In response to the claim by certain quarters that the *Sharī'ah* is Roman law in Arab garb as discussed in the previous chapter, I have cited, inter alia, the *maqāṣid* doctrine and provided specific examples indicative of the influence having been in fact the other way round—that is, the influence of the *Sharī'ah* on western jurisprudence and not just English law. I propose now to go a bit deeper into the subject incorporating the classical positions as well as the contemporary interpretations and reformulations but as for the final prescription this will be discussed in the last chapter under the topic of rethinking the *Sharī'ah.*

In this regard, earlier references to terms like *istiṣlāh*, *maṣlaḥah* and *istiḥsan* should be seen as being subsumed under the umbrella doctrine of the *maqāṣid al-Sharī'ah. Istiṣlāh* is different from *istiḥsan* in that it is limited to its technical use being more closely defined in content and sharing an etymology with *maṣlaḥah* from the root "*ṣāluha.*" *Istiṣlāh* is therefore governed by the concept of *maṣlaḥah mursala*, that is to say, considerations of public interest where a decision is made guided by the demands of human welfare in the widest sense. The Mālikīs are regarded as principal champions of *istiṣlāh*, notably through the efforts of the Andalusian *faqīh* and philosopher al-Shāṭibī (d. 790/1388) in his discourse on the *maṣlaḥah* and the *maqāṣid* as the central principle for the advancement of the *Sharī'ah.*[38]

What appears to be lost in the discourse of the *maqāṣid al-Sharī'ah* is the fact that it is the product of *ijtihād*. In his *Kitāb al-Muwāfaqāt fī uṣūl al-Sharī'ah*, al-Shātibī referred to *ijtihād* as an "intellectual exercise based on two pillars," the first being mastery of the grammar and syntax of the Arabic language and the second being "knowledge of the purposes behind the legislation of the Lawgiver."[39] Most of his predecessors were content on searching for the *'illah* (following al-Shāfi'ī) as the principle cause for legislation.[40] Al-Shāṭibī made it clear that knowledge of the purposes of the *Sharīʿah* was essential in understanding the legislation of the Lawgiver. And with that understanding of the purposes, there was a need to advance or promote the higher objectives of the *Sharīʿah.* Nevertheless, this aspect of his thought was not taken seriously at that time probably because of the traditional notion that it was not permissible for the *ʿulamāʾ* to seek reasons for legislation by the Lawgiver because that would be engaging in the realm of speculation or second guessing the Almighty.[41] Another significant aspect of al-Shāṭibī's contribution which tends to be overlooked is his pioneering approach in *maqāṣid*-based legal hermeneutics and Qur'ānic exegesis as an essential part of his *fiqh* methodology. This particular approach in effect makes him the precursor to the modern exegetic paradigm known as *al-tafsīr al-mawḍūʿī.* [42]

It is true that more than two centuries earlier, in *al-Mustaṣfā min ʿilm al-uṣūl,* al-Ghazālī had already expounded the doctrine of *maṣlaḥah* as "considerations for what is aimed at for mankind in the law" of which there are five categories: maintenance of religion, of life, of reason, of lineage and property. These were graded into the *ḍarūriyyāt* (essentials), the *ḥājiyyāt* (complements) and the *taḥsīniyyāt* (embellishments)—the triple gradations. Any measure which secures these categories comes within the domain of *maṣlaḥah,* and is therefore lawful, while anything which violates them is *mafsadah* (evil), and it therefore becomes incumbent on the people to prevent its occurrence.[43] But al-Ghazālī, along with his mentor, al-Juwaynī and others such as al-ʿIzz ibn ʿAbd al-Salām were focused on the static part of the *Sharīʿah* objectives primarily fixated with the concept of protection (*ḥifẓ*) as the ultimate objective of the *Sharīʿah.* It was al-Shāṭibī who advocated the concept of the advancement of the *maqāṣid,* a dynamic approach that marked a paradigm change in the discourse. As if to anticipate the charge of engaging in frivolous speculation, al-Shāṭibī contended that the new theories of *maqāṣid* were derived from the inductive process of reasoning which would attain to "certainty" (*qatʿiyyah*) rather than "uncertainty" (*ẓanniyyah*).

He departed from the Māliki *madhhab* by giving precedence to the triple gradations as expounded by al-Ghazālī over the partialities and minutia (*juz'iyyāt*).[44] Thus the welfare of the people is in principle good grounds for the derivation of legal principles as well as in judicial decision making.[45]

It is said that Qur'ānic legitimacy for the *maqāṣid* doctrine is to be found, among others, in the *āyah*: "We have sent thee not save as a mercy for the peoples."[46] It appears rather farfetched at first blush to suggest this *āyah* as legitimizing the *maqāṣid* doctrine considering its rather general tenor and purport. Asad renders *li al-'ālamīn* as "towards all the worlds," that is to say, towards all mankind. Indeed the profound importance of this *āyah* is not in question in as much as it is a manifestation of "the universality of the Qur'ānic revelation" which is self-evident from the reference to *li al-'ālamīn* apart from the other manifold proofs throughout the Qur'ān. Asad posits that it also appeals exclusively to the *'aql* and "does not postulate any dogma that could be accepted on the basis of blind faith alone." If anything, this could well be the rationale that may be invoked for expounding the *maqāṣid* doctrine. Thirdly, the Qur'ān has remained immutable and intact since the first verses were revealed to the Prophet and will remain so till eternity as promised by the Almighty: "it is We who shall truly guard it."[47]

Now, there is also no direct evidence of the doctrine being founded on the Sunnah and to suggest otherwise is counter-intuitive for the simple reason that if it were based on the Sunnah then the principle established would be sui generis, a direct *naṣṣ* with the force of law, and no longer a doctrine of *siyāsah*. There is, however, substantive authority by way of the practice of the Companions and the leading jurists of the past for the proposition that laws may be enacted in pursuance of public considerations, even though that may constitute a departure from the strict application of Qur'ānic rulings.

With the passing of the Prophet and the end of law-making by way of the Qur'ān and the Sunnah, the Rightly-Guided Caliphs (*al-Khulafā' al-Rāshidūn*) continued the process of legislation as the empire expanded and new situations arose alongside questions of dealing with Byzantine law in Syria and Egypt and the Safavid law of Persia. As a rule, the caliphs applied the principles of the Qur'ān and the Sunnah but in situations not covered directly by the primary sources, customary law, including the rules derived from Byzantium and Persia which had become the *corpus juris* in those lands, were left intact as long as they were not at odds with the Qur'ān and the Sunnah, continued to be applied.[48]

By virtue of the divine authority to legislate positive law as grounded in Sūrah an-Nisā', *āyah* 59, the Rightly-Guided Caliphs, as "those in authority," passed edicts to complement what was silent in the Qur'ān and for which no precedent was found in the Sunnah. For example, Abū Bakr decreed 40 lashes as the penalty for wine-drinking. This was subsequently increased to 80 lashes by 'Umar and maintained as such by 'Ali.[49] Indeed, there is *khilāf* (difference of opinion) on this matter but the majority of scholars agree it is set at eighty lashes for a free man and forty for others. 'Umar had on several other occasions departed from the decisions of the Prophet on the ground that no exact precedent could be derived arising from the same set of facts and circumstances. In other words, 'Umar applied *ijtihād* after reasoning that the Prophet would have decided likewise if the same situation had presented itself during his time. He occasionally even exercised *ijtihād* on a matter already stated in the Qur'ān on the grounds that the divine purpose would be better served and, in this regard, we may say that he was the first of the caliphs to have applied the doctrine of *maqāṣid al-Sharīʻah.* For instance, the Qur'ān prescribes the various categories of people entitled to receive *zakāh*: the poor, the needy, those employed to collect it, for bringing hearts together (*mu'allafah al-qulūb*), for freeing captive, or those in debt and for the cause of Allah and for the traveller. 'Umar stopped the practice of distributing *zakāh* for the purposes of *mu'allafah al-qulūb.*[50] So, rather than parcelling out the conquered territories among the soldiery which was the prevailing practice, he kept them for the Muslim community at large as public property and allowed the lands to be occupied on payment of a land tax (*kharāj*), thereby introducing a new concept of land tenure.[51]

'Umar also suspended the execution of the prescribed punishment for theft in a year of famine despite the clear ruling of the Qur'ān concerning the punishment for *sariqah*—the crime of theft punishable with amputation of the hand.[52] Significantly too, he and the Companions were in agreement that the literal purport of *qiṣas* would not apply in the case of the murder of an innocent life by a group of criminals, that is, that the prescription of "a life for a life" as ordained in the Qur'ān would have to be modified by the dictates of public interest. In this case, all the culprits must be punished by execution as well because otherwise society would be exposed to grave danger and people would literally get away with murder. The doctrine, however, cannot be invoked out of every frivolous need that comes to mind. The considerations must be cogent and clearly defined. The individual's rights must give way to that of the whole community's.[53] Other examples include 'Umar's suspension of the established part of the punishment for fornication (which was exile for one year) when an exiled fornicator defected to the enemy. 'Umar also invalidated the rule (set by the Prophet and continued under Abū Bakr and for two years during his ('Umar's) time that three pronouncements of "*ṭalāq*" executed in a single sitting were tantamount to only a single divorce and not a "triple *ṭalāq*" in which case the husband will lose the right to take his wife back by saying so or by having sexual contact with her. The early *fuqahā'* were generally in agreement that the "triple *ṭalāq*" was unlawful based on various *hadīth* and also on the reasoning that the pronouncement of divorce must be followed by a waiting period and recognizing the triple *ṭalāq* uttered in one single sitting would be a mockery of the Qur'ānic injunction:

> "… When you divorce women, divorce them with a view to the waiting-period appointed for them, and reckon the period, and be conscious of God, your Sustainer …"[54]

'Umar, however, enforced the "triple *ṭalāq*" but for a good reason, that is, to deter the frivolous practice by Muslim husbands of habitually intimidating and emotionally tormenting their wives by uttering the triple pronouncements.[55] The jury is still out on this issue considering the differing views cited by various sides but the "triple *ṭalāq*" practice has nevertheless persisted throughout the history of Islam and is widely used in Saudi Arabia.[56]

To be sure, this was not a situation of the caliphs acting the part of legal maestros conducting the affairs of society with the broad sweeping strokes of the jurisprudential wand, making and unmaking laws as they pleased. It could not be said that they were "tampering with divine law" in their efforts at fulfilling the Prophet's Sunnah which is nothing if not the constant endeavour to uphold God's commands. Compared to the *'ulamā'* later in their *fiqh*, this was undertaken with a zeal that was "more macrocosmic and less textual."[57] Nevertheless, for the most part, the injunctions of the Qur'ān and the Sunnah were enforced without question, but where existing legal systems were found in the conquered lands, a flexible approach was taken as long as they did not violate any religious strictures. The rationale of advancing the *maqāṣid al-Sharī'ah* was paramount in giving sanction to all efforts at law-making.

Along these lines, much new legislation was also made in the name of public security.[58] When Mu'āwiyah became Caliph, heralding the birth of the Umayyad dynasty (40 to 132/661 to 750), a newly constituted state saw the *Sharī'ah* being applied across the Muslim empire. However, in matters pertaining to the law of personal status such as marriage and divorce, adoption, inheritance, Jews and Christians were governed by Rabbinical and Christian laws. The question that is raised is: Did the implementation of the *Sharī'ah* in totality include the imposition of *ḥudūd* laws, and if so, did its jurisdiction include non-Muslims? The answer is yes and no. "Yes," as there was no bifurcation between *Sharī'ah* law and criminal law as such and "no" because *ḥudūd* laws were not applicable to non-Muslims in so far as they had their own religious laws governing such matters already in their *corpus juris*. That seems rather superficial in as much as Islam as *dīn* means more than just the imposition of laws according to the *Sharī'ah*. In any event, there is the view that the imposition of God's law in totality is subject to certain conditions precedent as the foregoing discussion of the practice of the Companions would indicate. At this juncture suffice it to say that the founder of the Umayyad dynasty might be likened to an "enlightened despot" in a loose sense but for all intents and purposes, Mu'āwiyah may be regarded as the first secular ruler of Islamic history.[59] But this did not prevent Mu'āwiyah from applying the *Sharī'ah*—according to its higher objectives as translated into *siyāsah* principles—on Muslims while non-Muslims continued with their religious laws. One view, the basis of which remains questionable, suggests that, even as they had transformed into a "dynastic caliphate," the appellation of being God's representatives on earth (*khalīfah Allāh fī al-arḍ*) was not lost on them and by virtue of that, they contributed positively to the definition of the *Sharī'ah* as law of the land.[60] Whether or not this may be regarded as the genesis of a jurisprudential *convivencia* that would be the hallmark of "enlightened despotism" until the absolutist rule of the Abbasids, as some would argue, remains a point of contention.

Islamic law is not a smorgasbord of disparate laws conveniently laid out on a jurisprudential platter just to serve the appetite of a growing empire. On the contrary, as regards customary usages and practices in the conquered territories, it may be said that even though some elements had been adopted, quite a number of original juridical creations emerged from there through the employment of *ra'y*, *qiyās*, and the application of *maqāṣid al-Sharī'ah*. As early as the first half of the second century Hijrah and on account of the diverse situations presenting themselves that warranted the exercise of *ijtihād* based on the *maqāṣid al-Sharī'ah*, three different schools of *fiqh* had developed in the Hijaz, Iraq and Syria which constituted the precursors of the later *madhāhib*.

As the law developed, it became clear that the exposition of the *Sharī'ah* proper fell within the domain of the *'ulamā'* while the *siyāsah al-Shar'iyyah* became the domain of the caliph or sultan through the state appointed *qāḍis*. Whether it is enlightened despotism or outright tyranny, it was an exercise in kingship.[61] It was therefore a symbiotic arrangement as we saw how the caliphs sought religious legitimacy from the *'ulamā'* who in turn secured political influence, both parties collaborating in the "sacralization" of the law. In this regard, *al-siyāsah al-Shar'iyyah* has been considered nothing but attempts at sacralizing political power.[62] The implications of this kind of "unholy" alliance are not lost on contemporary Muslim societies where the *'ulamā'* are often seen to be working hand in glove with the powers that be. It is the nature of this relationship which has led both present-day Islamist movements as well as civil society organizations to have a rather dim view of the *'ulamā'* of the establishment. As for the emasculation of the office of the *qāḍī* or the self-imposed subservience of the judiciary *vis-à-vis* the rulers, it is true that this state of affairs took root more than 1000 years ago and perhaps ought to be seen in the context of the era as well as in the light of similar dispensations in other parts of the world at that time. But history of course has a tendency to repeat itself. It may be recalled that servility of the *'ulamā'* towards the ruling classes—or at least a preponderance for that—was a matter that al-Ghazālī dealt with in the *Ihyā'*, himself having gone through that life-changing experience.[63]

The weaknesses of the Islamic judiciary notwithstanding, the *maqāṣid* doctrine is not only conceptually sound but is well-suited to be the driver for reform and renewal of the ummah. To invoke the *maqāṣid* doctrine, the essential feature that binds *istiḥsān* and *istiṣlāh* is therefore the absence of a ready rule either in the Qur'ān or the Sunnah applicable to the particular circumstances or facts of the case and that no *ijmā'* on the matter is known to exist. This approach is endorsed by al-Āmidī, al-Bayḍāwī, al-Isnawī, Ibn al-Ḥājib and al-Qarāfī with the five essentials generally adopted in modern day discourse though, as we shall see, this limitation to the five essentials is now considered arbitrary while the approach to the *maqāṣid* needs a systemic rethink.

In Chapter 4, I considered the parallels or affinities of the concept of *maslaḥah* with the English jurisprudential doctrine of utilitarianism. As a clear reaffirmation of the universality of the Qur'ānic message, 'Abduh by virtue of his firm grounding in the *maslaḥah* (as influenced no doubt by the *Muwāfaqāt*) had no problem advocating the Benthamite theory to his fellow Muslims. In reinterpreting the law and adapting it to modern problems, 'Abduh extended the doctrine of *maslaḥah* by giving it a far wider interpretation than originally expounded by the classical theorists. Thus, while under the Mālikī *madhhab*, the promotion of human welfare could only be advanced as an exegetical tool of the Qur'ān and the Sunnah, 'Abduh applied it for deriving specific laws from general principles of social morality as revealed by God. Since only the general principles had been revealed, the *'aql* must be employed to apply them to the specific problems of social life, guided not by fixed principles but by the general welfare of mankind at that time. This is essentially utilitarianism minus the Benthamite tag. This was no doubt far-reaching in implication: if adopted fully, it stands out against the static juristic landscape of the classical doctrine of *taqlīd*. According to Hourani, while the latter purportedly stood for certainty and definitiveness in juridical interpretation, 'Abduh's doctrine meant that principles prescribed for social problems should never be hidebound simply because society was always in a state of flux and the problems generated likewise change.[64] Certainty in the law should not be procured at the expense of the people's welfare which eventually reflected the workings of justice, and Islam is nothing if not justice. In other words, the *maqāṣid al-Sharī'ah* must prevail over so-called time-honoured conventions founded on the supposed primacy of the *Sharī'ah* as law.

What appears to be lost on modern day Islamists when they wave the fundamentalist banner in the name of 'Abduh is that for him, the ideal Muslim society is not founded on law only (and certainly not a rigid adherence to the letter of the law) but also reason which guides the true Muslim in affairs of the world and religion. To 'Abduh, infidelity to religion is not merely a question of committing transgressions against moral teachings but to close one's eyes to the light of truth and refusing to examine rational proofs.[65] It is from this prism that 'Abduh's *maqāṣid* formulations should be viewed. This rationalist bent of mind should come as no surprise considering that he was influenced by the French Enlightenment, his ideas believed to be forged on the schema of Comtean positivism. In this paradigm, it was posited that the glorification of personal opinion on a pedestal of independent inquiry led to too much diversity and a lack of conceptual cohesiveness. The prescription was a system of ideas universally acceptable embodied in religious symbols but necessarily elitist to lord over morals. In Comte's opinion, this could be reached by extending the rational methods of science and mathematics to society and developing a rational system of social morality. 'Abduh's purpose was "to show that Islam contained in itself the potentialities of this rational religion, this social science and moral code which could serve as the basis of modern life."[66] There is the alternative narrative concerning his rationalist inclination attributable to a supposed attachment to Mu'tazilī teachings which as far as the general Sunnī world was concerned was heresy. According to one account, 'Abduh, however, disavowed any such affiliation by proclaiming his rejection of *taqlīd* to one group but this is said to be unlikely because necessity for *taqlīd* was generally accepted by all at al-Azhar. So, to deny one heresy by professing another would have got him nowhere.[67]

One of the lasting influences on 'Abduh's outlook was Francois Guizot's *History of Civilization* in Europe, even as it was particularly influential on Guizot's three great European contemporaries, Karl Marx, John Stuart Mill, and Alexis de Tocqueville. The overarching theme concerning the significance of class conflict to drive societal change as well as the cultural impact of a pluralistic European tradition reinforced Abduh's Islamic Weltanschauung as one that is universalistic and characterised by compassion and justice. 'Abduh's doctrine was eventually brought to fruition in the context of his general prescriptions for the modernity of Muslim societies.

Modernist Legislation

In the last two centuries, beginning from the latter half of the 19th century, *siyāsah al-Shar'iyyah* under the Ottomans began to lose its *Sharī'ah* moorings, or whatever semblance of it, as Islam came face to face with the West. This was, however, not an encounter of equivalence, let alone of dominance with which it used to enjoy in the heyday of the spread of the Islamic empire, as we have noted earlier. In that earlier encounter, the conquered Byzantine and Persian legal heritage was incorporated into the *Sharī'ah* corpus and where the *'ulamā'* were given due recognition by the Abbasid caliphs and later even under the Ottomans there were attempts to bridge the gap between the *Sharī'ah* and the *siyāsah.* However, with the onslaught of Western imperialism and spurred on directly by the infusion of Western political ideas, the movement of modernist legislation gained momentum initially in the realm of constitutional law and eventually into municipal laws.[68]

This was an encounter that the world of Islam had never experienced before in its history for the challenge was mounted on all fronts that would constitute the essence of its civilization. With its *ummah* subjugated by a Western civilization at the apogee of its military and political power, both its constitutional and legal foundations crumbled. Bereft of the power to overcome or the ability to assimilate the dominant civilization, it lay impotent as a Western constitutional and legal system was superimposed on its existing indigenous *Sharī'ah* structure. As one commentator puts it,

> "...the massive reforms carried out in almost all Islamic legal systems in the world (during this period of colonization) left this law totally mutilated...."[69]

But was it really that tragic a situation as made out to be? One could well contend that there was nothing tragic about it for in response to European imperial expansion, eventually after the initial stupor, modernist Islamic political thought emerged. By the middle of the 19th century, there emerged two broad streams of modernist Muslim scholars with one side leaning on what it regards as the enlightening aspect of European civilization and therefore advocating assimilation while maintaining a foundational Islamic character. Into this category we may include the likes of Rifā'ah Rāfi' al-Ṭahṭāwī (d. 1289/1873), Sayyid Ahmad Khan (d. 1315/1898), and Shihabuddin Marjani (d. 1306/1889). Without getting too deep into this discourse which should occupy us in a separate monograph on political Islam, suffice it to say that Ṭahṭāwī, who translated the French Charter of 1814 into Arabic, went as far as proposing it as a model for Muslim societies: "What they [the French] hold dear and call liberty is what we call equity and justice, for to rule according to liberty means to establish equality through judgments and laws, so that the ruler cannot wrong anybody, the law being the reference and the guide."[70] Muḥammad Iqbāl (d. 1356/1938), hailed European imperialism as a progressive political force in as much as democracy, according to him, was one of England's greatest achievements where "English statesmen have boldly carried this principle to countries which have been, for centuries, groaning under the most atrocious forms of despotism." At the other end were those modernists who rejected European imperialism among whom the most influential being Jamāl al-Dīn al-Afghānī (d. 1314/1897) and 'Abduh, even as he was, as mentioned earlier, influenced by the French Enlightenment and both advocated *iṣlah* and *tajdīd* through education, science and technology. Their rantings against imperialism are documented for posterity in the journal *al-'Urwah al-Wuthqā* (The Firmest Bond). Then there were those who not only rejected but actively advocated *jiḥād* against the West such as Abū al-A'lā Mawdūdī (d. 1399/1979) and Sayyid Quṭb (d. 1385/1966).[71]

Putting things in perspective, the pre-modern period saw the rise of the Ottoman Empire in the new Near East and the Mogul Empire in India where *Sharī'ah* law gained token primacy as the law of the land having incorporated a substantive constitutional and legal paradigm based on the *siyāsah al-Shar'iyyah* state. In this process of internal adaptation, *Sharī'ah* law clearly demonstrated its effectiveness as a practical and dynamic law until the subsequent decadence of the empire led to its weakening and subsequent disintegration in 1908. Meantime, reform initiatives begun under Mahmud II (1808-39) saw a clash with the *Shari'ah*. In the 1850s, there began the legislation of the *Tanẓīmāt* after European models with the Code of Commerce (1850) as the first important manifestation signalling as it were the eventual demise of the *Sharīʿah*. Nevertheless, the *Sharīʿah* was not officially abandoned as yet. Ottoman Turkey in fact made a courageous attempt to codify the law of contracts and obligations and of civil procedure. The outcome was the *Majallah al-Ahkām al-ʿAdliyyah*, promulgated as the Ottoman Civil Code in 1877 in order to provide the institutions of the *siyāsah al-Sharʿiyyah* with an authoritative statement of the *Sharīʿah* law without having to resort to the works of Islamic jurisprudence which had proved cumbersome and impracticable.[72]

As for British India and French Algeria, there was a convergence of *Sharīʿah* law and Western laws leading to the emergence of two unique legal systems, Anglo-Muhammadan law and *Droit muṣūlman Algerien*. Though by no means *Sharīʿah* law in the comprehensive sense as defined in Chapters 1 and 2, they provided the *modus vivendi* for Muslims to live by a legal system which recognized their personal status as Muslims with its distinctly *Sharīʿah* content governing inheritance, marriage, divorce, and family. Positive law in the area of public administration and penal laws remained in the hands of the colonial masters using common law and continental law. Purists will object to what they regard as the "hybridization of *Sharīʿah* law with Western law" brought about not by the will of the people but by the fiat of colonial overlords but on closer inspection it would be clear that the antipathy is borne of political rather than jurisprudential concerns. In reality, there was no hybridization as such in the sense that the principles governing *Sharīʿah* law were never mixed with the principles of common or continental law and passed off as Islamic law. What was practised or imposed was a dual system of laws with *Sharīʿah* courts operating in tandem with civil courts implementing different sets of laws. While the civil courts dealt with matters pertaining to general penal laws, constitutional and administrative laws and contractual and tortious laws, the *Sharīʿah* courts dealt essentially with the law of personal status as alluded to earlier as well as certain *taʿzīr* laws enacted under the principle of *siyāsah al-Sharʿiyyah.*

Self-styled purists decry that God's law is being adulterated with the importation of modernist Western concepts. This is not something that can be dismissed summarily or ignored as inconsequential. In any event, the issue of extraneous adulteration of the *Sharīʿah* has a certain Hegelian determinism to it dating back to the early days of Islam. According to Gibb, "From the very first, the *Sharia*, as administered in the Muslim states, was modified … by the addition or substitution of administrative rulings, and at the present day it is menaced by the growth and expansion of Western codes and courts of law."[73] In modern times, even without bringing in the question of the imposition of colonial laws, the issue remains as to whether *siyāsah al-Sharʿiyyah* itself could be regarded as addressing the entire community as a state and formulating the subject matter of its administrative and public law in a manner that meets the demands of the *Sharīʿah*? Is the resulting law arbitrary, reflective of the particular prejudices and predilections of the law makers or has it stayed faithful to the dictates of the Qur'ān and Sunnah? In theory, it should not go astray from the foundations of the divine law because from the *Sharīʿah* standpoint, as our definition indicates, *siyāsah* law can only be promulgated in line with the spirit of the *Sharīʿah* and must not contravene any fundamental principle of the *Sharīʿah*.

The fundamental question that is raised is, considering that *siyāsah al-Sharʿiyyah* was already adopted in place of the *Sharīʿah*, could the *ummah* really continue to exist as a community of Muslims living the Islamic way of life? This is the community as declared by God:

> "You are indeed the best community that has ever been brought forth for [the good of] mankind: you enjoin the

doing of what is right and forbid the doing of what is wrong, and you believe in God ..."[74]

Has there been such a community in reality? The answer to this is not a straightforward "yes" or "no" because it will depend on one's interpretation of the various key phrases in the verse. At one level, it is said there is no specificity in the tense whether it is in the present or in the past. Interpreting it as the future, one view suggests that indeed it has been written in stone, that is, in the Preserved Tablet (*al-lawḥ al-maḥfūẓ*), that Muslims are fated to be the best community, and must therefore live up to the expectation. Another view suggests that these words are spoken to Muslims in Paradise to describe their life in the world. It could also be that they "become" the best ummah on condition that they enjoin right and forbid evil.[75]

Now, on the interpretation that it refers to the present existence, and that Islam is seen as *dīn* ("religion" in the ordinary sense), the answer from a moderate's point of view is in the affirmative, on condition that the *siyāsah al-Shar'iyyah* is adopted not in place of the *Sharī'ah*, but as an essential supplement to fulfil the ever changing needs of the *ummah*. The argument is that in the Islamic conception of law as *fiqh*, enforcement of the law in matters governing beliefs and ritual and devotional practices, is not required. Thus, if the state failed to enforce the law, the believer is still obliged to observe it, bearing in mind the earlier discussion on the *forum internum/externum* dichotomy. The sanction of the law is, strictly speaking, irrelevant because, according to the tenets of Islam, the object of the *Sharī'ah* is to place the believer on the right path. This stands in contrast with the Western conception of law as rules backed by sanction.[76] So, in Western jurisprudence, it is not law if there is no punishment whereas, if we recall as stated in Chapter 1, the *Sharī'ah* is "the totality of divine categorizations of human acts"—*al-aḥkām al-'amaliyyah*. The question about it being backed by sanctions does not arise. If there are sanctions, as indeed there are as in the *ḥuḍūd* crimes and the *ta'zīr* offences, these are incidental to the law not definitive of it. Similarly, *qiṣās* allows for monetary compensation and even full pardon from the victim or his or her kin. In other words, sanction is not mandatory but by no stretch of the language can it be said that on account of this, *qiṣāṣ* is not law.

Now, at the other end of the polarity, for those who take the position that the religion of Islam including the laws of the *Sharī'ah* were already completed by the time of the famous *ḥajjah ul-wiḍā'*, the adoption and implementation of *siyāsah al-Shar'iyyah* is pernicious innovation (*bid'ah*) pure and simple regardless whether it purports to substitute the *Sharī'ah*, in which case such a community cannot be regarded as being the best. As will be recalled, the revelation concerning the perfection of "your religious law for you," occurred at 'Arafah in the afternoon of Friday, the 9th of *Dhū al-Ḥijjah*, 10 A.H., after which no legal injunction whatsoever was revealed.[77] Secondly, there is the school of thought that advocates the establishment of an Islamic State without compromise, that is to say that all the *siyāsah al-Shar'iyyah* would come to naught as long as the *Sharī'ah* is not enforced in full because Islam is regarded as inclusive of a political system requiring the setting up of a state based on the Qur'ān and the Sunnah. A system which falls back on just the so-called spirit of the *Sharī'ah* while in effect bypassing the letter of the law with the *siyāsah al-Shar'iyyah* is, therefore, a sham system.[78] For example, if one were to refer to Ibn Taymiyyah's *al-Siyāsah al-Shar'iyyah*, which is essentially a treatise on the imperatives of setting up an Islamic State, the discourse makes it clear that *siyāsah al-Shar'iyyah* remains firmly grounded in the *Sharī'ah* and on account of the overarching Qur'ānic injunction on "enjoining good and preventing evil," the state must be given broad and sweeping powers to enforce the *Sharī'ah*.[79] In other words, merely calling it *siyāsah al-Shar'iyyah* will not pass muster.

In light of the preceding argument, it might well be contended that, apart from the introduction of its legal system and the substantive laws governing societal relations in commerce and the economy, the influence of European political ideas was but a natural consequence of the vacuum created by the nature and substance of Islamic political philosophy which was essentially characterized by autocracy and an overarching theme of subservience to authority. Proponents of the Islamic state will object to such an assertion on the grounds that principles of Islamic constitutionalism were expounded way before John Locke or Rousseau came on the scene.[80] But this seems to be a stock response by conservative pundits upon being confronted with the challenge of modernist legislation: The *Sharī'ah* is comprehensive and all-encompassing. Everything is already there, so why do we need to borrow from the West?[81] Other than exhibiting ignorance of the historical development of the *Sharī'ah* and the process of juristic law-making as discussed earlier, such a statement also betrays the cultural cringe often associated with a large section of so-called Islamic purists. The question of the percolation of extraneous sources into Islamic law has been considered and the conclusion is that the sacral nature of the *Sharī'ah* is not fundamentally undermined. The historical record shows that original *Sharī'ah* legal doctrines have foreshadowed the subsequent evolution of modern Western jurisprudence in various aspects while certain principles of pre-Islamic natural law founded in the Greco-Roman tradition were already in place in lands subsequently coming under the expanded Islamic empire.

Our discussion in Chapter 4 on the bifurcation of church and state will be considered heretical if we take the Ibn Taymiyyah path which advocates the return of the "glory days of the *Khilāfah*." His views on the *siyāsah al-Shar'iyyah* must be seen as being subsumed under the concept of the *Sharī'ah* as "the be-all and end-all for the *ummah*."[82] But this is not to say that he advocates blind fealty to the rulers at all costs. While the people owe a primary duty of obedience to the rulers, he stresses that sovereignty over the *ra'iyyah*, that is, the citizenry, is a trust—*amānah*. It remains arguable what exactly this trust is: reductionist apologists insist that it means "to rule justly and to protect constitutional rights" while detractors dismiss it as merely "ruling according to the *Sharī'ah* under an Islamic state." Indeed, the apologists will argue that there is no difference between the two for an Islamic state is synonymous with ruling with justice and fairness.

Again, detractors rejoin that such a statement is not empirically proven at all, not only in the historical but the contemporary context as well. In any event, both sides agree that according to Ibn Taymiyyah obedience to the ruler and by extension authority or government is only warranted on condition that those in power do not violate this trust. Translated into simple language, certain *ʿulamāʾ* including Ibn Taymiyyah and many others since—down the line to Ḥasan al-Bannā, Mawdūdī and Sayyid Quṭb—regard as infidels rulers who fail to implement the *Sharīʿah* as the law of the land. Rebellion is therefore sanctioned.[83] In his *Maʿālim fī al-Ṭarīq*, which is nothing if not a manifesto for the modern Islamic State, Sayyid Quṭb charges that the *ummah* has reverted to a state of *jāhiliyyah* for the last few centuries because Muslims have failed to follow the *Sharīʿah*—the laws of God. In Quṭb's view, *jāhiliyyah* is not just ignorance in the ways of God but rather a classic case of secularism where the sovereignty of man over man constitutes the guiding philosophy in defining the principles of right and wrong conduct.[84] In Quṭb's political philosophy, the Qur'ān enjoins that all existing systems are antithetical to the spirit of Islam except the *Sharīʿah* whose observance by Muslims is mandatory.[85] Hence, those who choose not to follow the *Sharīʿah* are therefore *kāfir* (infidels). Any system of government that is not based on the *Sharīʿah* is "evil and corrupt … and all man-made systems of government and political ideologies would lead to enslavement by the one in authority."[86] Training his sights on personalities, he first castigates those who would separate the *ʿibādāt* from the *muʿāmalāt* intoning that anyone who understands religion should know it could not be separated from worldly affairs. He singles out ʿAbduh and Iqbāl for attack as those who had sacrificed the divine lordship (*rabbāniyyah*) on the altar of modernity and for having "poured Islam into the foreign mould of philosophy."[87] The course of sanctimonious condemnation is predictable and would not have merited mention but for the fact that Quṭb has remained a highly iconic figure for radical Islam. So, as expected, Iqbal is upbraided for having conceived Islam from the prism of secular philosophers (by

Quṭb's reckoning) such as Hegel and Kant. For the sin of equating *aql* with *naql*, a *de rigueur* charge meted out against anyone who employs reason more than revelation harking back to the days of Aḥmad ibn Ḥanbal and the Ash'arite *mutakallimūn*, Quṭb chastises 'Abduh's alleged preponderance towards that. While lacking the profundity and analytical incisiveness of al-Ghazālī in his *Tahāfut al-Falāsifa*, Quṭb nevertheless did not let pass the opportunity of dismissing the mediaeval Muslim philosophers such as al-Fārābī, Ibn Sīnā and Ibn Rushd as "mere imitators of their Greek predecessors." He also warns of the "dangerous philosophical equations" which not only diminish the status of the Qur'ān as first source but legitimizes the entry into Islam of Western secular culture.[88] There is also a third position which may first be simply stated as rejecting both the above-stated polarities but it requires a revisiting of the fundamentals of the *Sharī'ah* as we will do in the next chapter.

Notes

1. For classical expositions on *siyāsah* see Ibn Qayyim al-Jawziyyah, *al-Ṭuruq al-Ḥukmiyyah fī al-Siyāsah al-Shar'iyyah*; al-Māwardī, *Kitāb al-Aḥkām*. See also Fauzi M. Najjar, "Siyasa in Islamic Political Philosophy," in *Islamic Theology and Philosophy: Studies in Honor of George F. Hourani*, edited by Michael E. Marmura (Albany, 1984), 92-111, 295-97.
2. Gibb, *op. cit.*, 132-33.
3. Bernard Lewis, *Istanbul and the Civilization of the Ottoman Empire*, (University of Oklahoma Press, 1963), 71; Stanford J. Shaw, *History of the Ottoman Empire and Modern Turkey: Volume 1, Empire of the Gazis: The Rise and Decline of the Ottoman Empire 1280-1808*, (Cambridge University Press, 1976), 25; Lewis, *The Political Language of Islam*, (Chicago: University of Chicago Press, 1988), 14.
4. Frank E. Vogel, *Islamic Law and Legal System: Studies of Saudi*

Arabia, (Boston: Brill, 2000), 171
5. Coulson, *History*, 129.
6. Sūrah al-Anbiyā', *āyah* 107.
7. Sūrah al-Sharḥ, *āyah* 5.
8. The two of them were the primary exponents of the doctrine from the Ḥanbalī *madhhab*.
9. Ibid., 204, citations omitted.
10. Ibn al-Qayyim, *Ṭuruq*, 100; idem, *I'lām*, 373-74. Vogel, 206-7.
11. *Shorter Encyclopaedia*, 527; Coulson, *Conflicts and Tensions*, 87-91.
12. See, Nyazee, *Theories of Islamic Law.*
13. For the early history of judicial administration, see Coulson, *History*, 21-35.
14. Tyan, "Méthodologie," 101-9.
15. Vogel, *Islamic Law,* 173.
16. Ibid. 174.
17. Ibid.
18. Ibid. 205; Of even greater import would be the practical transformation of his doctrines into a full-blown constitutional paradigm that would be brought about with rise of a Wahhābī regime in Arabia in the 12th/18th century.
19. H. A. R. Gibb and Harold Bowen, *Islamic Society and the West.* Vol I: Islamic Society in the Eighteenth Century, Part I. 12, 386 pp. Issued under the auspices of the Royal Institute of International Affairs, Oxford University Press, 1950, 35; Schacht, *Introduction*, 89.
20. Schacht, *Introduction*, 89-90.
21. Ibid. 91.
22. Ibid. 92-93.
23. Vogel, *Islamic Law,* 205.
24. Schacht, *Introduction,* 92
25. Haim Gerber, *State, Society, and Law in Islam: Ottoman Law in*

Comparative Perspective, (State University of New York Press, 1994) Chapter II—The Making of Ottoman Law—The Rise of the *Kadi* and the *Shari'a* Court, 58-78; Vogel, 207.

26. Schacht, *Introduction*.
27. Ironically, though while both these concepts did not gain full recognition in the development of Islamic legal theory, centuries later, the principle of *ra'y* was to be expounded by Dicey in his Constitution pertaining to the doctrine of the rule of law except that it goes by the name of "discretion." Judicial precedent particularly in jurisdictions which have adopted the English common law including the United States is now a central feature flowing from the doctrine of *stare decisis*.
28. Brockelmann, *History*, 111.
29. *The Princeton Encyclopedia of Islamic Political Thought*, edited by Gerhard Bowering, (Princeton University Press, 2013), 501.
30. Ibid.
31. Cosgel, Metin, Rasha Ahmed and Thomas Miceli, "Law, State Power, and Taxation in Islamic History," *Journal of Economic Behavior & Organization* 71, no. 3 (2009): 704-717.
32. There are suggestions that this was pioneered by the 5th Umayyad Caliph 'Abdel Malik Ibn Marwan (685-705), not an implausible claim considering that he was credited for standardizing imperial coinage and collecting a corpus of hadith to be interpreted by appointed *fuqahā'*, causing hadith to emerge as a cornerstone of Islamic scholarship. Among his most significant contributions was his Arabization program which led to the development of Arabic-language sciences, particularly Adab literature, and the emergence of Arabic as the empire's official language. During his reign, the Dome of the Rock was constructed, Jerusalem was appropriated as a holy place for Islam, and the first Arabic-script coinage of the Islamic empire was struck: *The Oxford Dictionary of Islam*, edited by John L. Esposito, *Oxford Islamic Studies*

Online, accessed 9 August, 2015, available at http://www.oxfordislamicstudies.com/article/opr/t125/e4.

33. For details on accounting see T. Hayashi, *On Islamic Accounting: Its Future Impacts on Western Accounting*, (Kyoto: International University of Japan, Monograph Series, 1988).
34. *PEIPT*, 256.
35. Ibid. See also Walther Björkman, *Beiträge zur Geschichte der Staatskanzlei im islamischen Ägypten*, 1928.
36. Gibb, *Mohammedanism: An Historical Survey*, 72-84.
37. The Local Government Act 1974 of the United Kingdom which established two commissions, one each for England and Wales. Certain matters such as decisions affecting the public generally and the conduct of criminal investigations are outside their jurisdiction.
38. See al-Shātibī, Abū Ishāq Ibrāhīm, *al-Muwāfaqāt fī Uṣūl al-Sharī'ah*, in two volumes, (Beirut: Dar al-Fikr, 1990); See Muhammad Khalid Masud, *Islamic Legal Philosophy: A Study of Abū Ishāq al-Shātibi's Life and Thought*, (Islamabad, 1977).
39. This is, of course, an oversimplification for there is much more required of a *mujtahid*—the practitioner of *ijtihād*—as Chapter 7 will show.
40. al-Alwānī, *Source Methodology in Islamic Jurisprudence*, 58
41. Ibid., 59.
42. Mohamed El-Tahir El-Mesawi, "From al-Shāṭibī's legal hermeneutics to thematic exegesis of the Qur'ān," Intellectual Discourse, 20:2 (2012) 189-214; accessed on 22 February 2016, available at: https://www.researchgate.net/publication/277118089_From_al-Shatibi's_legal_hermeneutics_to_thematic_exegesis_of_the_Quran
43. al-Ghazālī, *al-Mustaṣfā min 'Ilm al-Uṣūl*, 2 vols. (Cairo: al-Maktabah al-Tijāriyyah, 1356/1937), I, 139-140; Vol. 1 was translated as Abu Hamid Al-Ghazālī's Juristic Doctrine in *al-*

Mustaṣfā min 'Ilm al-Uṣūl by Hammad, Ahmad Zaki, (University of Chicago Press, 1987).

44. Tawfique al-Mubārak, "Imām al-Shātibī," accessed June 2015 available at www.iais.org.my/e/attach/Imam_al-Shatibi.
45. The traditional pigeon-holing of the *maqāṣid* into five categories has been viewed by some as inadequate to deal with the problems of modernity and the contemporary challenges facing the *ummah.* This is discussed further under in Chapter 9.
46. Sūrah al-Anbiyā', *āyah* 107.
47. Sūrah al-Ḥijr, *āyah* 9; Asad, *The Message of the Qur'ān.*
48. Schacht, *Introduction*, 76-79.
49. Coulson, *History*, 26; R. M. Savory, *Introduction to Islamic Civilization*, (Cambridge University Press, 1976), 59.
50. Sūrah al-Tawbah, *āyah* 60. There is *ijmā'* that 'Umar's decision, though unprecedented, does not violate this verse, taking into consideration the *maqāṣid al-Sharī'ah.* See Ibn Qayyim al-Jawziyyah, *al-Ṭuruq al-Ḥukmiyyah fī al-Siyāsah al-Shar'iyyah*, edited by Muhammad Jamil Ghazi, (Jeddah: Matba'at al-Madāni), 16; also Mahmassani, *Falsafāt al-Tashrī' fī al-Islām*, 207.
51. Coulson, *History*, 23.
52. Sūrah al-Māidah, *āyah* 38.
53. See Abū Zahrah, *Uṣūl*, generally on the conditions (*shurūṭ*) of *maṣlaḥah.*
54. al-Ṭalāq, *āyah* 61.
55. Vogel, *Islamic Law,* 185-186, citations omitted.
56. Natana J. DeLong-Bas, *Wahhabi Islam: From Revival and Reform to Global Jihad*, (I.B. Tauris, 2007), 123-192
57. Vogel, *Islamic Law,* 186.
58. Coulson, *History*, 26.
59. Ibid., 27.
60. P. Crone and M. Hinds, *God's Caliph: Religious Authority in the First Centuries of Islam* (Cambridge, 1986), 43.

61. Amyn B. Sajoo, "Ethics in the Civitas" in *Civil Society in the Muslim World: Contemporary Perspectives*, edited by Amyn B. Sajoo, (London and New York: I.B. Tauris Publishers, 2004), 225.
62. See the discussion in Chapter 4 on the treatises of al-Māwardī, al-Juwaynī and al-Ghazālī on the *fiqh* of rebellion and the duty of enjoining good and forbidding wrong.
63. Amyn Sajoo, *Ethics* op cit.
64. Albert Hourani, *Arabic Thought in the Liberal Age, 1798-1939*, (Cambridge University Press, 1983), 148-53.
65. Ibid., 148.
66. Ibid., 139-141.
67. Mark Sedgwick, *Muhammad Abduh*, (Oneworld Publications, 2014)
68. Schacht, *Introduction*, 100.
69. Gerber, *State, Society, and Law in Islam*, 26.
70. *PEIPT*, 349.
71. Ibid., 349-50.
72. Schacht, *Introduction*, 92-93.
73. H. A. R. Gibb, *Studies on the Civilization of Islam*, (1962) (Routledge, 2013), 200.
74. Sūrah Āl ʿImrān, *āyah* 110.
75. Nasr, *Study Quran*, 9397.
76. H. L. A. Hart, *The Concept of Law*, (Clarendon Press, 1997).
77. Sūrah al-Māidah, *āyah* 3; Asad, *Message of the Qur'ān*.
78. Ibn Qayyim al-Jawziyyah, *al-Ṭuruq al-Ḥukmiyyah fī al-Siyāsah al-Sharʿiyyah*, edited by Muhammad Jamil Ghazi. Jeddah: Matbaʿat al-Madani, n.d. *passim*.
79. Sadakat Kadri, *Heaven on Earth: A Journey Through Shari'a Law from the Deserts of Ancient Arabia*, (Macmillan, 2012), 139.
80. See for instance, Asad, *Principles of State*.
81. This sentiment coincided with the rise of modernism, nationalism and then fundamentalism in the Muslim countries.

82. His best exposition on political philosophy remains *Minhāj al-Sunnah al-Nabawiyyah* from which much credo on the Islamic state is to be derived discussion of which is, however, beyond the scope of this monograph.
83. Richard Paul Mitchell, *The Society of the Muslim Brothers*, (Oxfonird University Press, 1993), 68-69; *cf.* discussion in Chapter 4 on the classical Shāfi'ī positions concerning rebellion versus duty to obey those in authority; Gilles Kepel, *Muslim Extremism in Egypt: The Prophet and Pharaoh*, (University of California Press, 1985), 196-200; Laoust, Henri. "Ibn Taymiyya." *Encyclopaedia of Islam*, Second Edition. Edited by: P. Bearman, Th. Bianquis, C.E. Bosworth, E. van Donzel, W.P. Heinrichs. Brill Online, 2016. Reference. 29 January 2016 http://referenceworks.brillonline.com/entries/encyclopaedia-of-islam-2/ibn-taymiyya-SIM_3388.
84. Muqtedar Khan, "A Fresh look at Sayyid Quṭb's *Milestones*," *The Milli Gazette*, accessed 21 August, 2015; available at http://gemsofislamism.tripod.com/milestones.html
85. Sayyid Quṭb, *Ma'ālim fī al-Ṭarīq*, (Egypt: Kazi Publications, 1964); translated as *Milestones*. (The Mother Mosque Foundation, 1981), 11, 19.
86. Omer Ali Saifudeen, "The Chosen" An Examination of Extremist Muslim Narratives, Discourse and Ideologies In Cyberspace. PhD Thesis, 13 citing the Arabic text.
87. *Islam: The Religion of the Future* (Delhi: Markazi Maktaba Islami, 1974), 21-22; cited in John Calvert, *Sayyid Quṭb and the Origins of Radical Islamism*, (Hurst and Company, London, 2010), 208.
88. The Islamic Concept and Its Characteristics, 2-16; *Khaṣā'iṣ al-Taṣawwur al-Islāmī wa Muqawwamātuhu* (The Characteristics and Values of Islamic Conduct), 1960, 5-22; Calvert, 208.

Chapter 7

Sharīʿah Sources Revisited

This chapter as the title suggests is a revisiting of the sources of the *Sharīʿah*, and not an attempt at re-inventing the wheel. The *Sharīʿah* sources have been thoroughly and exhaustively studied, extracted and defined by the *fuqahā'* of the ages and anyone who pretends that he can formulate a "new" source is either suffering from delusions of grandeur or knowingly engaging in self-mockery. As we have seen in Chapter 2, the classical theory of Islamic law—*uṣūl al-fiqh*—came about during the third century of the *Hijrah*. Experts in this discipline spent probably their entire lives trying to fathom not just the sources but the exact nature and scope. As raised at the very outset of this study, Imām Mālik regarded the Sunnah of the people of Medina as a source of law but do the other mujtahids agree? While there is general agreement concerning *ijmā'* there is *khilāf* with regards to the scope of its legal purport such as whether it is binding on all as well as the subject matter. Can there be *ijmāʿ* on theoretical issues? Nevertheless, as a result of the unceasing efforts of the *'ulamā'* in attempting to ascertain the sources of the *Sharīʿah* law, they effectively mapped out the jurisprudential landscape of the Islamic world. The question is: Is this a permanent immutable landscape or is it a map with shifting boundaries and changing perimeters? According to a generally held view, the *Sharīʿah* law is derived from four major sources, namely, the Qur'ān, the Sunnah, the *ijmāʿ* of the scholars of the orthodox community, and *qiyās*.[1]

What we propose to do is to suggest that this conventional ascription of the "major" sources may no longer be the best approach if we are to do justice to the comprehensiveness of the *Sharīʿah* as an all-encompassing paradigm for the advancement of the *ummah* in its broadest sense. In this regard, a fundamental point that needs to be stressed is that the foundational pillars of the *Sharīʿah* are not four but only two—the Qur'ān and the Sunnah. These two, and only these two, are the immutable divine sources of *Sharīʿah* law. Everything else—*ijmāʿ*, *qiyās* and others such as *istiḥsān, istiṣḥāb, al-maṣālih al-mursalah*, and all else that have been diligently worked out by the great jurists of Islam—is secondary as a source of law derived through the process of *ijtihād*. For example, it is contended that even *ʿurf* and *ʿādah* if accepted as a source of law is first derived via the process of *ijtihād*. Issues such as which part of the *ʿurf* and *ʿādah* and at which level of importance it occupies may only be resolved by *ijtihād*. The bifurcation of primary and secondary sources—without purporting to add or subtract them—is warranted by the fact that failure to separate them is the main cause of confusion and uncertainty in drawing the line between God's law and juristic law. To put that into perspective, that is equivalent to drawing the line between *naql* and *ʿaql* or *strictu sensu* between *Sharīʿah* and *fiqh*, in that while the *Sharīʿah* is the Divine law (in the sense as explained in Chapter 1), *fiqh* is the derivative law with the rules derived (*ahkām al-mu'tasaba*) from the Qur'ān and the Sunnah. While the *Sharīʿah* may thus be considered as the divinely ordained and immutable law, *fiqh*, on the other hand, cannot be treated as such. To reiterate our point as made at the outset, the contention that *fiqh* is God's law for all time and unchangeable, is therefore groundless. Immutability of the law lies only within the domain of God, not the *fuqahā'* or the *mujtahid*s who themselves were God-fearing men of virtue and supreme piety and would never have pretended to confer upon themselves the mantle of infallibility. Again, in making this assertion, we are not trivializing the importance of *fiqh* rules.

Indeed, by separating the secondary from the primary sources, we can free *Sharī'ah* from the imposition of unwarranted constraints that has led to Islamic law being seen as ossified desert law unable to respond to the dynamic changes of society. By placing *ijtihād* in its proper place, that is, the use of the intellect—*'aql*—within the boundaries of the revealed texts—*naql*—the ensuing rulings will blend with and not run counter to the *Sharī'ah.* The question that arises is will not the use of reason, being merely a kind of interpretation, lead us into error? On the contrary, it is submitted that it is the use of our intellect when such use is warranted that will save us from error. The evidence is abundant:

> "And they will add: 'Had we but listened [to those warnings], or [at least] used our own reason, we would not [now] be among those who are destined for the blazing flame![2]"

God bestowed on man the faculties *sam'* and *'aql*, the first being the capacity to listen and understand and the second being reason, intelligence or intellect. *'Aql* employed within the bounds as we have stated will thus lead man to the realization that the distinction between right and wrong is to be found through the medium of the revelation provided that he either listens or uses his faculty of reason (*law kunnā nasma'u wa na'qilu*—had we but listened or used our reason). The Qur'ān—the paramount source of the *Sharī'ah*—abounds with references calling on man to contemplate and think as well as to use reason.[3] The Prophet was instructed to transmit through recitation part of the speech of God communicated verbatim from Angel Gabriel. That part is the Qur'ān. The rest of the speech the Prophet transmitted by expressing its meaning in his own words or in his deeds, that part is the Sunnah.[4] It is the Qur'ān first as the font of Islamic law that we shall now revisit.

The Qur'ān

The general view is that there can be no doubt about the Qur'ān's final authority and infallibility or that it had been handed down intact.

Hence, the Qur'ān has always been the first and most highly esteemed source of law.[5] Nevertheless, one should not lose sight of the fact that the Qur'ān is not a legal code because its main purpose "is to awaken in man the higher consciousness of his relation with God and the universe" even as it appears to mandate the integration of religion and state, ethics and politics "much in the same way as Plato does in his Republic."[6] What is clear is that the dynamic outlook of the Qur'ān and the non-territorial character of Islam combine to draw "adherents from a variety of mutually repellant races, and then transforming this atomic aggregate into a people possessing a self-consciousness of their own."[7]

It is this "dynamic outlook" and "non-territorial character" as opposed to "passive" and "parochial" nature as some would have it that sets the Qur'ān as the first and foremost foundation for the realization of the commands of the Lawmaker: "And We reveal the Scripture unto thee as an exposition of all things," read with "We have neglected nothing in the Book (of Our decrees)."[8] Fundamentalists cite these verses as proof that the *Sharīʿah* law is all-encompassing and all that is needed to govern the *ummah* is found within the four walls of the Qur'ān because the Book of Allah clarifies all things with nothing neglected. This is essentially an incorrect, literalist and exceedingly narrow reading. According to al-Ṭabarī and al-Zamakhsharī, the Qur'an is a "clarification of all things" in that it contains all the religious knowledge that individuals need. We have taken some trouble in Chapters 1 and 2 to explain the difference between *dīn* as religion and *fiqh* first as knowledge and then technically as law. Obviously, "religious knowledge" as stated here is not "legal knowledge," the former being the concern of *uṣūl al-dīn* or *ʿilm al-kalām* and the latter being associated with *uṣūl al-fiqh*. As for nothing being neglected, Fakhr al-Dīn al-Rāzī (d. 606/1210) comments that although the Qur'ān may not contain detailed knowledge of all things, it contains the essential and principal knowledge from which all the Islamic sciences and all spiritually beneficial knowledge may be derived.[9] Again, it does not appertain to law as such.

Does this mean that the Qur'ān is incomplete as far as *Sharī'ah* law is concerned and that there is more that needs to be done? The answer is no first and then yes, oxymoronic as it might seem. Even though we have noted earlier that the Qur'ān is not a legal code, it is nevertheless God's Law and it is counter-intuitive to speak of God's law as being incomplete. As evidenced by the first verse of the revelation—"Read in the name of thy Lord who created"—Islam is an "epistemic faith anchored in sophisticated spiritual, rational, and practical knowledge."[10] From the first revelation and through almost the entire period of the prophethood spanning 23 years, the Qur'ān was revealed mostly in response to situations and problems with which the Prophet had to deal (*asbāb al-nuzūl*). We have discussed earlier the significance of the Prophet's death and the implications in respect of the extent and scope of the *Sharī'ah* law as laid down by then. The much-cited *āyah*

> ("This day have I perfected your religion for you, completed my favour upon you, and have chosen for you Islam as your religion")

may be taken as "a profound closure of God's Law," giving a sense of completion, and a code of behavior with broad principles as well as specific rules, "and a general invitation for further reflection over legal matters."[11]

The Qur'ān is, in a sense, the primary document for the purposes of laying down the generic principles of the law and in respect of this, it is complete, preordained and immutable. The answer to the second part is in the affirmative. Yes, more needs to be done because man's knowledge of the *Sharī'ah* is incomplete, being limited to the level of his *fiqh*. Indeed, the Qur'ān has neglected nothing in terms of the general principles that may be derived for man to attain a balance between the temporal and the spiritual but, as noted earlier concerning the difference between *fiqh* and *Sharī'ah*, Islamic law did not come down in one package but had to be articulated by the *fuqahā*. This means that it developed over time against a vast and varied geo-political and cultural landscape. And undoubtedly this landscape was not static but one that continued to evolve with the march of time. According to Asad, the limited scope of the explicit ordinances contained in the Qur'ān and the Sunnah was "meant to provide a most essential deliberate safeguard against legal and social rigidity" and that the Law-Giver never intended the *Sharī'ah* to cover in detail all conceivable exigencies of life:

> "He intended no more, no less to stake out, as it were, the legal boundaries within which the community ought to develop, leaving the enormous multitude of 'possible' legal situations to be decided from case to case in accordance with the requirements of the time and of changing social conditions."[12]

A distinct feature of Qur'ānic legislation is the broad and general tenor of its prescriptions as to what the aspirations of the *ummah* should be. Because the Qur'ān is concerned with fundamentals essential for the establishment of a civilized society, it commands the believer to do this, and not do that; or if a certain transaction is intended, what conditions must be fulfilled; or if one transgresses a certain prohibition, such will be the punishment. It enjoins, as desirable norms of behaviour, compassion for the weak and the marginalized, fairness and good faith in commercial dealings, and incorruptibility in the administration of justice.[13]

As for the contention that the Qur'ān is complete in the sense that nothing more needs to be added to the *corpus juris* of *Sharī'ah* law, some hard facts will suffice to counter it. The quantity of Qur'ānic legislation (*al-āyāt al-shar'iyyah*) amounts to no more than 500 *āyahs*. This represents only a fraction of the Qur'ān. And of these 500 *āyah*s, the majority is concerned with ritual practices pertaining to worship, fasting and the pilgrimage. No more than 80 *āyah*s deal with legal issues of a military or political nature.[14] Spread out over the Qur'ān are ordinances governing civil and commercial transactions, as for example,

> "… and who are faithful to their trusts and to their pledges,"; "and [truly pious are] they who keep their promises whenever they promise"; and "Be true to your covenants."[15]

The Qur'ān is not concerned with laying down precise rules governing those transactions or situations. For example, in respect of the last quoted verse, the term *'aqd* ("covenant") denotes a solemn undertaking or engagement involving more than one party. But what exactly are these covenants and how many categories are there, no fixed rule is provided in the Qur'ān which is then left to be explicated by the jurists whose first recourse would be other verses in the Qur'ān, if any. If not, then they would refer to the Sunnah by sifting through the voluminous *aḥādīth*. Again, if no clear *naṣṣ* could be derived, then they would resort to *ijtihād*. Contrary to popular understanding, the exercise of *ijtihād* need not be confined to efforts to derive legal principles (notwithstanding the technical definitions of a *mujtaḥid*) for when stripped to its bare semantic foundations, *ijtihād* is any wholehearted and steadfast endeavour to fully understand God's speech and later by extension the Sunnah. (Nevertheless, as we shall see, al-Āmidī's technical definition of *ijtihād* straitjackets it to only *aḥkām* or legal principles). According to al-Rāghib al-Iṣfahānī (d. 502/1108)[16], the covenants referred to in this verse "are of three kinds: the covenants between God and man (*i.e.* man's obligations towards God), between man and his own soul, and between the individual and his fellow-men" rendering therefore only the third category to be within the realm of commercial transactions. But the beauty of such a short and succinct (part of a) verse lies in its capacity to embrace "the entire area of man's moral and social responsibilities,"[17] which would not be grasped if constrained to a mere legalistic reading. In modern times, the failure to grasp this fundamental aspect of Qur'ānic legislation is one of the root causes of the inability of traditionalists and conservative *'ulamā'* to articulate a dynamic and vibrant *Sharīʿah*-based legal system. There are exceptions of course to this generic feature where in certain instances, the Qur'ān is explicitly specific. For example, specific sanctions are prescribed such as the punishment of flogging, of 100 stripes for the crime of *zinā'* (adultery) on the adulterer and the adulteress, or 80 stripes for the crime of *qadhf* (calumny) on the person who accuses someone of committing *zinā'* but fails to bring forth the requisite number of witnesses. Another exception is the set of Qur'ānic injunctions on inheritance constituting the law of *farāid*, specifying fixed portions of the estate of the deceased as the entitlement of certain nominated relatives. This Qur'ānic legislation, nevertheless, is by no means comprehensive and recourse must still be made to the Sunnah for a full explication of the quantum of apportionment.

Another key aspect of Qur'ānic legislation is the element of a combination of decisive or clear verses (*āyāt muḥkamāt*) and those that are open-textured or allegorical (*āyāt mutashābihāt*). The Qur'ān (vide Sūrah Āl 'Imrān, *āyah* 7) itself provides its exposition on this point, as has been dealt with in Chapter 3 but that was in the context of justifying the use of hermeneutics (*ta'wīl*) in respect of the discourse pertaining to *kalām*. Here, we shall focus on the implications in respect of extracting *aḥkām* from the Qur'ān as the primary source in respect of *āyāt mutashābihāt*. The majoritarian position concerning *āyāt mutashābihāt* is that hermeneutics is prohibited in terms of *fiqh* for it involves speculation and speculation cannot take the place of certainty and God has made it clear that "no one knows its hidden meanings except God" (*wa mā ya'lamū ta'wīlahu illa Allāh*). On the other hand, a contrarian position taken by Ibn Rushd maintains that "those who are firmly grounded in knowledge" (*al-rāsikhūnā fī al-'ilmi*) are also able to interpret the allegorical verses. As we have noted in Chapter 3, Ibn Rushd in his *Kitāb Faṣl al-Maqāl* considers it a duty for "those whose powers of theoretical understanding have attained the dialectical level" to engage in *ta'wīl* and in this regard the Mu'tazilites are generally sounder in their statements. He, however, lodges the caveat that hermeneutics is only meant for the initiated while the laity, being incapable of understanding beyond the exoteric meaning, are forbidden from engaging in *ta'wīl*.[18] He, however, rejects the notion that *ta'wīl* is unfathomable. The logic of Ibn Rushd's argument is compelling: if knowledge of the meaning of allegorical verses resided exclusively with God, with no possibility for mortals—regardless of their *maqām* (the station or level attained in the gradation of knowledge)—to grasp, what would be the point of revealing them in the first place?[19] The rejoinder to this is that these verses are intended as a reminder of man's limited capacity in his knowledge and that though he may not comprehend, by reason alone, the vast unseen realities of the universe, he should have the humility to believe in their existence.[20]

But where do we draw the line between *tafsīr* (exegesis) and *ta'wīl* (hermeneutics)? The distinction appears to be quite obvious. *Tafsīr* is a conventional method of understanding the Qur'ān by exoteric interpretation employing formalist textualism through examining the *asbāb al-nuzūl* (causes for revelation/historical context), the *lughah* (linguistic/grammatical context), the *aḥādīth* (the Traditions) and the employment of *manṭiq* (logic), and to a certain degree *'aql* (reason). In this sense, it is more accessible to the well-trained *fuqahā'*. *Ta'wīl*, on the other hand, is pre-conditioned on a necessarily rare and elitist quality that appertains to "those who are firmly grounded in knowledge" in a sense that goes beyond the meaning conventionally associated with the *'ulamā'* in general. *Ta'wīl* presupposes esoteric understanding, necessitating intuition and creative imagination that is only accessible with knowledge at the highest level including *ma'rifah Allāh* (the knowledge of God) associated with the master practitioners of *tasawwuf* (Sufism) or knowledge associated with *falsafah* among the adepts such as Ibn Rushd himself. In light of this, it appears to be too tall an order for anyone except the chosen few to exercise *ta'wīl*, not to mention the disconnect generally between *fuqahā'* and Sufis.

As such there is also a "more mundane level" of *ta'wīl* recognised by the *'ulamā'* as merely a departure from the manifest (*ẓāhir*) meaning of a text in favour of another meaning where there is evidence to justify the departure. *Ta'wīl* of this kind is generally accepted based on traditions of the Prophet's companions having used it at deriving rules from the primary sources. Apart from the general prohibition against applying *ta'wīl* for commands and prohibitions in as much as they are as a rule not expressed in *mutashābihāt* terms, *ta'wīl* which is otherwise properly constructed constitutes a valid basis for judicial decisions.[21] However, the conventional position is that as a rule, *mutashābihāt* verses are not amenable to either *tafsīr* or *ta'wīl* for the purposes of deriving the *nuṣūṣ* (legal textual authorities).

Ibn Rushd's position on this would therefore be unorthodox but it was in reality neither new nor that radical for more than 150 years before that, Ahmad ibn Muhammad al-Tha'labī, in his *al-Kashf wa al-Bayān 'an Tafsīr al-Qur'ān* (*Tafsīr al-Tha'labī*) had posited that there are no verses in the Qur'ān which are not amenable to *tafsīr* because "scholars are partakers in God's knowledge of every aspect of Qur'ānic interpretation" and the *mufassirūn* never refrained from interpreting any verse just because it was *mutashābih*.[22] That is because for al-Tha'labī, *mutashābih* carries an entirely different meaning and has nothing to do with being ambiguous or allegorical. It means verses which resemble each other in manner and style. Thus, there are two categories of verses: clear as in *muḥkam* and similar as in *mutashābih*.

The approach advocated by al-Tha'labī in widening the berth of *ta'wīl* to such an extent could well open the floodgate of interpretations leading to a free-for-all exegetic slugfest, as it were, causing doctrinal clashes as each *tafsīr* is being validated on the grounds of "consistency with the surrounding context." This goes back to the first principle: what precisely are the criteria for the determination of validity? It appears that this confusion is symptomatic only of the sceptics because in al-Tha'labī's book, there is only one criterion for accepting or rejecting *ta'wīl* which is the compatibility with the Qur'ān and the Sunnah (*ba'da an yakūna muwāfiqan li al-Kitābi wa al-Sunnah*).[23] The compatibility, however, is in respect not of philological but doctrinal fundamentals by virtue of which, al-Thaʿlabī being a Shāfiʿī Ashʿarite, had no qualms about rejecting wholesale the interpretation of the Muʿtazilites.

One significant aspect of al-Thaʿlabī's *tafsīr* doctrine is the conception of a salvific Qur'ān, which for the purposes of this chapter —and for this monograph as a whole—is not merely of academic interest but for practical reason when we consider the Qur'ān a source of law for the *ummah*. Apart from the traditional teaching concerning the untold benefits of Qur'ānic recitation for the soul of the believer which will be bestowed on him from on high as a reward, what we are interested here is the notion of the Qur'ān as a vehicle of salvation for both the individual and the community as well that will inhere from a proper interpretation of the text itself. The salvific message, according to al-Thaʿlabī, is at the core of the Qur'ān and is an overarching theme in his *ta'wīl* paradigm, guiding the nature and direction of his hermeneutical enterprise.[24] One example suffices to illustrate the point as in the verse:

> "He mixed the two seas such that they meet one another. (But) between them lies a barrier that they transgress not."[25]

During al-Thaʿlabī's time, this was understood as a reference to the meeting of salt and fresh water. As the predicate in "they transgress not" is in the dual form, most interpret it as a reference to the two seas themselves. They meet but, because of their distinct natures, will not intermingle and thus compromise one another.[26] Another interpretation views the two seas as a metaphor for the sky and the earth.[27] Yet others regard one sea representing formal religious knowledge and the other an allusion to spiritual knowledge (*maʿrifah*). In the complete individual, the two meet but do not mix so that the formal does not stifle the spiritual and the spiritual does not compromise the formal.[28]

Rising from these somewhat mundane and predictable interpretations, al-Thaʿlabī offers a refreshingly novel *tafsīr*: "There exist two seas between the creature (*al-ʿabd*) and his Lord. The first one is the sea of salvation (*al-najāh*) and it is the Qur'ān; whoever upholds the Qur'ān is saved. The second is the sea of perdition (*halāk*) and it is the world; whoever grasps on to it and takes it as his resort, he shall perish."[29] This was indeed a tour de force in interpretation. By ascribing the metaphor of salvation to the Qur'ān, al-Tha'labī did what no exegete before him had done. It is argued that in incorporating mystical interpretation into his commentary, al-Tha'labī made the Qur'ān "the most polyvalent text in Islamic culture: it was the only text decipherable both philologically and mystically." This may be true in respect of the interpretations before and during his time, but it is now well established that the interpretations of the Sufi masters and the accomplished *falāsifah* of Islam too have contributed to the manifold layers of meanings of the Qur'ānic text: the likes of Muḥyī al-Dīn Ibn 'Arabī (637/1240) and his *Futūḥāt al-Makkiyyah* or Ibn Sīnā's *al-Ḥikmah al-Mashriqiyyah*, Suhrawardī's *Ishrāq* and the interpretative writings of Mullā Ṣadrā just to name a few. Nevertheless, it is true that he was a pioneer in this regard "making the mystical vision a part of the general culture and not the object of a *Kulturkamph* in early medieval Islam" evidenced by the fact that shortly after al-Tha'labī, "mysticism, as an intellectual current, would move from the periphery to the centre."[30]

The Sunnah

While the Qur'ān was preserved textually soon after the demise of the Prophet, that is, way before the Uthmānic Recension, the Prophet's Sunnah, however, remained uncertain for decades. A preliminary issue concerning the Sunnah as an immutable divine source centres on this uncertainty: to what extent it played a role as an integral pillar of the *Sharī'ah* to early Muslims. This is because early Muslims focused on the Qur'ān to the exclusion of everything else and partly because the definition of the Sunnah was far from certain. In addition to this normative uncertainty, the logistical difficulties of retrieving the Prophet's Sunnah posed additional barriers. Mostly oral and some written *aḥādīth* circulated in different parts of the emerging Islamic empire. But the task of separating the true from the false *aḥādīth* and verifying both the substance and the source of each reported *hadith* was a huge undertaking, particularly because opposing political groups used and even manufactured *aḥādīth* as weapons to legitimize their respective political, theological, social, and familial viewpoints.

In any event, it has been resolved that there are three strata of the Sunni *ḥadīth* canon, the first and foremost being the two foundational classics of al-Bukhārī and Muslim commonly known as the *Ṣaḥīḥayn.* Next there is the four-book selection that adds the two *Sunan*s of Abū Dāwūd (d. 275/889) and al-Nasā'ī (d. 303/915). There is also the Five-Book canon which incorporates the *Jami'* of al-Tirmidhī (d. 279/892). The final stratum is the Six Book canon that adds either the *Sunan* of Ibn Mājah (d. 273/887), the *Sunan* of al-Dāraquṭnī (d. 385/995) or the *Muwaṭṭa'* of Mālik ibn Anas (d. 179/796).[31] It should be noted that the Mālikīs traditionally reject the *Sunan* of Ibn Mājah naturally asserting the pre-eminence of the *Muwaṭṭa'* over the former.[32]

Another preliminary issue concerns the confusion arising from the usage of "Sunnah" and "*ḥadīth*" interchangeably as if they are synonymous. "Sunnah" is a term of pre-Islamic origin for established customs and usages in the social and commercial context of the Arabs. With the advent of Islam, it attained a specific meaning denoting exclusively the actions and activities of the Prophet but it is incorrect to say, as some writers do, that this Prophetic Sunnah must be taken entirely as a source of the *Sharī'ah*, as we shall discuss more fully later. The *ḥadīth* (pl. *aḥādīth*) is a written record of the sayings of the Prophet as transmitted via a verifiable chain of narrators (*isnād*). *Aḥādīth* emerged in the course of the first *hijrī* century, comprising predominantly reports from the Companions. Eventually, *aḥādīth* circulated in very large numbers and several collections of those deemed authentic were made from the mid-third/mid-ninth century onward. As detailed earlier, six of these became canonical. There is definitive *ijmā'* (universal consensus) that an authentic *ḥadīth* is an integral part of the Sunnah and, subject to the finer divisions on the categories of the Sunnah, is prima facie a source of the *Sharī'ah.*[33]

There remains also some dispute concerning the normative

hierarchy of the Qur'ān and the Sunnah. According to the principles of *uṣūl al-fiqh*, the rule is that the Qur'ān takes precedence over the Sunnah in terms of the weightage to be assigned to its normative commands and prohibitions. Common sense would therefore suggest that no *ḥadīth* can modify the Qur'ān, let alone abrogate it. On the subject of abrogation and avoiding the technical obfuscation that this subject is notorious for, it should first be seen broadly as a theory of the repeal of an earlier ruling by a later ruling. Thus, an earlier Qur'ānic rule may be abrogated by a subsequent Qur'ānic ruling. Likewise, a ruling by the Prophet or a Sunnatic ruling may be abrogated by a subsequent Sunnatic ruling. The problem arises in the case of a principle which says that a Sunnatic ruling may also abrogate an earlier Qur'ānic ruling, counter-intuitive as it may sound. Indeed, not all Sunnatic rulings may have this abrogative effect, only those that are based on a *mutawātir ḥadīth*, which is the strongest of the *ḥadīth* in the hierarchy that can be used as a source for extracting a principle of law.[34]

Al-Āmidī defines abrogation as "addressed speech of the Legislator that obstructs the continuing operation of a rule established by means of preceding speech."[35] Several essential factors must therefore be fulfilled before a judgment on a text as abrogated can be pronounced. There must be a genuine contradiction between two texts. Only a text that preceded another may be abrogated. The categories of texts must be such as to permit an abrogation.[36] Now, the main problem with Sunnatic abrogation is of course the difficulty of accepting that Allah's messenger can override His command. The logic of this objection is not difficult to fathom. Since all rulings of the Prophet are those issued during his lifetime which would therefore be also the lifetime of the period of Qur'ānic revelation, why would it be necessary for the Prophet to issue his own ruling to override the Qur'ān? Why confound subsequent inquiry when it would have been just as easy for the primary Lawgiver to come out with another ruling (via revelation) to repeal an earlier one? Why leave certain rulings to be repealed by the Qur'ān and others by the Prophet? In light of the anomalies and doubts raised, certain scholars have categorically rejected this doctrine altogether while others have rejected this aspect of the abrogation.[37]

On the whole, however, abrogation makes sense and is reflective of the dynamic nature of legislation. In certain instances it also reflects the gradualism of legislation in line with the persuasive manner in which the rules were imparted and the transitional character of the earliest Muslim community.[38] Consider, for example, the legislation pertaining to the prohibition of wine drinking. Initially, the rule was that one should not perform the ritual prayers while still intoxicated. Put in another way, you could still drink, but if you wanted to be in communion with God, stay sober. Is this a correct interpretation? Certain scholars say that this is incorrect because the principle must be read in the light of another which is one of the five pillars of the religion, that is, the commandment for every Muslim to pray five times a day. Getting drunk will therefore mean being unable to perform this duty which in turn means failure to practise as a Muslim. While that is true, the argument is misconceived because the ruling at this juncture is correct and even if interpreted literally is acceptable because the formula for the five daily prayers did not come into existence until after the Isrāʾ and the Miʿrāj incident when the Prophet is believed to have ascended to heaven and among other things was finally given the order to set the specific number of times of worship for Muslims.

So, to the Arabs who were the early converts to the faith, wine was not forbidden but they should by no means desecrate the sanctity of prayer and annoy fellow worshippers in the congregation. This was reverse psychology. That itself would be a powerful antidote to the need for that quick fix. But then came a more powerful message appealing to the rational mind of the believer—that wine has beneficial as well as harmful effects and that the latter outweighs the former.[39] For temporal reasons alone, this could be taken as a message to avoid it though at this stage, there was still no outright ban. To be sure, the final clear prohibition came much later when it was evident that the Muslims were mentally and, we would imagine, spiritually prepared for the final nail in the coffin for wine drinking:

> "O ye who believe! Strong drink and games of chance and idols and divining arrows are only an infamy of Satan's handiwork. Leave it aside in order that ye may succeed."[40]

This verse repeals the legal rulings of all the previous verses concerning wine drinking but it had yet to become a *ḥadd* offence punishable by 80 lashes until the time of the Caliph 'Umar, his predecessor Caliph Abū Bakr having prescribed only 40 lashes, a subject that we have already dealt with in Chapter 2.

The doctrine of abrogation is therefore particularly relevant in the discussion on *ḥudūd* crimes when the question arises concerning the applicability of certain punishments within the broad spectrum of the *Sharī'ah*. For example, if a Sunnatic rule is allowed to abrogate a Qur'ānic injunction, then stoning for adultery, purportedly ordered by the Prophet, will be recognised as a *ḥadd* punishment. This flies in the face of a specific injunction prescribing the punishment of 100 lashes as ordained in the Qur'ān. It is contended that a rationalist approach to the subject of abrogation is needed in order to take the discourse of practical jurisprudence to a level that is not counter-intuitive. However, the scope of this present study does not permit venturing into the detailed expositions concerning the correctness or otherwise of specific *ḥudūd* punishments.

The Sunnah, while explicating certain general commands and prohibitions laid down in the Qur'ān, did not provide for every legal issue that may arise in the course of personal, commercial or international dealings. According to Yusuf al-Qaraḍāwī, "the Sunnah distinguishes what the Qur'ān combines, it disentangles what the Qur'ān intertwines, and it specifies what the Qur'ān deals with in general terms."[41] There is nothing in the biographical accounts of the Prophet or the Traditions to suggest that it was ever the Prophet's intention to create a legal system during his life time which was to regulate the whole life of his followers. The relative paucity of legislative *āyah*s in no way constituted a drawback on Islamic law because essential aspects of worship as well as juridical and political matters were regulated simply by the Sunnah, in the Prophet's role as the ultimate arbiter entrusted to interpret the general provisions of the Qur'ān and passing judgments with absolute finality.

"In the Prophet's role as the ultimate arbiter"—that leads us to a crucial point in considering the subject of the nature of prophetic authority. We stated earlier that a preliminary issue concerning the Sunnah as a divine *Sharīʿah* source centres on the uncertainty of ascertaining the Prophet's Sunnah and that this lack of certainty appears to be finally resolved by the time the canonical *ḥadīth* collections were compiled. But that is not the end of the story because tied with the concept of prophetic authority is the doctrine of *ʿiṣmah* or infallibility. It posits that all prophets are *maʿṣūm*, that is, shielded from falling into error or sin by God's decree. However, this is not a doctrine supported by textual evidence and is conceptually at odds with Sunni orthodoxy. On the other hand, *ʿiṣmah* fits snugly within the matrix of Shīʿite theology which, among other things, places the infallibility of the *imām*s as a fundamental article of faith. Nevertheless, *ʿiṣmah* was an important guarantee of the integrity of the Qur'ān as it was revealed to mankind through the vehicle of prophecy which perforce must be via a Prophet who is free from error. But from the point of the *Sharīʿah*, a more significant reason is that it provided the essential foundation for the authority of the Prophetic Sunnah. Thus, by the third/ninth century, the doctrine found its way into mainstream Sunni theology.[42] The question then is: what is the scope of this authority? The *fuqahā'* distinguished *al-sunnah al-ʿādiyyah* (the Prophet's personal habits and preferences) from *sunnah al-hudā* (the Prophet's mission-related activity) and considered only the latter as legally enforceable and in this regard the great majority of them agreed that in all matters pertaining to revelation the Prophet was *maʿṣūm*. To be precise, in his missionary role, the sayings and actions of the Prophet were divinely guided, manifesting God's will and provided a primary component of the *uṣūl* *al-Sharīʿah* (sources of the law). The *sunnah al-ʿādiyyah,* however, would not constitute a *Sharīʿah* source being non-binding and within the five-tier *ḥukm* categorisations, was graded as *mandūb* (recommended). This was the approach adopted by the *fuqahāʾ*.[43]

This was generally the norm over the ages until the advent of the early modernists such as Sayyid Aḥmad Khān and Muḥammad ʿAbduh who "downgraded" the *sunnah al-ʿādiyyah* from *mandūb* to *mubāḥ* (permissible/indifferent). Khān extended this category to the bulk of the Prophet's political and civil activity. It reached the point where only Sunnah connected with *dīn* (religion) as supported by authentic *aḥādīth* could be classified as *waḥy* (revelation) effectively eliminating a major aspect of Prophetic activity from the *uṣūl al-Sharīʿah.* As for the rejection of precedents in civil and political affairs, the contention was that if worldly matters require detailed Prophetic guidance then every age will require a new prophet to accommodate changing circumstances.[44]

ʿAbduh, a conservative by present standards, did not go that far but nevertheless took the not-so-conventional position that "it is in any event very difficult to come by any rational proof or decisive dogmatic evidence for the view many take about prophetic freedom from error"[45] which is diplomatic speak for questioning the validity of the *ʿiṣmah* doctrine. ʿAbduh cites the case of the *ḥadīth* that says that the Prophet initially prohibited the pollination of date palms but subsequently permitted it because he wanted to teach the believers that their practices in economic and practical matters are the outcome of their own research. Such practices are valid as long as the Divine laws are observed and the virtues maintained.[46] ʿAbduh also took the position of advocating that "no one should be blamed as an unbeliever if he withholds acceptance" of a *ḥadīth* that he does not regard as authentic.[47] The early modernists therefore paved the way for the later modernists to launch their attack on traditionalism by advocating the theology of secularism as exemplified by the likes of ʿAlī ʿAbd al-Rāziq whose views we have already discussed in Chapter 4. Suffice it here to say that the secularist argument essentially undermines the *ʿiṣmah* doctrine rendering it totally irrelevant, except as a guarantee for the authenticity of the Qur'ān. But not all detractors of the doctrine advocate abandonment of the Sunnah in political and worldly affairs as al-Rāziq's thesis would suggest, one that was later taken up by Khalid Muhammad Khalid (d. 1416/1996) in his *Min Huna Nabda'* which was banned for its "Communist" overtones and "assault" on Islam. Later modernists posited a sophisticated theory of authority which, while still based on the thesis that "the Prophet's duty is but to proclaim (the Message)"[48], advanced the concept of the Prophet also taking on the role of establishing a political system known as *niẓām*. There is an odd rider to this system in that the Prophet in this capacity is not a Ruler by divine decree but purely an *amīr* (administrator) whose task was not to pass laws but purely to administer the *Sharī'ah*, the Divine law.[49] In other words, what they give by the right hand, they take by the left. In denigrating the role of the Prophet to one of mere administrator, all the *sunnah al-hudā* pertaining to the Prophet's legislative function in political and civil affairs is thrown out the window, lock, stock and barrel including the *'iṣmah* doctrine. As for the well-known injunction "Obey God and obey the Messenger," they employ the circuitous logic that obeying the Messenger is no different from obeying God for the Messenger's duty, as *amīr*, was just to implement God's law. This renders the command on obedience to the Prophet as virtually tautologous for in the same *āyah* there is the command to obey "those in authority among you" (*wa ūlī al-amri minkum*)—a concept we have dealt substantively in Chapter 5. As advanced by Parwez and others, in the context here, both the role of the Prophet as administrator and that of successive *amīr*s merge into a seamless continuum where obedience to the rulings of the Prophet *qua amīr* could be disregarded by the *amīr*s of later generations as was exemplified by the *Khulafā' al-Rāshidūn*, 'Umar in particular being the *amīr* par excellence after the Prophet. As *amīr al-mu'minīn*, he exercised *ijtihād* on many occasions departing from the Prophet's Sunnah and applying his own *tafsīr* of the Qur'ān in order to deal with new situations and circumstances, as noted in our discourse on the *maqāṣid al-Sharīʿah*. According to Parwez, Prophetic authority should now be manifested through the conception of the *markaz-i-millat*, an institution of central authority that would be part and parcel of an Islamic state. Principles of governance can be gleaned from the Qur'ān while the *aḥādīth* would be of no consequence.[50] These scripturalist advocates have one essential message: follow the Qur'ān for it is all encompassing and follow it the way the Prophet has followed. In the Prophet is a paradigm, not a paragon, a broad framework for Muslims to order their lives and community by resorting to reason and revelation, not by blind and unthinking mimicking of the Sunnah as the traditional *'ulamā'* would have us do.

As expected, this new wave of *aḥādīth*-denying-revisionist modernists was fervently met by a counter-wave of vigorous defenders of orthodoxy bent on upholding "the specificity, the indivisibility, and the universality of Prophetic authority." The logic was compelling: If the Prophet's word could not be relied upon even in worldly matters, then *a fortiori* in religious matters. Trustworthiness cannot be bifurcated into distinct spheres.[51] The *ḥadīth* deniers cannot blow hot and blow cold. The Prophet's sayings cannot be authoritative and unauthoritative at the same time. Who is to judge between the two?[52] Mawdūdī attempts to reconcile the polarities by first conceding that the Prophet was not completely *maʿṣūm* as the Qur'ān itself would show and secondly rejecting any suggestion that Prophetic authority is thereby undermined. Errors made by the Prophet were in fact minor and formed part of God's plan to teach believers that even minor aberrations came within the divine purview and must be corrected. What then would be the rationale of righting such minor infractions if not to show that even these mistakes are part of the prophetic mission?[53] It would appear that these attempts were rather futile because till today these differences have not dissipated and some would say have actually accentuated beyond any possibility of reconciliation. The crux of the matter finally centres on the question of who actually has the authority to represent the Prophet.

One important aspect of *Sharīʿah* development which tends to be overlooked is *taqrīr* or confirmation exemplified by the Prophet himself during his "farewell" pilgrimage where he meticulously went through the rituals to make it clear what was authentic and what was pagan accretion.[54] Textual support for this is strong:

> "He has sent down upon you, [O Muhammad], the Book in truth, *confirming* what was before it."

In another verse:

> "And We have revealed to you, [O Muhammad], the Book in truth, *confirming* that which preceded it of the Scripture and as a criterion over it."[55]

That the Sunnah constitutes the second most important source is also beyond dispute, although there remains, apart from the *ʿiṣmah* issue, much disagreement on what are good and bad traditions in terms of their derivability into law. Abū Ḥanīfah, for example, gave priority to *istiḥsān* or juristic preference over traditions of a purely legal import and Iqbal considers his attitude to be "perfectly sound" and if modern liberalism considers it safer not to make any indiscriminate use of them as a source of law, it will be only following one of the greatest exponents of Islamic law. However, this is not to downgrade the role of the traditions particularly in insisting on the value of the concrete case, as against the tendency to abstract thinking in law.[56]

Some *aḥādīth* are considered spurious in terms of its authenticity or line of transmission and are not accepted by certain *madhāhib* while others may rely on them to support a particular position. However, wholesale rejection of the Sunnah as indicative of some of the aforementioned positions, is heresy though recently, Islamic revivalism has led to a reexamination of some of the conventional postulates governing the process of deriving *fiqh* from the Traditions. This has led to some heated polemic between those who advocate the importance of the authenticity of the *aḥādīth* and those who advocate the importance of the subject matter.[57] We have noted earlier the "juristic wars" between the *ahl al-ḥadīth* and the *ahl al-ra'y* in the early days of Islamic jurisprudence. The present-day tension may be seen as a revival of sorts and has yielded interesting insights pertinent to the discourse on modernity and contemporary political Islam, a subject though most pertinent, is however beyond the scope of this monograph.

But what is of concern in the present age, as it was even during the classical period of Islam, is the simplistic reliance on the text, particularly the *aḥādīth* by all and sundry to make pronouncements on law without reference to context as well as the *asbāb al-nuzūl* (causes or reasons for revelation), the *maqāṣid al-Sharīʿah* and the principles of abrogation. As we know, historically, certain hardliners belonging to the Ḥanbalī School who took literalism to extremes were not prepared to tolerate any other position on the interpretation of the text and were not averse to resort to physical violence. This is where the approach taken by al-Shāfiʿī which is the middle-way takes on greater significance. For him then, it was a struggle not to be caught between the two polarities as stated earlier—those of the *ḥadīth* and those of *ra'y*. For the former group, the subtleties of linguistic analysis, logical reasoning and contextual reading were part and parcel of a sophistry that bordered on heresy apart from being a pure waste of time. As for the latter, we have seen how adepts in the use of opinion and rational analysis emanating from the school of Abū Ḥanīfah tended to ignore the text altogether where a literal reading will yield manifestly unjust or counter intuitive legal rulings. For al-Shāfiʿī, the literalists were easy game in the debates since disputations were by definition analytical and rational, two essential qualities of which the *ahl al-ḥadīth* were notoriously in deficit. That was then but even today there are self-proclaimed *'ulamā'* whose competency in citing chapter and verse to support a particular *fiqh* ruling or position far exceeds their competency in intellectual discourse and logical analysis. Literally following a *ḥadīth* without the proper *fiqh* is the road to damnation, as one popular saying goes.[58]

Ibrāhīm al-Nakha'ī used to say, "When I hear a *ḥadīth* I look to see what part of it is applicable and I apply that and leave the rest."[59]

In his *fatwa* on the necessity for *taqlīd* for those who are not *mujtahid*s, the renowned Mauritanian Shaykh Murābiṭ al-Ḥājj said that on the chapter concerning inferential reasoning, from *Marāqī al-Sa'ūd*, [Sidi 'Abd Allāh] says, "As for the one who is not a *mujtahid*, then basing his actions on primary textual evidence [Qur'ān and *hadīth*] is not permissible." He says in *Nashru al-Bunūd*, "It means that it is prohibited for other than a *mujtahid* to base his actions upon a direct text from either the Book or the Sunnah even if its transmission was sound because of the sheer likelihood of there being other considerations such as abrogation, limitations, specificity to certain situations, and other such matters that none but the *mujtahid* fully comprehends with precision. Imam al-Qarāfī[60] says, 'And whoever interprets an *āyah* or *ḥadīth* in a manner that deviates from its intended meaning without proof [dalīl] is a *kāfir*.'"[61]

Ijmā' [62]

By the early third/ninth century, the legal fraternity recognized *ijmā'* as a fundamental principle of *uṣūl al-fiqh* and could be legitimately employed for *tafsīr*. But what was not recognised was a universal definition of *ijmā'*. Al-Shāfi'ī restricted it to only universal consensus—the vox populi of the *ummah* though he does not elaborate how the consensus works in relation to rules not clearly stated in the Qur'ān and Sunnah. He rejected *ijmā'* of the *mujtahids*. The universal *ijmā'* includes consensus on matters such as the number of daily prayers or the obligation to perform the pilgrimage.

Al-Āmidī, on the other hand, has given a more comprehensive definition of *ijmā'* as "the agreement of the entire body of *mujtahids* of Muhammad's community in a particular generation upon a rule of law pertaining to a particular case." (*Al-ijmā'u 'ibāratun 'an ittifāqi jumlati ahli al-ḥalli wa al-'aqdi min ummati muḥammadin fī 'aṣrin min al-a'ṣāri 'alā ḥukmi wāqi'atin min al-waqā'i'*).[63] It should be noted that al-Āmidī uses the term *ahl al-ḥall wa al-ʿaqd* (those who loosen and bind) and not *mujtahid*s but they are synonymous because in the scheme of those who qualify to be *mujtahid muṭlaq* are those who loosen and bind. Al-Āmidī's definition may be compared with that of the Muʿtazilī al-Naẓẓām (d. 220/835) and that of al-Ghazālī. Al-Naẓẓām gave *ijmāʿ* a wide berth incorporating any opinion of which the truth has been incontrovertibly established (*ḥujjah*) even that of a single person. Al-Ghazālī defines it as the agreement of Muhammad's community in particular upon a religious matter. Al-Naẓẓām's definition is free-rein respecting neither common nor technical usage. In *uṣūl al-fiqh,* a *dalīl* (proof) is an indication in the sources of the *Sharīʿah* from which a *ḥukm* (practical rule) is derived. The *ḥukm* so deduced may be *qaṭʿī* (definitive) or *ẓannī* (speculative).[64] Thus, a legal matter that has been incontrovertibly established would be *ḥukm qaṭʿī* derived from the Qur'ān, the Sunnah, *ijmāʿ* or *qiyās* though for the latter, as we shall see, the jury is still out whether *qiyās* could ever give rise to a definitive ruling. What is clear at this point is that the Muʿtazilī definition of *ijmāʿ* does not pass muster. Al-Ghazālī's definition, according to al-Āmidī, is also defective from at least three perspectives. First, by referring to "Muhammad's community," it becomes neither period nor time constrained throwing open the interpretation of "a trans-generational conception" of the *ummah,* that is, the entire Muslim community throughout the ages till *yawm al-qiyāmah* (the Day of Resurrection) which is absurd because no *ijmāʿ* will ever be attained before such a day by which time it will be of no consequence. Second, being silent in respect of *mujtahid*s, the definition leaves open the possibility and legitimacy of an *ijmāʿ* being determined wholly by those who do not qualify as *mujtahid*s. Thirdly, while the previous two objections point to the latitudinal nature of the definition, the final objection centres on its unwarranted restrictiveness in confining the subject matter of *ijmāʿ* to only religious matters, that is, *naqliyyah* (transmitted from revelation). Matters which are *ʿaqliyyah* (derived via rational inquiry or proofs) will be excluded from the realm of *ijmāʿ*. Such a requirement goes against the general notion that *ijmāʿ* could be established in respect of any matter whatsoever deliberated and agreed upon among *mujtahids*. Al-Āmidī's definition, on the other hand, incorporates the latter including agreements expressed verbally, or in deed or even in silence but sufficiently exclusive to discount non-*mujtahid*s as well as the agreement of *mujtahids* of other scriptural communities.[65] *Ijmāʿ* in this regard represents the third source of the *Sharīʿah*.

Apart from the fact that it serves as source of law, a legitimate question raised is what is the role that is played by *ijmāʿ* within the larger context of the *Sharīʿah*? Firstly, *ijmāʿ* defines the limits of *tafsīr* and the perimeters of the interpretive community. Secondly, in tandem with the *madhāhib*, *ijmāʿ* provided the juridical matrix for religious discourse authorising only *fuqahā'* to engage in it. The Mālikīs accord the *ijmāʿ ahl al-madīnah* the status of binding authority but this is rejected by others. Also rejected were the opinions of the *mutakallimūn*, on the grounds that they lacked proper legal training. This was in reality a stratagem to undermine the authority of the Muʿtazilites, who, as we have seen in Chapter 3, had worked hand in glove with the Abbāsid caliphs to foist the doctrine of the createdness of the Qur'ān on the people. Needless, to say, also excluded were the opinions of the Shi'ites and the Khārijites. *Muḥaddīthīn* (compilers of *aḥādīth*), caliphs, and other rulers were also not spared. This was in line with the phenomenon of *taqlīd* whereby such rejection was made possible and effective via the *madhāhib*. This was to give finality on issues already decided and avoid undue uncertainty. After the third/ninth century, no *faqīh* could voice opinions on *Sharīʿah* law except through the *madhāhib*. In his study on *ikhtilāf al-fuqahā'*, al-Ṭābarī excluded Aḥmad ibn Ḥanbal from the list on the grounds that he was merely a *muḥaddīth* and not a *faqīh*. The caliphs, who in an earlier period had been able to set precedent and change Islamic law of their own accord, were no longer granted the authority to do so. The espousal of legal opinions in contradiction to those established consensually within the established *madhāhib (mukhālafah al-ijmāʿ*) or departing from an established *ijmāʿ* (*al-khurūj ʿan al-ijmāʿ*) was a serious matter that might lead to the invocation of *takfīr* whereby a believer is excommunicated and declared a disbeliever (*kāfir*). By the mid-fourth/tenth century, the fear of excommunication eventually brought about marriages of convenience of the various *kalām* denominations with the *madhāhib*: Ashʿarites with the Shāfiʿīs and Muʿtazilites with the Ḥanafīs. Even Shīʿites and Khārijites sometimes chose affiliation with a Sunni legal *madhhab* in order to participate in authoritative religious discourse.

Though the *fuqahā'* were theoretically independent and equal and consensus was described as the end result of a free battle of *fatwas*, in many Islamic societies there was a recognized hierarchy of authority among the jurists. As alluded to earlier, al-Āmidī mentions the *ahl al-ḥall wa al-ʿaqd* as those *fuqahā'* whose opinions can establish *ijmāʿ*. These are none other than the *mujtaḥid muṭlaq*. Later usages talk about "greater jurists" (*akābir*), who voice opinions on pressing issues and "lesser jurists" (*aṣāghir*), who follow the greater jurists instead. The important classical works on *ijmāʿ* include *al-Ijmāʿ* by Abū Bakr Muḥammad ibn Ibrāhīm ibn al-Naysābūrī (d. 308/921), *Marātib al-Ijmāʿ* (The Degrees of Consensus) by Ibn Ḥazm, and *Naqd Marātib al-Ijmāʿ* (Refutation of the degrees of consensus) by Ibn Taymiyyah (d. 921/1328). In a sense, *ijmāʿ* and *khilāf* are two sides of the same coin: the dissenting opinions of jurists whose opinions are taken into account in consensus are also considered valid contributions to legal debate. *Ijmāʿ* and *khilāf* together represent precedents providing the historical record of opinions that must be taken into account by later jurists in arriving at an independent ruling.[66] A description of the levels of consensus by Fakhr al-Islām al-Bayḍāwī (d. 481/1089) emphasizes this historical aspect. He distinguishes the consensus of the Prophet's Companions, claiming that it is as strong as the Qur'an or a report attested by multiple chains of transmission (*khabar mutawātir*); the consensus of those after the Companions, which is of the same level of reliability as a well-known hadith report (*ḥadīth mashhūr*); and a consensus that comes into being after dispute, the validity of which is comparable to a *ḥadīth* report attested through a solitary chain of transmission.[67]

Owing to the binding authority of *ijmā'* a consequential *ḥukm* derived therefrom is considered to be infallible and not amenable to change or challenge. This may lead to the intractable situation where there exist two parallel but conflicting *ijmā'* on an identical issue. While the respective schools are free to choose one or the other, the rule book does not allow for a third opinion. This appears to limit inquiry severely and dictate strict adherence to a traditional corpus of legal rulings. In practice, however, it was possible for jurists to propose new rulings by distinguishing the issue at hand from that which had been debated earlier or by showing that the earlier claims of consensus were not actually valid.

What is the significance of *ijmā'* in the contemporary world? The modern reformists regarded it as a stumbling block to their *iṣlāḥ* and *tajdīd* enterprise because *ijmā'* by definition according to the classical theorists engendered *taqlīd*. Hence, for the likes of 'Abduh et al, the only viable room for *ijmā'* must be by way of rational inquiry and therefore should be subject to revision and change with the changing circumstances of Islamic societies. The limitation set by the classical scholars on those qualified to give opinions that would eventually lead to *ijmā'* is so stringent that in practical terms no one but a handful will be able to fit the bill. The circle of adepts in the law must therefore be considerably widened and their opinions included so as to break the monopoly on authoritative religious discourse.

One is tempted to compare *ijmā'* to the ecumenical Catholic councils or the Synods of churches where ecclesiastical dignitaries and theological experts convened to settle doctrinal and liturgical matters.[68] Historically, the councils were defined more by their failure to agree than coming to a consensus, a phenomenon that may be likened to the process of *ikhtilāf* which used to be a defining feature in the development of the *Sharī'ah*. However, unlike the *ikhtilāf* which helped to cement rival *madhāhib* into staking their respective *fiqh* positions while advancing the cause of *ijtihād* generally, the disputes of the Catholic Councils/Synods led to permanent schisms. For example, after the second council, Bishops of the "Church of the East" boycotted the event and as further schisms erupted over Christological and other issues, later councils were attended by bishops of only parts of the Catholic Church. But it would be a fallacy to assume that they have fallen into desuetude. The institution remains a force for the multitude of Christians today. The Pope sets the topic and participation is governed by a set of rules. Thus, we can find an Orthodox listing of councils and synods.

However, they are fundamentally different from the consensus doctrine of *ijmā'*. To begin with, the classical doctrine did not arise from any kind of formal convention of *'ulamā'* sitting in council. The principles considered as *ijmā'* are deemed *ex post facto*. *Ijmā'* is reached instinctively and automatically and its existence on any point is perceived only on looking back and seeing that such an agreement has actually been attained. Only then is *ijmā'* consciously accepted as a source of law. To be sure, not unlike the councils in terms of failure to reach consensus, *ijmā'* has had its fair share of controversy arising mainly from the question as to whose consensus really constitutes the *ijmā'*. As noted earlier, Imām Mālik recognized only the *ijmā'* of the scholars of his own locality, Medina, the practice of the people of Medina taking precedence over everything after the Qur'ān and the most authoritative Sunnah. The Ẓāhirī School restricts *ijmā'* to the first generation of Muslims who lived alongside the Prophet only.[69] As alluded to earlier, al-Shāfi'ī gave higher authority to the consensus of the community at large.[70] In the latter part of *al-Risālah*, al-Shafi'ī says, "... but in the community as a whole there is no error concerning the meaning of the Qur'ān, the Sunnah, and analogy" the basis of which is to be found in a tradition which states "My people will never agree on an error."[71] Though both kinds of *ijmā'* count as final arguments in the ancient schools of law, the *ijmā'* of the scholars is of much greater practical importance while the reliance on the community at large was opposed even by al-Shāfi'ī's own disciples including al-Ghazālī who, in turn, was corrected by al-Āmidī in respect of the definition of *ijmā'*. In any event, a body of principles of law has developed over the years which may find its genesis in *ijmā'*. It is, however, clear that *ijmā'* is not revealed law which would necessarily remove it from the realm of divinity, notwithstanding comments to the contrary.

At least in terms of theological matters, Ibn Rushd is of the view that it is impossible to achieve consensus. In his *Faṣl al-Maqāl*, Ibn Rushd asserts that only the metaphysician employing *al-qiyās al-burhānī* (certain proof through syllogism) is capable and competent (as well as obliged) to interpret the doctrines contained in the *Sharī'ah*, and not the *mutakallimūn* who rely on dialectical arguments. The revealed law is superior to the Greek nomos (law) and everyone is entitled to his share of happiness. Only the *Sharī'ah* cares for all believers which justifies speculation because the *Sharī'ah* demands that the believer should know God. While this knowledge is accessible to the naive believer in mere metaphors, the inner meaning is intelligible only to the philosopher with the help of demonstration. Hence, it is the prerogative of the philosopher—as well as incumbent on him—to interpret the doctrines of religion in the form of right beliefs and convictions. The *Sharī'ah* contains teachings that surpass human understanding but must be accepted by all believers because they contain divinely revealed truths.[72]

In his search for truth the philosopher is bound by Arabic usage and certain proof. Conversely, he is not bound to accept what is contradicted by demonstration. This covers such matters as belief in the creation out of nothing since Aristotle demonstrated the eternity of matter. Hence creation is a continuing process. Ibn Rushd justified this position on the ground that a Muslim is bound only by *ijmā'* of the *'ulamā'* in a strictly legal context where actual laws and regulations are concerned. Yet, since there is no consensus on certain theoretical statements, such as creation, he is not bound to conform.

According to Ibn Rushd, *ijmā'* on theoretical matters (*al-naẓariyyāt*) is never determined with certainty (*bi ṭarīq yaqīnī*), as it can be on practical matters (*al-'āmaliyyāt*). In other words, it is not possible for *ijmā'* to be determined about a particular question at a particular epoch unless that epoch is delimited by us; we know all the learned men existing in the period; the doctrine of each one of them on the question has been handed down by means of an uninterrupted transmission; certified that the learned men existing at the time agreed that there is not an apparent and an inner sense to the Law, that it is obligatory that knowledge of every question be concealed from no one, and that there is only one method for people to know the Law.[73] According to certain detractors, Ibn Rushd dismisses the doctrine of *ijmāʿ* because its practice is essentially a stumbling block to his doctrine of *ta'wīl.* In order to determine what should be interpreted hermeneutically and what should be taken at face value, Ibn Rushd cannot have recourse to *ijmāʿ* for *ta'wīl* and *taqlīd* are diametrically opposed.[74]

Countering the Rushdian analysis, *ijmāʿ* proponents use textual and rational arguments to uphold its authority and notwithstanding that it is said the rational method (as employed by Ibn Rushd) yields real certainty—*al-maslak al-ʿaqlī al-yaqīnī*—al-Āmidī prefers the textual arguments, as evidenced in his *Muntahā* and the *Iḥkām*. The rational arguments in support of *ijmāʿ* are said to be completely ineffective and even though textual arguments may not yield full certainty they are nevertheless adequate in establishing the authority of *ijmāʿ*.[75] Effectively, opinion suffices. But because opinion was the sense of a thing's being probable, any *ḥukm* derived from an *ijmāʿ* of this nature, could only be a probable rule. Nevertheless, such a rule could be fully operative as positive law applicable to concrete cases in a court in line with the maxim that in the absence of solid knowledge of the divine law, considered opinion as to what constituted that law was binding upon the judge and the parties. Issues pertaining to *ʿamal* (conduct) were generally placed in the class of *masā'il ẓanniyyah* while issues on matters of great importance such as the existence of God and the prophethood of Muhammad were *masā'il qaṭʿiyyah* and could never be resolved through mere opinion. It may be said that apart from such fundamental issues of faith, for al-Āmidī, the textual indicators were not decisive enough to allow one to claim absolute confidence and were in fact all *dalīl ẓannī*.[76] Additionally, failure of the *fuqahā'* to reach a consensus upon the authority of the *ijmā'* in no way impeded the functioning of that authority as the authority of consensus cannot by itself rest upon a consensus, as this would entail a *petitio principia* or *circulus in demonstrando*.[77] This must be determined entirely on the basis of the Qur'ān and the Sunnah.

Qiyās

In the usage of *uṣūl al-fiqh*, *qiyās* is the deduction of legal prescriptions from the Qur'ān and the Sunnah by analogical reasoning. Where a clear rule is to be found in the Qur'ān or the Sunnah or even the *ijmā'*, the use of *qiyās* is prohibited in as much as the need for it should not arise in the first place. The traditional and logical view is that the need for *qiyās* would have arisen only after the death of the Prophet when the growing interest in theological and juridical speculation raised entirely new questions the answers to which could not be found in the Qur'ān or the Sunnah.[78] However, there are Traditions to the effect that during the lifetime of the Prophet, *ijtihād* was exercised by the Prophet himself as well as some of the Companions, in certain situations (though not many) where no definitive Qur'ānic ruling or principle was in place at the relevant time. In resorting to *ijtihād*, *qiyās* might or might not have been employed. Hence, it is *qiyās* that has given rise to much disputation because this process is directly related to the issue of *ijtihād*. According to al-Shāfi'ī, the use of *qiyās* would entail the exercise of intense intellectual exertion in order to arrive at a particular ruling which is effectively the definition of the *ijtihādic* process. Epiphanies or flashes of brilliance would not count as deduction by analogy, inspiring as they may be. But if indeed *qiyās* and *ijtihād* are considered two terms for the same idea it would appear then that jurists had been using it to formulate legal rules ever since the need arose. The crux of the issue was really in the terminology applied.

Let us probe a little further into the concept. Anyone trained in Western law will be familiar with the doctrine of *ratio decidendi*, which is the core principle of the law upon which a case is decided. In applying precedents in judicial decision-making, as is the method in common law jurisdictions, the doctrine of *ratio decidendi* is essentially the extraction of the *ratio* of the decision of a particular case to another case with similar facts.[79] In this regard, it might be noted that in statutory interpretation, there is also the doctrine of *ratio legis* which is the underlying rationale for the legislature to enact a particular law which is necessary to be ascertained in order to help the court to construe the language and purport of certain provisions of a statute. The doctrine of *ratio legis* is, in a limited sense, comparable to the doctrine of *asbāb al-nuzūl* in Qur'ānic hermeneutics but the latter, in the context of the doctrine of *qiyās*, has greater significance and legal impact. In English jurisprudence, the principle of *ratio decidendi* is key to the application of judicial precedents and *ratio legis* facilitates in clarifying the law. But that is about all there is to it in terms of the legal effect. The process does not create new law or rules. On the other hand, in *uṣūl al-fiqh*, the doctrine of *qiyās*—by resorting to the *asbāb al-nuzūl* as well as various other criteria in hermeneutics including *tafsīr mawḍūʿī* (purposive interpretation) and *lughah*-related postulates (linguistic factors in ascertaining the sources)[80]—has enabled jurists to make new laws by extracting the *ratio* or *ʿillah* of a particular Qur'ānic injunction or a ruling of the Prophet to new situations. Of course, it could still be argued that in common law jurisprudence, the process of ratiocination and statutory interpretation by judges does lead to the development of judge-made law but that is the exception rather than the rule apart from the argument that the outcome is, strictly speaking, not new law but mere lacunae-filling, that is, filling gaps in the law or situations where there is no applicable law. *Qiyās*, on the other hand, as first employed by Abū Ḥanīfah and later given a firmer methodical structure by al-Shāfiʿī in his *al-Risālah* is an established source of law for both the Shāfiʿī and Ḥanafī schools about which more will be said later.[81] There is also the use of *ra'y* where reasoning takes precedence over a textual referent.

As noted earlier, the use of reason itself is nothing new when the methodology of personal opinion or *ra'y* is considered, a process which evolved into various forms going by different names such as *istiḥsān* and *istiṣlāḥ*.[82] *Istiḥsān* literally means "approval, consent, or discretion," being derived from "*ḥasuna*," which means "to be handsome, beautiful, lovely" or "to be expedient, advisable, suitable."[83] Juristically, it is defined as "a form of *ijtihād* in which jurists use their personal discretion within the guidelines of the *Sharīʿah* to choose the better legal judgment in a case which has more than one possible solution."[84] Imām Mālik, credited for having remarked that "*istiḥsān* represents nine-tenth of human knowledge" used the expression in connection with legal decisions for which he could not find authority in tradition. About the same time, Abū Yūsuf said that "according to the *qiyās*, this and that would be prescribed but I have decided according to what I deem preferable (*istaḥsantu*)."[85] As expounded by the Ḥanafī School, this doctrine posits that where harsh consequences may result or where injustice may be occasioned if a rule is applied too strictly, then the judge is allowed to come to a different ruling to avoid the hardship being set on the concerned party.

In later centuries, the term *istiḥsān* meant a method of finding the law which for any reason would be contradictory to the usual *qiyās*. In al-Shāfiʿī's *al-Risālah*, an entire chapter is devoted to the subject though on closer analysis one is hard pressed to discern the difference between the two. The exercise of *istiḥsān*, according to *al-Risālah*, is only permissible if done through the process of *qiyās* and subject to the same conditions required for the exercise of *ijtihād*. In other words, as far as al-Shāfiʿī is concerned, you can call it whatever you want but at the end of the day, the derivation of law must be exercised by way of *qiyās*. This is diplomacy at its finest, no doubt conducted in accordance with the etiquette rules governing the polemics of disagreement (*al-adab al-ikhtilāf*), a subject that we shall pursue in the next chapter. On balance, it may be said that al-Shāfiʿī fundamentally rejected the doctrine for fear that it might lead to arbitrariness in making a judicial decision. "God has not permitted any man since His Messenger to present views unless from knowledge that was complete before him."[86] This was a clear rejection of *istiḥsān* though the word was not used in this context. We have seen earlier that on the principle that the validity of religious issues is only upheld by certainty, and that speculation cannot lead to the truth, the Ẓāhirī school does not accept *qiyās* as a source of *Sharīʻah* law, nor do they accept the practice of *istiḥsān* (juristic discretion), pointing to the *āyah* in the Qur'ān to the effect that "nothing has been neglected in the revealed texts."[87]Proponents of the doctrine of *istiḥsān*, however, respond by saying that their principle in diverting from the *qiyās* does not arise from personal whims but by purely material considerations provided for in the law. It is a concealed *qiyās* (*qiyās khafī*), a divergence from an externally obvious *qiyās* to an inner or self-conditioned decision. This is, of course, not the direct response of Abū Ḥanīfah or even his immediate disciples such as Abū Yūsuf or Muḥammad al-Shaybānī but the later Ḥanafī jurists such as Pazdāwī (d. 481/1089), al-Sarakhsī (d. 482/1090), and al-Nasafī (d. 709/1310) to name but a few.[88]

Nevertheless, as alluded to earlier, according to Syed Ameer Ali, the early use of private judgment was not unilaterally started by the Ḥanafīs but, in fact had been consecrated by the Prophet and strictly followed by his immediate descendants. This had induced the development of a liberal spirit among the Fāṭimides, and from there, exerted legitimate influence on the mind of Abū Ḥanīfah.[89] Though the author does not explain what he means by "consecrated" here, it would be safe to surmise that it is in reference to the famous *ḥadīth* regarding the sanction given by the Prophet to Muʻādh ibn Jabal when he sent him to Yemen as *qāḍī*. According to this *ḥadīth*, when asked by the Prophet how he would decide when a question arises and no answer is found either in the Sunnah or in the Book, Muʻadh said, "Then I shall come to a decision according to my own opinion (*ajtahidu ra'yī*) without hesitation."

If there seems to be a jump from *istiḥsān* to *ra'y* it is because both are sometimes used interchangeably. *Al-ra'y* must be viewed as a generic expression for *ijtihād* employed when warranted and *istiḥsān* is one of the ways with which this *ijtihād* is exercised. It would be clear therefore that *istiḥsān* used in this sense (as the exercise of *ijtihād*) is a perfectly legitimate way of coming to a legal decision where the texts are silent on a matter. Herein lies the problem of dealing with *qiyās* as the fourth source of the *fiqh* where the terms lose their exactitude and the perimeters become blurred: *qiyās* (as syllogistic reasoning or, as alluded to at the outset, commonly translated as analogical deduction), *ijtihād* (as intellectual striving in respect of ascertaining a juridical view) and *ra'y* (considered opinion) are arguably synonymous terms when one is looking at the outcome but become contentiously ambiguous when one is looking at the process. For example, in the case of *ra'y*, with the passage of time, and in any event, by the fourth/tenth century, Traditionists (*ahl al-ḥadīth*) totally rejected it as a source of law labelling it as "idiosyncratic opinion" while accepting *qiyās* in its place. On the other hand, the Ḥanafī jurists have sanctioned it as a source of law. Historically, it was the socio-economic milieu prevailing in the conquered territories of *Dār al-Islām* that first prompted Abū Ḥanīfah to resort to speculative reasoning in interpretations. There is the view that recourse to Aristotelian logic at that stage of the growth of the Muslim community as an *ummah* was likely to be detrimental to the development of *fiqh*. Imposing rules logically deduced from lofty conceptions and using them as the compass for the intricate behaviour of life was seen as problematic. In this regard, it is said, albeit rather hyperbolically, that in aspiring for a logically perfect system based on pure reason, the Ḥanafī *madhhab* tended to ignore the creative freedom of life.[90] Opposed to them, the Hijāzī Traditionists argued that the scholastic subtleties of the Ḥanafīs and their tendency to imagine unreal cases would turn the *Sharīʿah* into a lifeless mechanism. Piling on the criticism against unbridled personal opinion, the Mālikīs and the Shāfiʿīs, however, took separate lines of attack. The upshot of these rancourous debates was a critical delineation of the scope of *qiyās* which eventually became a source of the *Sharīʿah*. In his typical catholic style, Iqbal portrays the clash in civilizational terms as "an effective Semitic restraint on the Aryan tendency to seize the abstract in preference to the concrete, to enjoy the idea rather than the event."[91] In the final analysis, taking the criticisms in stride, the School of Abū Ḥanīfah forged that critical balance of the concrete with the abstract by incorporating the dynamics and multi-dimensionality of life in their mechanics of *tafsīr* and *ta'wīl*. Thus, at both the conceptual as well as the empirical level, the Ḥanafī *madhhab* may rightfully be described as "absolutely free in its essential principle and possesses much greater power of creative adaptation than any other school."[92]

While al-Shāfiʿī's *qiyās* doctrine was indeed a profound contribution to the field of theoretical jurisprudence, it has been said that it also led to the constraining of the metaphorical imagination of Muslim legal and ethical thought. *Qiyās*, in this sense, is seen as a methodology that is moulded on a template of the past and the quest for answers in the modern world based on such a template will yield answers that cannot attain to the present let alone the future. It will not save the day to argue that *qiyās* applies only to *fiqh* matters as if it is cast in stone that matters of law have no direct bearing on the foundations of *dīn* and *kalām*. The contention is that if Muslim thought is to be effective, Qur'ānic hermeneutics must take a radical course breaking free from the *taqlīd* of *qiyās* even if it may cause disruptions and displace the inherited notions of exegesis and revelation.[93] On this, al-Juwaynī says that those who deny *qiyās* (*al-qiyās al-jalī*) cannot even be reckoned among the *ʿulamā' al-ummah* (the learned of the Islamic community) or *ḥamalah al-Sharīʿah* (the bearer of the law) but must simply be equated with the ignorant rabble.[94]

One significant aspect of the *Sharīʿah* discourse that is seldom pursued at the *fiqh* level is the doctrinal underpinnings of *qiyās* which is essentially syllogistic reasoning. In this regard, it may be stated that it is in *qiyās* that *uṣūl al-fiqh* meets *falsafah*. And ironically it is here too that the two part company. That is because while the two are essentially a procedural paradigm dependent on the exercise of the intellect, *qiyās* in respect of *fiqh* is anchored on the textual sea-bed (*naqliyyah*) while *qiyās* in respect of *falsafah* is afloat on the ocean of intellect (*al-qiyās al-ʿaqlī*). As Ibn Rushd puts it, the process of inferring and drawing out the unknown from the known is "syllogistic reasoning or by means of syllogistic reasoning" (*wa hādhā huwa al-qiyās aw bi al-qiyās*) and it is therefore obligatory that we go about reflecting upon the existing things by means of intellectual syllogistic reasoning (*fa wājib an najʿal naẓaranā fī al-mawjūdāt bi al-qiyās al-ʿaqlī*). [95] *Qiyās*, taken at this broad and expansive level in a free and open-sky and not an Orwellian or panoptic sense, can therefore pave the way for a new *ijtihād* to meet the challenges of the *ummah* of the contemporary and future world about which more will be said in the next chapter.

Conclusion

Indeed, a fundamental weakness in the discourse of the Qur'ān as the supreme source of the law is the general assumption of *Sharīʿah* law being "*sui generis* in the history of human social regulation" as if other *Sharīʿah*—as we have noted at the very commencement of this study in respect of the Judaic and Christian faiths—were not also *sui generis* in human history. As a matter of fact, we have seen that when it comes to setting the paradigm of religion as law, it is the Judaic faith and the paramountcy of the Torah as the all-encompassing legal code that sets it apart from the Christian faith and to a lesser extent even the Islamic faith. The natural corollary to such a misconception—that *Sharīʿah* law was in a most unique sense cast in stone as the be-all and the end-all of Islam—rendered it to be regarded as impractical by nature. Even if it was widespread in its use for a while, it somehow fell into desuetude having crumbled under the pressure of "hair-splitting scholastic authority that doomed it to irrelevancy" as well as marauding conquerors from Europe. It is all the more tragic that recent studies have uncovered, from Ottoman court documents, "the absolute centrality of Islamic law to the day to day lives of Ottoman

Muslims, and indeed to Ottoman Christians and Jews." The courts, however, eventually failed because of the doctrinal rigidity espoused by the *'ulamā'* and not because of any inherent inability of the *Sharīʿah* to accommodate new scenarios. As we have indicated in the preceding chapter, the *Sharīʿah* courts were doomed to a premature end because of "the wave of social change that accompanied European hegemony and the new nation-state order."[96] Nevertheless, all is not lost for if *Sharīʿah* law could indeed have occupied that position of "absolute centrality" in the lives of the *ummah* during the reign of the Ottomans, it could not have been as impractical and ossified as made out to be. What inherent qualities are subsumed under the *Sharīʿah* or extrinsic phenomena that are generated by it that could inject dynamism in its permanence is an overriding question that warrants examination. It is towards this line of inquiry that we now turn.

Notes

1. Ṭāhā Jābir al-Alwānī, *Uṣūl al-Fiqh al-Islāmī—Source Methodology in Islamic Jurisprudence: Methodology for Research and Knowledge* (Herndon: The International Institute of Islamic Thought, 1990); Syed Ameer Ali, *Muhammadan Law Compiled from Authorities in the Original Arabic*, Vol. 1 (New Delhi: Kitab Bhavan, 1986), 9-10; Coulson, *History*, 76.
2. Sūrah al-Mulk, *āyah* 10.
3. *Fikr: afalā tatafakkarūn/tatafakkaru/awalam yatafakkarū. 'Aql: afalā taʿqilūn/in kuntum taʿqilūn/afalam takūnū taʿqilūn.*
4. Bernard Weiss, "Exotericism and Objectivity in Islamic Jurisprudence," in *Islamic Law and Jurisprudence*, edited by Nicholas Heer (University of Washington Press, Seattle and London, 1990), 56.
5. *Shorter Encyclopaedia*, 612.
6. Iqbal, *The Reconstruction of Religious Thought*, 131-132.

7. Ibid., 133.
8. Sūrah al-Naḥl: 89—"*Wa nazzalnā 'alayka al-kitāb tibyānan li kulli shay'in wa hudan wa raḥmatan wa bushrā li al-muslimīn*"; Sūrah al-An'ām: 38—"*Mā farraṭnā fī al-kitābi min shay*'"
9. All citations from Nasr, *Study Quran*, and translations from Asad, Pickthall.
10. Sūrah al-'Alaq, *āyah* 1; L. Ali Khan & Hisham M. Ramadan, *Contemporary Ijtihad: Limits and Controversies* (Edinburgh University Press, 2011), 7.
11. Ibid., 7-8.
12. Muhammad Asad, *The Principles of State and Government in Islam* (Kuala Lumpur: Islamic Book Trust, 1980), 12.
13. Coulson, *History*, 11.
14. Ibid., 12; *Shorter Encyclopaedia*, 612; As usual, there is *khilāf* on this with al-Ghazālī limiting it to no more than 500 while there are other scholars who go as far as 900.
15. Respectively, al-Mu'minūn, *āyah* 8; al-Baqarah, *āyah* 177; al-Māidah, *āyah* 1.
16. Literally, "the monk of Iṣfahānī," Abū al-Qāsim al-Ḥusayn ibn Mufaḍḍal ibn Muḥammad was an Ash'arī *mufassir* and man of letters, his *ta'wīl* and *falsafah* predisposition notwithstanding. In his *al-I'tiqādāt*, he criticises the Mu'tazilī and the Shī'ī school and also rejects the pantheistic philosophy of emanationism of the *Ikhwān al-Ṣafā'* (Brethren of Purity), which, briefly stated, posits that the creation process happened in two stages: first, God creates *ex nihilo* the Intellect; immediately after the Intellect's emanation (*fayḍ*), it proceeded gradually, giving shape to the present universe: *Encyclopaedia of the Qur'ān*, edited by Oliver Leaman (London: Routledge, 2005), 156; *Internet Encyclopedia of Philosophy—A Peer-Reviewed Academic Resource*, "Ikhwān al-Ṣafā'."

17. Asad, *Message of the Qur'ān.*
18. *Supra.* Notes 72-73, Chapter 3.
19. L. Ali Khan, Hisham M. Ramadan, *Contemporary Ijtihad: Limits and Controversies* (Edinburgh University Press, 2011), 19-21.
20. Ahmad Von Denffer, *'Ulūm al-Qur'ān—An Introduction to the Sciences of the Qur'ān* (The Islamic Foundation, 1983,) 84; Kamali, 102.
21. Hashim Kamali, *Principles of Islamic Jurisprudence* (Cambridge: Islamic Texts Society, 1989), 88-89, citing al-Āmidī, *Iḥkām*, III, 53; Badrān, *Uṣūl*, 400.
22. Walid A. Saleh, *The Formation of the Classical Tafsīr Tradition: The Qur'ān Commentary of Al-Tha'labī (d. 427/1035)* (Brill, 2004), 94; al-Tha'labī, *Al-Kashf* (M100) fols. 4(b)-(b).
23. Saleh, *The Formation of the Classical Tafsīr Tradition*, 98.
24. Ibid. 108.
25. Sūrah al-Raḥmān, *āyahs* 19-20.
26. Nasr, *Study Qurān*, citing Ibn Kathīr, al-Qurṭubī.
27. Al-Ṭabarī, *Jāmi' al-Bayān*, v. 27: 128; likewise, al-Zamakhsharī, v. 4: 31—*al-Kashshāf.*
28. Nasr, citing Ibn 'Ajībah.
29. Saleh, ibid, 108-09; *al-Kashf*, M106 fol. 37(a).
30. *The Blackwell Companion to the Qur'an*, edited by Andrew Rippin (John Wiley & Sons, 2008), 332.
31. Jonathan A. C. Brown, *The Canonization of al-Bukhārī and Muslim: The Formation and Function of the Sunnī Ḥadīth Canon* (Brill Publishers, 2007), 10.
32. For an excellent study of a small collection of aḥadīth antedating the six canonical works of al-Bukhārī and the rest, see M.M. Azami, *Studies in Early Ḥadīth Literature* (Islamic Book Trust, 2000).
33. Khan and Ramadan, *Contemporary Ijtihad*, 24.

34. A *mutawātir ḥadīth* is one which has been reported by such a large number of narrators that it is deemed to be free from inaccuracy or error. The strength in numbers is traceable in every link of the *isnād* of narrators, from the Companions, down to a Follower, down to the time when it was recorded. For example, the *ḥadīth*: "Whoever fastened a lie on me may find his abode in Hellfire," is ranked as *mutawātir* as it has been narrated by more than 62 Companions with corresponding huge numbers down the chain of narration. Generally, *aḥādīth* in respect of rituals in worship such as the five daily prayers, fasting, *zakāḥ*, performing the Hajj and recitation of the Qur'ān are of *mutawātir* status.
35. Weiss, *God's Law,* 504: *Al-naskhu 'ibāratun 'an khiṭābi al-shāri'i al-māni'i min istimrāri mā thabita min ḥukmi khiṭābin shar'iyyin sābiqin* (*Ihkām*, 155).
36. Weiss, *Spirit*, 97.
37. The doctrine of abrogation (*naskh*) is generally founded on the Qur'ānic verse: None of our revelations do we abrogate or cause it to be forgotten, but we substitute something better or similar: knowest thou not that God has power over all things?"—al-Baqarah, *āyah* 106. One view suggests that this abrogation here refers to those revelations before the Qur'an, that is to say, they have now been abrogated by the Qur'an itself. For a concise explanation of this doctrine, see Von Denffer, *'Ulūm al-Qur'ān*, 104-113; for a detailed discussion see Weiss, *God's Law,* Chapter 11.
38. Weiss, *Spirit*, 90.
39. al-Baqarah, *āyah* 219.
40. al-Māidah, *āyah 90.*
41. *Kayfa nata'āmalu ma'a al-Sunnah al-Nabawiyyah* (El-Mansura, 1990), 23 as cited in Daniel W. Brown, *Rethinking Tradition in Modern Thought* (Cambridge: Cambridge University Press, 1996), 119.

42. Brown, *Rethinking Tradition,* 60-61.
43. Ibid. 61-62.
44. Ibid. 66. Aḥmad Khān, *Tafsīr*, III, 19
45. Muḥammad 'Abduh, *The Theology of Unity,* being a translation from the Arabic *Risālah al-Tawḥīd* by Isḥāq Musa'ad and Kenneth Cragg (London: Allen & Unwin, 1966), 80.
46. Ibid.
47. Ibid., 155-157; Suha Taji-Farouki, Basheer M. Nafi, *Islamic Thought in the Twentieth Century* (I.B.Tauris, 2004), 71.
48. al-Māidah, *āyah* 99
49. Ghulām Aḥmad Parwez, *Mi'rāj Insāniyyāt*, 315-317; Aslam Jayrājpūrī, *Ta'līmāt*, 128-130, Abū al-A'lā Mawdūdī, *Tafhīmāt*, 257-260.
50. Parwez, *Mi'rāj Insāniyyāt*, 436-38; Brown, *Rethinking Tradition,* 68-72.
51. Muḥammad Ismā'īl al-Salafī, *Ḥujjiyyāt-i-ḥadīth*, Lahore n.d. 188; Brown, 73.
52. Muḥammad Ayyūb Dihlawī, *The Mischief of Rejection of Ḥadīth*, Karachi, n.d., 18-20.; Brown, 73.
53. Mawdūdī, *Tafhīmāt*, 279-281; Brown, 78-80.
54. Muhammad Baqir as-Sadr, *Lessons in Islamic Jurisprudence*, translated by Roy Parviz Mottahedeh (OneWorld, Oxford, 2003), 9.
55. Respectively, Āl 'Imrān, *āyah* 3; al-Māidah, *āyah* 48.
56. Baqir as-Sadr, op cit, 137.
57. Brown, *Rethinking Tradition,* 112.
58. *Al-ḥadīthu maḍillatun illā li al-fuqahā'*—"*Ḥadīth* is a source of error except for the jurists."
59. "Imām al-Shāfi'ī: The Worshipping Saint," accessed 19 June 2015, https://www.youtube.com/watch?v=bUxc-g4rP4g.

60. Aḥmad ibn Idrīs Shihāb al-Dīn al-Ṣanhājī al-Qarāfī al-Mālikī (d. 684), one of the greatest Mālikī scholars known for his work in *uṣūl al-fiqh*. His 14-volume magnum opus *al-Dhākhirah* concerns Mālikī *fiqh* with proofs from *uṣūlī* sources.
61. "Shaykh Murabtal Haaj's Fatwa on Following One of the Four Accepted Madhhabs," Translated by Sheikh Hamza Yusuf Hanson; accessed on 2 March 2014; http://www.masud.co.uk/ISLAM/misc/mhfatwa.htm.
62. For a classical definition of *ijmā‘* and generally a comprehensive study see Ahmad Hassan, *The Doctrine of Ijmā‘ in Islam* (Islamabad: Islamic Research Institute, 1978).
63. al-Āmidī, *Iḥkām*, 1: 281-82; Weiss, *God's Law*, 185.
64. Kamali, *Islamic Jurisprudence*, 9-11.
65. Weiss, 184-186.
66. Devin J. Stewart, *PEIPT*, 111.
67. *Kashf al-Asrār ‘an Uṣūl Fakhr al-Islam al-Bazdawī* (Unveiling the Secrets of the Sources of Fakhr al-Islām al-Bazdawī) edited by Muḥammad al-Mu‘taṣim bi Allāh al-Baghdādī, 4 vol. (Beirut: Dār al-Kitāb al-‘Arabī, 1994).
68. Philip Schaff, *The Seven Ecumenical Councils*, series editor. Henry Wace.
69. Chiragh Ali, "The Proposed Political, Legal and Social Reforms," *Modernist Islam 1840-1940: A Sourcebook*, Edited by Charles Kurzman (New York City: Oxford University Press, 2002), 281.
70. *Shorter Encyclopaedia*, 157.
71. Majid Khadduri, *Al-Shāfi‘ī's Risāla, Treatise on the Foundations of Islamic Jurisprudence* (Islamic Texts Society, 1987), 287.
72. *Kitāb Faṣl al-Maqāl*, Butterworth, 11.
73. Ibid.
74. Ibid. 52-53; for a critical analysis of the Rushdian conception of *ijmā‘* and *ta'wīl* and the polemics with the Ghazālian approach,

see I. A. Bello, *The Medieval Controversy between Philosophy and Orthodoxy: Ijmāʿ and Ta'wīl in the conflict between al-Ghazālī and Ibn Rushd* (Leiden: E. J. Brill, 1989).

75. al-Āmidī, *Muntahā al-Sūl fī ʿIlm al-Uṣūl* (Cairo: Muḥammad ʿAlī Sabīh, n.d.), 1: 50-52; Weiss, *God's Law*, 196-7.
76. Ibid. 197-8.
77. Weiss, *God's Law*, 210, that is to say, begging the question: *petitio* (an assumption from the beginning); *circulus in demonstrando* (circle in demonstrating) which occurs when the conclusion of an argument is assumed as a premise of that same argument. Weiss uses the term "*principio principii*" which, it is submitted with respect, could have been a typographical infelicity.
78. Khadduri, *Al-Shāfiʿī's Risāla op. cit.*, 304-332.
79. Arthur L. Goodhart, "Determining the Ratio Decidendi of a Case," *The Yale Law Journal* 40, no. 2 (1930): 161-83.
80. On *lughah*-related postulates, see Weiss, *God's Law*, 117-150.
81. But his greatest jurisprudence is recorded for posterity in his *Kitāb al-Umm*, compiled by (or as some accounts have it, dictated to) his pupil al-Rabīʿ ibn Sulaymān al-Murādī (d. 270/884) with the latter's commentaries inserted across the board. For students of *uṣūl-al-fiqh*, this is a veritable goldmine containing the works of al-Awza'i (d. 157/774), Malik b. Anas (d. 179/796), Abū Yūsuf (d. 182/798), and Muḥammad b. al-Hasan al-Shaybāni (d. 189/804 or 805), and the legendary intense discourses al-Shāfiʿī had with other fuqahā. See Ahmed El Shamsy, "Al-Shāfiʿī's Written Corpus: A Source-Critical Study," *Journal of the American Oriental Society* 132, no. 2 (2012).
82. See M. Hashim Kamali, *Equity and Fairness in Islam* (Cambridge: The Islamic Texts Society, 2005), where the author deals substantively with the twin doctrines of *istiḥsan* and *maslaḥāh* and relate them to contemporary application through the

principles of *qabd* (taking possession) and *awqāf* (charitable endowments.)

83. Hans Wehr, *A Dictionary of Modern Written Arabic*, edited by J Milton Cowan, 4th Edition (Wiesbaden: Otto Harrassowitz, 1979).
84. Saim Kayadibi, *Istiḥsān—The Doctrine of Juristic Preference in Islamic Law* (Islamic Book Trust, 2010), xxix.
85. *Shorter Encyclopaedia*, 184.
86. Khadduri, *op. cit.*, Chapter on *Istiḥsān.*
87. Devin J. Stewart, "Muhammad b. Dawud al-Zahiri's Manual of Jurisprudence," *Studies in Islamic Law and Society* Volume 15: Studies in Islamic Legal Theory. Edited by Bernard G. Weiss. (Leiden: Brill Publishers, 2002) 111.
88. *Shorter Encyclopaedia*, 185.
89. Ali, *Muhammadan Law*, 25.
90. Iqbal, *Reconstruction*, 140.
91. Ibid.
92. Ibid., 141
93. Fazlur Rahman, *Revival and Reform in Islam —A Study of Islamic Fundamentalism*, edited and with an introduction by Ebrahim Moosa (OneWorld Publication, 2006), 205.
94. Goldziher, *The Ẓāhirīs*, 103-104.
95. Averroës, *The Book of the Decisive Treatise*, 2.
96. A. Kevin Reinhart, "Chapter 12: Law," in Jamal J. Elias, *Key Themes for the Study of Islam* (Oneworld Publications, 2014).

Chapter 8

Dynamism and Permanence

Ijtihād as Doctrinal Dynamics

Ijtihād is the resort to intellectual exertion in order to form an opinion, and in Islamic jurisprudence, it refers to the effort to determine God's will in a case in order to arrive at a rule of law.[1] To take a more technical definition offered by the classical texts, the following by al-Āmidī would be instructive, if not altogether daunting: "a total expenditure of effort in seeking an opinion regarding a rule of divine law such that the one [putting forth the effort] senses within himself an inability to do more [than he has done]." (*Istifrāgh al-was'i fī ṭalabi al-ẓannī bi shay'in min al-aḥkāmi al-Shar'iyyati 'alā wajhin yuḥassu min al-nafsi al-'ajzu 'an al-mazīdi fīhi*).[2] Further elucidation of this rather abstract definition yields the following: a total expenditure of effort in seeking an opinion as to what constitutes a probable rule of divine law relative to a particular case under consideration. Total means one has done one's utmost and can do no more. The phrase "in seeking an opinion" excludes those rules that can be known with certainty while "rule of divine law" excludes *ijtihād* that has some other aim than seeking an opinion regarding the divine law.[3] Thus, cogitations on *kalām* and *falsafah*, no matter how profound and exhausting they may be, do not count as *ijtihād* in this technical sense. On the question of probability, it is to be noted that it covers a wide range: from that which borders on certainty (*al-ẓann al-muqārib li al-qaṭ'*) to "overwhelming opinion" (*ghalabah al-ẓann*). However, high probability is not a mandatory requirement for the formulation of a *ḥukm* though, naturally, the slighter the degree of probability the greater will be the likelihood of subsequent repeal or reformulation. This aspect of *uṣūl al-fiqh* is of profound importance for it provides "the salvation of Muslim legal hermeneutics" and this "probabilism enables (the *fuqahā'*) to combine a steadfast intentionalism with a realistic recognition of the uncertainties entailed in the interpretive enterprise."[4] The question of probability also entails discussion on inductive corroboration and certainty too expansive for inclusion here but suffice it to note that in the preceding chapter on sources of the *Sharīʿah*, mention was made about the *ḥadīth* as a written record of the sayings of the Prophet as transmitted via an *isnad*. The unbroken transmission might have been effected via a single line in which case it yields a *āḥād* (one-time) report or it may be through numerous parallel lines yielding a *mutawātir* (recurrent) report. The channels of transmission are so numerous as to preclude any possibility of collaboration on a forgery. Epistemologically, it yields immediate knowledge (*ʿilm ḍarūrī*) in the mind of the hearer, that is, a knowledge that is not inferred but directly imposed on the intellect. Hence, its authenticity is absolutely certain.[5] Nevertheless, this does not mean that *āḥād* reports are inconsequential. On the contrary, by virtue of their quality of being uninterrupted in transmission going back to the Prophet, such solitary reports are accorded a degree of probability in excess of 0.5. Sunni *fuqahā'* are unanimous with regard to the *ẓannī* status of *āḥād* reports. The *fuqahā'* also recognised degrees of probability higher than 0.5 but lower than 1.0,[6] covering, as stated earlier, a wide range, from bordering on certainty to "overwhelming opinion."

We may look at *ijtihād* as intellectual dynamics comprising inductive and deductive reasoning, objective contextualism and multi-dimensional hermeneutics with its doctrinal moorings in the Qur'ān and the Sunnah. It has led to a flowering of the intellect which was indeed crucial for the developmental advancement of the *ummah* after the passing of the Prophet and, as will be argued in this chapter, remains absolutely relevant today. As the contestation of ideas is essential for the advancement of an intellectual society so does the law attain its relevancy and utility through the avenue of "ijtihādic debate" where intense discourse is done openly among the learned of the community, that is, the *fuqahā'* in their various gradations within their self-regulating hierarchy. On account of the fact that the authority of *ijmā'* was often a matter of opinion, as we have resolved in the previous chapter, the law so derived may at best be only tentative if not altogether shrouded in uncertainty. Hence, it is said that both the meanings and the texts from which they are drawn, float on "a sea of opinion, a sea of *ijtihād*."[7] Obviously, the key question is what constitutes the sea and what constitutes the shore? While a great part of the *Sharī'ah* stays afloat, whatever that remains on the shore resides there as securely and immutably as the ordainment that "indeed Judgment [as to what is right and what is wrong] rests with God alone" (*ini al-ḥukmu illā li Allāhi*)[8]. And these are the fundamentals that are cast in stone: The overarching commandments and prohibitions of God as are spelt out in the Qur'ānic text which, by virtue of its miraculous character and error-free transmission process, is fully authentic, the prophethood of Muhammad and the clarity and firmness of its most fundamental themes encapsulated in the *āyāt muḥkamāt*—these and these alone delineate the province of the *Sharī'ah* law into which no *ijtihād* may trespass. These rules have become manifest through indicators that yield certainty (*al-adillah al-qaṭ'iyyah*) as, for example, the five basic religious duties of Islam or the six articles of faith. *Ijtihād* is, however, permitted in regard to matters adrift in the sea, rules of law whose indicators will yield nothing higher than opinion (*mā kāna min al-aḥkāma al-shar'iyyatī dalīluhu ẓannī*).[9]

In the preceding chapter it was suggested that it would be counter-intuitive to say that the Prophet had to resort to *ijtihād* in arriving at a legal rule for the obvious reason that he would be divinely guided on such matters and would not need to consciously exercise intellectual exertion for such a purpose. Nevertheless, this matter remains a subject of contention. There is also still the nagging issue whether *ijtihād* was possible during the era of revelation where two overriding controversies tend to cast a shadow of doubt on the role of the Prophet in legislation.

The first point of contention centered on the question whether the Prophet was obliged to follow the dictates of his own *ijtihād* when precise guidance on a particular question of law was not available from a revealed text. Aḥmad bin Ḥanbal and Abū Yūsuf took the position that the Prophet was indeed duty-bound while Shāfiʿī considered it possible though not conclusively proven. Several of his followers and the Muʿtazilī *mujtahid*s, namely, ʿAbd al-Jabbār and Abū al-Ḥusayn al-Baṣrī follow Shāfiʿī's thinking while another two, Jubbā'ī and his son Abū Hāshim oppose such a notion. Interestingly, al-Āmidī adopts the Ḥanbalī-Abū Yūsuf position effectively departing from Shāfiʿī's cautiousness on the strong conviction that not only is it possible that the Prophet engaged in *ijtihād* but it is an actual fact that he did.[10] The very idea of a prophetic *ijtihād* presupposes that revelation was not an ongoing experience in the Prophet's life, guiding him on every matter that came before him. The Prophet could therefore make pronouncements that did not constitute the Sunnah, much less the Qur'ān.

The second controversy concerned whether others, namely, his Companions, were free to rely on *ijtihād* while the Prophet was alive. The majoritarian position affirmed such a practice as the famous *ḥadīth* concerning Muʿādh ibn Jabal would clearly show. There were, however, some qualifications: the Companions could only engage in *ijtihād* when not in the presence of the Prophet, or only when the Prophet had authorized them to engage in *ijtihād*. Now, being free to exercise *ijtihād* is one thing but actually engaging in it is another matter concerning which it appears that the majoritarian position suggests that no evidence could be found to that effect. Again, al-Āmidī disagrees and asserts there were no such qualifications and that the evidence makes it at least probable, if not certain, that it did actually occur.[11]

From a one-dimensional view point of the *Sharīʿah*, *ijtihād* is the other side of the coin against *taqlīd* which may be defined at this preliminary stage as adopting without question the opinion of a *mujtahid* on an issue pertaining to the *Sharīʿah*. Using Newton's first law of motion analogy, we may say that the body of *Sharīʿah* law remains at rest unless an external force acts on it. The body at rest represents the legal corpus at a given time as maintained by *taqlīd* while the external force generates new legal principles as propelled by *ijtihād*. In light of this, this chapter is so titled as to reflect the interrelatedness of the two necessitating discussing *ijtihād* and *taqlīd* conjointly. However, for structural purposes we bifurcate the two here in terms of perspective presenting first *ijtihād* before moving on to *taqlīd* and finally looking at *ikhtilāf* which is both process and outcome. While *ijtihād* is a process through which the *fuqahā'* explore and define the parameters of Islam's sacred law (setting down values, mores, and boundaries of the *ummah*), *taqlīd* is the outcome whereby ordinary Muslims follow the guidance for they are not experts in the field of religious and legal study. This is common sense. But *taqlīd* is practised not just by lay Muslims but by other *fuqahā'* as well. Why this is so and what the ramifications are of such a process will be answered when we come to *taqlīd* proper.

It may be said that if there had been no *ijtihād*, the *madhāhib* would not have come into existence and Islam would be purely monochromatic, one-dimensional and a completely intolerant religion where the entire *ummah* would subscribe to one and only one version of Islam as *dīn*. The closest possibility to that realization may be traced to those who claim that, indeed, they are the followers of that true pristine Islam, a *dīn* that had not been adulterated by *ijtihād* as yet by those who used their reason to practice the religion. As we have alluded to in Chapter 2, present-day claimants to that ideal Islam are the Salafis tracing their titular eponym to the mythical *salaf* of early Islam, who apparently evolved along the way to become Ḥanbālis, Wahhabis, fundamentalists, neo-fundamentalists, jihadists, Talibanis, and so on, culminating at this point in history in ISIS. It would be obvious by now that even this supposedly monolithic brand of Islam has splintered into these diverse groups each claiming to be more "Salafist" than the other and competing among themselves as to who could do greatest disservice to the term Islamic State.

In any event, thanks to *ijtihād*, the *mujtahids* were able to stake out their own territory of the law arising not from hegemonic claims to purity to the *dīn* but from the *Sharīʿah's* inherent nature that allowed for the cycle of change and permanence to continually generate dynamic growth of the law. The smaller schools such as the Ẓāhirī and Jarīrī *madhāhib* died natural deaths so that by the mid-fourth/tenth century, only four Sunni schools remained together with the Twelver Shīʿī, Zaydī Shīʿī, and ʿIbādī Khāriji *madhāhib*. After that period, it is claimed that *taqlīd* set in for good until the advent of the modern era. If that were so, then every *faqīh* during those successive generations would have been only a *muqallid* no more exercising *ijtihād* but only blind imitation. But this was not the case. Recent scholarship has emphasized that, according to the works on legal theory and even according to the evidence of practice, *ijtihād* in the sense of the independent investigation of legal questions did not simply come to an end at any point in the premodern period. *Ijtihād* had never stopped though in terms of magnitude and impact it atrophied into insignificance until the advent of the 19th century when it latched on to the legal-politico phenomenon of the push for modernity in the Muslim world.

Ijtihād is required of a *faqīh* who sets out to answer a legal question, and attainment of the rank of *mujtahid* is based on a thorough education in the law, legal interpretation, and the sciences that are ancillary to it, such as Arabic grammar and rhetoric.[12] Indeed, having delineated the province of *ijtihād*, and definitively mapped out its terrain, it would appear to be superfluous to define *mujtahid* but for the fact that it is a different matter to talk about the conditions a *faqīh* or *ʿālim* or a *mutakallim* must fulfil in order to be recognised as a *mujtahid* described generically by al-Āmidī as "anyone characterized by *ijtihād*."[13] There are two primary qualifications which effectively encompass the six to ten conditions often referred to by standard textbooks: knowledge of the basics of *kalām* (speculative theology) and a profound mastery of *uṣūl al-fiqh* (theoretical jurisprudence).[14] As for the former, al-Āmidī specifies knowledge of God's existence, and that He exists *ex necessitate* through Himself,[15] knowledge of His attributes, and that He is living, all-knowing, omnipotent, so that the *mujtahid* understands that God should impose obligations, and knowledge that God establishes the veracity of the Prophet and the *Sharī'ah* he brings, so that the *mujtahid* can be a true expounder (*muḥaqqiq*) of what is transmitted from the Prophet.[16] In respect of the condition pertaining to *uṣūl al-fiqh*, it is indeed a tall order: inter alia, knowledge of the indicators of the rules of law (*madārik* rather than *adillah*) and all the categories, classifications, the hierarchy and conditions of applicability, knowledge of resolution of conflicts between indicators and the rules governing them. This would necessitate familiarity with the transmitters and the ways of distinguishing the trustworthy from the untrustworthy, the sound from the weak, the *asbāb al-nuzūl*, knowledge of the factors and circumstances surrounding the abrogation of certain *āyah*s, knowledge of both lexicography and grammar, although he need not be as learned as al-Aṣma'ī in lexicography or as Sībawayhī in grammar. A *mujtahid* must have full command of the language of the Arabs which would include knowing semantics and territorial and customary usage as well as the ability to differentiate between similar but variant verbal expressions. All these qualifications are only requisite in the case of the *mujtahid mutlaq*, that is, the "unrestricted *mujtahid*" who formulates rules and gives opinions on the entire range of legal questions. Below that is the *mujtahid muqayyad* or the restricted *mujtahid* who may pass rulings according to the confines of his particular *madhhab*, or matters that pertain to his chosen field.[17]

Ijtihād has also been used to refer to the degree of freedom a *faqīh* enjoyed in formulating and propagating his opinions. While *ijtihād* did not grind to a halt, the *fuqahā'* in the 13th and later centuries knew that the days of unrestrained exposition of opinions were gone. When the renowned Shāfiʿī scholar Jalāl al-Dīn al-Suyūṭī (d. 909/1505) claimed to be a *mujtahid* at par with the founders of the *madhāhib* and that he could depart from the opinions of Imām Shāfiʿī, he was roundly rebuked.

It has been said that Islamic law is not a corpus of legislation but the living result of legal science.[18] No other legal system exists which gives so much attention to the science of *uṣūl al-fiqh* than to the law itself. Nevertheless, the divine law was not given in the form of a ready-made body of precise rules, but more often by way of general and sometimes specific words and phrases that provide the foundational reference points or indicators for the rules. It is the business of the *fuqahā'* to construct rules on the basis of these indicators.[19] *Sharīʿah* law, therefore, is to a large extent law of the *fuqahā'* or 'jurists' law'. In the earliest usage, as we alluded to above, *ijtihād* was equated with *qiyās* by al-Shāfiʿī in *al-Risālah.* It was practically the same as *rā'y* and since the *mujtahid* was one who by his own exertions formed his own opinion, he was the opposite of the *muqallid*, or imitator, that is, one who takes the saying of another without knowledge of its basis. Hence, the word *taqlīd* which means acceptance without knowledge.[20]

We have examined the question why there was a need to differentiate between matters of belief and matters of practice which led to the separation between *kalām* and *fiqh* and could not see any basis for making these polarities. As mentioned earlier, *fiqh*, as used in al-Tawbah, *āyah* 122, encapsulates the study of the religion as *ʿilm*—as a science in the pursuit of knowledge concerning all matters related to the Qur'ān, and later expanded to include the study of the Sunnah and all attendant matters, not necessarily of a juristic or legalistic kind. It is contended that the Qur'ānic reference in this *āyah* specifically linking *fiqh* directly to *dīn* (*liyatafaqqahu fī al-dīn*) sows the seeds of intellectual expansion of the concept of the *Sharīʿah.* By inductive reasoning, we can take the concept of *fiqh* in a static sense out of the general semantic sense of knowledge or understanding to the active, conscious and deliberate pursuit of knowledge and understanding—in matters of *dīn*. On this premise, the answer to the question is "no." It is argued that not only is there no legitimate reason why *fiqh* should be separated from *dīn, kalām* or *qawā'id*, but rather that there is every reason for the two to be taken holistically.

The pursuit of *fiqh* beyond the time-honoured tradition of the *'ulamā'* in constraining *fiqh* to just "legal and juristic matters concerning human conduct" would open new vistas to accommodate the dynamics of change. Why then has the province of *fiqh* been limited to purely legalistic matters? The strict emphasis on the legalistic side of the science of *fiqh* has much to do with a view of the *Sharī'ah* where form tended to prevail over substance. Externalization of ritual tended to prevail over internalization of beliefs. Traditional proofs (*dalāil naqliyyah*) took precedence over rational proofs (*dalāil 'aqliyyah*). As in the refrain "Theirs not to make reply, Theirs not to reason why, Theirs but to do and die,"[21] the onslaught of legalistic and rigid approaches eventually led to the emergence of an overarching attitude where one was not allowed to have an independent mind to investigate the doctrines of the Qur'ān. This was the inevitable consequence of an approach which denied the legitimacy of resorting to the intellect, where rationalizing was seen as prima facie rejection of revealed proofs and where the challenge to orthodoxy bordered on disbelief (*kufr*).

Now, the argument is that even allowing for the alternative approach where the exercise of the intellect is permitted—which must perforce be the case or else the concept of *ijtihād* itself will be meaningless—it should not be forgotten that under the traditional regime of *uṣūl al-fiqh*, the derivation of *aḥkām* (rules) from legislation verses must abide by certain criteria. Words may be categorised as *'ām* (general), *kḥāṣṣ* (specific), *muṭlaq* (absolute), *muqayyad* (restricted) *mujmal* (comprehensive) or *mubayyan* (explicit). The *faqīh* must have knowledge of not just parts of but the entire Qur'ān, in order to undertake a fully inclusive and comprehensive *tafsīr* of the prescriptive verses, not to mention the other qualifications. As we have considered earlier in respect of the criteria and conditions of being a *mujtahid* (as outlined by al-Āmidī), the *faqīh* would have fulfilled the conditions for the exercise of *ijtihād* in its entirety if he is to be considered a *mujtahid muṭlaq*. The reality is that from the Sunni perspective, a *mujtahid muṭlaq* no longer exists in this day and age. What we have are the *mujtahid muqayyad* who are authorised to pass rulings according to the confines of his particular *madhhab* or particular area of specialization and even in this category there are few and far between. The question then is: how does the *ummah* deal with new situations and issues that present themselves as civilization progresses?

Perhaps to talk of "civilizational progress" is rather presumptuous, as our discussion in Chapter 3 has pointed out, but at least when pitted against the contemporary world, it would appear that the stringent attitude towards *ijtihād* would have little traction with the *ummah* except for the tradition-bound *'ulamā'*. Although the general perception is that it was only by the turn of the last century, that there emerged a drive for *tajdīd* (renewal) and *iṣlāḥ* (reform) in the Middle East and certain parts of Asia, recent studies have shown that this renaissance occurred earlier—in the 17th and 18th centuries —via a robust, rich and cosmopolitan interplay of intellectual forces that constituted one of the most dynamic periods in the history of Islam since its Golden Age.[22] Networks of *'ulamā'* centered in the Haramayn (Mecca and Medina) hailing from all corners of the Muslim world driven by a conviction for *tajdīd* and *iṣlāḥ* of the *ummah* which, to their mind, was in a state of intellectual and socio-moral stagnation. Emerging from this melting pot in the Ḥaramayn was a non-Arab community called *aṣḥāb al-Jāwiyyīn* where the term *Jāwī* came to signify anyone from the Malay-Indonesian world. Among the great contributions made by them was the reconciliation between *Sharī'ah* and *Taṣawwuf* although such a marriage had already been advocated by the likes of al-Qushayrī and al-Ghazālī. However, it had to take the renewed commitments by the Haramayn revivalists to give the merger a solid and virtually unshakeable synthesis that would have great impact particularly on the brand of Islam that finally prevails in Southeast Asia today. This is Islam of the archipelago or Nusantara Islam as distinct and formally structured as the other textures and shapes of Islam in other parts of the world such as the Middle-East or Pakistan and India. However, owing to its geographical remoteness (or at least the perception of it) in the Muslim world, there was (and still remains) a tendency among scholars to exclude the Malay-Indonesian world from any serious discourse of Islam[23] save for the relatively recent surge of attention consequent on several violent episodes of militant radicalism. Apart from that, Islam in the archipelago has long been regarded as not "real Islam" being merely a façade on a heathen foundation prodded no doubt by an array of myths, the most bandied about being the abangan/santri bifurcation of Muslims in Java. According to American anthropologist Clifford Geertz, the majority of Muslims in Java and by extension Indonesia in general, were *abangan*, that is, nominal Muslims while only the elite constituted the *santri*, that is, strict and practicing Muslims. Afflicted with a pathological loathing of recognizing the "Islamic nature" of Islam in Java, or even in Southeast Asia for that matter, and influenced, subconsciously perhaps, by Max Weber's interpretative social science, Geertz considered Islam in Java as only a "thin veneer of symbols attached to a supposedly solid core of animistic and Hindu-Buddhist meaning."[24] Islam is therefore regarded as having no significant impact on Southeast Asia and the region consequently is regarded as marginal and peripheral vis-à-vis Middle Eastern Islam.[25] Perhaps it could be contended that much of the renewalist phenomenon then was leaning towards the transmission of learning more by way of *taqlīd* and less of *ijtihād*. It is, however, beyond the scope of this present study to venture into the nature and extent of *tajdīd* and *iṣlāḥ* that the region was experiencing during the said period but suffice it to say that it was no winter of intellectual hibernation.

Nevertheless, the zeal and conviction for change has cumulatively transformed the meaning of *ijtihād*, taking it out of the ironclad technical confines to a broad society-centric paradigm which renders it as a cognate of *tajdīd* and *iṣlāḥ*. As I have stated at the outset, *ijtihād* as in renewal and reform taken collectively must mean effecting change for the betterment of the *ummah* and at the same level a rejection of any kind of *taqlīd* that would be a stumbling block towards that path of progress.

This usage coincides with the emergence of modern Islamic legal scholarship and a parallel development in societal reform which would be a natural corollary considering that the *Sharīʿah* does not recognize any bifurcation between law and society. The terms had mass appeal to modernist reformers like Muhammad ʿAbduh (d. 1323/1905) and Rashīd Riḍā (d. 1353/1935), religious liberalists, utilitarians, and even fundamentalist thinkers. As we have seen in Chapter 6 with reference to the *maqāṣid al-Sharīʿah*, *ijtihād* in this sense signified breaking free from the constraints of certain time-honoured legal rules based on the higher objectives of the *Sharīʿah*, expounded by resort to *ʿaqliyyah* arguments that resonate with utilitarian, welfarist and society-centric advocates.

Notwithstanding the force of *taqlīd*, major figures continued to claim the ability for creative adaptation, rethinking and expansion of the legal tradition.[26] For example, the compilation of the monumental *Fatāwā-i ʿĀlamgīriyyah* under the reign of the Mughal Emperor Aurangzeb ʿĀlamgīr (d. 1118/1707) was ostensibly justified to make judicial practice less varied in the opinions of the most widely accepted authorities in the Ḥanafī school. This lament regarding the diversity of legal opinions testifies to the flexibility in the legal practice of the time. But a variety of differing opinions is routinely noted in this compilation giving the judges considerable discretion in dealing with the cases before them and conferring on jurists the freedom to suit the application of the law to changing times.[27]

A leading *ʿālim* Taqī ʿUthmānī has argued that those who are steeped in the Islamic juristic tradition ought to be able to venture beyond their own school of law and expound on new matters.[28] The modern age has brought with it new intellectual and practical issues and challenges that warrant continuous *ijtihād*. By the exercise of *ijtihād* we are not concerned here with intra-*madhab* disputations or legalistic controversies stemming from variant interpretations of the Qur'ān and the Sunnah. Our idea of a reopening of the gates of *ijtihād* and the resolve to leave them permanently open is grounded on the conviction that the spirit of the faith demands that law-making be regarded as a dynamic process of renewal. It is in this spirit that present day experts should be able to exercise "absolute *ijtihād*," that is, *ijtihād* which might lead to a fundamental disagreement with an established authority. According to Waḥīd al-Dīn Khān the problem is not that people have come to lack the ability for *ijtihād*, but the tolerance for criticism has declined and that in later centuries it was the gate of criticism and disagreement that came to be closed, not the gate of *ijtihād*.[29]

The Tunisian project is a classic case in point where the oft-cited Qur'ānic verse which had served as the *naṣṣ* for the practice of polygyny was given an entirely new interpretation:

> "... but if you have reason to fear that you might not be able to treat them with equal fairness, then [marry only] one."[30]

Applying new *ijtihād* it was interpreted that the verse meant that no husband would be able to treat co-wives equally as enjoined by the Qur'ān and this provided the legal proof to outlaw polygyny instead. Whatever might be the merits or demerits of such an interpretation, this new-fangled approach manifested the radical—in an intellectual sense—change that would be required in order to break out from a *fiqh*-centric paradigm that had provided the Muslim world with what was seen as an established legal and juristic system. This was *ijtihād* with a vengeance and a radical departure from even the most "liberal" classic interpretation which essentially gives the impression that polygyny is not *mandūb* (recommended) but stops short of ruling that it is *makrūh* (discouraged) let alone *ḥarām* (forbidden). For example, according to Sa'īd ibn Jubayr, Qatādah, and other successors of the Companions, the purport of the passage is that one must apply careful consideration to the interests and rights of the women whom one intends to marry. Al-Ṭabarī gives it his unequivocal approval. The number of wives must not exceed four. It was in this sense that 'Abduh understood the verse. Modern scholars such as Asad advocate a reductionist *tafsīr* of the *āyah* to hone in on the rational and logical conclusion that must be derived from the requirement of "equal fairness," concluding that because it is virtually impossible to treat wives with equal fairness, monogyny would therefore be the best course. However, being well-grounded in *uṣūl al-fiqh*, Asad never suggests that there is any textual foundation for the prohibition of polygyny. However, he makes it clear that contrary to the popular view and the practice of many Muslims in the past centuries, neither the Qur'ān nor the Sunnah gives any sanction for sexual intercourse without marriage.[31]

We considered in the previous chapter how certain modern trends in *ijtihād* have advocated proposals as radical as the rejection of certain *aḥkām* derived from Qur'ānic *āyahs* revealed in Mecca and the excision of the entire corpus of *aḥādīth* as textual material of the Sunnah, hence removing it as one of the *uṣūl* of the *Sharī'ah*. It is therefore hardly surprising that modernist *ijtihādic* calls for reforms in Islamic legal hermeneutics also lean on the repudiation of *ijmā'* while making a case for the *ijtihād* of non-conventional *'ulamā'* such as scientists, medical experts and scholars in areas not traditionally related to *uṣūl al-fiqh* or *fiqh*.[32] Indeed, the natural corollary to such *ijtihādic* developments eventually converge on a modernistic, contemporary approach to the doctrine of the *maqāṣid al-Sharī'ah*.

Taqlīd—And attempts to break free

The phenomenon of *taqlīd* is one of the most misunderstood in the history of the development of the *Sharī'ah* and is often described coterminously with what has been fashionably termed as *insidād bāb al-ijtihād* or the closing of the door of *ijtihād*. According to Schacht, this had occurred by the beginning of the 10th century where "a consensus gradually established itself to the effect that from that time onwards no one could be deemed to have the necessary qualifications for independent reasoning in religious law, and that all future activity would have to be confined to the explanation, application, and, at the most, interpretation of the doctrine as it had been laid down once and for all."[33] Dismissing Schact's theory as "pure fiction," Iqbal posits that the situation was more complex entailing partly "the crystallization of legal thought in Islam," and partly "intellectual laziness which, especially in the period of spiritual decay, turns great thinkers into idols." Now, even if some of the later *fuqahā'* may have upheld this fiction, contemporary Islam "is not bound by this voluntary surrender of intellectual independence."[34] Thus, while brushing off any suggestion of legitimacy in "closing the door of *ijtihād*," Iqbal recognizes the reality of the phenomenon of *taqlīd*.

Taqlīd, therefore, (according to conventional wisdom) set the stage for the hibernation of intellectual activity in the field of *Sharī'ah* law, with the *'ulamā'* particularly the *fuqahā'* moving away from the practice of *ijtihād* towards blind and uncritical acceptance of the prevailing dogma and opinions concerning the law. This is the clichéd conception of *taqlīd* but it suffices for now—only momentarily—as we shall see later. *Taqlīd* defined simplistically was the taking of a *mujtahid*'s viewpoint without evidence. *Taqlīd* in matters of *fiqh* may therefore only be understood in the context of the four orthodox schools of Sunni jurisprudence wherein adherents are obliged to accept without question the principles of law as professed by the school. Undoubtedly, there were other schools notably the Ẓāhirī associated with the famed Ibn Ḥazm of Andalusia and the various Shī'ī schools but, within the Sunni world, the law books of these four schools became the authoritative texts on all points of law and any departure by way of dissenting views or new interpretation was not permitted. Within these schools some degree of manoeuvrability was permitted in that a follower of one particular school may choose to convert to another on condition that he did so completely.

The general view as held by Schacht, Gibb, Coulson, Watt, Khadduri and Fazlur Rahman was that by the end of the 10th century, intellectual stagnation finally set in and the *Sharīʿah* was to remain fossilised for another 700 years. The four Sunni schools had reached their peak output capacity and the *ʿulamāʾ* were of the view that whatever that could be discoursed and elucidated in respect of *fiqh* was already undertaken. As no new rules needed to be formulated anymore, *ijtihād* on *fiqh* matters was not only unnecessary but harmful.[35] But the operation of *taqlīd* meant that everyone was now bound to what had been authoritatively laid down by the predecessors. No one may any longer consider himself qualified to give a verdict of his own in the field of *fiqh*, independent of that of an earlier *mujtahid* save, as we have seen earlier, the *mujtahid muṭlaq*.

We saw in Chapter 2 the phenomenon and significance of the role of the *madhāhib* and why *taqlīd* is necessary, even essential within a specific context. The conventional wisdom is that unless one has reached the level of a *mujtahid muṭlaq*, and thus possesses the requisite credentials and qualifications to exercise *ijtihād* to formulate a new rule, one should just follow the rules of the established schools of law. To be a *muqallid* in matters of *fiqh,* faithfully following the practice and understanding of a particular *madhhab,* is by itself an achievement, an act of humility and valour at the same time, manifesting recognition of the wisdom of the ages in the genesis of *fiqh* teachings handed down through an unbroken chain of transmission. On the other hand, to be a *ghayr muqallid*, that is, to reject the need to follow the masters (because *taqlīd* is regarded as *bidʿah* or for whatever reason) is a sign of arrogance.

Nevertheless, the conventional view concerning *taqlīd* has increasingly come under attack as being unfaithful to the facts of history. Hallaq proffers a different position with regard to the role of *taqlīd*. The loss of faith in the *fiqh* of traditionalists is said to be grounded in the failure of Western trained Muslim lawyers and judges to grasp the epistemological and hermeneutical framework of legal thinking. The doctrine of *taqlīd* should not be seen as the death of freedom in legal speculation or as diametrically opposed to *ikhtilāf* but rather should be seen as primarily buttressing the defence of a particular *madhhab's fiqh*.[36]

A *madhhab* was defined by its substantive boundaries informed by a certain body of positive doctrine. Far from working in opposition to *taqlīd*, the process of *ikhtilāf* was part and parcel of the discourse that encouraged robust disputation but it was not unbridled. Limits were set and transgressing them invoked the risk of being labelled a heretic bordering dangerously on apostasy. The authority of a *madhhab* depended largely on the doctrinal corpus distilled over the years from principles and rulings expounded by the founder with accretions of his followers and pupils lending credence to the assertion as advanced in Chapter 2 that *Sharī'ah* law, after making allowance for the law directly attributed to the Qur'ān and the Sunnah, is essentially "*fuqahā'* law" as expounded and concretized by *mujtahid*s and eminent jurists of the four Sunni *madhāhib*.

Pedalling back into history, *taqlīd* in a generic sense denotes the acceptance of legal authority and as early as the second/eighth century, it meant specifically following unquestioningly the teachings of the *Ṣaḥābah* (Companions) and the *Tābi'ūn* (Followers).[37] In later usage, it was confined to following the authority of a *mujtahid* which, however, could be used at two distinct levels. First, it referred to following unquestioningly the *mujtahid*'s authority in respect of either his textual evidence or the line of reasoning adopted in a particular case. *Taqlīd* here denotes "following the totality of the founder's legal doctrines as a methodologically systematic structure, without the *muqallid* being bound by all the individual opinions within the corpus of those doctrines."[38] It is in this sense that the term is employed in traditional works of theoretical Islamic jurisprudence, applicable across the board to the public and the non-*fuqahā'*. Secondly, *taqlīd* also denoted *madhhab* fidelity (that is, bindingness of authoritative legal doctrines within one's school) with full knowledge of the means by which the rulings were arrived at."[39]

Taqlīd was therefore practised in both senses of the term. In the context of a single case, it could operate as a multi-layered and vertically composite principle. In other words, for one question there could be at least two or more possible answers with overlapping nuances and implications and permutations in between semantically and normatively. For the average *fiqh* manual, the *faqīh/mujtahid* engages in all manner of *taqlīd*, ranging from simple restatement of authority to quasi-exposition of a given position.[40] At its most advanced level, it constituted a full ratiocination of established *aḥkām* and re-articulation of textual evidence as explicated by the early masters. At this level, the line between *taqlīd* and *ijtiḥād* becomes blurred.[41]

The predominance of *taqlīd* within a particular *madhhab* signified that it had come of age manifesting the internal juridical dynamics that led to the crystallization of its principles and doctrines. This explains why *taqlīd* plays an absolutely essential role in holding the fort of the *madhhab* as "a methodological and interpretive entity" constituted of identifiable principles discoursed via *uṣūl al-fiqh* and to a certain extent *uṣūl al-dīn*. In formulating its body of positive doctrine, such a *madhhab* also carved out, as it were, its substantive boundaries, beyond which the *faqīh* traversed only on pain of being excommunicated or disowned by the school.[42]

Nevertheless, embedded in the discipline of *uṣūl al-fiqh* is a doctrinal antipathy towards *taqlīd* because the very nature of *uṣūl* discourse is brought about by the need for the contestation of ideas. The thinking and outlook of the *fuqahā'* must by necessity be latitudinous and multi-dimensional in order to develop a sound and vibrant *ijtihādic* methodology. *Taqlīd* among such circles is naturally greeted with contempt and ridicule as borne out by the voluminous literature dealing with this kind of intellectual derision under the rubric *fī dhamm al-taqlīd* (in condemnation of *taqlīd*) regardless of the *madhhab* they were affiliated with though among the four the Ḥanafīs received the least of the brickbats.[43] That is within the realm of expectation on account of the fact that historically among the Sunni *madhāhib* the Ḥanafī *mujtahids* were the most receptive to rationalist interpretations which enabled them to be less rigid and more tolerant of variant opinions.

Ibn 'Abd al-Barr (d. 463/1070), a contemporary of Ibn Ḥazm, in his *Jāmi' Bayān al-'Ilm wa Faḍlihi,*[44] condemns *taqlīd* as invalid, being a practice contrary to the Qur'ān, the Sunnah as well as *ijmā'*. Detractors say this was just a case of semantic hair-splitting for while *taqlīd* is forbidden for the *faqīh* in religious matters, *ittibā'* is permitted. There is, however, a difference. Whereas *ittibā'* entails following an opinion based on strong evidence, *taqlīd*, which is adopting an opinion without knowledge, is nothing but blind imitation.[45] However, the detractors cite the purported fact that Ibn 'Abd al-Barr himself was a *muqallid* in religious matters as evidenced by his position in respect of *kalām* where he had allegedly opposed the *mutakallimūn* by citing Ibn Khuwayz Mindād al-Baṣrī who had stated that "every *mutakallim* is from the people of *bid'ah*—whether he is an Ash'arī or other than an Ash'arī. His testimony is never accepted in Islām. Indeed ... he should be punished for his *bid'ah* and must repent," citing Imām Mālik and various Companions as authorities. This supposed citation has, however, been discredited by al-Qāḍī 'Iyāḍ (d. 544/1149) as totally unreliable considering that Ibn Khuwayz Mindād who had not risen to the rank of *muḥaddith* was only a Māliki *faqīh* who died in 390/999 and was therefore not a companion of Imām Mālik making his claim concerning what Imām Mālik supposedly said as unworthy of merit in the absence of an *isnād* let alone independent corroboration.[46]

Up to the fifth/eleventh century, when an opinion was introduced in a particular context the reason for which it was introduced is known though it may not be articulated. By way of illustration, the question was whether a *qāḍī* should be personally liable to make good loans taken (from the *aḥbās*—revenues of mosque endowments), at his behest, for renovation works to a grand mosque if it turns out that subsequently income due to the mosque were insufficient to service the debt. Ibn Rushd issued a *fatwā* to the effect that the *qāḍī* is not liable[47] but he did not specifically cite an authority for the opinion. It was nevertheless established among the *fuqahā'* in Andalucía on the basis of Mālikī jurisprudence that the surplus generated from endowments may be used to defray costs incurred on other endowments in the event of insufficient funds. It is clear that in this situation, Ibn Rushd did not exercise *ijtihād* in any sense and may be rightly said to have practised *taqlīd* instead but this is one done "with full knowledge of a prevailing authority" and does not constitute blind imitation.[48]

In *fiqh* discourse centering on positive law, the main purpose appears to be the exposition of principles as may be instanced in the vast corpus of *fiqh* literature. In the case of the *Mukhtaṣar* of the Ḥanafite Ṭaḥāwī, a classic example concerns the sale of a house to a third party by the owner whilst a valid lease was still running. According to Abū Ḥanīfah and his protégé Muḥammad al-Shaybānī, the lessee may nullify the sale before the end of the lease in which case the sale will be rendered void *ab initio*. However, nullification of the sale after the expiry of the lease will be ineffective. This was the old position. The *aṣḥāb al-imlā'* (pupils-cum-scribes) related that subsequently, Abū Yūsuf opined that nullification by the lessee was in all instances ineffective and that the lease should be treated merely as a defect (*'ayb*) in the subject matter of the sale. The buyer's knowledge of the defect prior to the execution of the contract would exculpate the owner/seller of any liability and the lessee may continue with the lease until expiry. However, where the defect is known only after the sale is executed, the buyer then retains an option (*khiyār*) either to rescind or ratify it.[49]

Another key aspect of the development of *taqlīd* is the formulation of a doctrine that could be applied across the board using inductive generalization in addition to casuistry. In this regard, the *muqallidūn* systematized the myriad instances of casuistry into sets of general principles that governed the major issues involved in each area of the law. It may be noted that Western scholars tend to emphasize the deficiencies and negative effects of casuistry on the normative structure of *Sharī'ah* law, ascribing its preponderance to the quest for abstract thought and jurisprudential (*uṣūlī*) verbiage. Against this, it has been contended that casuistry pertains to a process of social differentiation that renders the universal validity of norms socially implausible and that the *fuqahā'* often engaged in casuistry in an effort to answer practical problems that evolve from this process of social differentiation.[50] Rather than being sheer casuistry, one contrarian approach posits *ḥiyal* as being based on a utilitarian doctrine that characterises them as *makhārij*, that is, normative exits which are informed by the rationalist paradigm of the Ḥanafi mujtahids.[51] Al-Bukhārī in his *ḥadīth* compendium uses the term 14 times in the *Kitāb al-Ḥiyal*, exceeding the number of times it occurs in the rest of his work.[52] This underscores the importance of *ḥiyal* in framing the clash between the Ḥanafis and the Traditionists, or the *aṣḥāb al-ra'y* and the *aṣḥāb al-ḥadīth*. For example, in the discussion on *nikāḥ mu'aqqat* in al-Bukhārī's *Kitāb al-Ḥiyal*, the impression given is that the Ḥanafis advocate *mut'ah* marriage.[53] The argument against *mut'ah* is aimed at an opinion of Zufar which appears to permit a time restricted marriage (*nikāḥ mu'aqqat*), although on further inspection, it means that the marriage is effected while the stipulation of time is held to be void. Although Zufar's opinion in this issue is not the official ruling in the school, clearly what he is not upholding is *mut'ah* marriage and al-Bukhārī's equating his verdict relating to *nikāḥ mu'aqqat* with the latter is itself, questionable.

By virtue of *taqlīd* and the preponderance towards generalizations, new types of legal discourse emerged among which of great import are *qawā'id al-fiqhiyyah* and *al-ashbāh wa al-naẓā'ir* encapsulating a systematic construction of higher juristic principles into legal maxims that are still very much in use in present day *fiqh* discourse.[54] In sum, it may be stated that *taqlīd* is far from the blind following of an authority. True, there were always *fuqahā'* who did mechanically follow legal authority and they have been roundly condemned. The search for the school's authoritative principles and the attempt to apply them to individual cases emerged as one of the mainstays of *taqlīd*. In fact, it is a salient feature of Islamic legal doctrine that the juristic authority embedded in the works of the immediate or near-immediate precursors was to come to constitute the chief source from which the jurists expounded their own doctrines, or at least on par with the teachings of the founders. *Taqlīd*, therefore, was not bound by any particular authority just because this authority was equated with an eponym or an early master. *Taqlīd* of the "moderns" (*muta'akhkhirūn*) was therefore as legitimate as that of the "ancients" (*mutaqaddimūn*). Another aspect of *taqlīd* is the re-enactment of the textual evidence and legal reasoning adopted by a master, signifying an *ijtihādic* activity in the course of defending the great *mujtahids* by vindicating the methods and outcome of their *ijtihād*.[55]

Hallaq contends that if the practice of *ijtihād* was the primary objective of *uṣūl al-fiqh* throughout Islamic history, in what way was the gate of *ijtihād* thought to have been closed? According to him, there was no basis in reality for the assumption that qualifications for a *mujtahid* had become so immaculate and rigorous and set so high that it became impossible to fulfil. An examination of the writings of the *fuqahā'* would expose that fallacy.[56] In his view, the conclusion that the gate was not closed therefore "requires a re-evaluation of the legal history of Islam" while the continuity of *ijtihād* "suggests that developments in positive law, legal theory and the judiciary have indeed taken place ..."[57] One may extol Hallaq's study as a paradigm shift on the subject or, on the other hand, one may be tempted to dismiss his theory as yet another classic instance of historical revisionism. But as Thomas Kuhn once said the social sciences are characterized by a "tradition of claims, counterclaims, and debates over fundamentals,"[58] this revision should therefore be taken as a positive development.

To be sure, the right to *ijtihād* was not surrendered without a fight. Protests against *taqlīd* were voiced on grounds of principle from various quarters such as the Ẓāhirīs led by their founder Dāwūd ibn ʿAlī, Ibn Ḥazm and other luminaries, who condemned it and established the obligation, even for the later scholars, to practise *ijtihād*. For this reason, the unorthodox Ẓāhirī school is historically the "preferred" *madhhab* of many famous Sufis, drawn to its strict ritualism and at the same time sharing its deep-seated aversion to *taqlīd* as well as dogmatics.[59] In coming up with their interpretations of the texts, the Ẓāhirīs no doubt resorted to *ijtihād*. But the misperception must be emphasized: the exercise of *ijtihād* does not necessarily lead to a modernist or liberal view though of course by definition *ijtihād* will enable a departure from the orthodox position. This also explains why the Ḥanbalī School, which was instrumental in making *taqlīd* fashionable, subsequently brought forth masters like Ibn Taymiyyah and Ibn Qayyim al-Jawziyyah, who advocated the break from *taqlīd* in its traditional form. Along these lines, the Wahhabīs naturally reject *taqlīd* too but sanction *ijtihād* only if this would lead to further divestment of the accretions of time, that is, *ijtihād* in order to return the religion to its pristine form which is really diplomatic speak for a return to conservatism. And in this case, the line of *ijtihād* took them to the conclusion that television is evil and must be prohibited. The Taliban took this kind of retrogressive *ijtihād* to its logical conclusion in the name of enforcing "Islamic religious iconoclasm" by ruling that allowing statues in the land of Islam was tantamount to honouring the practice of idol-worship. So, in March 2001, they took the outrageous action of blasting the statues of the Buddhas of Bamiyan in Afghanistan, effectively bombing 2500 years of history into oblivion. But even though theoretically both ends of the spectrum from modernity to conservatism may advocate the practice of *ijtihād* over the imposition of *taqlīd*, in reality at least in the last century it is the modernists who are louder and certainly the more unequivocal in their condemnation of *taqlīd*.[60]

Ikhtilāf and the Culture of Dissent

The hallmark of the early development of the *Sharīʿah* is the phenomenon of *ikhtilāf*, which is the difference of opinion among the *ʿulamāʾ* on law and scholastic theology and of details of religious practice and doctrine. In contrast to *ijmāʿ*, which is the consensus of views, *ikhtilāf* spawned dynamic debates and vibrant disputations that led to a diversity of views and the registering of these differences has produced considerable literature since the foundation of the study of *fiqh*.[61] While leaving the fundamental principles intact, *ikhtilāf* in respect of the law led to the development of the *madhāhib* no doubt encouraged by the famous saying attributed to the Prophet: "Difference of opinion in the Muslim community is a sign of divine favour."[62] This saying has become authoritative in bringing about the conviction in Muslim orthodoxy that the different schools are of coterminous if not altogether equal value. Herein were sown the seeds of the freedom of legal speculation which contributed no doubt to the inclusive nature of Islam until the subsequent development of ideological rigidity became a predominant feature in jurisprudential discourse. For now at least, this freedom of legal speculation saw the genesis of a multitude of major and minor schools each headed by a *mujtahid muṭlaq* drawing his own circle of disciples.[63] By virtue of it being juristic law, disagreements were not only tolerated but became an essential sub-discipline under *uṣūl al-fiqh*.[64] Another way of looking at this phenomenon is to term it "*ijtihādic* pluralism" whose permanency has outlived the crystallization of the *madhāhīb* throughout the entire history of Islamic law. This concept therefore poses structural challenges to the doctrine of *ijmā'* and *taqlīd* pitting it in a doctrinal zero-sum game. It has to be more of one and less of the other. Thus, where *ikhtilāf* and *ijtiḥād* is on the ascent, using the term collectively, *ijmā'* and *taqlīd*, representing consistency and certainty, will have to be on ebb.

However, while legal pluralism as such was not an issue, ascertaining the most authoritative opinion proved to be problematic. *Ijtihādic* multiplicity could not be allowed to fester at the expense of consistency and certainty which meant that at the end of the day, what was needed was still a single authoritative opinion. This warranted a further hermeneutical process by which plurality was reduced to a minimum in a discourse termed *tarjīḥ*, namely weighing conflicting evidence.[65]

To be sure, there was no lack of inter-school vituperative but on balance there was a tolerant attitude on the part of the Muslim community towards their leading *mujtahids*, who favoured *ikhtilāf* rather than *ijmā'*. No doubt there was a natural tendency towards uniformity fed by the forces of particularism and precedents and constricted by intense parochialism but this was to a large extent ameliorated by the personal influence of the leading *mujtahid*s themselves. If they had wanted to, they could certainly stir up their followers from a state of benign contentment to one of volatile extremism as some leaders are wont to do in this day and age.

There is a story that Mālik ibn Anas (d. 179/795) was requested by the Caliph al-Mansur to permit the adoption of his great work, the *Kitāb al-Muwaṭṭa'* as the canon for the caliphate. Mālik refused preferring instead the enforcement of a variety of law books. A single standard text would have undoubtedly established his authority beyond dispute but *al-Muwaṭṭa'* was written in fulfilment of a spiritual calling, not to satisfy egotistical desires.[66] But his humility did not prevent his fame from spreading. Imām al-Shāfi'ī is reported to have said "After the Book of Allah, there is no book on the face of the earth sounder than the book of Mālik."[67] But freedom in legal speculation also opened the way for a free-for-all in *ijtihād* and further intensified rivalry and pettifogging. Eventually, the law of diminishing returns set in. Some minor and less popular schools died a natural death. In due course, as alluded to earlier, speculative freedom succumbed to the tyranny of intolerance and *ijtihād* gave way to *taqlīd*. As alluded to earlier, the general view—though not necessarily an overwhelmingly correct one—considers this to be the start of the long winter of intellectual hibernation that was to see the ossification of Sunni Islamic law into a monolithic system of four, and only four, orthodox schools of law while others were systematically reduced to oblivion. Thus, by the fourth/tenth century only these four schools survived in Sunni orthodoxy, namely, the older schools of Abū Ḥanīfah in Iraq and Mālik in Medina and the relatively "modern" school of Shāfi'ī in Egypt (modern in the sense of being the first to undertake a thorough and structured investigation into the principles of jurisprudence), and the ultra-conservative school of

Aḥmad ibn Ḥanbal.

In terms of its significance to the *Sharīʿah*, *al-Muwaṭṭa'* is regarded as the earliest surviving Muslim law book and represents the earliest stage of literary development which was common to both *fiqh* and *ḥadīth*. Its object was to give a survey of law and justice, ritual and practice of religion according to the Qur'ān and the most reliable *aḥādīth*, followed by the *ʿamal* (practices and usages) of the people in Medina, because in his estimation, the practices of the first three generations there constituted evidence of the Sunnah in practice—the living Sunnah—superior to isolated *aḥādīth*. By "practice" here in relation to the *fiqh*, Mālik accepts it only as far as it is recognised as *ijmāʿ* by the *fuqahā'*. Hence, *ʿamal* becomes the highest criterion for ascertaining the Sunnah, no doubt a position which is said to be controversial and needless to say rejected by the other schools with the possible exception of the Ḥanafī *madhhab*. It was also to set a theoretical standard for matters which were not settled from the point of view of *ijmāʿ* and Sunnah.

At that time, the usage of *Sharīʿah* to refer to any kind of Islamic law as we understand in later usage would be a rarity, if used at all. In a period of recognition and appreciation of the canon law under the early Abbasids, there was a practical interest in pointing out a "well-trodden path" (hence *Muwaṭṭa'*) through the far-reaching differences of opinion even on the most elementary questions. Mālik wished to help this interest on the basis of the practice in the Ḥijāz and to codify and systematize the customary law of Medina. Tradition, which he interprets from the point of view of practice, is with him not an end but a means. The success of *al-Muwaṭṭa'* is due to the fact that it always takes an average view on disputed points. "Sharīʿahtization" of the law had been already concluded in terms of the essential *fiqh* principles being expounded and laid out even before Mālik but many generations had still to work at its systematization. Mālik's achievement may therefore be seen as being contributory to the formation of a legal system.[68] By merely recording the usual consensus of opinion in Medina without any special contribution of the author's own, *al-Muwaṭṭa'* came to be regarded as authoritative as the expression of compromise, manifesting the stage reached in the development of "*Sharī'ah* as *fiqh*" in his time. However, as a strict textualist he would not compromise on *bid'ah* (pernicious innovation) and was vehemently opposed to *kalām* (scholastic theology) and under no circumstances would *fiqh* reasoning prevail over the primary texts.[69]

That aspect of the *Sharī'ah* was already spearheaded by Abū Ḥanīfah by the methodology known as *ra'y* (personal view) which by the prevailing standards was the earliest form of rationalistic method of establishing rules in matters of *fiqh*. On account of this preponderance to "rationality" its pioneer, Imām Abū Ḥanīfah, became the target of attacks by later Ḥijāz scholars who reproached him for persistent neglect of *ḥadīth*. However, the *Musnad Abū Hanīfah*, a collection of traditions, compiled by his disciples and later Ḥanafīs, clearly shows up the lack of basis for such criticism. In the *Sharī'ah* discourse, Abū Ḥanīfah's contribution may be regarded as significant particularly in respect of *kalām* which explains why his tradition has been kept up especially in the school of al-Māturidi and its adepts in Samarqand. As for the *fiqh* part of the *Sharī'ah* which significantly contributed to the moulding of the Ḥanafī *madhhab*, it should be noted that it was his two most important pupils, Abū Yūsuf Ya'qūb and Muḥammad Ḥasan al-Shaybānī, who were in fact the primary architects in the development of the teaching of the school.[70] Among the more significant later works of *fiqh*, mention must be made of *al-Hidayah fī Sharḥ Bidāyah al-Mubtadi* (593/1197), commonly referred to as *al-Hidayah* (The Guidance) by Shaykh al-Islam Burhān al-Dīn al-Farghānī al-Marghinānī.[71] Failure to mention this magnum opus in a discussion on the impact of Ḥanafī *fiqh* on *Sharī'ah* law would be akin to leaving out Shakespeare when talking about Elizabethan drama. This tome has presided over the landscape of the Ḥanafī *fiqh* for the last eight centuries having been the primary text relied on for the issuance of *fatwās* and judicial rulings.

Apart from the epochal founders of their eponymous *madhāhib*, two more iconic Muslim scholars discussed in other contexts earlier must be mentioned, namely, Ibn Ḥazm and Ibn Rushd, to showcase their significant contributions in the field of *ikhtilāf*, which in turn attest to their supreme competence in *uṣūl al-fiqh*, an aspect often overshadowed on account of their reputations as Andalusian polymaths and leading Muslim thinkers whose works covered a comprehensive spectrum which included history, ethics, linguistics, aesthetics, physical and life sciences, theology, comparative religion, logic and philosophy.

Ibn Ḥazm's magisterial 12-volume *Kitāb al-Muḥallā bi al-Āthār* is a commentary of an earlier extensive two-volume work called *al-Mujallah* which, together with the other 90 percent of his written works were publicly burnt on the orders of Caliph al-Muʿtaḍid of Seville (d. 461-1069). Seen as the encyclopaedia of Islamic *fiqh*, *al-Muḥallā* is, from the standpoint of a *khilāf* treatise, a comprehensive study of the rulings by a multiplicity of *mujtahid*s including those among the *Tābiʿūn* such as al-Ḥasan al-Baṣrī (d. 110/728) and ʿAṭā' ibn Abī Rabāḥ (d. 114/732), and the *Tābiʿ al-Tābiʿīn* such as al-Layth ibn Ṣaʿd (d. 175/791), Sufyān ibn Saʿd al-Thawrī (d. 161/777) and al-Awzāʿī (d. 157/773). According to Shaykh Muḥammad Abū Zuhrah, the problem with *al-Muḥallā* is the use of intemperate language in the discourse of dissent and the lack of tolerance of other positions. Had it not been for this, it would have been the best book ever on Sunni *fiqh*.[72] Belonging to the Ẓāhirī *madhhab*, Ibn Ḥaẓm's literalist approach to the revealed texts has in modern times earned him a large following among Salafists who, regrettably, use his writings on Judaism, Christianity and Shīʿism as justification for hatred and animosity. The Almohads sought to canonize his legal thought into official creed as part of their power strategy to counter the pervasive influence of the mainstream Māliki doctrines in line with the internal movement for societal reform. In driving home his minimalist approach to the *Sharīʿah*, Ibn Ḥazm also took on an antagonistic position towards all of the major religious and philosophical factions of his time which led to his isolation in the community of believers.

The kind of synthesis towards which he strove was not realised.[73] One could characterize his activities on the whole as a twofold struggle for the rule of Islam over Andalusia and the truth of its beliefs over all other religions. He lived during the twilight of the Umayyad Caliphate and the beginnings of its fragmentation into city-states. He was also disturbed at the presence of Jews and Christians in well-placed positions in Muslim Spain and the wilful neglect of its rulers to enforce God's law.

Ibn Rushd must be singled out as a *faqīh* of the high calibre required for *uṣūl al-fiqh*, even as his reputation as the Muslim philosopher who has had the greatest influence on the Latin Medieval world remains unassailable. Thus, embodying a philosophical perspective, Ibn Rushd's *Bidāyah al-Mujtahid wa Nihāyah al-Muqtaṣid* (translated as *The Distinguished Jurist's Primer*[74]) stands out as discourse par excellence on *ikhtilāf*. Being a Mālikī *mujtahid* himself and Chief *Qāḍī* as well, one would have thought that his *magnum opus* on *fiqh* would be a definitive manual on Māliki law but Ibn Rushd chose instead to take the bigger challenge of writing a book of comparative jurisprudence which entails examination of the minority positions and not just the major schools. For Ibn Rushd, *ikhtilāf* was not just about giving variant rulings but a methodology of eliciting the principles which engender differences while keeping at bay his own doctrinal leanings. It required absolute objectivity as the goal of the treatise was to demonstrate the importance of a multiplicity of views as opposed to the singularity of vision that would be the natural consequence of *taqlīd* to a particular *madhhab*. Indeed, Ibn Rushd's method truly exemplifies the Almohad approach as founded by Ibn Tumart (d. 524/1130) which advocated the marriage of law with philosophy and science. This engendered a doctrine that rested on an entirely positive system of law on the one hand and a rational theology, on the other. This *madhhab al-fikr* (doctrine of thought) by way of rationalization was seen to be essential to justify to man's innate intellect the authority of the divine decree as well as the positive character of *fiqh*. Thus, for Ibn Rushd there was no question of any departure from the strictures of divine imperatives for "God commanded only by the demands of reason."[75]

By way of illustration, Ibn Rushd's laconic treatment of the subject of *khiyār* testifies to his catholic and objective approach in demonstrating the widespread and multi-dimensional *khilāf* among the *madhāhib*. Thus, he observes in his *Bidāyah* that al-Thawrī, al-Ḥasan ibn Jinnī and several others permitted the stipulation of an absolute *khiyār* where the option remains indefinite. Mālik opined that an absolute option is permissible provided a reasonable period for its exercise is stipulated. Abū Ḥanīfaḥ and al-Shāfi'ī ruled out any kind of absolute and indefinite option. On the contrary, such a *khiyār* would render the sale null and void. They, however, disagreed in respect of an option exercised within three days of an absolute *khiyār*. For Abū Ḥanīfa, it is legal. For al-Shāfi'ī, it is void.[76] Thus, *ikhtilāf* attests to the culture of dissent that prevailed in classical Islamic jurisprudence discourse and sets the reality bar much higher than the general notion of *taqlīd* would suggest.

Navigating between the high road of divine revelation and the byways of human reasoning, al-Shāfi'ī emerged with his brand of middle-of-the-road jurisprudence. Appropriately described as an eclectic or cynically as a maverick because he subscribed to no particular doctrine or school of law of his time, al-Shāfi'ī took an intermediate path between the *ahl al-ḥadīth* of Imām Mālik and the *ahl al-ra'y* of Imām Abū Ḥanīfah. Al-Shāfi'ī himself had the double distinction of having been a pupil of Mālik, and after his death, a self-ascribed pupil of Abū Ḥanīfah. It would only be natural that in the juristic polemics between the two schools he was sandwiched between them. However, unlike both the earlier masters, who tended to be partial to their respective avenues of divining the law, al-Shāfi'ī worked through the whole material of the law, and not finding the ultimate answer to his inquiry, he took on the task of expounding what he considered to be the methods and principles of jurisprudence. The upshot was *al-Risālah* recognised as a pioneering foundational text for *uṣūl al-fiqh*.[77] On the key issue of *ijtihād*, he lays down strict rules for its application through the process of *qiyās*, as discussed earlier, while he rejects the Ḥanafī doctrine of *istiḥsan*, in place of which the principle of *istiṣḥāb* is said to be advocated, but it seems this was only introduced by the later followers of al-Shāfiʿī. As noted earlier, a canonical collection of al-Shāfiʿī's writings and lectures is handed to posterity under the title of *Kitāb al-Umm*, which essentially represents his views and position while in Egypt (*qawl jadīd*) on *fiqh* matters. This constitutes his *khilāf*—difference of opinions—from his own position articulated while he was in Iraq (*qawl qadīm*). True to the spirit of *ikhtilāf*, it also incorporates the opinions of the other great *mujtahids* who had disagreed with him.[78]

The medial position of al-Shāfiʿī in advocating the use of analogical deduction elicited hostile reaction from those who were steadfastly against the use of human reasoning in law and subscribed to the doctrine that each and every legal rule could be found in the textual evidence (the Qur'ān and the Sunnah). This spawned another two schools, namely, the Ḥanbali and Ẓāhirī noted among other things for their deep-seated antipathy towards Shāfiʿī's doctrine.[79] According to some authorities, the anticipated atmosphere of intolerance drove Shāfiʿī to settle in Egypt. Ironically though, it was in Egypt that Shāfiʿī was mortally wounded at the hands of the fanatic followers of a Mālikī jurist, Fityān, who had been defeated in a public debate with him.[80] What this episode and many others subsequently say about *ikhtilāf* is quite simply that disagreement as articulated through forums and debates must be conducted within the rules and confines of proper *ādāb*. Unrestrained and unstructured *ikhtilāf* can turn into violence because of a combination of factors—egotistic motivations (*hawā*) of wanting to show that one is always right, holier-than-thou feelings of religiosity, intellectual myopia where one is unable to see beyond one's perspective and so on—that would "penetrate deep into a person's psyche and take hold of his mind, attitudes and feelings."[81] One thing leads to the other and soon recriminations proliferate, those who disagree are labelled *fāsiqun* (sing. *fāsiq*) and others are declared *kuffār* (sing. *kāfir*). At the hands of blind followers and inexperienced folk, the *madhāhib* and *fatāwā* of the *mujtahid*s are twisted and distorted along with the verses of the Qur'ān and the *aḥādīth* and used arbitrarily to support one position against another. Intolerance breeds fanaticism which in turn could lead to the sanctification of violence in the name of *jihād*. Muslims then revert to the days of *jāhiliyyah* "when the prevailing dictum was: the liar of the tribe of Rabī'ah is better than the one who tells the truth from the tribe of Muḍar. In other words, my people, right or wrong."[82]

Aḥmad ibn Ḥanbal emphasized the primacy of the *aḥādīth* as a primary source of the *Sharī'ah* and rejected any kind of middle path, giving his *madhhab* its distinct character of being dogmatic in both *fiqh* and *kalām*. As a rule, the Ḥanbālīs reject *kalām* as a legitimate discourse but when pressed to choose between the Mu'tazilī and the Ash'arī position on theological matters, they will absolutely reject the former on account of its preponderance towards *'aql* in textual interpretation. Aḥmad ibn Ḥanbal's emphasis on the Traditions bordered on fanaticism which accounts for his having collected more than 80,000 *aḥādīth* (*Musnad Aḥmad ibn Ḥanbal*) and the anecdotal story of his never having eaten water melon because he had not come across any *ḥadīth* of the Prophet having done so. This was a man of exceptional moral courage who would rather suffer corporal punishment and imprisonment, even death, rather than profess a doctrine he did not believe in. Thus, he vehemently condemned the Mu'tazilī doctrine of the "creation of the Qur'ān" in favour of the orthodox Ash'arī view of its eternal nature as co-existing with God. It was within the labyrinths of incarceration that one of his most frequently quoted works was written, a polemical treatise dedicated to the refutation of the Mu'tazilī doctrine of *ta'wīl*.[83] But this same ideological steadfastness also led to rigidity in outlook and a propensity to stir up controversy which eventually led to the Ḥanbalī School's decline from the eight/fourteenth century until the arrival of the Wahhabis four centuries later. The Wahhabi movement fast gained notoriety for its intolerant attitude not only towards non-Muslims but Muslims of the other schools as well. Nevertheless, while the totalitarianism of this doctrine is legendary, it should also be understood in the context of the strategic benefits attendant on its adoption as the state creed of Saudi Arabia. Contrary to popular perception, however, Wahabbism's major impact on the Saudi Kingdom was not on its social structure but as "the banner of the Arab national movement against the Turkish influence in Arabia" under the leadership of ʿAbd al-ʿAzīz ibn ʿAbd al-Raḥmān ibn Fayṣal al-Saʿūd.[84] Today, Wahhabism has mellowed considerably and is the main force in Saudi Arabia going officially under the banner of the Ḥanbalī *madhhab*. Unfortunately, the events of 9/11 and the murderous acts of Osama bin Laden and al-Qaeda have reinstated Wahhabism to its pristine notoriety without even going into the myriad extremist variations culminating today in ISIS.[85]

Therefore, even before the onset of *taqlīd* on a full scale, the history of legal speculation is not without its blemishes on the freedom of opinion. As between the various *madhāhib*, differences of opinion were not necessarily resolved amicably, if resolved at all. Even as persecution against other religions was the exception to the rule, as between the different schools of law, street skirmishes often broke out. The intolerance sometimes led to Inquisition-like witch hunts. For instance, al-Shāfiʿī was driven out of Iraq by Ḥanafī jurists when it appeared that he was getting the upper hand over al-Shaybāni in the debate between the use of Traditions over *al-ra'y*, which al-Shāfiʿī had regarded as pseudo *qiyās*. (As noted earlier, he finally formulated his middle ground position between the two polarities). And we saw in Chapter 3 how in 211/827 Caliph al-Ma'mūn raised the Muʿtazilī doctrine to a *confessio fidei*, ushering the *miḥnah*—a period of toil and hardship and political persecution for those who refused to subscribe to the creed, in particular the createdness of the Qur'ān. In addition to the infamous episode of Aḥmad Ḥanbal being incarcerated as well as tortured, naturally no *qāḍi* who did not subscribe to this doctrine was allowed to hold office. In the fifth/eleventh century, there was often fighting in the streets between the Ḥanbalīs and the Shāfiʿīs in Baghdād, and between the latter and the Ḥanafīs in Isfahan.

Ibn Qayyim al-Jawziyyah said, "Verily, the *Sharīʿah* is founded upon wisdom and welfare for the servants in this life and the afterlife. In its entirety it is justice, mercy, benefit, and wisdom. Every matter which abandons justice for tyranny, mercy for cruelty, benefit for corruption, and wisdom for foolishness is not a part of the *Sharīʿah* even if it was introduced therein by an interpretation."[86] Indeed, it is duly acknowledged that in citing Ibn Qayyim, one runs the risk of being accused of sympathizing with the so-called proto-fundamentalists. Even today, the accusation against Ibn Taymiyyyah that he was the "father of Islamic fundamentalism" rarely includes Ibn Qayyim explicitly, but it does cast a certain suspicion on him.[87] Nevertheless, the passage quoted clearly debunks the notion that within the Ḥanbali mould, no room for the exercise of the *ʿaql* is allowed. Notwithstanding their strict *ḥadīth*-bound *fiqh*, there is room indeed for the exercise of *ijtiḥād*. Therefore, when the Qur'ān enjoins on goodness by way of commands and prohibitions the objective is justice for all. When the Sunnah teaches the right way it is infused with wisdom and intended as a mercy. When believers of different *madhāhib* claim they follow "the right way"—according to their respective *madhhab*—the *ādāb fī al-ikhtilāf* warrants that no adherent of one *madhhab* should pass judgement on the other, let alone attempt to compel observance.

Conclusion

In light of the foregoing discussion, it needs to be stressed that the *Sharīʿah* is not an over-the-counter prescription with a limited shelf life intended only for a particular ailment. Detractors may point out that the comparisons made in our earlier comparative survey in Chapters 4 and 5 are superficial ignoring the reality of the structural differences in both jurisprudential systems, one being essentially God's law and the other secular law. To this the reply is that they are really missing the entire point of the discussion, which is to emphasize the convergence in the streams of jurisprudence in spite of the perceived differences. By convergence, two streams may flow together side by side their waters mingling in the middle sharing the same overarching purpose of the *Sharīʿah* which, as asserted from the outset of this monograph, is the way of God given to humanity based on wisdom and the common good. And this convergence is possible because of the inherent dynamism of the *Sharīʿah* which allows for the interaction and coalescence of the tri-phenomena of *ijtihād*, *taqlīd* and *ikhtilāf*.

Notes

1. For a brief but highly original discourse on the phenomenon of *ijtihād*, see al-Alwānī, *Uṣūl al-Fiqh al-Islāmī,* Chapter 6.
2. *Iḥkām*, 218; Weiss, 683.
3. Ibid.
4. Ibid., 684-5.
5. Hallaq, "Inductive Corroboration, Probability and Certainty," in Heer, *Islamic Law and Jurisprudence*, (University of Washington Press, 1990), 10; sources omitted.
6. Ibid. 19
7. Weiss, 687.
8. Sūrah Yūsuf, *āyah* 40, 67.
9. Weiss, *op. cit.* 687-90.
10. Ibid., 690-91.
11. Ibid., 693-95.
12. *PEIPT*, 244
13. Weiss, *God's Law*, 687-88.
14. For *kalām* and *uṣūl al-fiqh* see respectively Chapters 3 and 2.
15. *Cf.* Descartes' argument on God's existence: the idea of God contains the idea of existence; therefore God must exist (the conclusion is not just that God does exist, but that God cannot not exist, *i.e.* God's existence is necessary). Kant argues that the Cartesian ontological argument is misconceived for postulating existence as a property (*Critique of Pure Reason*, Book II, Ch. 3, s.

4). While things may 'have' other properties, they do not 'have' existence in the same way. Existence does not add anything to, or define, a concept itself; to say something exists is to say that some object corresponds to the concept. To say that the concept "God" contains the idea "Existence" is therefore a mistake: Michael Lacewing, "Descarte's Ontological Argument," Routledge, Taylor and Francis,
http://documents.routledge-interactive.s3.amazonaws.com/9781138793934/A2/Descartes/DescartesOntological.pdf.

16. Weiss, *op cit.*, 687-88.
17. Ibid.
18. Schacht, *Introduction*, 71.
19. Weiss, *God's Law*, 16-18.
20. *Shorter Encyclopaedia*, 158.
21. Lord Alfred Tennyson, "The Charge of the Light Brigade."
22. Azyumardi Azra, *The Origins of Islamic Reformism in Southeast Asia*, (Allen & Unwin, 2004).
23. Ibid. 1-3.
24. Clifford Geertz, *The Religion of Java* (University of Chicago Press, 1976).
25. Robert Day McAmis, *Malay Muslims: The History and Challenge of Resurgent Islam in Southeast Asia*, (Wm. B. Eerdmans Publishing, 2002), 44; Clifford Geertz, *The Interpretation of Cultures,* (Basic Books, 1973); for a more nuanced criticism of Geertz's theory of religion, see Talal Asad, "Anthropological Concepts of Religion: Reflections on Geertz," *Man*, New Series, Vol. 18 No. 2 (1983): 237-59. Talal Asad is the son of the late Muhammad Asad whose translation of the Qur'ān is used throughout this study as a default choice.
26. Muhammad Qasim Zaman, *The Ulama in Contemporary Islam—Custodians of Change*, (Princeton: Princeton University Press, 2002), 19-20.

27. Ibid., 99.
28. Ibid., 182 quoting Wahid al-din Khan.
29. Brown, *Rethinking Tradition*, 141.
30. Al-Nisā', *āyah* 3: "And if you have reason to fear that you might not act equitably towards orphans, then marry from among [other] women such as are lawful to you—[even] two, or three, or four: but if you have reason to fear that you might not be able to treat them with equal fairness, then [only] one—or [from among] those whom you rightfully possess. This will make it more likely that you will not deviate from the right course.
31. Asad, *Message of the Qur'ān.*
32. Stewart, *PEIPT*, 245.
33. Schacht, *Introduction*, 70-71.
34. Iqbal, *Reconstruction*, 141.
35. Norman Calder, *Islamic Jurisprudence in the Classical Era*, edited by Colin Imber, (Cambridge University Press, 2010).
36. Hallaq, "Can the *Sharī'ah* be Restored?"
37. Hallaq, *Authority, Continuity, and Change in Islamic Law*, (Cambridge University Press, 2001), 86; citing Abū Bakr Aḥmad ibn 'Umar al-Khaṣṣāf's *Kitāb Adab al-Qāḍī* in Ibn Māzah, *Sharḥ Adab al-Qāḍī*, 18; Joseph Schacht, *The Origins of Muhammadan Jurisprudence*, (Oxford: Clarendon Press, 1950), 18, 32.
38. Hallaq, *Authority*, 86.
39. Ibid., citations omitted.
40. For a full illustration of how *taqlīd* operates at these variant levels, see Hallaq, *Authority*, 88-113.
41. Hallaq, *Authority*, 113.
42. Ibid., 86 citing Muḥammad ibn Muḥammad Ḥaṭṭāb, *Mawāhib al-Jalīl li Sharḥ Mukhtaṣar Khalīl*, Vol. I, 30-31, 37, on the authority of Mālikite and Shāfi'ite jurists, including al-Ghazālī and Ibn al-Ṣalāḥ.
43. Hallaq, 87; an extensive list of citations is given but suffice it to

mention only the following: al-Suyūṭī, *al-Radd*, 196, 117, 120, where he mentions a number of prominent jurists who wrote in condemnation of *taqlīd*, including al-Muzanī, al-Zarkashī, Ibn Ḥazm, Ibn 'Abd al-Barr, Ibn Abī Shāmah, Ibn Qayyim al-Jawziyyah, al-Majd al-Shīrāzī and the Shāfi'ite jurist Ibn Daqīq al-'Īd, who wrote a treatise titled *al-Tasdīd fī Dhamm al-Taqlīd.*

44. *Jāmi' Bayān al-'Ilm wa Faḍlihi wa Mā Yanbaghī fī Riwāyatihi wa Ḥamlihi,* (Compendium Exposing the Nature of Knowledge and Its Immense Merit, and What is Required in the Process of Narrating it and Conveying it); 2 vols. (Cairo: Idārah al-Ṭibā'a al-Munīriyyah, n.d.), II, 109-19; Hallaq, *Authority,* 116-7.
45. Hallaq, *Authority,* 117.
46. al-Qāḍī 'Iyāḍ, *Tartīb al-Madārik* (Moroccan ed. 7:77-78) in G.F. Haddad, "Ibn 'Abd Al-Barr," accessed 2 May 2015 http://www.sunnah.org/history/Scholars/ibn_abd_al_barr.htm.
47. Ibn Rushd, *Fatāwā*, III, 1268; Hallaq, *Authority*, 89.
48. Baber Johansen, "Casuistry: Between Legal Concept and Social Praxis," *Islamic Law and Society* 2 (2) (1995), 154-56.
49. Hallaq, *Authority*, 90; It should be noted that according to Ḥanafī law of transactions, *khiyār al-'ayb* constitutes the purchaser's or lessee's option to return the subject matter of the purchase, hire, or rental on account of a defect in it, thereby effecting a rescission —al-Marghīnānī, al-*Hidāyah*, III, 35 ff.
50. Johansen, "Casuistry: Between Legal Concept and Social Praxis," *op. cit.*
51. Muhammed Imran Ismail, "Stratagems (Ḥiyal) and Usury In Islamic Commercial Law," PhD Thesis, University Of Birmingham, 2010, 89-90.
52. Ibid. citing 'Abd al-Majīd Maḥmūd, *al-Ittijāhāt al-Fiqhiyyah 'inda Aṣḥāb al-Ḥadīth fī al-Qarn al-Thālith al-Hijrī*, cited in Abū Ghuddah, *Taqdimah*, 32.
53. *Nikāḥ al-mut'ah* is a marriage contracted for a limited period of

time at the end of which the contract automatically expires.

54. For a definitive summation of the discourse on legal maxims within the Ḥanafī *madhhab*, see Khadiga Musa, *A Critical Edition of 'Umdah al-Nāẓir 'alā al-Ashbāh wa al-Naẓā'ir*, (Prince Muhammad bin Fahd University, 2016), being a critical edition of the twelfth/eighteenth century manuscript on the subject of legal maxims, written by a distinguished Ḥanifite jurist Abū al-Su'ūd al-Ḥusaynī and is a commentary on an earlier seminal text *al-Ashbāh wa al-Naẓā'ir* authored by Ibn Nujaym in the tenth/sixteenth century.
55. Hallaq, *Authority*, 120.
56. Hallaq, "Was the Gate of Ijtihad Closed?" *International Journal of Middle East Studies* 16 (1984): 3-41, at 5.
57. Ibid., 33-34.
58. Thomas Kuhn, "Logic of Discovery or Psychology of Research," in *Criticism and the Growth of Knowledge* edited by Imre Lakatos and Alan Musgrave, (Cambridge: Cambridge University Press, 1972), 6.
59. Goldziher, *The Zahiris*, 165.
60. *Shorter Encyclopaedia*, 564.
61. Ibid., 161-162; On the rules of disagreement—*al-ikhtilāf*, see Tāhā Jābir al-Alwānī, *Ethics of Disagreement in Islam*, prepared from the original Arabic by 'Abd al-Wāḥid Ḥamīd; edited by A.S. Shaikh Ali, (Herndon: The International Institute of Islamic Thought, 1993).
62. *Ikhtilāf ummatī raḥmah*; the Shāfi'ī scholar Taqī al-Dīn al-Subkī and the great Andalusian *faqīh* and a leading figure of the Ẓāhirīs Ibn Ḥazm say there is no *isnād* for this *ḥadīth*. In his *al-Iḥkām fī Uṣūl al-Aḥkām,* Ibn Ḥazm states, "... if *ikhtilāf* were a mercy, then agreement would be a punishment, something which no Muslim would say, because there can only be agreement or disagreement, and there can only be mercy or punishment." Nevertheless, the

narration is supported by other *āthār* (sayings, action and consent of the Companions) from the likes of 'Umar ibn Abdul Aziz and the meaning is established in many narrations. For a laconic discussion on the sources, with no frills, see Dr G. Fouad Haddad, "*Ikhtilāf* among the *Madhhabs* in Islam" in: http://masud.co.uk/ISLAM/misc/ikhtilaf.htm.

63. Khadduri, *War and Peace*, 35.
64. Norman Calder, "Ikhtilāf and Ijmā' in Shāfi'ī's *Risāla*," *Studia Islamica* 58 (1984): 55-81; G. Makdisi, *The Rise of Colleges* (Edinburgh: Edinburgh University Press, 1981), 107-11.
65. Hallaq, "Can the Shari'ah be Restored?" 21-53.
66. Ibid, 35, citing Ibn 'Abd. Al-Barr, *Kitāb al-Intiqa' fī Faḍā'il al-Thalāthah al-A'immah al-fuqahā'*, (Cairo, 1350/1931), 40-1; according to another account, this episode is apocryphal: *Shorter Encyclopaedia*, 321.
67. Recounted by Jalāl al-Dīn al-Suyūti in the introduction to his *Tanwīr al-Hawālik Sharḥ al-Muwaṭṭa'*, as quoted in the Introduction, *al-Muwaṭṭa' of Imām Mālik ibn Anas*, translated by Aisha Abdurrahman Bewley, (Madinah Press Granada, Spain, 1989), xxxiv.
68. For a laconic account in English see Umar Farouk Abd-Allah, *Malik and Medina: Islamic Legal Reasoning in the Formative Period*, (Brill, 2013).
69. The Mālikī doctrine spread mainly in the west of the Muslim world; after it had succeeded in driving out the *madhhab* of al-Awza'ī and the Ẓāhirī school, it prevailed not only in the Maghrib (Tunis, Algeria, Morocco, including Muslim Spain) but almost in all the rest of Africa, so far as it has adopted Islam. The Māliki *madhhab* has many followers in Egypt: in Upper Egypt it occupies about the same position as the Shāfi'ī *madhhab* in Lower Egypt.
70. The school originated in the Iraq and was in the time of the Abbasids the prevailing official doctrine. It spread to the East and

flourished particularly in Khurāsān and Transoxania. Numerous famous jurists of this school came from there. From the fifth century till well into the time of the Mongols, the family of Ibn Māzah wielded political power in Bukhārā as hereditary *ra'īs* (chief) of the Ḥanafīs of the town, with the title of *ṣadr.*

71. Charles Hamilton (trans.) *The Hedaya: Commentary on the Islamic Laws* (Delhi: Islamic Book Trust, 1870); Nyazee (trans.) *Al-Hidayah: A classical manual of Hanafi Law* (Bristol, 2006).
72. *Ibn Ḥazm of Cordoba: The Life and Works of a Controversial Thinker*, Edited by Camilla Adang, Maribel Fierro and Sabine Schmidtke. (Brill, 2012)
73. James Pavlin, "Sunni *Kalām* and Theological Controversies," in Nasr, Seyyed Hossein & Leaman, Oliver. Ed. *History of Islamic Philosophy*, (London & New York: Routledge, 2001), 109.
74. Ibn Rushd, *Bidāyat al-Mujtahid wa Nihāyat al-Muqtaṣid*, translated by Imran Ahsan Khan Nyazee as *The Distinguished Jurist's Primer*, (Garnet Publishing, 2000).
75. Dominque Urvoy in *History of Islamic Philosophy*, 331-334.
76. Ibn Rushd, *Bidāyat al-Mujtahid*, Vol. II, 250-51.
77. Khadduri, *Al-Shāfi'ī's Risāla.*
78. As we may recall from the earlier chapters, among notable and important Shāfi'īs were: the Traditionist al-Nasā'ī (d. 915), al-Ash'arī, al-Māwardī, al-Juwaynī, al-Ghazālī, and al-Nawawī (d. 1277).
79. Coulson, *History*, 71.
80. Khadduri, *Al-Shāfi'ī's Risāla*, 12–16.
81. al-Alwānī, *Ethics of Disagreement in Islam*, 6.
82. Ibid.
83. Aḥmad ibn Ḥanbal, *Kitāb al-Radd 'alā al-Zanādiqah wa al-Jahmiyyah*, "Refutations of the Heretics and the Jahmites" (Cairo: 1973).
84. For an unconventional account, see Alexei Vassiliev, *The History*

of Saudi Arabia, translated by P. A. Seslavin, (London: Saqi, 1998).

85. See also Brockelmann, *History of the Islamic Peoples*, 127; Schacht, *Introduction*, 66.
86. *I'lām al-Muwāqqi'īn 'an Rabb al-'Ālamīn*, edited by Muḥammad Mu'taṣim bi Allāh al-Baghdādī, 4 vols. Beirut: Dār al-Kitāb al-'Arabī, 1418/1998.
87. Birgit Krawietz, "Ibn Taymiyya, Vater des islamischen Fundamentalismus?: Zur westlichen Rezeption eines mittelalterlichen Schariatsgelehrten," in *Theorie des Rechts und der Gesellschaft*, edited by Manuel Atienza et al. (Berlin, 2003), 39-62.

Chapter 9

Fundamental Rethink of the Sharīʿah

The debate on the validity or suitability of the *Sharīʿah* as the law of the land has reached the stage where it threatens to drown the real issues in a sea of acrimonious polemics. In these stormy yet murky waters wafts a flotsam of divergent and opposing views that one risks being swept away by the undercurrents.

Two Broad Positions

But if we step back it would be apparent that two broad positions have crystallized at opposing ends of the spectrum with varying shades of intensity or lightness in between: At one extreme, there is the view that the *Sharīʿah* is the be-all and end-all for humankind, having been laid down by the Almighty to cater to the complete needs and requirements of the *ummah* which comprises all members of a community regardless of race, class, wealth or religion. Attempts at interpreting the established sources within a modern context are tantamount to "secularizing" the *Sharīʿah* as positive law. This is post-colonial heresy under the guise of a reductionist Weltanschauung. At the other end of the spectrum is the view that the *Sharīʿah* is obsolete and totally unsuited for modernity and if taken would lead to the path of absolute political serfdom. The adoption of the *Sharīʿah* would be "nothing less than the legalization of irrationalism,"[1] the legitimization of human rights violations and the death of constitutional liberties. According to this view, the law of the desert that was developed more than a thousand and four hundred years ago cannot conceivably be of any use in the modern world. The *pax Islamica* of Muḥammad was a mere federation of Arab tribes and to suggest that a political system based on such a simple construct could be relevant today is an act of impious intellectual obstinacy.

In response to this latter position, it is contended that coming from scholars supposedly well versed in the subject, these expressions of aversion and loathing towards the *Sharī'ah* are not the product of naiveté or ignorance. The sting in the statements lies not in their obvious meaning but in the implication that they carry. Sure, desert law used 14 centuries ago cannot possibly be the ideal model of law in the new world, nor can it be disputed that at the time of the Prophet's death the empire of Islam had not gone beyond the shores of Arabia. But the *Sharī'ah*, as we have already seen above, is not about desert law. It is founded on the Qur'ān and the Sunnah, and by the Second Century after Hijrah it bore the features of a formative legal system resulting from the syncretization of the various components of the laws of the empire from Baghdad to Andalusia. As the renowned historian Edward Gibbon puts it:

> "We should vainly seek the indissoluble union and easy obedience that pervaded the government of Augustus and the Antonines; but the progress of the Mahometan religion diffused over this ample space a general resemblance of manners and opinions. The language and laws of the Koran were studied with equal devotion at Samarcand and Seville: the Moor and the Indian embraced as countrymen and brothers in the pilgrimage of Mecca; and the Arabian language was adopted as the popular idiom in all the provinces to the westward of the Tigris."[2]

To suggest that the call for the implementation of the *Sharī'ah* today is a call to return to desert law and the practice and usages of primitive tribes is therefore to betray either sheer ignorance or devious misrepresentation. As regards the claim that the nation of the

Prophet Muḥammad was but a mere federation of Arab tribes the innuendo is facetious, apart from the fact that it is a symptom of myopia of historical reality.[3] It also entirely misses the point about the process of Islamic legislation as we have amply demonstrated. As canvassed earlier, the process of legislation continued as the Islamic empire expanded and new situations arose. In doing so, it was guided by the principles of the Qur'ān and the Sunnah even as new legislative activity sometimes tended to go on its own course. If anything, this demonstrated the internal dynamism of the *Sharīʿah*.

Yet while this line of reasoning seems unassailable its validity appears to be predicated upon a purely *a priori* proposition. Here is the response to the other extreme stated at the start. What ought to be may not be what is. It is all well and good to talk of the inherent dynamism of the *Sharīʿah* and that it is indeed meant to be for all time but as the saying goes the proof of the pudding is in the eating. When the ideals are subjected to a reality check, the question remains: after 1400 years, what is there to show for the proposition that the *Sharīʿah* caters to "the complete needs and requirements of the *ummah*"? The golden age of Islam is what it is—an age, reminding us of the glory days of Islam gone by. But if we are to fall back on history, we have to take the good with the bad. Viewed in a chronological continuum, the halcyon days of Islam pale before the long and protracted history of internecine conflict within the Muslim world itself which subsists till today. In any event, the question is, after all these years, what has the *Sharīʿah* to offer to modern society in terms of its essential needs socially, economically and politically? For example, has the *Sharīʿah* been able to provide a comprehensive financial system for the running of the modern economy in a global context? It is true that *Sharīʿah* proponents will chant the mantra about Islamic finance and capital markets gaining increasing acceptance even by non-Muslim sectors and communities but there is a substantive body of opinion which says that many so-called Islamic financial instruments are essentially rebranding exercises of Western financial modalities with Islamic labels? What welfare system is in existence or can be proffered by the *Sharī'ah* model that is not already being applied— probably far more effectively—in the Scandinavian countries? Can any existing *Sharī'ah* legal and constitutional model guarantee a politico-constitutional system that secures the rule of law, freedom from oppression by arbitrary executive power and equality before the law? How does the *Sharī'ah* deal with issues of overlapping consensus and the protection of fundamental liberties? A full answer to these questions and many more would warrant more space than is available but we will address them as substantively as possible towards the end of the chapter but suffice it to say at this juncture that in the last century, those countries that have one way or another attempted to implement the *Sharī'ah*—as defined by placing it as the law of the land—have demonstrated dismal results at best and catastrophic failure at the worst.

The debate exposes the deep fissures in modern Muslim intellectual history over the meaning of revelation, the exact nature of the *ummah* now as compared to the society as established by the Prophet, the role of the *'ulamā'* now and then, and the general lessons of history of the civilization of Islam itself. In other words, ideals are one, realities another. *Sharī'ah* advocates in the contemporary Muslim world draw on what they regard as a treasure trove of sources in classical Islamic thought and re-interpret them in the light of modernity. The opponents of the *Sharī'ah* would draw on these same sources and deconstruct them to arrive at a conclusion in diametric opposition. Essentially, the revivalist phenomenon that emerged in the 19th century and continues even today has called for a renaissance of Islam by a reopening of the gates of *ijtihād* in order to achieve the ideals of the religion. The view that the gates were never really closed in the first place as discussed earlier may have some validity with reference to the traditional viewpoint on *taqlīd* during the early and classical periods of Islamic history, but the reality is that in recent and modern times the need for *ijtihād* is real and pressing in as much as a comprehensive *Sharī'ah* system needs to be formulated *de novo* in the modern world with primary emphasis on socio-economic advancement, governance, rule of law and the securing of constitutional freedoms.

Direction of Iṣlāḥ

In contemporary times, the direction of *iṣlāḥ* sees a firm call for the Qur'ān to be returned to its rightful place as the supreme arbiter of the authenticity of the *aḥādīth*. According to Shaykh Muḥammad al-Ghazālī, this is not to weaken *ḥadīth* but to bring it within the boundaries of the Qur'ān.[4] Essentially, this approach advocates that wherever a *ḥadīth* is in conflict with Qur'ānic teaching, it loses its validity regardless of the strength of its transmission. Great scholars have fallen into error when they ignore this principle. For example, when an American engineer was killed in Saudi Arabia, the *qāḍī* ruled that *qiṣāṣ* could not be applied on the basis of the *ḥadīth* "*lā yuqtalu muslimūna fī kāfirīn*" (there shall be no killing of a Muslim in respect of the killing of an unbeliever). Applied literally, this saying would fly in the face of the doctrine of the sanctity and dignity of life which is the basis for the law of *qiṣāṣ*. The Saudi government was forced into bypassing the strict prohibition of the *Sharīʿah* (as literally interpreted from the said *ḥadīth*) by invoking the principle of *siyāsah sharʿiyyah* in order to invoke the death penalty.[5] The point is that obsession with *ḥadīth* without reference to wider concerns will lead to a distraction from issues of real importance. Conservative *'ulamā'* dismiss Shaykh al-Ghazālī's approach as a smoke screen for unbridled personal opinion. They contend that his use of the Qur'ān to invalidate the Sunnah runs counter to the *ijmā'* and that it is in reality "the free rein of *ra'y*." Harsher criticism attributes his views to the influence of rationalist schools of thought, and orientalists such as Goldziher, and to his affinity to Europe and the West.[6] But why is there the need for such scorn to be heaped on a scholar who is merely exercising the right of *ijtihād*? Bearing in mind the tenor of the Qur'ān against unlawful killing and the protection of the sanctity of life, one would have thought that the practice of the Companions would have provided the best example in such situations, that is, the use of *istiṣlāh*, public policy considerations, to rule accordingly. As referred to earlier, the precedent established by Caliph 'Umar in invoking the doctrine of public interest to circumvent a specific Qur'ānic ruling is instructive. It is contended that there is nothing extreme about the approach advocated by Shaykh al-Ghazālī in essentially proclaiming the paramountcy of the Qur'ān over the Sunnah in the event of an apparent conflict between the two. It would, however, be understandably disputable if the order were reversed but to suggest that allowing a Qur'ānic text or evidence to prevail over a proof based on the Sunnah can be an abandonment of the *Sharī'ah* is to misunderstand the foundational doctrines of *uṣūl al-fiqh* in particular the doctrine of *naskh wa al-mansūkh* where the Qur'ānic abrogation of the Sunnah has historical precedents.[7]

Another leading Islamic revivalist, Shaykh Yūsuf al-Qaraḍāwī aims to define the role of the Sunnah not merely in isolation, but in the broader context of the *Sharī'ah*. Sheikh al-Qaraḍāwī outlines three general characteristics of the Islamic program as it is reflected in the Sunnah: universality, balance, and simplicity. If the Sunnah represents all of these things, then any *ḥadīth* that contradicts them does not represent true Sunnah. And the Sunnah can only be known within a broader framework of legal principles. As noted earlier, the Sunnah distinguishes what the Qur'ān combines and disentangles what the Qur'ān intertwines. Consequently, the Qur'ān can be fully understood and applied only with the help of the Sunnah. But the Sunnah must be viewed in the context of the Qur'ān.[8] An overriding theme of the *Sharī'ah* is freedom and liberty on the Qur'ānic presumption that everything is lawful unless and until made unlawful. That the *Sharī'ah* is not meant to be a burden on the people is clearly stated in the Qur'ān: "Allah doth not wish to place you in a difficulty" and "Allah doth wish to lighten your difficulties."[9] It is also echoed in the saying of the Prophet: "Ease the way, and do not make it rougher ..."[10]

While these trends including the revival of the *maqāṣid* approach are indicative of a positive development in the direction of *iṣlāḥ* and *tajdīd*, there remains an overarching modern and contemporary concern that the *ummah* is still hidebound by what is termed as the "tyranny of legalism." Hence, it is said that even while "the Islamic intellectual tradition is highly developed and profound," it is "strikingly undeveloped" in matters of political philosophy.[11] Because of the "colonial" emphasis on legal thought "where Islam is equated with the *Sharīʿah*," the upshot is that "hundreds of thousands of legal scholars" are being churned out by Islamic educational institutions with hardly any political philosophers being produced.[12] One may not be faulted to think this was a radical and harsh criticism typifying the so-called contemporary and liberal attitude towards the *Sharīʿah* but this is hardly so. More than a millennium ago, commenting on the *ummah* of his time, Imām al-Ghazālī said there was a wrong emphasis on Islam as law whereas the essence of religiosity was ethics and morality which was so in the early history of Islam. After five centuries of the demise of the Prophet, this order of priorities was reversed, with morality being suppressed under the pressure of the law. He lamented that everywhere one went, one saw the multitude of *madrasahs* that produced experts in the *Sharīʿah* but not raised on morality as if "it was totally dead." Hence, there was a dire need to revive religion in order to reform it and restore the balance. These lamentations share a common nexus with different luminaries of Islam though motivated by different considerations. We have stated at the outset that there was no foundational justification for excising *kalām* from *fiqh* which, pursued in isolation or discoursed only within legal-centric silos, had contributed to the intellectual impoverishment of Islamic thought and the ossification of *Sharīʿah* jurisprudence. Hence, ideas on political philosophy such as those espoused by al-Fārābī or Ibn Sīnā were considered heretical, profound as they may seem to the contemporary thinking. Even al-Ghazālī, despite bemoaning the overemphasis on *fiqh*, and a Muslim philosopher in his own right, was essentially hostile towards Neoplatonist and Aristotelian conceptions of state for the *ummah*.

Islamic Renaissance

The term "Islamic Renaissance" has attracted some controversy. With reference to the political developments that started almost simultaneously in Muslim countries from Indonesia to Egypt in the 19th century, these revivalist movements were animated by a single conception of religion and though their efforts imparted credibility to Islam as a moral code of life, the negative implications were also far reaching. I am not plunging headlong into the usage of the term in the sense associated with the European or more specifically the Florentine Renaissance. The overriding feature of that Renaissance was that theological skepticism got the upper hand over religion and was reinforced by an enthusiastic belief in science amid a period of history alternatively known as "the age of moral release."[13] The European Renaissance then became a movement to liberate the mind from the tyranny of organized control and a pretext for anarchy and toleration of sensate culture.

In a sense, an Islamic Renaissance or *al-Nahḍah al-Islāmiyyah* could find some parallel in the European Renaissance in terms of the need for freedom "from the tyranny of thought control" exerted by conservative minds but surely no one is suggesting that it is to be a pretext for anarchy and indulgence in sensate culture. It should signify a period of resurgence of intense and vigorous intellectual activity in the Muslim *ummah* sustained by a deep-seated and passionate commitment to return to the foundational principles of the Qur'ān and the Sunnah. In historical terms, such a renaissance coincided with the rise of modernity and the ensuing intellectual reform in the Muslim world in the late 19th and early 20th centuries with its epicenter in Egypt, spreading eastward to the Levant, the Indian subcontinent and Southeast Asia. There are several perspectives concerning this renaissance but the prevailing position takes the Arabic-centric viewpoint in the Middle East lands under the Ottomans. As we noted in Chapter 6 concerning the legal and constitutional developments in the Ottoman Empire, this was the period of major Western style legislative changes under the rubric of *Tanẓīmāt* reforms. Contrary to the supposed Islamic-centric viewpoint which regards this in a negative light, it is contended that this was in fact the lightning rod that triggered the renaissance and unleashed the rise of modernist Islamic political thinkers such as al-Rifa'a al-Tahtāwī[14] of Egypt and Khayr al-Dīn al-Tūnisī (d. 1307/1890). Through his works on political and moral philosophy, al-Tahtāwī, among the prime movers of Egyptian modernity, introduced ideas such as secular rule and fundamental liberties. Khayr al-Dīn, who was largely responsible for the modernization of Tunisia, no doubt bolstered by the reformist ruler Ahmad Bey and Butrus al-Bustani (d. 1310/1893) was also much influenced by the political philosophy of the European Enlightenment and naturally advocated constitutionalism. In Lebanon, al-Bustānī, a Maronite Christian who converted to Protestantism, played a central role in the cultural aspect of the renaissance. Advocating a revival of literature and scholarship in the Arabic language, his early proselytizing fervor notwithstanding, he was instrumental in pushing for a secular education for Arabs. Among other achievements, his greatest was no doubt the compilation and publication of the Arabic encyclopedia which remains the most complete work of its kind in the language.[15] Iqbāl, emerging from the Indian subcontinent, blazed the trail for this renaissance while earning the wrath of conservative *'ulamā'* as he welcomed European imperialism as the essential antidote for the Muslim world's intellectual slumber. However, those who rejected European imperialism were not necessarily antagonistic towards Western thinking such as the likes of al-Afghani and 'Abduh. Across the board, the defining creed of *al-Nahḍah* was that reforms had to be introduced within the matrix of Islamic culture. This was strongly advocated by al-Afghani who artfully synthesized faith with anti-colonial rhetoric and a clarion call for Pan-Islamic solidarity while unobtrusively championing European democratic principles in place of authoritarian monarchies. As alluded to much earlier in Chapter 6, the coup de grace was left to be executed by 'Abduh who launched a full-frontal assault on the traditional *ʿulamāʾ* accusing them of intellectual malaise as well as moral corruption. Through their ideological mouthpiece *al-ʿUrwa al-Wuthqa*, the contention was that the ideal Muslim society which was already in existence at the time of the Prophet would never see the light of rejuvenation as long as the doctrinaire brand of Islam as preached by the traditional *ʿulamāʾ* continued to be imposed on the gullible and uncritical masses.

The question is raised whether an Islamic renaissance necessarily entails the abandonment of *taqlīd*.[16] Our position is that it is not required. At least not *taqlīd* in the technical sense of adhering to a particular *madhhab* or school of *fiqh*—a subject we have already explored in some detail in the preceding chapter. *Taqlīd* to a *madhhab* in matters of ritualistic practice is not only acceptable but absolutely essential to ensure that the structure and form of the orthopraxis of Islam remains intact as indeed it has over the ages until of course lately with the advent of new supposedly "more puristic" and "authentic" movements claiming greater affinity with the rituals and practices of the early Muslims. In repudiating *taqlīd*, and the established *madhāhib*, these groups generally going under the banner of salafis, wittingly or unwittingly impose their own "*madhhab*" on their followers who take it upon themselves the mission of correcting the "wrongs and deviant ways" of the rest of the *ummah* who are supposedly still tied to the pernicious innovative practices (*bidʿah*) taught by the *ʿulamāʾ* through the centuries of Islam. Indeed, that is no renaissance but a regression into puritanism, reminiscent of the days of Lutheran Protestantism and Calvinistic Reformation noted for self-righteous intolerance and religious fanaticism. While this is not the forum to delve deeper, suffice it to say that these nascent Muslim movements bear the same overzealousness as their Lutheran-Calvinist predecessors and in fact was one of the primary causes that led to the emergence of militant radicalism.

This is not the renaissance we have in mind. What we need is a renaissance that will take us from "the road to serfdom" to the path of intellectual, cultural and political enfranchisement.[17] It is going back to the *shir'ah minhāj*—the open way—by first reasserting the foundational principles of the Qur'ān and the Sunnah. This is not a new call but a resounding of the clear message made by the modernists of *al-Nahḍah.* In light of the foregoing discussion, they were undoubtedly forward looking intellectuals and enlightened scholars who were too early for their time whose ideas bordered on heresy to the minds of those unaccustomed to terms such as *iṣlāḥ* and *tajdīd*, let alone *tanwīr* (enlightenment). These were essentially calls for the reemergence of *ijtihād* to be exercised with less rigidity and more openness in order to give a fresh impetus to an enlightened reinterpretation of the texts.[18] According to Anwar Ibrahim, undoubtedly one of the prime movers of *iṣlāḥ-tajdīd* not just for Southeast Asia but for the Muslim world at large, the renaissance of Islam would "entail the flowering of Islamic communities based on a certain vision of perfection, imbued with truth and the love of learning." In this reflowering, "renewal of faith and the assertion of multiculturalism would be integral" while "justice and compassion, mutual respect and freedom and responsibility" constitute a collective new spirit to drive the *ummah* to move forward.[19] Some historians have pointed out that the Islamic Renaissance has already gone through two phases and the third one is about to begin soon. The first was supposed to be in the period of the "Golden Age of Islam" generally associated with the rule of the Abbasids while the second was brought on by the reign of the Ottoman Empire. Where and when the third one will begin still remains in the realm of speculation. Anwar Ibrahim's ascription of the renaissance of Islam, to my mind, appears to be more aspirational rather than empirical though there are ample references to the reformist ideas of the 19th century modern Islamists.[20]

We should not get bogged down with argumentation about when and where this has started or when it is going to end. Suffice it to say that on account of the myriad manifestations of turmoil, internecine strife, sectarian conflicts and the abysmal performance of Muslim majority nations in the Human Development Index, any suggestion of any Islamic Renaissance being under way in the present age is indulgence in fantasy. A condition precedent to such a renaissance would warrant, as a first step, the restudying of the religion by the *'ulamā'* particularly with reference to the *aḥādīth*, with their hearts firmly rooted in the rich intellectual tradition of the Islamic past but with their minds liberally open to doubt—in a Cartesian sense of *de omnibus dubitandum*. If the maxim "to accept nothing as true until established beyond doubt" resonated with *mujtahid*s of the past, *a fortiori*, it should apply to present day *mujtahid*s in their quest to provide alternative analyses of the *Sharī'ah*. Even in the first two centuries of the Islamic era, the quest for certainty about the authenticity of texts supporting the Sunnah was already a matter of primary concern for the *ahl al-ḥadīth*. Travelling the land in search of knowledge (*ṭalab al-'ilm*) was undertaken as an alternative to early juristic theorizing seen as being too speculative and productive of mere *ra'y*.[21] Reform precedes renaissance and as the pre-occupation with *fiqh* might have, in the past, directed the *'ulamā'* to miss the woods for the trees, a re-orientation in the approach is warranted.

Return of Rationality

Rationality is a much misused word. In religious discourses, it tends to be employed in contra-distinction to revelation in which case it stands for reason as in the general reference to the so-called clash between *naql* and *aql*. This study has used the term reason and rationality thus far without much qualification in similar fashion. It is time to make that qualification: the use of the term "reason" throughout the discourse in this book is with the foundational understanding that it refers to the use of the intellect—and not just reason in the general western sense.

And we are not here splitting hair over semantics that the difference lies in reason being a cause while intellect is the cognitive faculty. To use reason is to exercise the rational/cognitive faculty no less but that is only one of the multivariate functions of the intellect whose chief functions, apart from reasoning, encompass conception, judgment, reflection, and self-consciousness. Conception encapsulates universal ideas as opposed to sensations and sensuous images which are germane to only one object. In judgment, the mind perceives the identity or dissimilarity of two concepts. In reasoning, the mind grasps the connection between conclusion and premises. In reflection and self-consciousness there is perfect identity between the knowing subject and the object known.[22] Thus, in the western Catholic conception of intellect, reason is not differentiated as such but forms part of the intellect which in itself is defined in contra-distinction with the world of sensations and sensuous images. However, in modern western secular usage, the fundamental distinction between intellect and reason is generally glossed over and both terms are used synonymously.

On the other hand, *al-'aql*, as used in the Qur'ān, denotes both reason and intellect with the rider that reason is dependent upon the intellect. *Al-'aql* is that faculty which binds man to his Creator by virtue of which man becomes man, partaking in the attribute of *al-'ilm* (knowledge) which ultimately belongs to God alone.[23] The Qur'ān's constant reference to the intellect underscores the central role it occupies in man's religious life:

> "And they will add: 'Had we but listened [to those warnings], or [at least] used our own reason/intelligence (*na'qilu*), we would not [now] be among those who are destined for the blazing flame!'"[24]

According to Asad, reason/intellect, properly used, must lead man to a cognition of God's existence and of the fact that a definite plan underlies all His creation. In other verses various forms of the verb *faqaha* are used with the same meaning as *'aqala*:

> "We have detailed Our signs for people who understand (*qaumin yafqahūn*)."[25]

But, as in the Catholic description of intellect, *al-'aql* is also used as reason, intelligence, perception, foresight, even common sense. There is also the misconception of reason or intellect being seen in opposition against revelation as in the so-called clash between *ḥukm ʿaqliyyah* and *ḥukm naqliyyah*. This should not be the case for it is revelation via the Archangel Gabriel, the Holy Spirit, which illuminates the intellect and enables it to function properly.[26] Hence, the intellect is not merely reason but intuition which enables man to penetrate into the meaning of God's word. To understand revelation, man must exercise his intellectual faculty imbued with faith.[27]

The question is raised in the context of the *Ahl al-Sunnah wa al-Jamāʿah* concerning the role of the intellect *vis-à-vis kalām*, particularly according to the Ashʿarite creed. As we would have gathered from Chapter 3, Ashʿarite theology is less about reaching the universal dimensions of the intellect than about understanding the will of God. It is based on a voluntarism which reduces the function of the intellect to the purely human level. The aspect of the Divinity as objective Truth and Knowledge is practically ignored.[28] Ashʿarite theology asserts that truth is what God has willed and the intellect has no function outside the external tenets of the religion. This rather extreme form of voluntarism was later modified by al-Ghazālī and Fakhr al-Dīn al-Rāzī, but nevertheless, Ashʿarite theology continues to treat the intellect as subservient to the will of God giving it no place or role in the scheme of *tawḥīd*. On the other hand, other schools of *kalām* such as the Muʿtazilī and Māturīdī in the Sunni world accord a greater role to the intellect in its interpretation of God's will, without, however, leading to the type of position known as rationalism in the modern West. In any event, the function of *kalām* has been limited to finding rational means to protect the citadel of faith (*al-īmān*), rather than enabling the intellect to penetrate into its inner courtyard "and become the ladder which leads to the very heart of the truth of religion."[29] In fact it is not so much in *kalām* but rather in *falsafah* and Sufism in particular Gnosticism that the intellect and intuition can best be explicated.[30] As supported by textual evidence in the Qur'ān and the Sunnah, it is in *maʿrifah* (gnosis) that the intellect finds its most profound expression:

"O Mankind! There has now come unto you an admonition

> from your Sustainer, and a cure for all [the ill] that may be in men's hearts, and guidance and grace unto all who believe [in Him]."[31]

This *mawʿiẓatun* (cure) is indeed the remedy for all that is contrary to truth and moral good. It is the knowledge gained by the heart which counts before the Divine for

> "Allah will not call you to account for thoughtlessness in your oaths but for the intention in your hearts; and He is Oft-Forgiving Most Forbearing."[32]

In light of the foregoing exposition, it should be clear that recourse to reason in the Islamic sense, as in intellectual intuition with its concomitant multi-dimensional activities, is not a frolic into a world of rationalism where the cornerstone is the abandonment of faith on the altar of reason, being "the chief source and test of knowledge" and where the paradigm of the truth is purely intellectual and deductive.[33] Reason, as used in our approach, is not couched in the language of rationalism, as used by atheists, free thinkers, anti-religionists, or secularists. Nor is it in terms of the philosophy of the humanist or materialist.[34]

In modern times from the 19th century, the *Sharīʿah*—as law—was very important to Islam and some have said that the Muslim civilization is a civilization of law. That, of course, is a gross overstatement. Nevertheless, even allowing for the opening of the gates of *ijtihād*, the exercise of rational thinking was circumscribed by reference to questions of law. In matters of morality, theology or philosophy, the thinking was that there could be no *ijtihād*—no resorting to the intellect—even among the modern Islamic reformists. There were, however, exceptions as exemplified in the person of Iqbāl. He was not an Islamic jurist even though he was a trained barrister. He was a philosopher and a poet. Unlike the others, his diagnosis of the disease of the Islamic *ummah* was that it was weak in philosophy rather than in jurisprudence. Reform therefore had to be philosophical rather than legal. That would necessitate nothing less than the reconstruction of thinking in Islam and in this regeneration, the time-honoured cosmological, teleological and ontological arguments proffered as logical proofs of the Absolute "betray a rather superficial interpretation of experience"[35] and must be swept aside to make way for a new *ijtihād*. According to Iqbāl, this ought to be pursued with the passion as that which drove the likes of Ibn Ḥazm, Ibn Taymiyyah, al-Suyūṭī, al-Sanūsī or even 'Abd al-Wahhāb—in a movement manifesting the spirit of freedom of inquiry—but "while it rises in revolt against the finality of the schools and vigorously asserts the right of private judgment, its vision of the past was wholly uncritical, and in matters of law it mainly falls back on the Traditions of the Prophet." The assimilative spirit of Islam is particularly manifest in the sphere of law and paradoxes remain a source of mystification as expressed in the following ascription: "When we read the history of the development of Mohammedan Law we find that, on the one hand, the doctors of every age, on the slightest stimulus, condemn one another to the point of mutual accusations of heresy and, on the other hand, the very same people, with greater and greater unity of purpose, try to reconcile the similar quarrels of their predecessors."[36]

Islamists of today must face headlong the perennial existential question for the *ummah* the answer to which, as proffered by Abdul Karim Souroush, is holistic reform, one that is larger than just the law. Unless we undertake reform in our philosophy, our outlook towards religion, unless we change our theology, our perception of God, of prophethood, of the process of creation of law by the Prophet himself, then we cannot a have a real *ijtihād* in law.[37] It is not only in Iran but other parts of the Muslim world that this kind of reform is emerging. The Egyptian Naṣr Abū Zayd advocates a philosophy-based approach in Qur'ānic textual hermeneutics resting essentially on rationalism. Detractors will allege that this is nothing but an attempt to smuggle Mu'tazilism via the back door. Nevertheless, the view is that reform in the Muslim world has taken this Mu'tazilite trajectory, without, however, having to formally subscribe to a Mu'tazilī creed whatever that is supposed to mean. It is said that Muʿtazilism—as rationalism—provides a promising phenomenon because rationality and rationalism supply the tools to undertake comprehensive *iṣlāh* and *tajdīd* in all major areas of Islam as encapsulated in the concept of the Sharīʿah. This raises the question: assuming that is true—that one can take the Muʿtazilite trajectory without having to formally subscribe to the creed—why should we be so caught up in labels? What is the basis to suggest that reason and rationality is the sole preserve of the Mu'tazilites? The fact is no party or creed has a monopoly on the use of reason and rationality. Indeed, it is agreed that the exposition of the Sharīʿah can no longer be tied to the umbilical cord of fundamentalist and legalistic mindsets of the era after the defeat of rationalism but such a path can be taken without having, as it were, "to take the high road of Mu'tazilism". The view is that Muʿtazilism—as rationalism—provides a promising phenomenon because rationality and rationalism supply the tools to undertake comprehensive *iṣlāḥ* and *tajdīd* in all major areas of Islam as encapsulated in the concept of the *Sharīʿah*.[38] Just to be sure, the terms "rationality" and "rationalism" used here are to be understood in the context of our earlier clarification concerning the real meaning of reason and intellect and it is only on that premise that *iṣlāḥ* and *tajdīd* is conceivable, and not otherwise.

In this context, there was a palpable shift to revive rationalism, spearheaded by the major intellectual reformers of the 19th/20th century where *iṣlāḥ* and *tajdīd* was understood to mean "a tryst with modernity, reason, and enlightenment." The Islamic past was not the enemy of change and intellectual innovation and modernity was compatible with traditional Muslim thought.[39] The *naql* and the *ʿaql* must therefore be restored to a proper balance. Lately, there have been attempts at denying the validity of the revealed text particularly the Sunnah of the Prophet but the Sunnah is so well entrenched in terms of the written Traditions that such attempts will end up as exercises in futility. On the other hand, the attitude towards learning poetry, metaphysics and philosophy remains generally negative among the traditional sectors of society. As a rule, Islamic schools and universities in the Muslim world today do not teach these subjects. It has been said that the Muslims who perpetrated 9/11 were highly educated people. But what exactly is this education that they have been brought up in? Was it a liberal arts curriculum? Were they educated in the humanities or subjects considered in classical Islamic history as central to a well-rounded education to build character and to interpret the Qur'ān? Is there a metaphysical tradition still in our education system? Answering these issues, Sheikh Hamza Yusuf says: "When religion loses metaphysics, it loses the ability to defend itself intellectually. And so, its defence becomes one of violence. When people don't have spokespeople who can articulate the highest truths with intelligence, then they are reduced to finding people to defend their religion that use brute force."[40]

The "Divine law and an open way" (*shirʿatan wa minhājan*) ordained to mankind must be interpreted to include Muslims as well and not, by negative elimination, only to other communities specifically excluding the Muslim *ummah*. An open way means a way that is not close which effectively opens up the myriad possibilities of expansion and growth of the *Sharīʿah* for Muslims. At the same time, it is not a wayward path that takes the *ummah* to perdition but an ordained way set by Allah and not those who know not. It is a way that is circumscribed but not closed by the Qur'ān and the Sunnah so as to allow for dynamic and organic growth of the *ummah* in all aspects. In terms of the law, this open way provides the key to unlock the treasure trove of *al-siyāsah al-sharʿīyyah* which derives its sanctity from the *Sharīʿah* itself to govern the affairs of mankind.

But in all circumstances the way of the *Sharīʿah* must be accompanied by its spirit which is none other than *ʿadl*—justice. As Imām Mālik once said: *man tashawraʿa wa lam yataḥaqqaq fa qad tafassaq* (He who learns *Sharīʿah* without learning the inner reality becomes a *fāsiq*). This is a manifestation of impure intentions as intentions are the fountain spring of the reward for our actions as is well known from one of the most profound *aḥadīth* of the Prophet. In other words, instead of just rewards, what we may end up with will be the accursed qualities arising from our impure intentions. As long as it follows this circumscribed path and grows in response to the demands of public interest and the dictates of the *maqāṣid*, the *Sharīʿah* will not only be relevant but indispensable in answering humankind's call for progress in the temporal world. It certainly nails the lie to the *Sharīʿah* detractors' derogation that it is desert law entrenched in an ossified legal system. The significance of the doctrine lies in the fact that there are clear historical precedents to substantiate the advocacy of extra-*Sharīʿah* legislation without rendering it as deviating from the *Sharīʿah* as long as the *ratio legis* falls within the *maqāṣid*.

In this regard, Asad's approach as referred to at the outset, appeals to our common sense in so far as it seems to say that whatever that has not been stipulated by the Law-Giver may therefore be stipulated by other than the Law-Giver. This is effectively a summation of the principle of *ijtihād* based on the textual authority of a well-known *ḥadīth* commonly cited by jurists. It is contended that there is a difference between Islam as *dīn* (as religion with its body of doctrine and articles of faith) and Islam as an ummah (a civilization of people in a political setting). As I have stated at the outset, Islam as religion has been perfected with the sending of the last Prophet and is ipso facto in no need of reform. The Muslim ummah, on the other hand, is in dire need of *iṣlah* and *tajdīd*.

In this regard, al-Ghazālī's magnum opus, Ihyā Ulūm al-Din, must be seen in that context—as a fervent and passionate attempt at reforming the ummah of his time by reviving the quest for knowledge of the dīn.[41] The subject matter is not so much reforming the body of doctrine and articles pertaining to the religion than to jolt the masses from their slumber. Though himself a *faqīh* and *mutakallim* of the highest standing, al-Ghazali's bêtes noires, as we have alluded to earlier, were in fact the *fuqahā'* and the *mutakallimūn* whom he savaged as being responsible in leading the ummah on the road to spiritual perdition whereas the only true path should be serfdom towards the Almighty—the difference was as clear as between *al-dunya* and *al-akhira* citing Surah Al Rum ayah 7: "They know what is apparent of the worldly life, but they, of the Hereafter, are unaware." In the context of the *Iḥya*, however, *al-dunya* and *al-akhira* could also be rendered (as would be clear from his point of view) as worldly sciences and otherworldly sciences. Al-Ghazālī's acerbic attacks was also seen by the powers that be of the Almoravids as a seditious challenge to their legitimacy to rule sparking a frenzy of book-burning reprisals. Successive generations have witnessed the likes of ‘Abduh, ‘Alī Sharī‘atī and others emerging as leaders advocating reform and renewal of the ummah.

New Paradigm

It is said that the *Sharī‘ah* has sustained the *ummah* for over 1,400 years. Yes, there were other structures but this law was "the core and kernel" of Islamic life. For many Muslims, it is inconceivable for the *ummah* to reject the *Sharī‘ah* for that is as good as rejecting faith. Embracing secularism, they say, is to short-change Islam for the modernity of the West whose fabric of morality and ethics is in tatters. The proponents of the *Sharī‘ah* contend that the *ummah* already has a full system: a cosmology consistent with the rational mind, a Weltanschauung that is both coherent and comprehensive, a nomocracy founded on the principles of the *Sharī‘ah* and a profound ethical and moral paradigm that is timeless and practicable. Who in his right mind would exchange that for so-called Western modernity and enlightenment?[42] But is that really so? Is that a statement of fact or a manifestation of aspiration? We know too well that between the idea and the reality falls that long shadow of unfulfilled expectations. The full system is there—if only there is the total capacity, will and conviction to operate it. The Weltanschauung is there too if only it is universally articulated by those who should articulate it. And nomocracy is always there—in any modern civilized constitutional system—if the powers that be allow it to be a reality. I daresay that pitted against the Muslim world, the verdict on all three scores is catastrophic failure.

Hallaq asserts that the *ummah* is undergoing "a formidable impasse." Muslim intellectuals are and will remain marginalized while the authoritarian and autocratic regimes of the Muslim states do not see how their interests will be served by a full-scale program of Islamization.[43] But what exactly does it mean to talk about Islamization? As Wittgenstein says, the meaning of a word is its use in the language. Waving the banner of *ḥudūd* laws may well serve the needs of political expediency but can hardly count as the restoration of the *Sharīʿah* in the true sense. On the contrary, a holistic approach towards the *Sharīʿah* would in fact put its implementation on the back burner—and a long one at that—if not abolish it altogether. As long as the *ʿulamāʾ* remain tied to the political umbilical cord of the powers that be, it will be wishful thinking to expect any meaningful reform to emerge that would contribute to a renaissance of Islam.

To Iqbāl, the claim of Muslim liberals to reinterpret the foundational legal principles according to their own experience and conditions of modern life is perfectly justified. The Qurʾānic teaching that "life is a process of progressive creation necessitates that each generation, guided but unhampered by the work of its predecessors, should be permitted to solve its own problems." Excessive conservatism on the part of the *ʿulamāʾ* may well imply that "while the peoples are moving, the law remains stationary."[44] Almost 100 years have gone by since those words were spoken. Do we need another 100 just to set the law in motion again? While *ijtihād* by itself is a vital tool, it will be ineffective if applied within the grid-lock matrix of the traditional theoretical *uṣūl al-fiqh*. A literalist approach in the hermeneutics of revealed texts constrained by lexical and grammatical interpretations will be plainly inadequate to meet the exigencies of modernity and contemporaneity. The *de rigueur* invocation of the doctrines of necessity (*ḍarūrāt*) and public interest (*maṣlaḥah, istiṣlāh*) subsumed under the *maqāṣid* paradigm without dynamic expansion beyond traditional confines would also be ineffective. "Religious utilitarianism" without more may at best yield shallow juristic devices to rationalize existing arbitrariness of state legislation.[45] Indeed, the entire approach to the *maqāṣid* doctrine needs a "total recall" to bring it up to speed so that it can "catch up" with the progress of modernity and contemporaneity and then, perhaps get ahead of the curve. It is true that there is now a reawakening of the importance of the *maqāṣid* doctrine with politicians, Islamist NGOs, think tanks and even governments mobilizing state enterprises to conduct "*maqāṣid* awareness" seminars and conferences inviting speakers from near and afar to "enlighten" the masses. This frenzy to project that face of religiosity may well be prodded by a sincere motivation to fulfil what may be considered to be a *farḍ kifāyah* duty but two major issues need to be addressed in this regard. First, what happens after the talks, the forums and seminars are over? Secondly, and more significantly, what is being said in these talk-fests which has not already been said in the past? The question may be rephrased as follows: are we still talking about the same "*maqāṣid* doctrine" paradigm that was crystallized by al-Shāṭibī or are there new ideas being injected into the discourse that might warrant a total reconceptualization? Those who live by the *Sharī'ah*, or more correctly, literally make a living from the *Sharī'ah*, tend to place legal formalism at the expense of the message and the essence behind the law. This comprises an ethical set of practices which should be internalized according to which one lives. In this regard, the phenomenon of cherry picking Qur'ānic *āyah*s and expounding them to suit specific purposes presents a greater crisis. In indulging in this rhetoric on the platform of Islamic reform, intolerance, rancour and pettifogging seem to prevail over *ikhtilāf* as practised in accordance with the *adāb* associated with it.

A holistic rethinking of the *Sharī'ah* must factor into consideration the divine imperatives by which believers are enjoined to establish a just legal system so that they "stand out firmly for justice, as witnesses to Allah" and when they judge between mankind they must judge justly and that they be steadfast witnesses for Allah in equity.[46] Believers are commanded with reiterative intensity to judge by what Allah has revealed or risk eternal damnation as disbelievers (*kāfirūn*), wrong doers (*ẓālimūn*), or evil livers/rebels (*fāsiqūn*).[47] These are three key *āyah*s centering on the phrase "*yaḥkum bimā anzalallāh*" (judge by what Allah has revealed) that have been a major source of contention on the question of the application of the *Sharīʿah*. Most modern *tafsīr* equates this to the general concept of *dīn* and the paramountcy of justice in all human affairs without limiting its application to purely judicial-decision making or that the reference is to *Sharīʿah* law. As for judicial decision-making the consensus is that it refers to the practices of the People of the Book and the warning on being disbelievers, oppressors and rebels (against God) is specifically to the Jews and the Christians. Commenting on these *āyah*s, Shaykh al-Ghazālī says that they cover the attitude of the People of the Book towards legislation relating to capital punishment and penalties for illicit and extramarital sex. Those who ignored, avoided, or violated the law are condemned as unbelievers, transgressors and sinners.[48] "*Kāfirūn*" here means those who cover or hide something and connotes those who try to hide the real meaning of the scripture for their own agenda.[49] There is therefore no justification for employing these *āyah*s as authority for condemning those who oppose the implementation of the *Sharīʿah*, let alone the *ḥudūd* penalties. These *āyah*s cannot support the proposition that the *Sharīʿah* must be the law of the land in totality—in the sense as stated at the outset on the definition of the *Sharīʿah* as "the totality of Allah's commandments relating to the affairs of man." Such a proposition also invokes the mandatory adoption of *ḥudūd* laws as well and the *āyah*s are often cited *seriatim* to remind those who oppose *ḥudūd* about the damnation of hell fire awaiting them.[50]

Demagoguery, therefore, takes the place of informed and rational discourse. The upshot is that many of those who call for the implementation of *Sharīʿah* law lack the astuteness and intellectual circumspection to expound and make a convincing case for it other than citing chapter and verse and tolerating no alternative view. These proponents may be from the *ʿulamāʾ* class, generally fundamentalist and ultra-conservative but not necessarily radicalized. Others may be fundamentalist and radicalized calling for the establishment of a total Islamic state and yet other proponents might well be just seeking temporal power on the altar of religion, classic examples being the likes of ISIS, Boko Haram, the Taliban and so on. Upon taking power, the first thing that they do is to "implement the *Sharīʿah*" which in their order of priorities is nothing short of the imposition of the *ḥudūd* laws: the mandatory amputation of limbs for theft, flogging for liquor consumption, stoning for adultery and so on. Apart from doctrinal arguments based on the Qur'ān and the Sunnah which do not support a legalistic conception of the *Sharīʿah*, there is the overarching question, as I raised earlier, concerning nomocracy—the rule of law which may only be secured within the framework of constitutional democracy and where, inter alia, independence and competence of the judiciary and other vital organs of state power is of paramount importance. Today, there are modern legal systems that are purportedly operating within such a constitutional framework but when put to the test, judicial independence takes a back seat as the judges are either cowed into subservience or on their own volition bend backwards to side with the Executive which becomes increasingly autocratic. In Muslim majority countries, it would appear that the malaise and dereliction of duty of the *'ulamā'*—as lamented by al-Ghazālī more than a thousand years ago—continue to plague the *ummah* with their servility to autocrats and tyrants alike. Recent history and contemporary events show, for example, how they issue *fatwā*s not in support of the rule of law but on the contrary in support of unconstitutional usurpation of authority and gross violation of human rights. Whether this pertains to the toppling of a democratically-elected government or the unlawful detention of political opponents and dissidents or even brutal suppression of political rallies and demonstrations, the pronouncements of *qāḍī*s and *muftī*s alike sanctioning such acts of oppression and repression manifest a stark reality of the limitless possibilities where the *Sharīʿah* can be misused on supposed grounds of the public good.[51] The elite members of the *velayāt-e-faqīh* (Council of the Jurisconsults) in post-Revolutionary Iran while towering over the elected representatives of the people, remain subservient to the supreme religious leader, the Ayatollah.[52] This has historical antecedents going back directly to Khomeini. It is said that there is evidence that Khomeini's view is that actual power of government is a moral one, and should belong to him and the fundamentalists while the modernists could provide the technical expertise to administer the state but only to advance the objectives of the fundamentalists.[53] In such a system, the *ʿulamā'* and their courts attain the status of guardians of the political process. Similarly, though more disproportionately in favour of the ruling class, Saudi Arabia is also said to be another classic case where royalty and clergy claim religious legitimacy.[54] Nevertheless, though few and far between, there are still state-appointed *imām*s and *muftī*s who do not condone this molestation by the powers that be and choose to resign rather than continue in compromising their religious convictions, some remaining non-partisan and some eventually joining opposition political parties and other dissident groups.

A fundamental rethink of the *Sharīʿah* warrants a reformulation of legal theory by abandoning the conservative approach for a new paradigm that is pragmatic and progressive. According to this model, advocated by Muḥammad Saʿīd Ashmawī,[55] there is a crucial distinction between "religion as a pure idea and religious thought as an elaboration of that idea." The former finds expression in the Qur'ān and the Sunnah and, being supra-human, is endowed with objectivity and unaffected by variation or permutation. On the other hand, religion *qua* religious thought, being connected to society, "is thoroughly human" and "can never be isolated from the particular reality and history of that society." The entire system of Islamic hermeneutics including textual exegesis is no more than a system of religious thought. In a similar vein, neo-Mu'tazilite Souroush reminds us that our conception of the *Sharīʿah* demands an epistemological theory of the contraction and expansion of religious interpretation where there is a clear bifurcation between religion and religious knowledge. While sacred scriptures are flawless, our understanding of religion is flawed. Religion is "heavenly and remains constant" but religious knowledge is "human, earthly" and in need of reconstruction as "the *Sharī'ah* never sits parallel to human opinions."[56] As I have stated at the outset, the difference is between divinity and humanity in as much as the *Sharī'ah* belongs to God and *fiqh* belongs to man.

A fundamental rethink along these lines will yield several universal principles of the *Sharī'ah*. The first, signaling a clear departure from the traditional position, defines the *Sharī'ah* as more than just "a magnificent totality of rules and penalties" and takes it to the realm of a Weltanschauung that "presumes the existence of a generous and loving spirit that pervades society."[57] This is indeed a point of fundamental importance in view of the predisposition of pro-*Sharī'ah* advocates in demanding for the imposition of God's law on the *ummah* without considering whether the condition precedent has been fulfilled, that is, that the *ummah* is fully imbued by this spirit that will yield "a genuine desire to conform to both the letter and lofty aspirations of the law." This is already proven empirically where countries that have introduced the *Sharī'ah* as the law of the land including the imposition of *ḥudūd* penalties are, as contended earlier, either failed states or are failing or are absolute monarchies or dictatorships, the latter being by definition also failed states. This was inevitable and will remain so as long as the *Sharī'ah* is forced on a society or nation without proper rule of law, where the standards of governance are below par and where the socio-economic conditions are such that would naturally prevent the permeation of the "generous and loving spirit" that is so crucial for a proper application of the *Sharī'ah*.

Secondly, the fundamental rethink warrants a correct interpretation of the *Sharī'ah* based on an understanding that the *Sharī'ah* was revealed for particular reasons that are related to a particular human reality. Indeed, this position is controversial in as much as it warrants a review of a doctrinal stand that should be founded not on a purely legalistic understanding of the *Sharī'ah* and the *minhāj* but a holistic appreciation of the universalistic immensities that Islam can offer to mankind. Nevertheless, while it is indeed controversial, it is crucial that we break through this self-imposed mental barricade. The majoritarian view of the *mutakallimūn* that the Qur'ān was pre-existent and that, ipso facto, human reality was post-eventum in order to justify the text, had a lasting influence on the minds of *fuqahā'*. The upshot: scriptural texts were subject to an interpretative mindset intellectually encrusted with the narrowed thinking of antiquated clerics. Qur'ānic hermeneutics, which should have been anchored on the ocean floor of *asbāb al-nuzūl*, was hijacked by medieval-minded theologians and straightjacketed into a myopic and linear approach which persisted in looking at the texts divorced from the context—that revelation is intended not just for the prescription of a static past but also for the dynamism of human reality moving forward. This has deep historical roots and will require major attitudinal transformation. This mindset still enslaves the thinking of many contemporary *'ulamā'* who are content to accept that what was or appeared to be pertinent more than a thousand years ago, is still relevant today because, the Qur'ān being uncreated must also remain immutable and devoid of any defect. This defence is completely unwarranted for the challenge is never aimed at the createdness or otherwise of the Qur'ān or that there is any suggestion that the scriptures could be anything but immutable and perfect. This predilection betrays the failure to grasp the epistemological binary that is so crucial for the reformulation: an understanding of the fundamental difference between religion and religious knowledge or religion *qua* religion and religion as an idea. Indeed, the discourse is not about whether the Qur'ān may be changed or that the textual revelation is defective but rather about the dialectical relationship between revelation as a text and the human reality that gives rise to it. Qur'ānic revelation did not occur in a vacuum or in a static situation. Revelation interacted dynamically with the day-to-day existence of the community throughout the prophethood. The Qur'ān is therefore "the basis not of abstract formulations but rather of human conduct in actual reality."[58] Where the reality changes, the interpretive response must change accordingly while the scriptural texts remain unaltered. There is, therefore, no cause for hysteria.

Thirdly, a total reformulation should necessitate a review of the general approach towards the *maqāṣid al-Sharīʿah*, a concept that has been gaining currency and sometimes freely bandied about without a proper understanding as to its purport. A new approach is needed lest it runs the label of mere rebranding or churning out old wine in new bottle.[59] To be sure, the *maqāṣid* concept is as old as the doctrine of *ijtihād* during the early Islamic period where the need arose for the *fuqahā'* to search from within the scriptural text answers to the problems posed by daily reality and practices. This venture led to an inquiry on the objectives, intents and goals of the *Sharīʿah*. We discussed *maṣlaḥah* and *maqāṣid al-Sharīʿah* briefly when considering the subject of independent legal reasoning. A slight elaboration and a more nuanced treatment is warranted now. The concept is best explained by reference to the classic definition given by al-Shāṭibī (d. 790/1388) that *maṣlaḥah* are the "concerns that promote the subsistence of human life, the completion of man's livelihood and the acquisition of all his physical and intellectual qualities which are required for him."[60] The key issue is no longer whether the *maqāṣid* is applicable[61] but whether it should be limited to just five essentials and whether the traditional categorizations have indeed outrun their utility, as it were. The five essentials were enumerated by al-Ghazālī and then by al-Rāzī neither of whom stated explicitly that they should be numerically constrained. It was al-Āmidī who later declared that they were limited to five on the ground that this was self-evident.[62] But even this apparent constraint can be rationalized on the understanding of al-Āmidī's Aristotelian methodology in problem-solving, which is built on a holistic epistemological approach. As for al-Shāṭibī, without diminishing his instrumental role in expounding the *maqāṣid* doctrine, according to one view, he restricted the universals to five but left the door of interpretation open as to which of the *maqāṣid* should appertain to the community and which to the individual.[63] Ibn 'Āshūr states that the overall intent of Islamic legislation is to preserve the order of the *ummah* and perpetuate its well-being and integrity through the well-being and integrity of those who safeguard this order, that is, the human race. Going beyond the traditional approach, Ibn 'Āshūr employs the *maqāṣid* doctrine to advocate equality, freedom and justice. According to him, equality is a principle which applies in all situations unless prevented by extenuating circumstances. Equal opportunity means freedom and the intent of the law is to identify the various types of rights and this concept of right is connected with the concept of justice.[64]

Modernist *'ulamā'* after Ibn 'Āshūr such as Muḥammad al-Ghazālī, Ahmad al-Khamlishi, Yusuf al-Qarḍāwī, Ahmad al-Raysuni, Ismail al-Hassan and others in addition to endorsing equality, freedom and justice, include social, economic and political rights among the higher intents of the law.[65] However, once we subject them separately to a more particularistic analysis, various shades of difference in emphasis may be discerned, no doubt indicative of the dynamic nature of *ijtihād*. Synthesizing these variant approaches and taking the holistic paradigm to a new level in advocating a systems approach, Jasser Auda suggests that the *maqāṣid* may best be likened to a "multi-dimensional structure" where the levels of necessity, scope of rulings, scope of people and levels of universality are all valid dimensions. Current conceptions are closer to addressing current issues than classic conceptions whose traditional classifications have now evolved and brachiated into more wide-ranging intents encompassing the dynamic needs of contemporary society. Hence, rather than "preservation of offspring" we now have "family care" and "a civil Islamic social system" while "preservation of mind" should be seen as "propagation of scientific thinking," "travelling for the pursuit of knowledge," or "avoiding brain drain"; rather than just "preservation of honour" of wider purport is "preservation of human dignity" and "protection of human rights." In this regard, Auda maintains that a *maqāṣid*-based approach could be applied to support the Universal Islamic Declaration of Human Rights (Islamic

Declaration). As for the "preservation of religion," it should be expanded to "freedom of belief" or "freedom of conscience" while "preservation of wealth" should denote "economic development" and "reducing income inequities." There is merit in Auda's proposal that the term *maṣlaḥah* itself be renamed "human development" as that will be all-encompassing as well as amenable to empirical measurement via the United Nations Human Development Index.[66] Detractors who oppose this idea warn against such reductionist attempts to equate the *Sharīʿah* with the secular law pointing out particularly the hazard of falling into the quagmire of the latter's conception of human rights where the divergence in religious and secular values will lead to confrontational or irreconcilable positions. For example, even from the point of view of moderate Muslims, there is legitimacy in the argument that the rationale for the "preservation of religion," doctrine is precisely what it overtly means—to protect the religion of the *ummah* (as in Muslims) from the onslaught of proselytization by other faiths. To suggest that it should instead be expanded to "freedom of belief" or "freedom of conscience" would be tantamount to putting the doctrine on its head. There is, in any event, the question of what freedom of conscience really entails. If absolute values are to be swept aside to make way for relativist predilections in all matters under this freedom rubric, where is the line to be drawn? We need not venture too far to bring the issue home: If gay marriage is recognised, what about incestuous relations? Can a father marry his daughter because they subscribe to freedom of conscience and as far their conscience tells them, love conquers all? The normal rejoinder to such a contention is that the issues raised, while indeed legitimate, are not, however, germane to Islam but apply across the entire spectrum of the community of nations world wide and represents a conundrum even in Europe and America. Be that as it may, these issues do not detract from the fact that pressing practical concerns still plague a legal and judicial system founded on the *Sharīʿah* as it stands: what is the status of religious minorities and their rights under the constitution? Will they be treated as equals in the sense understood according to the Universal Declaration of Human Rights? Can the concept of *Dhimmī*s be compatible with such a declaration? Will Muslim women be treated equally in the complete sense of the word or will there be the usual qualifications and rationalizations as to why they must be subservient to men in certain situations? There is, again, the thorny question of LGBTs. It would be easy to grand stand and answer these questions in the appropriate fashion in view of the demands of modernity and contemporaneity but how would the formulators of change reconcile their reinterpretations with the revealed texts?

In light of the above, it is contended that there is a dire need for a complete overhaul of the entire traditional system of dealing with the challenges faced by the *ummah* which is to embrace the dynamics of change. While *iṣlāḥ* and *tajdīd*" is not rocket science, neither is it just about giving lip service to progressive sound bites and performing Band-Aid therapy. A slight re-orientation in hermeneutics, a rephrasing of the principles and axioms or the *qawāʿid* of the *fiqh*, a relook at the *madhāhib*—these would still be patchwork re-engineering of the *Sharīʿah* unless and until modern scholars and *ʿulamāʾ* get together to rethink the *Sharīʿah*. If the promotion of "human development" is seen as a basic purpose of law or legislation, then the *maqāṣid* doctrine will enable a virtually endless permutation to the possible solutions to society's problems.

Finally, the proposed full reformulation of the *Sharīʿah* can be attained only by realigning it to the *ummah's* exigencies which are never static. But majority Muslim societies have for centuries subjected themselves to a "restrictive and reactive vision" of the *Sharīʿah*. As Tariq Ramadan says, today's Muslims need a "holistic philosophy of ends" rather than "the chaotic management of means." To undertake a comprehensive review of the *maqāṣid* so that the *Sharīʿah* will not be reduced merely to a body of God's intangible laws, what the *ummah* needs is nothing short of a "radical intellectual revolution."[67] To stem the tide of opinion calling for the abolition of the *Sharīʿah* altogether, what is needed is therefore a transformation of the Islamic Weltanschauung into a model of rationality built on the Qur'ān and the Sunnah. It is contended that the failure to grasp the importance of this fundamental doctrine has contributed much to the intellectual paralysis of the *'ulamā'* and even many modern scholars alike. Till today, in spite of the conviction that the religion of Islam is for all time, being a mercy and a blessing to humanity at large, and not just to a tribe, sect, community or nation, there is as yet no "Islamic" blue print for the governance of a state, let alone for the entire *ummah*. Until we break free from the bondage of the past accretions and mindset that the *Sharī'ah* is stagnant and immutable, no real progress will be made and the *ummah* will remain behind in mankind's advance with the tide of times. This requires true courage of conviction and collective political will.

Much ink was spilt in the first two chapters just trying to get to the bottom of two terms—*Sharī'ah* and *fiqh*—not because of some pathological penchant for semantic hairsplitting but to lay the groundwork for the proposition that there is indeed more to *Sharī'ah* and *fiqh* than just law and legal principles and that *tafsīr* may and sometimes must go beyond the literal meaning. And we know that even in the realm of the legalistic there are at least four ways to skin the jurisprudential cat of the Sunni kind. Other schools of law are also part and parcel of the Muslim world and should not be summarily dismissed or branded as heretical. Let us not forget that in the *Risālah 'Ammān* (the Amman Message) of 1425/2004 eight *madhāhib* and the varying schools of Islamic theology were recognised,[68] underscoring the multiplicity and dynamism of *Sharī'ah* and *fiqh* as well as the inherent characteristic of diversity in theological matters.

Ultimately, there is the need to remember the primary objective of the *Sharī'ah* as the Qur'ān reminds that

> "Those who have believed and whose hearts are assured by the remembrance of Allah ... Unquestionably, by the remembrance of Allah hearts are assured."[69]

In going beyond a legalistic and doctrinaire conception of the

Sharīʿah, such an approach opens up vistas for the *ummah* to chart its course for the future, to be guided by *ḥikmah* (wisdom). Bereft of that wisdom the law operates within the confines of a mill pond constrained by limitations of space and functionality. And that will be an injustice to ourselves, a travesty indeed for forsaking the vast ocean of possibilities that the *Sharīʿah* has in store, and forfeiting the ecumenical divine beneficence that Islam can offer to mankind.

Notes

1. Ibrahim M. Abu Rabiʿ, *Contemporary Arab Thought—Studies in Post-1967Arab Intellectual History,* (London: Pluto Press, 2004), 204.
2. Edward Gibbon, *The History of the Decline and Fall of the Roman Empire,* Volume 5, Chapter LI. "Conquests By The Arabs," Part VII; accessed on March 23, 2015; available at http://www.gutenberg.org/files/25717/25717-h/files/735/735-h/735-h.htm.
3. See Montgomery Watt's analysis and the epithet of a "super tribe."
4. Shaykh Muḥammad al-Ghazālī, *al-Sunnah al-Nabawiyyah bayn Ahl al-Fiqh wa Ahl al-Ḥadīth* (Cairo, 1989), 24.
5. Brown, *Rethinking Tradition,* 118.
6. Ibid.
7. Wael Hallaq, *A History of Islamic Legal Theories: An Introduction to Sunni usul-al-fiqh,* (Cambridge University Press, 1997), 72.
8. Brown, *Rethinking Tradition,* 131, citing Ibn Abd al-Rahim, Jinayat, (53-84), see n.41, 281.
9. al-Māidah, *āyah* 6; *al-Nisāʾ*, *āyah* 28.
10. *Yassirū wa lā tuʿassirū wa bashshirū wa la tunaffirū* (al-Bukhārī and Muslim).

11. M. A. Muqtedar Khan, "The Primacy of Political Philosophy," in Khaled Abou El Fadl, *Islam and the Challenge of Democracy*, edited by Joshua Cohen and Deborah Chasman, (Princeton University Press, 2004), 63.
12. Ibid.
13. Will Durant, *The Renaissance: A History of Civilization in Italy from 1304-1576 A.D.*, (Simon and Schuster, 1953), 607.
14. Newman, Daniel, *An Imam in Paris, Al-Tahtawi's Visit to France* (1826–31), London: Saqi Books (2004).
15. Albert Hourani, *Islam in European Thought*, (Cambridge University Press, 1991), 165.
16. See Hallaq, "Was the Gate of *Ijtihad* Closed?" supra.
17. This is borrowed from A.F. Hayek's "Road to Serfdom" though in this case I use the phrase in a different context altogether.
18. Alfred Guillaume & Thomas Arnold, ed., *The Legacy of Islam*, (London: Oxford University Press, 1952), 289.
19. Anwar Ibrahim, *The Asian Renaissance*, (Times Book International, 1996), 19.
20. Ibid., *passim*.
21. Weiss, *Spirit*, 96-97.
22. This is essentially the Catholic conception of Aristotle's *De Anima* as developed by Albertus Magnus and St. Thomas, which comprises the main features of the common doctrine of Catholic philosophers: "Intellect," *Catholic Encyclopedia*, accessed 14 January 2015. http://www.newadvent.org/cathen/08066a.htm.
23. Seyyed Hossein Nasr, "Intellect and Intuition: Their Relationship from the Islamic Perspective," *Studies in Comparative Religion*, Vol. 13, No. 1 & 2. (Winter-Spring, 1979); accessed 23 March 2015. www.studiesincomparativereligion.com.
24. Sūrah al-Mulk, *āyah* 10.
25. Sūrah al-An‘ām, *āyah* 98.

26. Nasr, "Intellect and Intuition," 3.
27. Ibid. Further references from Nasr: "On the relation between faith and intellect or revelation and reason see F Schuon, *Stations of Wisdom,* (trans. GEH Palmer, London, 1976). "If 'no man cometh unto the Father but by Me,' this truth or this principle is equally applicable to the pure Intellect in ourselves: in the sapiential order—and it is only in this order that we may speak of intellect or intellectuality without making implacable reservations—it is essential to submit all the powers of the soul to the pure Spirit, which is identified, but in a supra formal and ontological manner, with the fundamental dogma of the Revelation and thereby with the Sophia Perennis" (F. Schuon, *Dimensions of Islam*, trans. by P. Townsend, London, 1970, P. 76).
28. Nasr, "Intellect and Intuition," 4-5; Further references by Nasr: On Ash'arite voluntarism see F. Schuon, *Islam and the Perennial Philosophy*, trans. J. P. Hobson, London, 1976, chapter 7. Although the above-mentioned book is out of print, readers can refer instead to Schuon's "Dilemmas of Moslem Scholasticism" in *Christianity / Islam: Perspectives on Esoteric Ecumenism: A New Translation with Selected Letters*, (World Wisdom, 2008.)
29. Nasr, "Intellect and Intuition," 4-5.
30. Space constraints do not permit further expansion on this theme. This matter is taken up cogently by Nasr who considers at least three schools which have dealt extensively with the methodology of knowledge and the full amplitude of the meaning of the intellect in its relation to intuition: Peripatetic (*mashshāʾī*) philosophy, illuminationist (*ishrāqī*) theosophy and the "transcendent theosophy" of Sadr al-Dīn Shirāzī: Nasr, "Intellect and Intuition," 4-8.
31. Sūrah Yūnus, *āyah* 57.
32. Sūrah al-Baqarah, *āyah* 225.
33. Vernon J. Bourke, "Rationalism," in *Runes* (1962), 263.

34. John Cottingham, *Rationalism,* (Paladi/Granada, 1984).
35. Iqbāl, *Reconstruction,* 23.
36. Ibid., 130, quoting Professor Christiaan Snouck Hurgronje, a Dutch critic of Islam. Like Richard Burton, because of his knowledge of the religion and the customs of the Arabs, he gave the impression that he had converted to Islam and was thus allowed to enter Mecca. In 1889, he became professor of Malay at Leiden University and official advisor to the Dutch government on colonial affairs. See his *Mohammedanism:* Lectures on its origin, its religious and political growth and its present state, (New York, 1916). Just to clarify, unlike Hurgronje, who had made it clear that he had only pretended to be a Muslim, Burton composed on his return journey from Mecca, the famous *Kasidah* which supports the theory that he had been accepted in the Bektashi Sufi order.
37. Panel discussion at City University of New York Forum entitled "The Rise of Intellectual Reform in Islam" accessed on June 12, 2014 available at https://www.youtube.com/watch?v=Q3IqSLy80nA.
38. Ibid.
39. Ravindra S. Khare, *Perspectives on Islamic Law, Justice, and Society,* (Rowman & Littlefield, 1987), 165. As noted earlier, the reformers include Khayr al-Dīn al-Tūnīsī (d. 1890), also known as Khayr al-Din Pasha who, among other things, introduced economic and administrative reforms in Tunisia to address the country's financial crisis. In *Aqwām al-Maslāik fī Ma'rifah Aḥwāl al-Mamālik*, he advocated constitutional government, the parliamentary system, and modernization of the educational system; Sir Sayyid Ahmad Khan (d. 1898) as mentioned in Chapter 6, and the well-known modernists such as Muhammad 'Abduh (d. 1905) and Muḥammad Iqbāl (d. 1938).

40. Sheikh Hamza Yusuf, "Zaytuna College Takes Religion Back From Extremists," at the World Economic Forum 2015, Davos, Switzerland;o accessed on 27, October 2015; available at: https://www.youtube.com/watch?v=oIArC2PHqBk; Sheikh Yusuf is one of the West's most influential Islamic scholars.
41. It may be recalled that Al-Ghazālī's acerbic attacks was also seen by the powers that be of the Almoravids as a seditious challenge to their legitimacy to rule sparking a frenzy of book-burning reprisals. For a scholarly account, see Kenneth Garden, *Al-Ghazali's Contested Revival: 'Ihya'Ulum Al-Din' and its Critics in Khorasan and the Maghrib* (Morocco, Tunisia, Algeria, Spain), PhD Dissertation, University of Chicago, 2005.
42. Hallaq, "Can the Shari'ah be Restored?"
43. Hallaq, *A History of Islamic Legal Theories.*
44. Iqbāl, *Reconstruction*, 134.
45. Hallaq, "Can the Shari'ah be Restored?"
46. Sūrah an-Nisā', *āyah* 135 and 58, and Sūrah al-Māidah, *āyah* 8.
47. Sūrah al-Māidah, *āyah*: 44, 45 and 47.
48. Muhammad al-Ghazālī, *A Thematic Commentary of the Qur'an*, (The International Institute of Islamic Thought, 2000), 101.
49. Nasr, *Study Quran*, 15407.
50. Nevertheless, according to Ibn Kathīr, the first two verses in respect of being disbelievers and oppressors, are with reference first to the People of the Book and then extended to include Muslims while the third in respect of being rebellious applies exclusively to Christians. In all three situations, however, they do not constitute outright disbelief, oppression and rebelliousness. Ibn Kathīr says: "Al-Barā' ibn 'Āzib, Hudhayfah ibn al-Yamān, Ibn 'Abbās, Abū Mijlaz, Abū Rajā' al-'Utaridī, 'Ikrimah, 'Ubay Allāh ibn 'Abd Allāh, al-Ḥasan al-Baṣrī and others said that this *āyah* was revealed about the People of the Book. Al-Ḥasan al-Baṣrī added that this *āyah* also applies to us. 'Abd al-Razzāq said

that L-Thawrī said that Manṣūr said that Ibrāhīm said that these *āyāt*, "Were revealed about the Children of Israel, and Allah accepted them for this *ummah*." Ibn Jarīr recorded this statement. ʻAlī ibn Abī Talḥah also stated that Ibn ʻAbbās commented on Allah's statement, (And whosoever does not judge by what Allah has revealed, such are the disbelievers,) "Whoever rejects what Allah has revealed, will have committed *kufr*, and whoever accepts what Allah has revealed, but did not rule by it, is a *ẓālim* (unjust) and a *fāsiq* (rebellious) and a sinner." Ibn Jarīr recorded this statement. ʻAbd al-Razzāq said, "Ma'mar narrated to us that Ṭāwūs said that Ibn ʻAbbās was asked about Allah's statement ... He said, "It is an act of Kufr." ʻIbn Tāwūs added, "It is not like those who disbelieve in Allah, His angels, His Books and His Messengers." Al-Thawrī narrated that Ibn Jurayj said that ʻAṭā' said, "There is *kufr* and *kufr* less than *kufr*, *ẓulm* and *ẓulm* less than *ẓulm*, *fisq* and *fisq* less than *fisq*." Waki' said that Sa'id Al-Makki said that Tawus said that, (And whosoever does not judge by what Allah has revealed, such are the disbelievers) "This is not the *kufr* that annuls one's religion." As for (such are the unjust) because they did not exact the oppressed his due rights from the oppressor in a matter which Allah ordered that all be treated equally and fairly. Instead, they defied that command, committed injustice and transgressed against each other. Earlier we mentioned the statements of ʻAṭā' and Ṭāwūs that there is *kufr* and lesser *kufr*, injustice and lesser injustice and *fisq* and lesser *fisq*. This refers to people of the Injīl. And if they not judge by what Allah has revealed, such are the rebellious, meaning the rebellious and disobedient of Allah who prefer falsehood and abandon truth. We mentioned before that this *āyah* was revealed about the Christians, and this is evident from the context of the *āyah*."

51. When ʿAbd al-Fattāh al-Sīsī engineered a military coup in 2013 toppling democratically-elected President Morsi, he announced it on state media. Lending moral support to his TV blitz were major religious leaders, including the Shaykh al-Azhar, Aḥmad al-Ṭayyib. More *ʿulamāʾ* bent backwards to support the ruthless and unconstitutional coup including ʿAlī Gumah, a former grand mufti and Shaykh al-Azhar, who likened obeying al-Sīsī to obeying the Prophet.
52. Sajoo, *Civil Society*, 226.
53. Cheryl Benard & Zalmay Kalilzad, *The Government of God: Iran's Islamic Republic*, (Columbia University Press, 1986), 104.
54. Sajoo, *Civil Society*, 226.
55. Muḥammad Saʿīd Ashmawī, *Uṣūl al-Sharīʿah* (Beirut, Dar Iqra', 1983) as summarized by Hallaq, *Islamic Legal Theories*, 231-235.
56. Abdolkarim Souroush, *Reason, Freedom, and Democracy in Islam —Essential Writings*, Translated, edited and with a critical introduction by Mahmoud Sadri and Ahmad Sadri, (Oxford University Press, 2000), 30-31.
57. Hallaq, *Islamic Legal Theories*, 232; Ashmawī, *Uṣūl al-Sharīʿah,* 55, 59.
58. Hallaq, 233; Ashmawī, 70.
59. New approaches that deserve review include: Gamal Eldin Attia, *Towards The Realization of the Higher Intents of Islamic Law—Maqasid al-Shari'ah: A Functional Approach*, Translated from the Arabic by Nancy Roberts, (The International Institute of Islamic Thought, 2007); and Auda, *Maqasid al-Shari'ah,* as cited earlier.
60. al-Shāṭibī, *al-Muwāfaqāt*, 2:15; Ahmad al-Raysuni, *Imam al-Shatibi's Theory of the Higher Objectives and Intents of Islamic Law,* (London: The International Institute of Islamic Thought, 2005)

61. The doctrine has been widely advocated by Muslim reformists and fundamentalists alike through the various epochs of Islamic history such as Muḥammad 'Abduh (d.1905), Ibn 'Āshūr (d.1973) and Sa'īd Ramaḍān al-Būṭī on the general rationale that the *Sharī'ah* was revealed, inter alia, to promote man's welfare. The medieval scholars, however, disagreed on the limits and the application of the doctrine resulting in it not being universally recognised as a source of law. As noted earlier, al-Shāfi'ī purportedly did not consider it as an independent *dalīl* for the exercise of *qiyās* because he believed that the classical sources of law were sufficient to cover the *maṣlahah*. Al-Ghazālī took a less restrictive view but placed three conditions precedent to the exercise of the *maqāṣid*, namely, *ḍarūrah* (necessity), *qat'iyyah* (absolute certainty) and *kulliyyah* (universality).
62. *al-Aḥkām* 3: 252; Attia, *Towards Realization*, 77.
63. al-Shātibī, *al-Muwāfaqāt,* 2:177.
64. Muḥammad al-Tāhir Ibn 'Āshūr, *Maqāṣid al-Sharī'ah al-Islāmiyyah* (al-Sharikah al-Tūnīsiyyah, 1970), 130-135; Attia, *Towards Realization*, 82.
65. Attia, *Towards Realization*, 83-90.
66. Auda, *Maqasid al-Shari'ah*, 247-249.
67. Tariq Ramadan, "Beyond Islamism," accessed 21 June, 2015; available at http://tariqramadan.com/english/2013/08/05/beyond-islamism.
68. These are Sunni Ḥanafī, Sunni Mālikī, Sunni Shāfi'ī, Sunni Ḥanbalī, Shī'ah Ja'farī, Shī'ah Zaydī, Ẓāhirī and 'Ibādī. It also forbade declaring an apostate anyone who is a follower of the Ash'arī/Māturīdī creed, real *taṣawwuf* (Sufism), and true Salafi thought.
69. Sūrah al-R'ad, *āyah* 28.

Bibliography

Abd-Allah, Umar Farouk *Malik and Medina: Islamic Legal Reasoning in the Formative Period.* Brill, 2013.

Abu Rabi', Ibrahim M. *Contemporary Arab Thought – Studies in Post-1967 Arab Intellectual History.* Pluto Press, 2004.

Abu Zahrah, Mohamed. *Usul Al-Fiqh.*

Affifi, A. E. *The Mystical Philosophy of Muhyid Din-ibnul Arabi.* Cambridge at the University Press, 1939.

Akasoy, Anna. & Giglioni, Guido. Ed. *Renaissance Averroism and Its Aftermath: Arabic Philosophy in Early Modern Europe.* Springer Science & Business Media, 2012.

Algar, Hamid. *Wahhabism: A Critical Essay.* Islamic Publications International, 2002.

Ali Shah, Zulfiqar. *Anthropomorphic Depictions of God: The Concept of God in Judaic, Christian and Islamic Traditions: Representing the Unrepresentable.* London: International Institute of Islamic Thought, 2012.

Al-Muwatta' of Imam Malik ibn Anas, translated by Aisha Abdurrahman Bewley. Madinah Press Granada, Spain, 1989.

Alusi, Shihab al-Din, al-. *Ruh al-ma'ni fi tafsir al-Qur'an al-'azim wa al-sab al-mathani.* Edited by Mohammad al-Amad and Omar al-Salami with an introduction by al-Taher bn Ashur. Dar Ihia al-Turath al-Arabi-Libanon.

Alwani, Ṭāhā Jabir al-. *Usul al Fiqh al Islami – Source Methodology in Islamic Jurisprudence: Methodology for Research and Knowledge*. Herndon: The International Institute of Islamic Thought, 1990.

______ *Ethics of Disagreement in Islam*. Prepared from the original Arabic by Abdul Wahid Hamid. Edited by A.S. Shaikh Ali, Herndon: The International Institute of Islamic Thought, 1993.

Amerini, Fabrizio & Galluzzo, Gabriele. (Eds.) *A Companion to the Latin Medieval Commentaries on Aristotle's Metaphysics*, Brill, 2013.

Amidi, Sayf al-Din al-. *Kitab al-ihkam fi usul al-ahkam*. Dar al-Kitab al-alamiyya, Beirut, 1985/1405.

Anjum, Ovamir. *Politics, Law, and Community in Islamic Thought: The Taymiyyan Moment*. Cambridge University Press, 2012.

Anwar, Sabieh. "Is Ghazali really the Halagu of Science in Islam?" *Monthly Renaissance* 18, no. 10, 2008.

Aquinas, Thomas. *Commentary on St. Paul's Epistle to the Ephesians* translated and introduced by Matthew L. Lamb. Magi Books Inc, New York, 1966.

______ *Summa Theologica*. In two volumes. The Franklin Library, 1985.

Arifin, Muhammad. "*Uṣūl al-Fiqh*: A History of Islamic Legal Thinking." *IIU Law Journal* 1, no. 2 (1989): 87-107.

Arkoun, Mohammed. "Rethinking Islam Today." *The Annals of the American Academy of Political and Social Science* 588 (2003): 18-39. http://www.jstor.org/stable/1049852.

Arnold, Thomas W. *The Caliphate*, Oxford at the Clarendon Press, 1924.

Arnold, Thomas & Guillaume, Alfred. *The Legacy of Islam*. London: Oxford University Press, 1952.

Asad, Muhammad. *The Message of the Qur'an*. Darul Andalus, Gibraltar, 1980.

______ *The Principles of State and Government in Islam*. Kuala

Lumpur: Islamic Book Trust, 1980.

______ *This Law of Ours and Other Essays*. Kuala Lumpur: Islamic Book Trust, 1987.

Asad, Talal. "Anthropological Concepts of Religion: Reflections on Geertz." *Man*, New Series, Vol. 18 No. 2 (1983): 237-59.

'Ash'arī, Abu al-Hasan 'Ali, al-. *Kitāb al-Lumā'*. ed. Father McCarthy. Beirut, 1953.

______ *Risālah fi Istiḥsan al-khawd fi al-kalām*. For the English translation of both: *The Theology of al-'Ash'ari: The Arabic Text of al-'Ash'ari's "Kitāb al-Lumā'" and "Risālat fi Istiḥsan al-khawd fi 'Ilm al-Kalām,"* Richard J. McCarthy. Beirut: Impremerie Catholique, 1953.

Ashmawi, Muhammad Said. *Usul al-Shari'a*. Beirut, Dar Iqra', 1983.

Aslan, Reza. *No god but God – The Origins, Evolution, and Future of Islam*. New York: Random House Trade Paperbacks, 2011.

Attas, Syed Muhammad Naquib, al-. *Prolegomena to the Metaphysics of Islām – An Exposition of the Fundamental Elements of the World View of Islām*. International Institute of Islamic Thought & Civilization, 1995.

Attia, Gamal Eldin. *Towards The Realization of the Higher Intents of Islamic Law – Maqāṣid al-Sharī'ah: A Functional Approach*. Translated from the Arabic by Nancy Roberts. The International Institute of Islamic Thought, 2007.

Auda, Jasser. *Maqāṣid al-Sharī'ah as Philosophy of Islamic Law – A Systems Approach*. The International Institute of Islamic Thought, 2008.

Austin, John. *The Province of Jurisprudence Determined*. (1832) The Lawbook Exchange, Ltd., 2012.

Averroes. *On the Harmony of Religion and Philosophy*. A Translation, with Introduction and Notes, of Ibn Rushd's *Kitāb Fasl Al-Maqāl*, With Its Appendix (*Damima*) and An Extract From *Kitāb Al-Kashf 'An Manāhij Al-Adilla* (Discovery of the Methods of Proofs) by George F. Hourani, Luzac & Co. 1976; See also entry under Ibn Rushd.

Awa, Mohamed S. El-, *Punishment in Islamic Law.* American Trust Publications, 1993.

Azra, Azyumardi. *The Origins of Islamic Reformism in Southeast Asia.* Allen & Unwin, 2004.

Badawi, Abd Al-Rahman. *Madhāhib al-Islamiyyin: al-Muktazilah.* Beirut, Dar al-Ilm li al-Malayin, 1970. Volume 1.

Barr, Ibn ʻAbd. Al-. *Kitāb al-Intiqa' fi-Fadhā'il al-thalātha al-Aʻimmah al-fuqahā.* Cairo, 1350/1931.

Bazdawī, Fakhr al-Islam al-. *Kashf al-Asrār ʻan Uṣūl Fakhr al-Islam al-Bazdawī* (Unveiling the Secrets of the Sources of Fakhr al-Islam al-Bazdawī) edited by Muhammad al-Muʻtasim bi Allah Baghdadi, 4 vol. Beirut: Dār al-Kitāb al-ʻArabi, 1994.

Becker, C. H. "Christliche Polemik und islamische Dogmenbildung." Festschrift fur Ignaz Goldziher, Herausgegeben von Carl Bezold. *Zeitschrift fµr Assyriologie und Verwandte Gebiete* (Strassburg: Karl J. Trubner, 1912): 175-195.

Bello, I. A. *The Medieval Controversy between Philosophy and Orthodoxy: Ijmā' and Ta'wīl in the conflict between al-Ghazālī and Ibn Rushd.* Leiden: E. J. Brill, 1989.

Benard, Cheryl & Kalilzad, Zalmay. *The Government of God: Iran's Islamic Republic.* Columbia University Press, 1986.

Bentham, Jeremy. *An Introduction to the Principles of Morals and Legislation.* Edited by J.H. Burns and H.L.A Hart. Clarendon Press, 1996.

Bhojani, Ali-Reza. *Moral Rationalism and Shariʻa: Independent Rationality in Modern Shiʻi Usul Al-Fiqh.* Routledge, 2015.

Bible - King James Version (KJV)

Binder, Leonard. *Islamic Liberalism: A Critique of Development Ideologies.* University of Chicago Press, 1988.

Bix, Brian. "John Austin." *The Stanford Encyclopedia of Philosophy.* (Spring 2015 Edition) edited by Edward N. Zalta <http://plato.stanford.edu/archives/spr2015/entries/austin-john/>.

Black's Law Dictionary, St. Paul: West Publishing Co., 1990.

Bowering, Gerhard. Editor, *The Princeton Encyclopedia of Islamic Political Thought.* Princeton University Press, 2013.

Brockelmann, Carl. *Geschichte der islamischen Völker und Staaten.* Mu̇nchen, Berlin, R. Oldenbourg, 1939. Translated by Joel Carmichael and Moshe Perlmami as *History of the Islamic Peoples.* G. P. Putnam's Sons, New York, 1947.

Brown, Daniel W. *Rethinking Tradition in Modern Thought.* Cambridge: Cambridge University Press, 1996.

Brown, Jonathan A.C. *The Canonization of al-Bukhārī and Muslim: The Formation and Function of the Sunnī Ḥadīth Canon.* Brill Publishers, 2007.

Bourke, Vernon J. "Rationalism," in *Runes* (1962).

Calder, Norman. "*Ikhtilāf* and *Ijmā'* in Shafi'ī's *Risāla.*" *Studia Islamica* 58 (1984): 55-81.

______ *Islamic Jurisprudence in the Classical Era.* Ed. Colin Imber, Cambridge University Press, 2010.

Calvert, John. *Sayyid Quṭb and the Origins of Radical Islamism.* Hurst and Company, London, 2010.

Calvin, John. *Institutes of the Christian Religion.* 1559.

Carter, Stephen L. *The Culture of Disbelief: How American Law and Politics Trivialize Religious Devotion.* New York: Basic Books, 1993.

Chittick, William. *The Sufi Path of Knowledge: Ibn Al-Arabi's Metaphysics of Imagination.* State University of New York Press, 1989.

Cook, Michael. *Commanding Right and Forbidding Wrong in Islamic Thought.* Cambridge University Press, 2000.

Cornell, Vincent J. *Voices of Islam: Voices of Change.* Greenwood Publishing Group, 2007.

Cosgel, Metin., Rasha, Ahmed and Thomas, Miceli. "Law, State Power, and Taxation in Islamic History." *Journal of Economic Behavior & Organization* 71, no. 3 (2009).

Cottingham, John. *Rationalism.* Paladi/Granada, 1984.

Coulson, Noel J. *A History of Islamic Law.* Edinburgh: Edinburgh

University Press, 1964.

______ *Conflicts and Tensions in Islamic Jurisprudence.* Chicago: University of Chicago Press, 1969.

Crone, P. and Hinds, M. *God's Caliph: Religious Authority in the First Centuries of Islam.* Cambridge, 1986.

Crone, Patricia. *Roman, Provincial and Islamic Law: The Origins of the Islamic Patronate.* Cambridge University Press, 2002.

Dabashi, Hamid. & Nasr, S.H. (Ed.) *Shi'ism Doctrines, Thought, and Spirituality.* SUNY Press, 1988.

Daher, Ayman. "The *Shari'a*: Roman Law Wearing an Islamic Veil?" *Hirundo: The McGill Journal of Classical Studies,* 3 (2004).

Dallmayr, Fred Reinhard. *Border Crossings: Toward a Comparative Political Theory.* Lexington Books, 1999.

Davis Jr, Donald. "A Realist View of Hindu Law." *Ratio Juris,* 19, no. 3, (2006).

Defilippo, Joseph G. "Aristotle's Identification of the Prime Mover as God." *The Classical Quarterly.* 44, no. 2 (1994): 393-409.

DeLong-Bas, Natana J. *Wahhabi Islam: From Revival and Reform to Global Jihad.* I.B. Tauris, 2007.

Dihlawī, Muḥammad Ayyūb. *The Mischief of Rejection of Ḥadīth.* Karachi, n.d.

Dreisbach, Daniel L. *Thomas Jefferson and the Wall of Separation of Church and State.* New York: New York University Press, 2002.

Duke, George. "The Sophists (Ancient Greek)." *Internet Encyclopedia of Philosophy.* Accessed on 27, June, 2014; http://www.iep.utm.edu/sophists/

Durant, Will. *The Renaissance: A History of Civilization in Italy from 1304-1576 A.D.* Simon and Schuster, 1953.

Ehler, Sidney Zdeneck and Morrall, John B, *Church and State Through the Centuries: A Collection of Historic Documents with Commentaries.* Biblo & Tannen Publishers, 1967.

Shamsy, Ahmed, El-. Al-Shāfiʿī's Written Corpus: A Source-Critical Study." *Journal of the American Oriental Society* 132, no. 2

(2012).

Emon, Anver M. "Conceiving Islamic Law in a Pluralist Society: History, Politics and Multicultural Jurisprudence." *Singapore Journal of Legal Studies* (2006): 331-355.

______ "*Huqūq Allāh* and *Huqūq al-'Ibād*: A Legal Heuristic for a Natural Rights Regime." *Islamic Law and Society*, 13 (2006): 325-391.

Fadl, Khaled Abou El-. *Rebellion and Violence in Islamic Law.* Cambridge University Press, 2006.

______ *The Great Theft: Wrestling Islam from the Extremists.* HarperOne, 2007.

______ *Reasoning with God: Reclaiming Shari'ah in the Modern Age.* Rowman & Littlefield, 2014.

Fakhry, Majid. *A History of Islamic Philosophy.* Columbia University Press, New York, 1983.

Faksh, M. A. "Theories of State in Islamic Political Thought." *Arab Journal of Social Sciences,* (1987).

Ficino, Marsilio. *Theologia Platonica de immortalitate animorum.* Olms; Nachdr. d. Ausg. Paris, (1559 edition), 1975.

Flannery, Kevin. *Acts Amid Precepts: The Logical Structure of Thomas Aquinas's Moral Theology.* Continuum International Publishing Group, 2007.

Frank, Richard M. "*Al-Ma'nā*: Some Reflections on the Technical Meaning of the Term in the *Kalām* and Its Use in the Physics of Mu'ammar," *Journal of the American Oriental Society*, 87 (1967): 248-259.

Freeman, M.D.A. *Lloyd's Introduction to Jurisprudence.* Ed. Sweet and Maxwell, London, 1994.

Friedmann, Yohanan. *Tolerance and Coercion in Islam: Interfaith Relations in the Muslim Tradition.* Cambridge University Press, 2006.

Fuller, Lon Luvois. *The Morality of the Law.* New Haven, 1964.

Garden, Kenneth. *Al-Ghazali's Contested Revival: 'Ihya'Ulum Al-Din' and its Critics in Khorasan and the Maghrib* (Morocco,

Tunisia, Algeria, Spain), PhD Dissertation, University of Chicago, 2005.

Geertz, Clifford. *The Interpretation of Cultures.* Basic Books, 1973.

______*The Religion of Java.* University of Chicago Press, 1976.

Gerber, Haim. *State, Society, and Law in Islam: Ottoman Law in Comparative Perspective.* State University of New York Press, 1994.

Ghaneabasseri, Kambiz. "The Epistemological Foundation of Conceptions of Justice in Classical *Kalām*: A Study of ʿAbd al-Jabbār's *al-Mughnī* and *Ibn al-Bāqillānī's al-Tamhīd.*" *Journal of Islamic Studies* 19:1 (2008): 71–96. doi:10.1093/jis/etm058.

Ghazālī, Abu Hamīd Muhammad al-. *Al-Mustasfa min 'Ilm al-Usul.* 2 volumes. Cairo: al-Maktabah al-Tijariyyah, 1356/1937.

______*Jawahir al-Qur'an* (Jewels of the Qur'an).

______ *Moderation in Belief, (Al-Iqtiṣād fī al-ʿitiqād)*, translated, with an Interpretive Essay and Notes by Aladdin M. Yaqub. The University of Chicago Press, Chicago and London, 2013.

Ghazālī, Muhammad al-. *al-Sunna al-nabawiyya bayna ahl al-fiqh wa ahl al-hadith.* Cairo, 1989.

______ *A Thematic Commentary of the Qur'an.* The International Institute of Islamic Thought, 2000.

______ *A Practical Approach to the Qur'an. (Kayfa Nata'amal ma'a al-Qur'an).* Nahdat Misr, Cairo, 2005.

Gianotti, Timothy J. "'Islamic Knowledge'—being a translation of the Introduction to al-Ghazali's masterwork, *Reviving Religious Knowledge*, immediately preceding his 'Book of Knowledge'," *Islamic Sciences*, 11 no. 2 (2013).

Gibb, H.A.R. *Mohammedanism: An Historical Survey.* London: Oxford University Press, 1950.

______ *Studies on the Civilization of Islam.* (1962) Routledge, 2013.

Gibbon, Edward. *The History of the Decline and Fall of the Roman Empire.* http://www.gutenberg.org/files/25717/25717-h/files /735/735-h/735-h.htm.

Glasse, Cyril. *The Concise Encyclopedia of Islam.* London: Stacey International, 1989.

Goldziher, Ignaz. *Vorlesungen uber den Islam.* Heidelberg: C. Winter, 1910, reprint 1958. Translated by A. Hamori and R. Hamori. *Introduction to Islamic Theology and Law.* Princeton University Press, 1981.

______ *The Zahiris: Their Doctrine and Their History, a Contribution to the History of Islamic Theology.* Leiden: E.J. Brill, 1971. Translated and edited by Wolfgang Behn first published as *Die Zahiriten, ihr lehrsystem und ihre geschichte : beitrag zur geschichte der Muhammedanischen theologie.*

Goodhart, Arthur L. "Determining the Ratio Decidendi of a Case." *The Yale Law Journal* 40, no. 2 (1930): 161-83.

Griffel, Frank. "Al-Ghazālī," *The Stanford Encyclopedia of Philosophy* (Fall 2007 Edition), Edward N. Zalta (ed.), URL = <http://plato.stanford.edu/archives/fall2007/entries/al-ghazali/>.

Guizot, Francois. *The History of Civilization in Europe.* New York, 1896.

Hallaq, Wael. "Was the Gate of Ijtihad Closed?" *International Journal of Middle East Studies* 16 (1984): 3-41.

______ "From Fatwas to Furu': Growth and Change in Islamic Substantive Law." *Islamic Law and Society* (1994): 17-56.

______ *An Introduction to Sunni usul-al-fiqh.* Cambridge University Press, 1997.

______ *A History of Islamic Legal Theories.* Cambridge University Press, 1997.

______ *Authority, Continuity, and Change in Islamic Law.* Cambridge University Press, 2001.

______ "Can the Shari'ah be Restored?" *Islamic Law and the Challenges of Modernity*, edited by Yvonne Y. Haddad and Barbara F. Stowasser. Walnut Creek: Altamira Press, 2004. Accessed on June 21, 2013; available at http://globalwebpost.com/farooqm/study_res/islam/fiqh/hal

laq_shariah.html.

______*The Origins and Evolution of Islamic Law.* Cambridge University Press, 2005.

______*Sharīʿa: Theory, Practice, Transformations.* Cambridge University Press, 2009.

Halverson, Jeffry R. *Theology and Creed in Sunni Islam: The Muslim Brotherhood, Ash'arism, and Political Sunnism.* Palgrave Macmillan, 2010.

Hamburger, Philip. *Separation of Church and State.* Cambridge, MA: Harvard University Press, 2002.

Hamid, Eltigani Abdulqadir. "Al-Mawārdī's Theory of State: Some Ignored Dimensions." *The American Journal of Islamic Social Sciences* 18, 4 (2001): 1-18.

Hamilton, Charles. (trans.) *The Hedaya: Commentary on the Islamic Laws.* Delhi: Islamic Book Trust, 1870.

Hart, H.L.A. "Positivism and the Separation of Law and Morals." *Harvard Law Review* 71 (1958): 593-629.

______*Law, Liberty, and Morality.* London: Oxford University Press, 1963.

______*The Concept of Law.* Clarendon Press, 1997.

Hassan, Ahmad. *The Doctrine of Ijma' in Islam.* Islamabad: Islamic Research Institute, 1978.

Hassan, Laura. "The Encounter of *Falsafa* and *Kalām* in Sayf al-Dīn al-Āmidī's Discussion of the Atom: Asserting Traditional Boundaries, Questioning Traditional Doctrines." The *SOAS Journal of Postgraduate Research*, 6 (2014): 77-98.

Hayashi, T. *On Islamic Accounting: Its Future Impacts on Western Accounting.* Kyoto: International University of Japan, Monograph Series, 1988.

Heck, Paul L. "Human Experience As Source of Moral Insight: Ibn Ḥazm's *Ṭawq Al-Ḥamāma*". *Islamochristiana* 39 (2013): 93–109

Heidegger, Martin. *Plato's Sophist,* Translated by Richard Rojcewicz and Andre Schuwer. Indiana University Press, 2003.

Heydon, Leeming & Turner. *Equity Doctrines & Remedies.* 5th edition. LexisNexis, 2014.

Hoffman, Valerie Jon. *The Essentials of Ibadi Islam.* Syracuse: Syracuse University Press, 2012.

Hourani, Albert. *Arabic Thought in the Liberal Age—1798-1939.* Cambridge University Press, 1983.

______ *Islam in European Thought*, Cambridge University Press, 1991.

Hughes, Austin L. "The Folly of Scientism." *The New Atlantis*, (Fall, 2012): 32-50.

Hourani, George F. *Islamic Rationalism: The Ethics of 'Abd al-Jabbār.* Oxford: Clarendon Press, 1971.

______ "Reason and Revelation in Ibn Ḥazm's Ethical Thought." in *Islamic Philosophical Theology*, ed. Parviz Morewedge. Albany, 1979: 142-164.

Ibn Ashūr, Muhammad al-Ṭāhir. *Maqāsid al-Sharī'ah al-Islamīyyah.* Al-Sharikah al-Tunisiyyah, 1970.

Ibn Farābī. *Fi Ihsa al-'Ulum.* Edited by 'Uthman Amin. Cairo, 1968.

Ibn Ḥanbal, Ahmad. *Kitab al-Radd 'ala al-Zanadiqa wa'l-Jahmiyya* "Refutations of the Heretics and the Jahmites". Cairo: 1973.

Ibn Ḥazm, *al-Fisāl fi'l milāl wa'l ahwa' wa'n nihāl* (Treatise on Religions and Schools of Thought), Cairo: Maktabat al-Khanji, no date; trans. M. Asín Palacios, *Abenházam de Córdoba y su historia crítica de las ideas religiosas*, Madrid: Real Academica de la Historia, 1927-32.

Ibn Khaldūn. *The Muqaddimah - An Introduction to History.* Translated by F. Rosenthal, 3 volumes. New York: Pantheon Books, 1958.

Ibn Manẓūr. *Lisān al-'Arab.* Dar Sadir, Beirut 1955-1956 (15 volumes).

Ibn Qayyim al-Jawziyyah, *al-Turuq al-Hukmiyyah fi'l-Siyāsah al-Shar'iyyah*, edited by Muhammad Jamil Ghazi. Jeddah: Matba'at al-Madani, n.d.

Ibn Qudāmah, Muwaffaq al-Dīn. *Tahrīm al-Nazār fi Kutūb ahl al-Kalām.* Translated and edited by George Makdisi as *The Censure of Speculative Theology of Ibn Qudama.* Gibb Memorial Trust, 1985.

Ibn Rushd, Abu Al-Walid Muhammad Ibn Ahmad. *Tahāfut Al-Tahāfut.* (The Incoherence of The Incoherence). Translated from the Arabic, with Introduction and Notes by Simon Van Den Bergh, The Trustees of The "E. J. W. Gibb Memorial".

______ *Tafsir ma ba'd at-tabi'at.* Averroes, Grand Commentaire de la Metaphysique Edition : Paris : les Belles Lettres, 1984.

______ *Kitāb Faṣl Al-Maqāl wa Taqrīr ma Bayna-l-Sharī'ah wal-Ḥikma min Al-Ittiṣāl,* (Manshurat al-Jamal, Beirut-Baghdad, 2009); Averroes, *On the Harmony of Religion and Philosophy,* A Translation, with Introduction and Notes, of Ibn Rushd's *Kitāb Fasl Al-Maqāl,* With Its Appendix (Damima) and An Extract From *Kitāb Al-Kashf 'An Manāhij Al-Adilla* by George F. Hourani, Messrs. Luzac & Co. 1976.

______ *Kitāb Faṣl Al-Maqāl wa Taqrīr ma Bayna-l-Sharī'ah wal-Ḥikma min Al-Ittiṣāl.* Translated by Charles Butterworth as *The Book of the Decisive Treatise - Determining the Connection between the Law and Wisdom,* Brigham Young University Press. 2001.

______ *Bidāyat al-Mujtahid wa Nihāyat al-Muqtaṣid,* translated by Imran Ahsan Khan Nyazee as *The Distinguished Jurist's Primer,* (Garnet Publishing, 2000) Vols. I & II.

Ibn Taymiyyah, *al-siyāsa al-shar'īyya fī iṣlāḥ al-rā'ī wa 'l-ra'īyya,* ed. Muḥammad Mubārak, Beirut 1386/1966, 3. (The Book of Governance According to the Sharī'ah).

Ibrahim, Anwar. *The Asian Renaissance.* Times Book International, 1996.

Iqbal, Allama Muhammad. *The Reconstruction of Religious Thought in Islam.* Institute of Islamic Culture: Lahore, 1986.

Islam, Politics, and Social Movements, edited by Edmund Burke III and Ira M. Lapidus. University of California Press, 1990.

Izutsu, Toshihiko. *God and Man in the Qur'an*. Ayer Co Pub, 1980.

______ *The Concept of Belief in Islamic Theology*. The Other Press, 2006.

Janin, Hunt. & Kahlmeyer, André. *Islamic Law: The Sharia from Muhammad's Time to the Present*. McFarland, 2007.

Johansen, Baber. "Casuistry: Between Legal Concept and Social Praxis." *Islamic Law and Society*, 2, 2 (1995): 136-156.

Kadri, Sadakat. Heaven on Earth: A Journey Through Shari'a Law from the Deserts of Ancient Arabia. Macmillan, 2012.

Kamali, M. Hashim. *Principles of Islamic Jurisprudence*. Cambridge: Islamic Texts Society, 1989.

______ *Punishment in Islamic Law: An Enquiry into the Hudud Bill of Kelantan*. Institut Kajian Dasar, 1995.

______ *Equity and Fairness in Islam*. Cambridge: The Islamic Texts Society, 2005.

______ *Sharī'ah Law: An Introduction*. Oneworld Publications, 2008.

Kant, Immanuel, 1787, *Critique of Pure Reason*, Norman Kemp Smith (transl.), New York: St. Martin's Press, 1965.

Kashani, 'Abd al-Razzaq al-. *Tafsir al-Qur'an al-karim*, 2 vols. Beirut: Dar al-Yaqzah al-'Arabiyya, 1387/1967.

Kayadibi, Saim. *Istiḥsān – The Doctrine of Juristic Preference in Islamic Law*. Islamic Book Trust, 2010.

Kepel, Gilles. *Muslim Extremism in Egypt: The Prophet and Pharaoh*. University of California Press, 1985.

Kerferd, G.B. *The Sophistic Movement*. New York: Cambridge University Press, 2009.

Kerr, M.H. *Islamic Reform: The Legal and Political Theories of Muhammad 'Abduh and Rashid Reda*. Berkeley: University of California Press, 1966.

Khadduri, Majid. *War and Peace in the Law of Islam*. Baltimore: The Johns Hopkins Press, 1979.

______ *Al-Shafii's Risala – Treatise on the Foundations of Islamic Jurisprudence.* Islamic Texts Society, 1987.

Khan, L. Ali & Ramadan, Hisham M. *Contemporary Ijtihad: Limits and Controversies.* Edinburgh University Press, 2011.

Khan, M.A. Muqtedar. "The Primacy of Political Philosophy." In Khaled Abou El Fadl, *Islam and the Challenge of Democracy.* Edited by Joshua Cohen and Deborah Chasman. Princeton University Press, 2004.

Khare, Ravindra S. *Perspectives on Islamic Law, Justice, and Society.* Rowman & Littlefield, 1987.

Kindī, Yaʿqub ibn Isḥaq al-. *Rasāʾil al-Kindī al-Falsafiyyah* (The Philosophical Treatises of al-Kindī), ed. M. A. H. Abū Ridah. Cairo: Dār al-Fikr al-ʿArabī, 2 vols in 1, 1953.

Krawietz, Birgit "Ibn Taymiyya, Vater des islamischen Fundamentalismus?: Zur westlichen Rezeption eines mittelalterlichen Schariatsgelehrten." *Theorie des Rechts und der Gesellschaft.* Edited by Manuel Atienza et al, Berlin, 2003.

Kuhn, Thomas. "Logic of Discovery or Psychology of Research." In *Criticism and the Growth of Knowledge* edited by Knysh, Alexander D. *Ibn 'Arabi in the Later Islamic Tradition: The Making of a Polemical Image in Medieval Islam,* SUNY Press, 1999.

Lakatos, Imre and Musgrave, Alan. *Criticism and the Growth of Knowledge.* Cambridge: Cambridge University Press, 1972.

Lane, Edward William. *Arabic-English Lexicon.* London: Willams & Norgate, 1863.

Lambton, Ann K. S. *State and Government in Medieval Islam: An Introduction to the Study of Islamic Political Theory: the Jurists.* Psychology Press, 1981.

Laoust, Henri. "Ibn Taymiyya." *Encyclopaedia of Islam*, Second Edition. Edited by: P. Bearman, Th. Bianquis, C.E. Bosworth, E. van Donzel, W.P. Heinrichs. Brill Online, 2016. Reference. 29 January 2016

<http://referenceworks.brillonline.com/entries/encyclopaedia-of-islam-2/ibn-taymiyya-SIM_3388>.

Lariviere, Richard W. "Law and Religion in India." In *Law, Morality, and Religion: Global Perspectives.* Edited by Alan Watson. Berkeley: University of California, 1996.

Lewis, Bernard. *Istanbul and the Civilization of the Ottoman Empire.* University of Oklahoma Press, 1963.

______*The Political Language of Islam.* Chicago: University of Chicago Press, 1988.

Locke, John. *Two Treatises of Government.* Edited by Peter Laslett. New York: Mentor, 1965.

______ *A Letter Concerning Toleration.* Originally written in Latin as *Epistola de Tolerantia.* Translated by William Popple (1689)

Lory, Pierre. *Les Commentaires ésotériques du Coran d'aprés 'Abd al Razzaq al Qashani.* Paris: Les Deux Océans. 1980.

Maghnisawi, Abu 'l-Muntaha al-. *Imam Abu Hanifa's Al-Fiqh al-Akbar Explained.* Compiled and Translated with an Introduction by Abdur-Rahman ibn Yusuf. White Thread Press, 2007.

Mahdi, Muhsin. "*Averroes'* Decisive Treatise" in *Islamic Theology and Philosophy: Studies in Honor of George F. Hourani.* Edited by Michael Marmura. SUNY Press, 1984.

Mahmassani, Subhi. *The Philosophy of Jurisprudence in Islam.* Falsafat Al-Tashri' Fi Al-Islam. Translated by Farhat Ziadeh. Leiden, E.J. Brill, 1961.

Makdisi, George. *The Rise of Colleges.* Edinburgh: Edinburgh University Press, 1981.

Makdisi, John. "An Inquiry into Islamic Influences during the Formative period of the Common Law." In *Islamic Law and Jurisprudence.* Edited by Nicholas Heer, University of Washington Press, Seattle and London, 1990.

Marmura, Michael E. *The incoherence of the philosophers: Tahafut al-falasifah: a parallel English-Arabic text.* Provo: Brigham Young University Press, 1997.

Marsham, Andrew. *Rituals of Islamic Monarchy – Accession and Succession in the First Muslim Empire.* Edinburgh University Press, 2009.

Martin, Richard C. and Woodward, Mark R. Defenders of Reason in Islam: Muʿtazilism from Medieval School to Modern Symbol, Oxford 1997.

Masud, Muhammad Khalid. *Islamic Legal Philosophy: A study of Abu Ishaq al-Shatibi's Life and Thought.* Islamabad, 1977.

Mawardi, Abu al-Hasan 'Ali ibn Muhammad ibn Habib al-. *Kitab al-Ahkam al-Sultaniyya.* Edited by M. Enger, Bonn, 1853.

Mayer, Ann Elizabeth. "The Shari'ah: A Methodology or a Body of Substantive Rules?" in *Islamic Law and Jurisprudence.* Edited by Mesawi, Mohamed El-Tahir El-. "From al-Shāṭibī's legal hermeneutics to thematic exegesis of the Qur'ān," Intellectual Discourse, 20:2 (2012): 189-214; accessed on 22 February 2016, https://www.researchgate.net/publication/277118089_From_al-Shatibi's_legal_hermeneutics_to_thematic_exegesis_of_the_QuranNicholas Heer. University of Washington Press, 1990.

McAmis, Robert Day. *Malay Muslims: The History and Challenge of Resurgent Islam in Southeast Asia.* Wm. B. Eerdmans Publishing, 2002.

Mitchell, Richard Paul. *The Society of the Muslim Brothers.* Oxford University Press, 1993.

Mottahedeh, R. "Some Islamic views of the pre-Islamic past." *Harvard Middle Eastern and Islamic Review* 1 (1994).

Motzki, Harald. *The Origins of Islamic Jurisprudence: Meccan Fiqh Before the Classical School.* Brill, 2002.

Mousourakis, George. *Roman Law and the Origins of the Civil Law Tradition.* Springer, 2014.

Mubarak, Tawfique al-. "Imam al-Shatibi" accessed June 2015 available at www.iais.org.my/e/attach/Imam_al-Shatibi.

Murata, Sachiko; William C. Chittick. *The Vision of Islam*. I. B. Tauris, 2000.

Musa, Khadiga. *A Critical Edition of ʻUmdat al-Nāzir ʻalā al-Ashbāh wa'l-Naẓā'ir*. Prince Muhammad bin Fahd University, 2016. This is a critical edition of the twelfth/eighteenth century manuscript on the subject of legal maxims, written by a distinguished Ḥanifite jurist Abū al-Suʻūd al-Ḥusaynī and is a commentary on an earlier seminal text *al-Ashbāh wa al-Naẓā'ir* authored by Ibn Nujaym in the tenth/sixteenth century.

Muṭahharī, Murtaḍā. *An Introduction to ʻIlm al-Kalām*. Translated from the Persian by ʻAli Quli Qara'i, Vol. II No. 2, 1985; accessed on June 19, 2014; available at http://www.muslimphilosophy.com/ip/kalam.htm.

Najjar, Fauzi M. "Siyasa in Islamic Political Philosophy." In *Islamic Theology and Philosophy: Studies in Honor of George F. Hourani*, edited by Michael E. Marmura, Albany, 1984.

Nasr, Seyyed Hossein. "Intellect and Intuition: Their Relationship from the Islamic Perspective." *Studies in Comparative Religion*, Vol. 13, No. 1 & 2. (Winter-Spring, 1979); accessed 23 March 2015. www.studiesincomparativereligion.com.

Nasr, Seyyed Hossein & Leaman, Oliver. Ed. *History of Islamic Philosophy*. London & New York: Routledge, 2001.

______ et al, *The Study Quran: A New Translation and Commentary*. HarperOne, 2015.

Neuhaus, Richard John. *The Naked Public Square: Religion and Democracy in America*. Grand Rapids, MI: William B. Eerdmans, 1984.

Neusner, Jacob & Sonn, Tamara. *Comparing Religions through Law: Judaism and Islam*. London: Routledge, 1999.

Nyazee, Imran Ahsan Khan. *Theories of Islamic Law: The Methodology of Ijtihad*. The International Institute of Islamic Thought, Islamabad, 1994.

______*Islamic Jurisprudence – Usul al-Fiqh.* Adam Publishers & Distributors, New Delhi, 2004.

______(trans.) *Al-Hidayah: A classical manual of Hanafi Law.* Bristol, 2006.

Pennington, Kenneth. *The Prince and the Law, 1200-1600: Sovereignty and Rights in the Western Legal Tradition.* University of California Press, 1993.

Pickthall, Marmaduke. *The Glorious Koran.*

Plato: Complete Works. Edited by John, M. Cooper. Hackett Publishing Company, Indianapolis, 1997.

Popper, Karl. *The Logic of Scientific Discovery. (1959)* Second Edition. Routledge, 2002.

Quṭb, Sayyid. *Ma'ālim fī al-Ṭarīq* (Signposts on the Road, or Milestones) 1964.

______ *Islam: The Religion of the Future.* Delhi: Markazi Maktaba Islami, 1974.

Rahman, Fazlur. "The Concept of *Ḥadd* in Islamic Law," *Islamic Studies* 4 (1965).

______ Fazlur. *Revival and Reform in Islam – A Study of Islamic Fundamentalism.* Edited and with an introduction by Ebrahim Moosa. OneWorld Publication, 2006.

Rawls, John. *Political Liberalism.* New York: Columbia University Press, 1993.

Raysuni, Ahmad al-. *Imam al-Shatibi's Theory of the Higher Objectives and Intents of Islamic Law.* London: The International Institute of Islamic Thought, 2005.

Rāzī, Fakhr al-Dīn al-. *Al-Maḥsul fī 'Ilm Uṣūl al-Fiqh.* 6 volumes. Edited by Tāhā Jābir al-Alwānī. Beirut: Mu'assasāt al-Risālah, 1992.

Raziq, 'Ali 'Abd. Al-. *Al-Islam wa usul al-Hukm.* Islam and the Bases of Political Authority. Cairo: 1925.

Reinhart, A. Kevin. *Before Revelation: The Boundaries of Muslim Moral Thought.* SUNY Press, 1995.

______ "Chapter 12: Law," in Jamal J. Elias, *Key Themes for the Study of Islam*. Oneworld Publications, 2014.

Renan, Ernest. *Averroès et l'averoïsme: essai historique*. Augusta Durand. 1852.

Rosen, Lawrence. *The Justice of Islam: Comparative Perspectives on Islamic Law and Society*. Oxford University Press, 2000.

Rosenthal, E. I. J. *Political Though in Medieval Islam*. Cambridge: Cambridge University Press, 1962.

Rosenthal, Franz & Marmorstein, Emile. *The Classical Heritage in Islam*, Psychology Press, 1992.

Roy, Olivier. *The Failure of Political Islam*. Harvard University Press, 1994.

Sadr, Muhammad Baqir as-. *Lessons in Islamic Jurisprudence*. (Durus fi 'Ilm al-Usul) Translated as *Lessons in Islamic Jurisprudence* with an introduction by Roy Parviz Mottahedeh. Oxford: Oneworld Oxford, 2003.

Said, Edward W. *Orientalism*. London and Henley: Routledge and Kegan Paul, 1978

Sajoo, Amyn B. "Ethics in the Civitas" in *Civil Society in the Muslim World: Contemporary Perspectives*. Edited by Amyn B. Sajoo. London and New York: I.B. Tauris Publishers, 2004.

Salafī, Muḥammad Ismā'īl al-. *Hujjiyyat-i-ḥadīth*, Lahore n.d.

Saleh, Walid A. *The Formation of the Classical Tafsīr Tradition: The Qur'ān Commentary of Al-Tha'labī (d. 427/1035)*. Brill, 2004.

Salvatore, Armando. "Public Religion, Ethics and Cultural Dialogue," in *Contemporary Islam: Dynamic, Not Static*. Edited by Abdul Aziz Said, Mohammed Abu-Nimer, Meena Sharify-Funk. Routledge, 2006.

Savory, R. M. *Introduction to Islamic Civilization*. Cambridge University Press, 1976.

Schacht, Joseph. *An Introduction to Islamic Law*. Oxford: Clarendon, 1964.

Schaff, Philip. *The Seven Ecumenical Councils*, series editor. Henry Wace.

Shabana, Ayman. *Custom in Islamic Law and Legal Theory: The Development of the Concepts of 'Urf and 'Adah in the Islamic Legal Tradition.* Palgrave Macmillan, 2010.

Shafiq, Muhammad. "The Meaning of Ra'y and Nature of its Usage in Islamic Law (An Examination of Select cases of the Legal Reasoning in the Period of 'Umar, the Second Caliph)." *Islamic Studies*, 23, no. 1 (1984): 21-32.

Shahidullah, Shahid M. *Comparative Criminal Justice Systems: Global and Local Perspectives.* Jones & Bartlett Publishers, 2012.

Sharif, M.M. ed. *A History of Muslim Philosophy.* Low Price Publications Delhi, 1999. Two-vol. Set

Sharif, M.M. ed. *A History of Muslim Philosophy.* Islamic Book Trust, 2016. Two-vol. Set

Shātibī, Abū Isḥāq Ibrāhīm al-. *al-Muwāfaqāt fī Uṣūl al-Sharīʿah.* 2 volumes. Beirut: Dar al-Fikr, 1990.

Shaw, Stanford J. *History of the Ottoman Empire and Modern Turkey: Volume 1, Empire of the Gazis: The Rise and Decline of the Ottoman Empire 1280-1808.* Cambridge University Press, 1976.

Shorter Encyclopaedia of Islam, edited by H.A.R. Gibb and J.H. Kramers. Leiden: E.J. Brill, 1974.

Sonneborn, Liz. *Averroes (Ibn Rushd): Muslim Scholar, Philosopher, and Physician of the Twelfth Century.* The Rosen Publishing Group, 2006.

Souroush, Abdolkarim. *Reason, Freedom, and Democracy in Islam – Essential Writings*, Translated, edited and with a critical introduction by Mahmoud Sadri and Ahmad Sadri. Oxford University Press, 2000.

St. Augustine, *De Civitate Dei contra Paganos*, translated in English as The City of God Against the Pagans and popularly as The City of God.

Steinschneider, Moritz. *Al-Farabi (Alpharibius) des Arabischen Philosophen Leben und Schriften.* (1869) http://www.archive.org/details/alfarabialphara00steigoog.

Story, Joseph, *Commentaries on the Constitution of the United States.* Boston: Hilliard, Gray, and Co., 1833.

Suyūṭī, Jalāl al-Dīn al-. *Tanwīr al-Hawālik Sharḥ 'alā Muwaṭṭa' Mālik* (The Enlightenment of Intense Blackness: Commentary on Malik's *Muwaṭṭa'*), with *Is'āf al-Mubaṭṭa' fī Rijāl al-Muwaṭṭa'* (Rescuing those Stalled Concerning the Narrators of Malik's *Muwaṭṭa'*).

Syed Ameer Ali, *Muhammadan Law Compiled from Authorities in the Original Arabic.* Vol. 1. New Delhi: Kitab Bhavan, 1986.

Ṭabarī, Abu Ja'far Muḥammad ibn Jarīr al-. *Al-Musammā Jamī' al-Bayān fī Ta'wīl al-Qur'ān (Tafsīr al-Ṭabarī)* (The Commentary on the Qur'an).

______*Tārīkh al-Rusul wa al-Mulūk) (Tārīkh al-Ṭabarī)* (History of the Prophets and Kings).

Taftāzānī, Sa'd al-Dīn al-. *Sharḥ 'Aqāid al-Nasafī* (A Commentary on the Creed of Islam), ScribeDigital.com.

Tahtawi, Rifa'a Rafi' al-. *An Imam in Paris: Account of a Stay in France by an Egyptian Cleric (1826–31)*, London: Saqi Books, 2004. Translated and Introduced by Daniel L. Newman.

Taji-Farouki, Suha & Nafi, Basheer M. *Islamic Thought in the Twentieth Century.* I.B.Tauris, 2004.

Ta'wīl, Shaykh Muhammad al-. "The Special Characteristics of the Maliki Madhhab." Translated by Abdullah bin Hamid Ali; accessed on August 2, 2014; available at http://www.muwatta.com/ebooks/english/special_characteristics_maliki_madhhab.pdf

Taylor, Alfred Edward. *Plato: The Man and His Work.* New York: Meridian Books, 1956.

The Oxford Companion to Philosophy. Edited by Ted Honderich. Oxford University Press, Oxford, 1995.

The Oxford Dictionary of Islam. Editor. John L. Esposito, *Oxford Islamic Studies Online*, accessed 9 August, 2015, available at http://www.oxfordislamicstudies.com/article/opr/t125/e4

The Princeton Encyclopedia of Islamic Political Thought. Editor. Gerhard Bowering. Princeton University Press, 2013.

Toynbee, Arnold J. *A Study of History*, Vol VI: *The Disintegrations of Civilizations.* Oxford University Press, 1939.

Treiger, Alexander. "Al-Ghazālī's Classifications of the Sciences and Descriptions of the Highest Theoretical Science," *Divan* 1, 2011.

Vanzo, Alberto. "Kant on empiricism and rationalism." *History of Philosophy Quarterly*, 30, no. 1, (2013): 53-74.

Vassiliev, Alexei. *The History of Saudi Arabia*, translated by P. A. Seslavin. London: Saqi, 1998.

Vico, Giambattista *The New Science of Giambattista Vico*, (1744 – original title Scienza Nuova) Translated by Thomas G. Bergin and Max H. Fisch. Ithaca: Cornell University Press, 1968.

______ *Universal Right* (Diritto universale). Translated from the Latin and edited by Giorgio Pinton and Margaret Diehl. Amsterdam/New York, Rodopi, 2000.

Vikør, Knut S. *Between God and the Sultan: A History of Islamic Law.* Oxford University Press, 2005.

Vogel, Frank E. *Islamic Law and Legal System: Studies of Saudi Arabia.* Boston: Brill, 2000.

Von Denffer, Ahmad. *'Ulūm al-Qur'ān – An Introduction to the Sciences of the Qur'ān.* The Islamic Foundation, 1983.

Wasti, Tahir. *The Application of Islamic Criminal Law in Pakistan: Sharia in Practice.* Brill Academic, 2009.

Watt, W. Montgomery. *Islamic Philosophy and Theology.* Aldine Transaction, 1962.

______*Muslim Intellectual: A Study of Al-Ghazali.* Edinburgh University Press, 1963.

______*Islamic Political Thought.* Edinburgh at the University Press,

1968.

______*The Formative Period of Islamic Thought.* Oneworld Publications, 1998.

Wehr, Hans. *A Dictionary of Modern Written Arabic*, edited by J Milton Cowan, 4th Edition. Wiesbaden: Otto Harrassowitz, 1979.

Weiss, Bernard G. "Exotericism and Objectivity in Islamic Jurisprudence," in *Islamic Law and Jurisprudence.* Edited by Nicholas Heer. University of Washington Press, Seattle and London, 1990.

______*The Search for God's Law: Islamic Jurisprudence in the Writings of Sayf al-Din al-Amidi.* Salt Lake City: University of Utah Press, 1992.

______*The Spirit of Islamic Law.* Athens and London: The University of Georgia Press, 1998.

Wellhausen, J. *The Arab Kingdom and Its Fall.* Calcutta: University of Calcutta, 1927.

Wolfson, Harry Austryn. *The Philosophy of the Kalam.* Harvard University Press, 1976.

Yu, Jiyuan. *The Structure of Being in Aristotle's Metaphysics.* Springer Science & Business Media, 2012.

Zaman, Muhammad Qasim, *The Ulama in Contemporary Islam – Custodians of Change.* Princeton: Princeton University Press, 2002.

Index

no distinction between morals and positive law...............138
Separation of church and state
Secular, Wallace (Governor of Alabama) v. Jaffree ...131, 133, 134
Separationism
Doctrine of the Two Swords..... 130
Evangelicals..........................131
Roma locuta sit, cause finita sit 131
St. Augustine of Hippo........131
Shāfiʿī, Muḥammad ibn Idrīs, al-14, 34, 35, 72, 144, 217, 263, 269, 272, 273, 274, 277, 283, 285, 294, 311, 316, 317, 319, 368
Sharīʿah, as v, ix, x, 1, 5, 10, 11, 12, 13, 15, 16, 17, 19, 21, 22, 27, 30, 34, 40, 41, 47, 51, 55, 59, 100, 119, 127, 136, 141, 184, 188, 200, 203, 211, 223, 225, 233, 243, 313, 329, 347, 351, 354, 358, 360, 371
a road to the watering place....1
all-embracing body of religious duties 13
as dīn...............41, 223, 231, 291
categorizations 11, 15, 32, 35, 36, 37, 60, 64, 168, 231, 356
divine law and a traced-out way 1, 22
not necessarily denote the revealed law of Islam 5
one-dimensional monolithic legal system................................17
path to salvation from death ..2
totality of Allah's commands13
Sharif, M. M......112, 113, 119, 388
Shāṭibī, Abū Isḥāq Ibrāhīm, Al-217
Shaybānī, Muḥammad al-275, 306, 313
Shaykh al-Islām 49, 207
Shīʿī 85, 111, 167, 169, 200, 280, 292, 301
Siyāsah al-sharʿiyyah
Sultan Meḥemmed II..........208
Souroush, Abdolkarim 344, 353, 367, 388
St. Augustine........... 131, 154, 388
State Power.......................237, 373
Sunnah..
abrogation ..255, 256, 257, 263, 264, 282, 293, 334
al-sunnah al-ʿādiyyah..........258
divine Sharīʿah source.........258
ḥadīth deniers 261
sunnah al-hudā 258, 260
Sunnī 226, 281, 373
Suyūṭī, Jalāl al-Dīn al-97, 294, 324, 344, 389
Syed Ameer Ali........ 275, 279, 389
Taʿzīr ....v, 51, 57
Ṭabarī, Abū Jaʿfar Muḥmmad ibn Jarīr al-9, 10, 12, 25, 30, 77, 172, 174, 245, 281, 300, 389
Taftāzānī, Saʿd al-Dīn al-75, 113, 389
Ṭalāq...239
Tanẓīmāt...........................229, 337
Taqlīd vii, 300, 301, 303, 304, 308, 324, 338
Taṣawwuf..................................296
Tawḥīd 32, 72, 73, 113, 116, 118, 283
āḥād....................................288
Divine Unity....................73, 74
Oneness of God 74

www.ingramcontent.com/pod-product-compliance
Lightning Source LLC
Chambersburg PA
CBHW022050210326
41519CB00054B/293
9789670957098